Lecture Notes in Computer Science

Commenced Publication in 1973
Founding and Former Series Editors:
Gerhard Goos, Juris Hartmanis, and Jan van Leeuwen

T0238286

Bettina Buth   Gerd Rabe   Till Seyfarth (Eds.)

Computer Safety, Reliability, and Security

28th International Conference, SAFECOMP 2009
Hamburg, Germany, September 15-18, 2009
Proceedings

 Springer

Volume Editors

Bettina Buth
Department of Informatik, Faculty TI
HAW Hamburg
Hamburg, Germany
E-mail: buth@informatik.haw-hamburg.de

Gerd Rabe
TÜV Nord SysTec GmbH & Co. KG
Competence Center Digital I&C Systems
SEELAB Software and Electronics Laboratory
Hamburg, Germany
E-mail: grabe@tuev-nord.de

Till Seyfarth
TÜV Nord SysTec GmbH & Co. KG
Competence Center Digital I&C Systems
SEELAB Software and Electronics Laboratory
Hamburg, Germany
E-mail: tseyfarth@tuev-nord.de

Library of Congress Control Number: 2009934307

CR Subject Classification (1998): B.8, C.4, D.2.4, D.4.5, H.2.7, K.4.4, K.6.5, D.4.6

LNCS Sublibrary: SL 1 – Theoretical Computer Science and General Issues

ISSN   0302-9743
ISBN-10   3-642-04467-0 Springer Berlin Heidelberg New York
ISBN-13   978-3-642-04467-0 Springer Berlin Heidelberg New York

springer.com

© Springer-Verlag Berlin Heidelberg 2009
Printed in Germany

Typesetting: Camera-ready by author, data conversion by Scientific Publishing Services, Chennai, India
Printed on acid-free paper   SPIN: 12753260   06/3180   5 4 3 2 1 0

Preface

Computer-based systems have become omnipresent commodities within our environment. While for a large variety of these systems such as transportation systems, nuclear or chemical plants, or medical systems their relation to safety is obvious, we often do not reflect that others are as directly related to risks concerning harm done to persons or matter as, for example, elevator control or mobile phones. At least we are not aware of the risk in our daily use of them.

Safecomp as a community and a conference series has accompanied this development for 30 years up to Safecomp 2009, which was the 28th of the series. During this time the topics and methods as well as the community have undergone changes. These changes reflect the requirements of the above-mentioned ubiquitous presence of safety-related systems. Safecomp has always encouraged and will further encourage academia and industry to share and exchange their ideas and experiences.

After 30 years, we as the organizers of Safecomp 2009, found it imperative to take stock: which methods found their way into the application areas; which new approaches need to be checked for their practical applicability. As different application domains developed their own approaches over the previous decades, we tried to attract people with different backgrounds for this conference. Although the years 2008 and 2009 were not easy with regard to the overall global economic situation, we succeeded with this goal.

We received 72 contributions from 14 countries, including 33 contributions from industry and research agencies. Of these, we selected 25 for the presentation as conference talks and for these proceedings. We invited two persons with a practical and theoretical background to provide the invited talks—our special thanks to Anne Haxthausen and Walt Boyes for their time and effort. The International Programme Committee further decided to include a joint session with the GfSE (Gesellschaft für Systems Engineering, German chapter of INCOSE) on model-based systems engineering in the conference programme in order to emphasize the system aspect and initiate a new liason. Unfortunately, it was not possible to include the related material in these proceedings since the session had a workshop character. Taking all this into account, we are positive that readers of these proceedings will gain as much insight into the current state of the art in safety engineering within various relevant application domains as the participants of the conference already have.

We would like to thank the International Programme Committee and the external reviewers for their work and the constructive comments regarding both the conference organization and the improvement of individual papers for Safecomp 2009. We look forward to further joint work for future Safecomp conferences. Special thanks go to Massimo Felici, who maintained the Cyberchair interface for the conference organization and always reacted immediately to any of our questions or cries for help. We would also like to thank those people at HAW Hamburg without whom the conference website would not have worked at all, especially Norbert Kasperczyk-Borgmann and Oliver Neumann. Last but not least we would like to thank Clarissa Hörnke and Markus Schweers of the TÜV NORD Akademie for supporting the local organization, registration and financial aspects of the conference.

During the organization of the conference and the preparation of these proceeding there were times where we were in panic and times where we had a lot of fun. Overall the fun prevailed. We do hope that this will also be the case for the local organizers of Safecomp 2010 in Vienna.

July 2009   Bettina Buth
                                                    Gerd Rabe
                                                    Till Seyfarth

Organization

Programme Chair

Bettina Buth, Germany
Gerd Rabe, Germany
Till Seyfarth, Germany

Local Organization

Bettina Buth, Germany
Gerd Rabe, Germany
Till Seyfarth, Germany

EWICS Chair

Francesca Saglietti, Germany

International Programme Committee

S. Anderson, UK
T. Anderson, UK
R. Bloomfield, UK
J. Braband, Germany
B. Buth, Germany
P. Daniel, UK
W. Ehrenberger, Germany
M. Felici, UK
F. Flammini, Italy
G. Glöe, Germany
J. Gorski, Poland
B. A. Gran, Norway
W. Halang, Germany
M. Harrison, UK
M. Heisel, Germany
C. Heitmeyer, USA
E. Hollnagel, France
M. Hübner, Germany
C. Johnson, UK
M. Kaniche, France
K. Kanoun, France

T. Kelly, UK
J. C. Knight, USA
F. Koornneef, The Netherlands
P. Ladkin, Germany
T. Lehmann, Germany
S. Lindskov Hansen, Denmark
B. Littlewood, UK
J. McDermid, UK
O. Nordland, Norway
A. Pasquini, Italy
P. Pareigis, Germany
J. Peleska, Germany
G. Rabe, Germany
F. Redmill, UK
F. Saglietti, Germany
E. Schoitsch, Austria
S. Schulze, Germany
T. Seyfarth, Germany
L. Strigini, UK
M. Sujan, UK
P. Traverse, France

J. Trienekens, The Netherlands   A. Weinert, Germany
M. van der Meulen, The Netherlands   S. Wittmann, Belgium
U. Voges, Germany   Z. Zurakowski, Poland

External Reviewers

O. Meyer   H. Unger
A. Tedeschi   A. Povyakalo
R. Lock   P. Hopkins

Scientific Sponsors

Austrian Research Centers
ENCRESS (European Network of Clubs for Reliability and Safety in
   Software-Intensive Systems)
DECOS (Dependable Embedded Components and Systems)
GfSE (Gesellschaft für Systems Engineering)
GI (Gesellschaft für Informatik)
ifip (International Federation for Information Processing)
IFAC (International Federation for Automatic Control)
OCG (Österreichische Computer Gesellschaft)
SCSC (Safety Critical Systems Club)

Table of Contents

Safety Guidelines

Automotive

Aerospace

Verification, Validation, Test

Fault Tolerance

Dependability

A Domain-Specific Framework
for Automated Construction and Verification of
Railway Control Systems
(Extended Abstract)

Anne E. Haxthausen

Informatics and Mathematical Modelling, Technical University of Denmark, Lyngby
ah@imm.dtu.dk

1 Introduction

The development of modern railway and tramway control systems represents a considerable challenge to both systems and software engineers: The goal to increase the traffic throughput while at the same time increasing the availability and reliability of railway operations leads to a demand for more elaborate safety mechanisms in order to keep the risk at the same low level that has been established for European railways until today. The challenge is further increased by the demand for shorter time-to-market periods and higher competition among suppliers of the railway domain; both factors resulting in a demand for a higher degree of automation for the development verification, validation and test phases of projects, without impairing the thoroughness of safety-related quality measures and certification activities. Motivated by these considerations, this presentation describes an approach for automated construction and verification of railway control systems.

2 Development and Verification Approach

We are suggesting a framework consisting of a domain-specific specification language, some tools, and a method for using the language and tools to construct and verify railway control systems that have a common kernel and only differ wrt. some configuration data.

2.1 Automated Construction

In recent years, domain-specific methods for software development have gained wide interest. One of the main objectives addressed by these techniques is the possibility for a given domain to reuse various assets when developing software, e.g. to develop a generic system from which one can instantiate concrete systems. Additionally, the use of domain-specific languages (DSLs) as front-ends for development tools is advocated. In contrast to general-purpose specification and programming languages, DSLs facilitate their utilisation by domain experts

B. Buth, G. Rabe, T. Seyfarth (Eds.): SAFECOMP 2009, LNCS 5775, pp. 1–3, 2009.

who are not specialists in the field of information technology, because they use the terminology of the application domain. Inspired by these considerations, our framework provides a generic railway control system model that can be instantiated with configuration data, a domain-specific language (DSL) for specifying application-specific parameters, and a generator from DSL specifications into configuration data. Hence, for each control system to be developed, the railway specialists specify the application-specific parameters (such as railway network geography and train routes) in the domain-specific language and apply the generator to automatically generate a control system model. An advantage of the front-end consists in the fact that it is much simpler to specify the parameters of a system in the domain-specific language and then apply the generator, than it is to program the configuration data directly. This speeds up the production time and reduces the risk of errors; furthermore, it can be done by domain experts without requiring the assistance of programming specialists. As "programming" language for the control system models we have chosen SystemC that both allows for formal reasoning based on an operational transition system semantics and can be compiled into executable code.

2.2 Automated Verification

Our method prescribes that verification shall be performed at three stages.

Static specification checking. First, when a domain-specific specification has been created, this has to be checked to be statically well-formed by a specification checker provided by the framework.

Bounded model checking. Secondly, when a control system model has been generated from the domain-specific specification, this has to be verified to satisfy required safety properties (as, for example, the requirement that trains never meet at a track segment). A common practise to perform such a verification task fully automated is to use model checking. However, conventional model checking would lead to state space explosions for train control tasks of realistic size. To overcome this problem, we have adopted a bounded model checking strategy combined with inductive reasoning.

Object code verification. Finally, when the control system model has been compiled into object code, it should be verified that the object code correctly implements the control system model. This process can be automated by tools that should also be provided by the framework. Automated object code verification for safety-critical control systems is motivated by the fact that applicable standards for these safety-critical applications, e.g. for railways [3], require a substantial justification with respect to the consistency between high-level software code and the object code generated by the applied compilers.

3   Related Work

The overview given in this presentation is based on results [4] that have been elaborated by the author and Jan Peleska during the last decade. For other complementary and competing approaches for the development and verification of railway control systems the reader is referred to the contributions in [5,6,2], and for a survey of new results and current trends the reader is referred to the paper [1].

References

1. Bjørner, D.: New Results and Current Trends in Formal Techniques for the Development of Software for Transportation Systems. In: Proceedings of the Symposium on Formal Methods for Railway Operation and Control Systems (FORMS 2003), Budapest, Hungary, May 15-16 (2003)
2. Ehrig, H., Damm, W., Desel, J., Große-Rhode, M., Reif, W., Schnieder, E., Westkämper, E. (eds.): INT 2004. LNCS, vol. 3147, pp. 1–8. Springer, Heidelberg (2004)
3. European Committee for Electrotechnical Standardization. EN 50128 – Railway applications – Communications, signalling and processing systems – Software for railway control and protection systems. CENELEC, Brussels (2001)
4. Haxthausen, A.E., Peleska, J.: A Domain-Oriented, Model-Based Approach for Construction and Verification of Railway Control Systems. In: Jones, C.B., Liu, Z., Woodcock, J. (eds.) Formal Methods and Hybrid Real-Time Systems. LNCS, vol. 4700, pp. 320–348. Springer, Heidelberg (2007)
5. Schnieder, E., Tarnai, G. (eds.): Proceedings of Formal Methods for Automation and Safety in Railway and Automotive Systems (FORMS/FORMAT 2004), Braunschweig, Germany. Technical University of Braunschweig (December 2004)
6. Schnieder, E., Tarnai, G. (eds.): Proceedings of Formal Methods for Automation and Safety in Railway and Automotive Systems (FORMS/FORMAT 2007), Braunschweig, Germany. GZVB e.V (2007) ISBN 13:978-3-937655-09-3

Model-Based Development of Medical Devices

Uwe Becker

Dräger Medical AG & Co KG
Moislinger Allee 53 – 55
23542 Lübeck, Germany
uwe.becker @ draeger.com

Abstract. Model-based development can offer many advantages compared to other techniques. This paper will demonstrate how models are used to develop safe systems in a medical devices company. The approach described uses a combination of model-driven analysis, model-driven design, model-driven test and model-driven safety analysis. Different approaches have been developed and followed in the past. The approach presented has been developed in an evolutionary manner and by combining approaches described in literature. It turned out to be well suited for the medical device domain and is considered to be a best practice approach. As such it is part of the development process that must be followed when developing new medical devices. The development process has to be defined in a written way and is checked by TÜV and FDA auditors on a yearly base. It is considered to be well above-average and thus may be adopted by other companies developing safety-relevant devices. During the audit process it is verified that the documentation of the process is as expected and that the actual development process is performed according to the defined process. This assures for companies adopting the approach that it is authenticated by daily practice and its use requires only modest overhead.

Keywords: medical devices, design process, model-driven analysis, MDRE, model- driven design, model-driven test, and model-driven safety analysis.

1   Introduction

There are more than 900 standards in the medical devices domain. By law, and in order to receive the respective certifications required, the devices must adhere to all applicable standards. Safety standards are very high to ensure patient safety even in the presence of a fault. Therefore companies in the medical devices domain have to spend considerable effort to fulfill the required level of safety. In addition, every company strives to improve the safety of their devices even further and thus has some internal standards with which the devices must comply. In some cases, formal verification is considered but it is currently only applied for small parts of the system. In most cases, though, formal verification is not considered applicable due to the very high complexity the products have today. Some parts of the devices may require different amounts of verification effort. Parts considered especially safety-relevant are tested very thoroughly in either case.

B. Buth, G. Rabe, T. Seyfarth (Eds.): SAFECOMP 2009, LNCS 5775, pp. 4–17, 2009.
© Springer-Verlag Berlin Heidelberg 2009

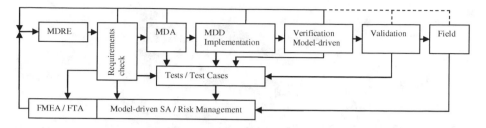

Fig. 1. Development Process Overview

As stated above, companies in the medical device field spend considerable amounts of time, and thus money, to ensure the safety of their devices. It would be very much appreciated by the industry if things could be automated without compromising safety. This is where model-based verification comes in. Using the right tools, many tests can be generated directly from the model and test execution can be automated. Especially regression tests which are applied very frequently benefit from this fact. Following the general trend in the industry, even software for medical devices is now written in a more agile way. In most cases, though, the development process is not purely agile but a mixture of traditional and agile methods. In addition, not every agile method is suitable for use in the medical device domain. Though the selection of the right software development method is not within the scope of this paper, it shall be mentioned that the method has to be chosen very carefully in order not to compromise safety.

This paper describes how safe systems are developed in a medical device company. The approach described uses a combination of model-driven analysis, model-driven design, model-driven test and model-driven safety analysis (see fig. 1). It is considered to be a best practice approach. When using concrete examples, the project of developing a new incubator system is used.

In order to demonstrate the different steps of the complete development process, this paper is organized as follows: Section 2 describes the requirements engineering process. This is partly interleaved with the risk management process described in section 3. Section 4 briefly describes the implementation process being followed by the testing and verification process described in section 5. The paper concludes with a short summary.

2 Requirements Engineering

Requirements engineering is a difficult task to perform. Even though the people writing requirements are skilled and trained to do so, a certain amount of ambiguity or room for interpretation may exist. This should of course be avoided because different people might interpret the requirements in a different manner. To cope with the ever increasing complexity, systems are divided in smaller subsystems or modules and subsystems from earlier projects are re-used. If two modules of such a system interpret requirements in a different way, this might only be noticed at a very late state of the development effort. Thus, it can be very costly to fix such a problem at the system

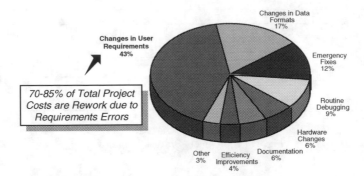

Fig. 2. Survey of 500 Major Projects Maintenance Costs

assembly stage. In addition, if a requirement is misinterpreted, development can be conducted incorrectly. The resulting product may not be what the customer wants. It is well known that the earlier errors can be found and corrected, the cheaper it is. Every later stage adds additional costs which may rise in an exponential manner. Detecting errors in the requirements, therefore, is very effective both in cost and in time-savings. An internal study including different projects showed that the main benefit of the model-based test approaches was in finding errors in the specification. Most of them were found in the early stage of creating models from the user requirements. Some other errors were found after the models had been created. Running the models showed that the system modeled did not exhibit the behavior required or desired. Here again most of the errors did not originate by creating a faulty model from a correct specification, but from an incorrect specification.

Fig. 2 illustrates that investment in requirements engineering pays off well. About three quarters of the development costs are caused by the 43% of changes related to user requirements [15]. Users expect high quality, functionality, and low costs. Unrealistic schedule and/or modification of or unclear requirements cause projects to be expensive, late to market, scrapped or to miss key features. Writing a good specification and finding/removing errors from it is time well invested. The time saved in later steps of development will even convince management that is reluctant to allow spending more time in the specification-writing phase.

Each requirement for a medical device has to be written in such a way that it is testable. At the end of the development cycle, verification and validation of the product has to be performed. This is meant to guarantee that the product developed is the product desired by the user. The verification step is simplified if the requirement specification is written in a form that every requirement is testable. Therefore, the test department is included in the process of writing the requirements. In generating a model and in writing the requirements in a testable way, the test department can plan and develop tests for the system verification phase. Having the tests be developed in parallel to the system itself saves valuable time and leads to shorter time to market. The verification phase is usually followed by a validation phase. This validation phase is somewhat comparable to a beta test phase common with software products. The devices are given to a defined number of users for validation. Of course, this phase should not lead to requirement changes.

Safety, in most cases, is not an explicit customer requirement. Customers do not ask for it; they just expect the device to be safe. They expect it to be a system property just like functionality or efficiency. For this reason there is a two-step requirements generation process. In the first step, the "real" user requirements are gathered. The user requirements are provided in the language of the users about the user domain. The vast majority of these are transferred into a model. The model describes use-cases and represents operational scenarios. They clearly demonstrate the results that operational users get from the device. Of course, there are different types of users. There are use-cases for end users, for training users, for maintenance, installation and service users as well as others. All theses kinds of users have different expectations and require different outcomes in certain situations. The modeling helps to clarify any discrepancy in the requirements from different use-types and the specification. In a second step, two very important users add their requirements. One part of these requirements represents the business aspects. This includes something like, "Function XY is an option the user has to pay for". The other part of those requirements represents the safety aspects. After the device type and the customer requirements for the device are clearly defined, the safety department can start to add the safety requirements to achieve the required goals. This is done using a combined approach.

The user requirements are used to generate the validation or acceptance tests. The system requirements are used to generate the system tests. The user requirements document is reviewed. After it is considered to be free of errors, the system requirements document is generated from it. The system requirements document is more detailed than the user requirements document. This document is input to the system architecture specification document. This document is at a very detailed level and describes the architecture of the system. For more complex systems, the architecture specification document is further detailed into component or sub-system specification documents. Once the architecture of the system is defined, the implementation phase of the system can start.

It is generally a good idea to have the test department develop the tests based on their own models and in parallel to the development activities of the hardware or software department. This, on one hand, keeps the test department or at least a part of it busy during the whole implementation phase. On the other hand, it shortens the gap between the end of the implementation phase and start of the tests in the test phase.

We had a student check the advantages of model-based testing in our development process. He found out that most errors were found in the specification. When deriving the model from the specification, the test department, having a different view on the product, uncovered many errors in the specification itself. The models they generated were different from the models the programmers derived. It is generally difficult to predict who generates the right model. It is our experience that on average, the developers had chosen the correct assumptions when generating the model only in 50% of the cases. This may vary from project to project. If the programmer is very experienced in the application domain, he already knows what to do and how. The models generated by these programmers are correct in most cases. However, the risk may be present that the programmers only have a cursory look at the requirements. Some details may go overlooked.

For some of the use-cases it is very hard to automatically generate test cases and tests. Other use-cases may be completely resistant to this approach. It is our experience that if the use-cases can be converted into state diagrams things are relatively easy. This holds true for both test generation and programming. Nevertheless, generating the model is always worth the work, even if there is no way to automatically generate tests from it.

Lately some tools have been developed advocating model-driven requirements engineering. These tools fit nicely in a development process that uses model-based testing. For this reason, a tool of this sort was used during the development of the new incubator system. The model-driven requirements engineering tool we use describes the requirements in two different ways. Every requirement that can be described with a use-case is described using a use-case model. There are, of course, some requirements that cannot be described by applying a use-case. Conformity to a standard is an example for a requirement that cannot be described by a use-case. Each use-case can contain additional data to further describe the requirement. The additional data, the requirements, and the use-cases are stored in a data base. For example: a user wants to change the O_2 concentration within the incubator. The respective standards require a certain level of accuracy and a maximum time in which the new O_2 concentration has to be reached.

The model-driven requirements engineering approach has three major advantages. The first is that users and product managers usually would rather think in terms of use-cases than in abstract and distinct requirements. The new product can be described in a more intuitive way. Therefore, it is easier to detect errors or gaps in the planned behavior. The second advantage is that there is already a model that can be used as input for model-based testing. There is no ambiguity in the requirements that leads to different models for tests and implementation. The correctness of the model, and thus the requirements themselves, can be verified easily. An additional advantage of this approach is that many of the use-cases can be converted to executable models. This allows product management to verify the requirements even by showing the executable models to customers. Customer input can be gained at a very early stage of development and thus costly errors can easily be avoided. This is a major advantage especially for new features. The user interface and operation of the new feature can be shown to customers. Valuable feedback can be gained and execution can be optimized even before the feature is really implemented. Such early feedback saves a lot of time and costly improvement loops. On the other hand the test department can already begin to design tests. For some of the requirements it may even be possible to automatically generate the appropriate tests. In either case, development of features and test cases can be performed in parallel. This keeps the test department busy and saves additional time at the end of the development phase. Testing can begin directly after the development is finished or with only a slight delay. There is no additional analysis and test generating phase which usually is in the range of some months.

3 Risk Management Process

The systems risk analysis is performed in two steps. As a first step there is a FMEA and a conventional fault tree analysis. This is done for two reasons. The FMEA is done at a very early point in the project. At this early stage, the system architecture definition is not yet complete. High level errors and possible unsafe states are identified using the user requirements. This information is added to the user requirements to form the system requirements. The latter are part of the input when defining the architecture of the new system. With a given initial system architecture in place, a high level FTA can be applied to it. The results of this FTA can be used to fine tune the system architecture and to increase system safety as a first step. The information gained from this step may be used to improve the system requirements. In terms of the incubator example there is the risk that the O_2 concentration is above the level set. This may harm the eyes of neonates. Risk management will require a measure to stop O_2 flow if measured concentration is above the desired value plus a tolerated limit. Based on the improved system requirements, a model is generated. This model is described in the SysML language and has some additional attributes when compared to other models. These additional attributes result from the fact that the model ought to serve two very different purposes. The first is to help the system test department. The model is either used to generate tests and test vectors directly from the model or used as a high level hierarchical model, which is refined in further steps of model-based testing. The other purpose the model ought to serve is for model-driven safety analysis. The approach thus independently developed is somewhat similar to other approaches [9, 10, 11, 14, 16, 17, 18]. It is our opinion that the analysis should start, as our approach does, in a very early stage of the project. The requirements and the architecture both may be changed based on the results. In addition, we take a combined approach both for the safety analysis of the system and from the test perspective. It is our experience that the main benefits of model-based testing are in the field of test automation and requirements check.

Safety analysis is an essential part in the development of medical devices. Safety is an essential property of the systems just like efficiency and reliability are. Some of the devices developed are life-supporting. This means that a failure of such a device may lead to the death of a patient if no adequate safety measures are applied. As complexity of the devices increases, the demand for automation in safety analysis grows. It is common sense that the traditional techniques are not necessarily complete. In addition, the results of such techniques largely depend on the experience of the analyst. Knowing that it is not sufficient to just replace the traditional manual techniques for automated counterparts, we follow a combined approach. The trend with new developments indicates a steady increase in the software portion of the systems. For some systems, the portion of total development time dedicated to hard-ware development is between 10 and 20%. This shift towards software is accompanied with an increase in the complexity of the systems. For this reason, the techniques used for safety analysis have to cope with the increased complexity. Automated tools can be effective in dealing with the inherent complexity of largely software-based systems. While for traditional techniques emphasis is placed on completeness, this changes to accuracy of the model for the automated techniques.

One part of the safety analysis is based on traditional manual techniques. The analysts perform an FMEA of the system. If the analysts are very experienced, first results from this step can be obtained very quickly. Despite these early results, the analysis based on the traditional techniques continues throughout the whole development cycle. The results are used to improve specification and design. It is our strong belief that model checking is a very effective technique if used with caution. For this reason, first models of the systems are being built in parallel with the manual analysis.

Two different types of models are used during this second step. One is an operational model. This model describes how the system operates. The other is a property-based model. This model describes the required system properties. The combined approach guarantees that no false confidence is obtained from model checking, and that no inappropriate guidance for risk reduction of the system is followed. Model checking can only confirm the presence of faults in the model, but not the absence thereof. Though safety analysis continues throughout the whole development cycle to evaluate every design change, it is advantageous if results are obtained in a relatively early stage of the design. This is crucial because of the huge costs for correcting defects later in development.

In order to have the risk management process continue throughout the whole development process, planning the different activities along the development chain is required. The international standard ISO 9126 defines a set of properties a system should have. For each of these properties, we defined a set of measures and a set of testing activities. The measures may well be split over different development steps.

The models generated have to be precise in describing the system and its environment. In addition, not only the desired behavior of the system but also the undesired hazardous behavior, together with component failures, has to be modeled.

Model-checking algorithms often explore the state space to determine whether the system satisfies the properties required. In general, the models generated are rather complex and state space is large. Therefore some abstraction steps are performed to reduce state space. Abstractions have to be done very carefully to avoid discarding details of the model during the transformation that could be the cause for a hazardous state. There are some well known algorithms for variable restriction and variable abstraction that can be used [6, 18]. To obtain valid results, the abstraction model has to be both sound and complete. Even though completeness cannot be guaranteed in every case, it is given in far the most cases. This is the trade-off that has to be made in order to be able to repeatedly apply the abstraction. The state space of the resulting model is reduced greatly – often by some orders of magnitude.

The operational model is less likely to omit required behavior. In addition, it is, in almost every case, executable. The property of being executable remains unchanged during model transformation. Therefore a more abstract model can easily be checked against functional requirements. Functional restrictions after transformation can be detected and the model or the abstraction step can be modified accordingly. The property-based model, on the other hand, is concise, abstract, and minimizes implementation bias. If the operational model shows the desired functionality, the model can be cross-checked with the property-based model. Inconsistencies between the two models can be found in a relatively easy manner.

4 Implementation Process

This phase again starts with generating models. The models in this phase usually describe the interfaces between the different parts of the software. Additional models refine the model down to the respective classes present in a specific module of the software. In general, model-driven architecture (MDA) is focused on forward engineering, i.e. producing code from abstract, human-elaborated specifications. One of the main aims of the MDA is to separate design from architecture. As the different concepts and technologies used to realize designs and architectures have changed at their own pace, decoupling them allows system developers to choose from the best and most fitting in both domains. The design addresses the functional (use-case) requirements while architecture provides the infrastructure through which non-functional requirements like scalability, reliability and performance are realized. MDA envisages that the platform-independent model (PIM), which represents a conceptual design realizing the functional requirements, will survive changes in realization technologies and software architectures.

Medical devices require a high safety level. A life-supporting device not safe enough could likely kill a patient. Thus, such devices have to be safe, even in the presence of a fault. If the fault can be detected during runtime, the system has to be safe in the presence of a single fault. If the system can only detect the fault during start-up, it has to ensure that safety is not compromised until the next start. If the system is not able to detect the fault, it is considered fault free and has to be safe even in the presence of a second fault. In general, life-supporting devices have a SIL safety level above 2 (acc. IEC 61508). A lot of testing is done while developing such devices. Most of the code is developed using the test-first approach. We determined that the advantages of such an approach are twofold. First, there is a test for every unit of code. This results in high code coverage of the tests. Second, and most important, there is no rush-to-code. Programmers consider the code more carefully and think more about the implementation and its advantages than they did before using the test-first approach. This in turn leads to higher code quality containing fewer errors.

Programmers often tend to consider unit testing as keeping them from their work. Furthermore, they consider writing tests a large waste of time. For these reasons, they often fear that they are not able to keep delivery dates. It is our practical experience that none of this is the case. Due to the higher quality of the code, they are more productive and spend less time debugging. There is no delay caused by the test-first approach. In addition, the tests have to be performed either way. If the programmers would not write the tests, the test people would. This would, on one hand, only shift the work from one group to another and, on the other hand, would take much longer. The test people first have to understand the code and then think about tests. The programmers know all about their code and thus can write tests faster. The only small disadvantage is that programmers have to possess some knowledge about testing. This requires some extra training. But this is worth the investment.

It is common practice to model the code before implementing it. An UML-based tool is used for this purpose. As a first step, the models were only used for documentation and to provide a standardized stub for classes and programs. As a second step, this changed to model-driven design and model-driven architecture. Thus a model-driven design using a test-first approach is used. Programmers and testers use different models. The models of the programmers are used to verify the models of the testers, but not to generate tests from them.

It is tempting to derive tests from pre-existing models. This is only a good idea for tests that the programmers need. The testers often have a very different view of things. Furthermore, they derive their models directly from the specification. This is the way to find errors on the path from specification to code. If programmers and testers come to a different model, the cause for this discrepancy must be investigated. For

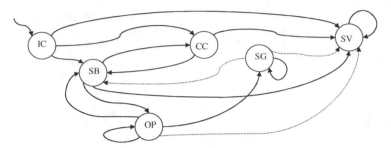

Fig. 3. State machine example from the project

instance, it may result from an ambiguous specification. If this is the case, the true customer requirement must be determined. This avoids developing a completely tested device which no customer wants.

It is our strong belief that producing a life-supporting device is not contradictory to a more agile development process. Software is developed using a test-first approach. Credo of Agility is to release early and to release often. Thus, only little functionality is added to a module in every release cycle. (Release in this context is an integration step with other modules or other parts of the software of that module). Programmers will realize the O_2 control loop in cycle #i and the superimposed warming control loop in cycle #n for instance. Every cycle consists of programming tests for a module in a first step. Module function is added in a second step. Practical experience shows that this leads to improved code quality. There is a test for each function of the module and there is no rush-to-code. Writing tests first causes programmers to think about the problem in a different way. Thinking about the code more thoroughly leads to better code quality. A programmer may only deliver code tested to work. Automatic code integration begins after code is delivered to the central code pool. There is a test for each piece of module functionality. Every test is run in the automatic integration stage. This gives three results. First, it is known if the code will compile with the other code of the module. Second, the results of the unit tests show if there are any side effects. If this is the case, unit tests from other parts of the module will fail. Third, there is always a functional base-line of the code. This can be tested as soon as hardware is available.

As far as possible, the automatic integration phase will also integrate a test using hardware-in-the-loop tests. This is a very interesting and a very important test. Some functionality or some behavior can only be tested with hardware in the loop. Timing issues may be mentioned as an example. It is our goal to test early and to find errors or undesired behavior as early as possible. The earlier an error is found the easier and the cheaper it is to correct it.

Let us consider the example state machine of figure 3. This is the usual way the designer develops such. The designer will draw a so-called bubble diagram. Arrows are used to indicate if the respective state is entered or left if a certain event occurs. Having completed the bubble diagram, there are two possible ways to get from it to code. The first way is to draw the bubble diagram in an UML tool. The tool will generate some stubs of code from the diagram. The code produced from the UML tool may or may not be easy to understand by a human being. The other way to get to code is again to start with the UML tool. Now the tool is not used to produce code directly, but is merely used as a drawing aid as far as code is considered. If a tool having some extensions to UML is used, the diagram can be used to generate tests from it. Some UML tools may support generating a state transition table from the bubble diagram. If this is not the case, some additional tool is used to generate such. Even if the UML tool is able to generate a state transition table, some additional work is required to convert it into code. Using an additional tool, generating the state transition table directly from the UML diagram may have the advantage that the table and additional code required can be generated in a single step. Using the BOOST library allows for generating the code for the state machine at compile time. Some kind of template meta-programming is used to perform the magic. This has the great advantage that the code is in a form that can be read and checked by humans very easily. Automatic generation of code from a bubble diagram helps to eliminate errors and to increase the maintainability of the code.

If the UML tool supports the extensions of UML, which are required for automatic test generation, the diagram really saves a lot of time and effort Automatic generation of test vectors and of the test suite for the state machine can be triggered by pressing a single button. This allows for automatic testing of the state machine behavior. It is well known that automated tests are capable of saving huge amounts of time, especially when performing regression tests. For safety-critical systems, such regression tests are performed rather frequently. If things are automated, the tests can run over night and thus do not keep the programmers from working. Safety-critical systems usually require adequate documentation. This again is easily accomplished if the code is directly derived from the bubble diagram. Furthermore, it is easier to check if the code exhibits the required behavior. During requirements inspection, the tester usually generates his/her own bubble diagram. It is much easier to perform the check on such a high level as on a bubble diagram. In some cases, it may even be possible to let a tool perform the comparison of the two diagrams. This, of course, is the preferred method because it will eliminate possible errors and omissions that can occur when humans compare the diagrams. Generally speaking, it is always a good idea to let things be tested or checked using a tool. Tools usually do not get tired and do not tend to overlook things. The time required to automate tests or to automatically generate tests is well invested if the respective test is performed frequently. It is, in most cases, not worth doing it if the test is performed only once or very seldom.

The use of some type of template meta-programming has the advantage of being very intuitive. It does not generate overhead after the compilation. Only the compilation itself will take somewhat longer. As this additional time is only in the range of a few seconds, this really is not an issue. As in the example above, the additional time required to resolve the template meta-programming is negligible. Traditionally, state machines are programmed using some kind of switch statements. If the state machine is in a certain state and a certain event is detected, a certain action is performed. There has to be an entry for every state in the switch tree. For every event there has to be a separate "if" or "case" statement in the respective switch block. If the programming scheme proposed is used, there is only a list of functions having the events as parameters. This is easy to check for omissions. In addition, the compiler will check if all the code required is available. If there is an event triggering a transition and the function describing the transition is not available, there will be an error at compile time. The code simply will not compile and thus everything required has been considered if the code will get compiled and linked. In addition, the usage of the templates will make the code type safe. If a programmer inadvertently changes the automatically generated code during code-writing, the compiler will detect this and will issue an error.

5 Testing and Verification Process

In the medical devices domain, users expect high quality, high safety and high functionality. When starting the implementation phase, functionality is prioritized as a first step. The functionality having the highest device or project risk is implemented first. The same holds true for software testing. The software portions generating the highest risk for the patient are tested with highest priority and highest amount of effort. Other parts of the software are tested with less effort. For a ventilator system, the functionality that might generate the highest risk to the patient is the pressure control of the respiratory pressure. If this pressure is too high or pressure limiting does not work as a result of an error, the patient may be injured or even die. For an incubator system, the functions having the highest risks are warming and control of the O_2 concentration. For this reason, very intensive testing is performed in the areas mentioned. Testers will check various settings and control system reaction using calibrated O_2 sensors to check accuracy and response time. Changing between day- and night-view, which is essentially applying a different skin to the GUI, imposes no risk to the patient. Testing effort in this area may thus be limited to a modest amount.

By law, the development process of medical devices has to be of high quality. The testing and verification process is an essential part of the development process of medical devices and systems because producing life-supporting devices requires a high amount of testing. Every function has to be tested. Virtually no function may slip through inadvertently and remain untested. Annual auditing helps to ensure this quality. Model-based testing and the test-first approach are used to reach this goal. Parts of the software can be generated right from the models. Model-based testing can be used for those parts of the software. The test department generates its own models and tests the software against this model. This allows for automatic generation of tests. Using the right tools, the tests generated can be applied to the software and automatic testing can be performed. It is essential, though, that tests and test cases are generated from different models than those from which the software is generated. This ensures that errors and omissions in the models used to generate the software can be detected. If the same model is used to generate both the software and the tests, errors in the model stay undetected. This would just check the automated generation process of the software which is assumed to be correct anyway.

Other parts of the software cannot be fully generated from models. In these cases, only stubs or parts of the software are generated. Some functionality has to be implemented by hand. It is part of the development process that this kind of implementation is performed using the test-first approach. A test is specified for each function. The automated testing will return an error for each function as long as it is not yet fully implemented. Each intermediate release of the software may only contain the functionality that does not return an error during the automated testing. The new functionality will be added in a later release. This ensures that there is always fully functional software available for testing.

To parallelize development, system software is divided into modules. Within a module, every class and some larger clusters both have their own unit tests. Every time a programmer commits code to the code repository of a module, a so-called build servant starts. In addition to compiling the code, this tool also executes the unit tests of the respective module. In this way, programmers are forced to deliver both code that compiles and tests for the code that run without errors. Basic code quality is improved. Integration tests may start earlier. Even if a module does not have all of its functionality implemented, integration tests may make sense. The interface at the module boundaries may be tested anyway. Errors may be found early and the interface may be corrected. From certain milestones on, regression integration tests are performed on a regular basis. These are automated tests that ensure that all modules of a system work together. The aim is to have a functional/running system after every integration/development step. Even though not all functionality is implemented, the test department may gain valuable insight from early tests. A design freeze is performed if the code of a module has reached a predefined level of maturity and all functionality is implemented. This is usually the point at which code reading starts.

The test department develops a verification test plan. To shorten time to market, test development or even some testing starts early and is largely done in parallel with the development of the systems itself. As far as feasible, models are developed to automatically generate tests and test suites. Regression tests that are performed with a certain frequency are automated, too. This allows for a large part of the tests to be automated and run frequently.

Usually some tests remain that either cannot be automated, require manual interaction, or are exploratory. Experience shows that some faults in the software or some behavior can only be found using exploratory tests. This holds true especially if models have been generated for modules but not for the combination of them. In addition, these kinds of tests are used to verify completeness of the models.

In general, the test department schedules testing effort with the help of a matrix. As a first step, the functionality of the system is split into sub-functionalities. The result may be a considerable list of functions to be tested. As a second step, the functions on the list will be prioritized. Usually, three variables are considered to determine the priority of a certain function. One is the criticality of a function. A function may gain a high value for criticality if it is of potential danger to the patient, as in the case of pressure control of breathing gas, for instance. It will gain a low value if it is not critical, as the input of a patient's name, for example. The second and third variables are marketing and user convenience respectively. In such a way every function of the system is equipped with a score. After that, clusters holding functions with certain ranges of the score are generated. The cluster holding the functions having the highest scores will be assigned the largest part of the testing time. The cluster holding the functions having the lowest scores will be assigned the shortest testing time. This will help to focus the testers on those parts/functions of the system that are most critical.

In a further step, each functionality's score is distributed across the properties set down by ISO 9126: Functionality, Reliability, Usability, Efficiency, Changeability, and Portability. The test department has defined a set of five test phases. These are: Unit testing, SW integration testing (integrating modules together), SW/HW integration testing, system testing, and acceptance/verification testing. The test department further defines to which extend the properties of ISO 9126 are tested in the defined test phases. Having all these parameters, testing time for the above- mentioned sub-functionalities may not only be scheduled as a whole block, but also split across the testing phases and thus along the development cycle of the product.

The final system has to undergo rigorous testing with regard to the respective standards. Company internal standards may require further qualification or may require that tests are more stringent than required by a standard. In addition, every requirement of the specification has to be checked by at least one test. If a system has passed all the required tests, it is ready to receive the CE mark, for example. At that point the system is given to so-called beta testers for clinical evaluation. The system will only be marketed if it has passed this additional clinical evaluation phase.

6 Conclusion

Successful projects spend considerably more time or effort in the requirements and concept phase than failing projects do. Safe systems require a good concept. Model-driven requirements engineering leads to more effort being spent in the requirements phase. Even though the supporting tools allow the requirements phase to be completed in the same amount of time as before when using the traditional method, there are more checks and a deeper analysis of the requirements. For these reasons, model-driven requirements engineering is one key feature for the development of a life-supporting medical device. Due to the fact that more effort is spent in the requirements phase, the probability for starting a successful project increases. If the test department starts generating models for model-based testing at an early stage of the project, this in turn will lead to further auditing of the requirements. All these activities aid in providing a sound base for the start of a new project.

In sum, the development process shown uses models throughout the whole development chain. Model-based safety analysis and the test-first approach, together with model-based design, lead to sound development concepts. Use of models provides the benefit that quality of design and design output are increased. Programmers do not "rush-to-code" but perform a more thorough analysis of the code to be written. Thus, the approach results in better code quality and better code design. The code produced contains fewer errors and thus less time is required for debugging and fixing bugs. The projects are more likely to be on schedule and thus are completed earlier than projects not using models, which are likely to be delayed. Crosby states that quality is free. We would like to add that it is not only free, but saves time and money and thus pays off instantly. We showed that around 75% of project costs are generated by faults and changes in the requirements. For this reason, the development process described using models and automated checking in very early phases definitely will save project costs.

Some improvements are still possible in the area of transferring models from certain phases into other phases. In addition, more formal auditing is much appreciated. We are rather confident that we can take benefit from the advances in the area of model-based requirements engineering and model-based safety analysis.

References

1. Cepin, M., de Lemos, R., Mavko, B., Riddle, S., Saeed, A.: An Object–Based Approach to Modelling and Analysis of Failure Properties. In: Daniel, P. (ed.) Proceedings of the 16th International Conference on Computer Safety, Reliability and Security (SAFECOMP 1997), September 1997, pp. 281–294. Springer, Berlin (1997)
2. Cepin, M., Riddle, S.: Object Modelling and Safety Analysis of Engineered Safety Features Actuation System, Technical Report TR ISAT 96/11 University of Newcastle upon Tyne (December 1996)
3. de Lemos, R., Saeed, A., Anderson, T.: On the Integration of Requirements Analysis and Safety Analysis for Safety-Critical Software, Department of Computing Science, University of Newcastle upon Tyne. Technical Report Series No. 630 (May 1998)
4. de Lemos, R., Saeed, A.: Validating Formal Verification using Safety Analysis Techniques, Computing Science, Technical Report Series, No. 668 (March 1999)
5. de Lemos, R., Saeed, A., Anderson, T.: On the Safety Analysis of Requirements Specifications. In: Maggioli, V. (ed.) Proceedings of the 13th International Conference on Computer Safety, Reliability and Security (SAFECOMP 1994), October 1994, pp. 217–227 (1994)
6. Heitemeyer, C., Kirby, J., Labaw, B., Archer, M., Bharadwaj, R.: Using Abstraction and Model Checking to Detect Safety Violations in Requirements Specifications. IEEE Transactions on Software Engineering 24(11) (November 1998)
7. Holcombe, M., Ipate, F., Groundoudis, A.: Complete Functional Testing of Safety Critical Systems. In: Proceedings of the IFAC Workshop on Safety Reliabity in Emerging Control Technologies, November 1995, pp. 199–204. Pergamon Press, Oxford (1996)
8. Hussey, A.: HAZOP Analysis of Formal Models of Safety-Critical Interactive Systems. In: Koornneef, F., van der Meulen, M.J.P. (eds.) SAFECOMP 2000. LNCS, vol. 1943, pp. 371–381. Springer, Heidelberg (2000)
9. Ortmeier, F., Reif, W.: Failure-sensitive specification: A formal method for finding failure modes, Technical Report 3, Institut fuer Informatik, University Augsburg (2004)
10. Ortmeier, F., Reif, W.: Safety optimization: A combination of fault tree analysis and optimization techniques. In: Proceedings of the Conference on Dependable Systems and Networks (DSN 2004). IEEE Computer Society, Los Alamitos (2004)
11. Ortmeier, F., Schellhorn, G., Thums, A., Reif, W., Hering, B., Trappschuh, H.: Safety Analysis of the Height Control System for the Elbtunnel. In: Anderson, S., Bologna, S., Felici, M. (eds.) SAFECOMP 2002. LNCS, vol. 2434, pp. 296–308. Springer, Heidelberg (2002)
12. Ortmeier, F., Thums, A., Schellhorn, G., Reif, W.: Combining formal methods and safety analysis – the forMoSA approach. In: Ehrig, H., Damm, W., Desel, J., Große-Rhode, M., Reif, W., Schnieder, E., Westkämper, E. (eds.) INT 2004. LNCS, vol. 3147, pp. 474–493. Springer, Heidelberg (2004)
13. Saeed, A., de Lemos, R., Anderson, T.: An Approach for the Risk Analysis of Safety Specifications, In: Proceedings of the 9th Annual Conference on Computer Assurance (COMPASS 1994), pp. 209–221 (June 1994)
14. Saeed, A., de Lemos, R., Anderson, T.: Safety Analysis for Requirements Specifications: Methods and Techniques. In: Proceedings of the 15th International Conference on Computer Safety, Reliability and Security (SAFECOMP 1995), October 1995, pp. 27–41 (1995)
15. Telelogic, A.B.: Writing Effective User Requirements; Education Material
16. Thums, A., Ortmeier, F.: Formale Methoden und Sicherheitsanalyse, Technical Report, University Augsburg, Institut fuer Informatik (2002)
17. Thums, A., Schellhorn, G., Ortmeier, F., Reif, W.: Interactive verification of statecharts. In: Ehrig, H., Damm, W., Desel, J., Große-Rhode, M., Reif, W., Schnieder, E., Westkämper, E. (eds.) INT 2004. LNCS, vol. 3147, pp. 355–373. Springer, Heidelberg (2004)
18. Chan, W.: Model Checking Large Software Specifications. IEEE Transactions on Software Engineering 27(7), 498–520 (1998)

Why Are People's Decisions Sometimes Worse with Computer Support?

Eugenio Alberdi[1], Lorenzo Strigini[1], Andrey A. Povyakalo[1], and Peter Ayton[2]

[1] Centre for Software Reliability, City University London, London, UK
[2] Psychology Department, City University London, London, UK
{e.alberdi,strigini,povyakalo}@csr.city.ac.uk,
P.Ayton@city.ac.uk

Abstract. In many applications of computerised decision support, a recognised source of undesired outcomes is operators' apparent over-reliance on automation. For instance, an operator may fail to react to a potentially dangerous situation because a computer fails to generate an alarm. However, the very use of terms like "over-reliance" betrays possible misunderstandings of these phenomena and their causes, which may lead to ineffective corrective action (e.g. training or procedures that do not counteract all the causes of the apparently "over-reliant" behaviour). We review relevant literature in the area of "automation bias" and describe the diverse mechanisms that may be involved in human errors when using computer support. We discuss these mechanisms, with reference to errors of omission when using "alerting systems", with the help of examples of novel counterintuitive findings we obtained from a case study in a health care application, as well as other examples from the literature.

Keywords: decision support, computer aided decision making, alerting systems, human-machine diversity, omission errors.

1   Introduction

It has long been known that introducing automation might have unexpected side effects on human performance [1, 2]. For instance, consider a computer tool designed to highlight targets of interest on a radar screen. If the computer does not highlight one such target, even an experienced radar operator could be led to miss that target, even if he would not have missed it without the computer aid. Such phenomena are often attributed to complacency, which makes operators abdicate their responsibility to the automated support. Given this interpretation, a tool designer may assume this to be the main risk, and so proper training and indoctrination is the natural defence (e.g. [3]); this attitude is widespread in practice. We argue that this view is too simplistic and present a much richer picture of unintended, subtle effects that automation may have and which a designer needs to be prepared to guard against.

Automation is increasingly taking on the role of *supporting* knowledge-intensive human tasks rather than directly *replacing* some of the human's functions. This actually makes the problem of computer-related human errors subtler. The responsibility

B. Buth, G. Rabe, T. Seyfarth (Eds.): SAFECOMP 2009, LNCS 5775, pp. 18–31, 2009.

for correct action rests with the user. One might think that user mistakes can be reduced by simple training or, sometimes, by a user interface that prevents those mistakes. But in practice computers and their users form human-computer systems, or "socio-technical systems", which need to be assessed as whole systems from the viewpoints of reliability and safety. Examples of these supportive systems are *alerting* systems: from spell-checkers to alarm-filtering systems for industrial control rooms through collision warning systems in transportation or computerised monitoring in health care. In these monitoring applications, automation typically assists the operator in judgement-oriented tasks – like dealing with anomalies and taking high-level decisions – by adding to situational data broadly "advisory" input: attention cues, prefiltered alarms, suggested diagnoses, or even recommended manoeuvres. If operators "trust" the computer's help too much or too little [4-6], compared to their own judgement skills, reliability and safety of operation may suffer. Labels used in the literature are: "automation bias", automation-induced "complacency" [7-9], "over-reliance" on automation [10], "automation dependence" [11] or computer induced "confirmation bias" [12].

The purpose of this paper is to both review and broaden the set of explanatory mechanisms proposed in the literature as potential causes of undesired effects of automation. We argue that such effects may indeed result from "complacency" but often, *instead*, from complex cognitive mechanisms in decision making under uncertainty. It is easy to view the user as culpable for reduced performance, but our analyses suggest that this is a simplistic, and thus often misleading, assumption. At each demand for a decision, the operator's use of computer help depends on the details of that individual demand as well as on the operator's skills and the computer's design. Performance can be influenced by all of these factors as well as interactions among them. We present a (non exhaustive) set of possible cause-effect mechanisms contributing to human error. Due to space restrictions, we focus on: *errors of omission* (human failure to react to target events) when using computerised *alerting tools*. The intention is to help designers of these socio-technical systems (i.e., the combination of computer algorithms, user interfaces, procedures, training protocols, etc.) to adopt appropriate defences to match these diverse threats.

In the rest of the paper, we present: an overview of the human factors literature on automation bias and related concepts (section 2); a brief description of a case study in the area of computer-assisted cancer detection, which has motivated many of the analyses and conclusions presented in this paper (section 3); an outline of the mechanisms contributing to errors of omission by computer-assisted operators (section 4); a discussion of the uses and limitations of this descriptive approach (section 5); and conclusions (section 6).

2   Literature on Automation Bias, Complacency and Trust

2.1   Scope and Terminology

This review focuses on computer assisted monitoring or decision making, where an automated alerting tool supports human decisions with some form of non-binding "advice", which can take the form of filtered or enhanced information, alerts and prompts.

The scenario of operation we envisage is that for the *user* or *operator*, *demands* for action may arise (for instance, a patient's vital sign indicate an impending crisis, two vehicles are approaching a potential collision, a word is misspelled in a document). The user sees the *raw data* about the situation (pulse, blood pressure, etc. for a patient; position and motion vectors of vehicles, visually estimated or displayed on a radar screen; the text of the document) in which s/he needs to detect *cues* (specific combinations of ranges of vital signs, or distance and velocities, or the misspelled word itself) and assess them and, if necessary, take an *alarm response*, such as recalling a patient for further examinations, initiate evasive manoeuvres, search for an alternative spelling of a word. A cue may indicate a *target* (real need for an alarm response: a demand implies the presence of at least one target), but the user needs to apply skill and knowledge to decide whether a given cue actually represents a target. To support the user, the computerised warning *tool* is designed to provide *prompts* (e.g. visual highlights on a screen) that point at cues for consideration. In this initial analysis, we do not consider the possibility that the tools also suggest specific actions. There is the possibility of the tool *missing* targets (*false negative* error, or *FN*), as well as of *false prompts* (*false positive* error, or *FP*). The tool can be assessed in terms of its probabilities of FN or FP errors, or equivalent pairs of measures (e.g. sensitivity/specificity are often used in signal detection theory and in the medical literature).

The errors of the human-computer system are also classified into false negatives (the user fails to initiate an alarm response despite a target being present) and false positives (the user initiates an alarm response in the absence of a target) and the system's dependability is described by FN and FP error probabilities (or equivalent pairs of measures). Another important figure is the *alarm response rate* – the cumulative frequency of alarm responses, either correct or spurious – since these are costly and most systems can only function if this rate is less than a certain threshold.

It is useful to introduce some terminology from the human factors literature to contextualise the scope of systems and of errors that we cover here.

Parasuraman and Riley [10] discussed different ways in which human-computer interaction can go wrong and talked about three aspects of ineffective human use of automation: *disuse*, i.e., underutilization of automation, where humans ignore automated warning signals; *misuse*, i.e., over-reliance on automation, where humans are more likely to rely on computer advice (even if wrong) than on their own judgement; *abuse*, when technology is developed without due regard for human needs or the consequences for human (and hence system) performance and the operator's authority in the system.

Skitka and colleagues [13] focused on the *misuse* of automation, in particular on the "automation bias" effects occurring when people used wrong computer advice for monitoring tasks in aviation. They distinguished two types of computer-induced error: a) *errors of commission*: decision-makers follow *automated* advice even in the face of more valid or reliable indicators suggesting that the automated aid is wrong; b) *errors of omission*: decision makers do not take appropriate action, despite non-automated indications of problems, because the *automated* tool did not prompt them.

Focusing on *warnings* generated by automated tools, Meyer [14], distinguishes between two alternative ways in which humans can "follow" or "conform to" the advice from a alerting system: compliance and reliance. *Compliance* indicates that the operator acts according to a warning signal and takes an action. *Reliance* is used to describe those situations where the alerting system indicates that "things are OK" and the operator accordingly – i.e. not merely coincidentally – takes no action.

As a result, combining Skitka's and Meyer's terminologies, undue *compliance* (complying with an incorrect automated warning) would lead to *errors of commission* and undue *reliance* (failing to take action when no automated warning is issued) would lead to *errors of omission*.

2.2 Automation Bias, Complacency and Trust

The phrase "automation bias" was introduced by Mosier et al. [15] when studying the behaviour of pilots in a simulated flight. In this study, they encountered both omission and commission errors. These findings were then replicated with non-pilot samples (student participants) in laboratory settings simulating aviation monitoring tasks [13]. They found that, when the automated tool was reliable, the participants in the automated condition made more correct responses. However, participants with automation that was imperfect (i.e. occasionally giving unreliable support) were more likely to make errors than those who performed the same task without automated advice. In Skitka and colleagues' studies, the decision-makers had access to other (non automated) sources of information. In the automated condition they were informed that the automated tool was not completely reliable but all other instruments were 100% reliable. Still, many chose to follow the advice of the automated tool even when it was wrong and was contradicted by the other sources of information. The authors concluded that these participants had been biased by automation and interpreted their errors (especially their errors of omission) as a result of complacency or reduction in vigilance.

Factors that have been investigated in empirical studies as possible influences in people's vulnerability to automation bias include: individual differences among operators [5, 13, 16, 17]; people's accountability for their own decisions [17]; the levels of automation at which the computer support is provided [12, 18]; the location of computer advice/warnings with respect to raw data or other non-automated sources of information [19, 20]; people's exposure to automation failures [21].

People's ineffective use of computerised tools is often described in terms of "complacency", which is said to cause over-reliance or "uncritical reliance" on automation [7-10]. However, there is no general agreement about what exactly is "complacency" and what are the best ways to measure it [16]. What seems to be common to most characterisations is a sense of contentment, unawareness of dangers or deficiencies and failure to look for evidence or to examine the raw data in a careful enough manner.

A problem with terms like "complacency" is that they suggest value judgments on the human experts. Moray [22] points out that the claim that automation fosters complacency suggests that operators are at fault and argues that the problem often lies in the characteristics of the automated tools, not in the human operators' performance.

Similarly, Wickens and Dixon [23] question the notions of complacency or reduced vigilance as explanations of automation bias. Instead, they argue that operators, whilst being aware of the unreliability of the diagnostic tools, choose to depend on the imperfect computer output to keep their cognitive processing resources for other tasks, particularly in situations with high workload.

Another concept that is frequently invoked when talking about automation bias or (over)reliance on automation is "trust" [4-6, 8, 10, 24-29]. The common assumption is that the more a human operator *trusts* an automated aid the more likely s/he is to *rely* on or *comply* with the advice provided by the aid. If a human trusts an aid that is adequately reliable or fails to trust an aid that is indeed too unreliable, appropriate use of automation should occur as a result. However if a human trusts (and therefore follows the advice of) an unreliable tool, then automation bias may occur (or misuse of automation as defined above). Similarly if a person does not trust a highly reliable tool, the person may end up disusing (as defined above) or under-using the tool, hence the full potential benefits of automation will not be fulfilled.

Subjective measures of the trust of human operators in a computer tool have been found to be highly predictive of people's frequency of use of the tool [5, 30]. Use of automation (or reliance in its generic sense) is usually assessed with observations of the proportion of times during which a device is used by operators or by assessing the probability of operators' detecting automation failures [19].

Factors that have been investigated in empirical studies as possible influences in people's trust in automation include: people's exposure to automation errors [5, 30, 31], the consistency of the tool's reliability [16, 32], the invasiveness or intrusiveness of the tool's advice [33, 34].

3   A Case Study: Computer Aided Detection (CAD) for Mammography

Many of the considerations we present originate from a case study we conducted in the area of CAD for breast cancer screening [35-40]. In breast screening, expert clinicians ("readers") examine *mammograms* (X-ray images of a woman's breasts), and decide whether the patient should be "recalled" for further tests because they suspect cancer. A CAD tool is designed to assist the interpretation of mammograms primarily by alerting readers to potentially cancerous areas that they may otherwise overlook. CAD is not meant to be a diagnostic tool, in the sense that it only marks areas, which should be subsequently classified by the reader to reach the "recall/no recall" decision. In the intention of the designers, it can only *avoid* a cancer being missed but *not cause* a cancer to be missed.

Our case study provided evidence of automation bias effects in the use of CAD; effects which could not be attributed to complacency and could actually coexist with users' reported mistrust towards the tool [35]. Previous studies had concluded that on average using CAD was either beneficial or ineffectual. Our analyses indicated instead that CAD reduced decision errors by some readers on some cases but increased errors by other readers on some cases. In short, this simple computer-assisted task hid subtle effects, easy to miss by designers and assessors [37].

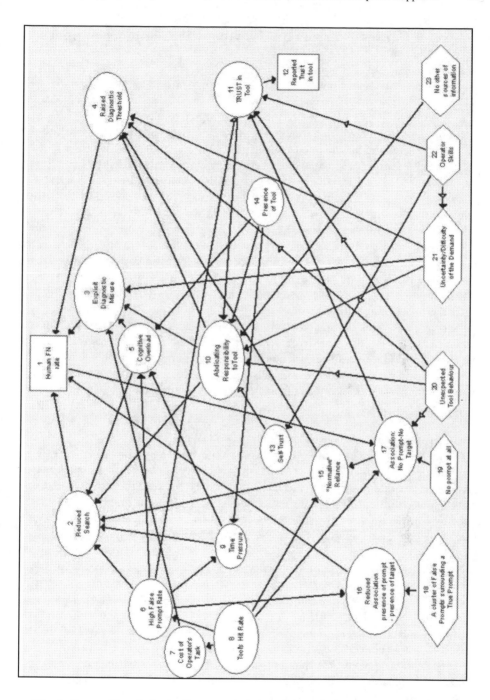

Fig. 1. Cause-effect chains leading to omission errors by computer-supported operators

4 Diverse Causes of Errors by Humans with Computer Support

Figure 1 shows a graphical representation of cause-effect chains involved in "errors of omission", as an incomplete but complex account of "automation bias". In the graph, rectangles denote observable behaviours; oval shapes represent causal factors (characteristics of the tool and/or of the user, including cognitive mechanisms and affective states) that may be present in the human-computer system, although perhaps not directly observable; and the diamond-like shapes (all at the bottom of the graph), characteristics of a specific demand and/or user that may trigger the effects of one or the other of the oval nodes. The lines between nodes indicate causal links. A black arrow indicates an "increase" relationship (i.e., an increase or intensification of the factor identified by the source node leads to a change in the same direction for the target node); a white arrow indicates a "decrease" relationship (an increase of the source node factor leads to a decrease of the target node factor); lines with both a black and a white arrow indicate that there is an influence but the direction of change can go either up or down depending on the circumstances. Multiple arrows into a node have an "OR" semantics: any one of the source nodes may affect the target node, irrespective of whether other source nodes do.

As noted, we focus on human errors of omission, exemplified by node 1 in the graph: "Human FN (false negative) rate". This node denotes the increased likelihood that a human's FN rate is higher when using computer support than when not using it. In mammography, a human FN is a radiologist's failure to recall a patient whose mammogram contains indications of cancer that s/he has missed or misinterpreted; in collision warning systems, a human FN is an operator's failure to notice the proximity between two vehicles or aircraft and her/his consequent failure to initiate evasive manoeuvres or give the necessary directions to colleagues.

We represent in nodes 2-4 our three main conjectures about how this increase in operator's FN rate comes about (possibly just three very plausible examples out of many other possible contributing mechanisms). Node 2 refers to the processing of raw data (the detection of or search for target cues). Nodes 3 and 4 refer to "diagnostic" aspects of the decision making (i.e., the interpretation or classification of the raw data once the operator has collected or detected them). More specifically:

- Node 2, "Reduced Search": the operator fails to either complete the search for all possible cues (e.g. suspicious features in a mammogram) or to examine all the necessary raw data to make a decision.
- Node 3, "Explicit Diagnostic Misuse": the operator, in deciding the value of a cue towards a decision, gives the tool's prompts more weight than intended by the designers. For example, in CAD for mammography, the prompts are meant as pure alerts, without diagnostic value and the procedure prescribed that if a user had decided to recall a case before seeing the prompts, s/he should not change her/his decision to "no recall" after seeing the prompts [37]. If a reader performs this forbidden action, it is explicit diagnostic misuse. By "explicit" we mean that such violations could be identified, e.g. by the user her/himself, differently from the form of potential tool misuse represented by the next node, 4.

- Node 4, "Raised Diagnostic Threshold": an operator raises the degree of "strength" or "severity" of cues that s/he requires in order to initiate an alarm response *without a prompt from the tool*. For certain borderline cases the user, when not using computer support, might be cautious and give an alarm response; for example, when seeing a moderately suspicious feature on a mammogram, a reader recalls the patient for further examinations even if it is not clear that she may have cancer. But if "supported" by the tool, the operator may become "less cautious" when interpreting those cues; for example, in a first examination, the reader decides not to recall the patient and waits to see the CAD prompts before committing her/himself to a recall decision.

Let us discuss some of the different paths that can lead to these three "top level" nodes (and, ultimately, to raised human FN rate).

We start with node 8, the tool's sensitivity ("Tool's hit rate"), an "obviously" beneficial characteristic. Increasing tool sensitivity is, in principle, desirable; and this is a goal tool designers normally aim for. However, it may actually lead to undesirable effects because increasing it usually increases the rate of false prompts (link to node 6 in the graph). Processing false prompts can be costly. Radiologists, for example, are known to be concerned with explaining why each prompt is present [37, 41]. Also, in aviation, pilots using TCAS (Traffic Collision Avoidance System) are strictly instructed to regard all automated messages as genuine alerts demanding an immediate, high-priority response [42]. Processing false prompts demands time and cognitive resources, and thus can lead to "Time Pressure" (node 9) and "Cognitive Overload" (node 5: presence of confusion that does not allow the operator to process information properly). Time pressure and cognitive overload are indeed interconnected and both reduce the operator's ability to complete the search for cues (links to node 2). It is important to note that none of the mechanisms just described (in connection with the tool's sensitivity) imply "over-reliance" on automation or "complacency". The tool affects the operators, but they are *not* conforming to its advice. In fact, operators' performance could be worse with computer support even for demands for which the tool provides *correct* advice. Evidence from the case study on CAD in breast screening strongly supports this view [35, 36]. Nodes 18 and 16, in conjunction with node 6, illustrate the "cry wolf" situation that may explain phenomena like this. Imagine that a true prompt (e.g., one signalling cancer in a mammogram) is surrounded by a cluster of many obviously false prompts (node 18). The user may infer that prompts in this case are *not* correlated with the presence of cancer (node 16); the value of the true prompt gets diminished for the radiologist, leading her/him to overlook correct prompts.

The tool's sensitivity (node 8) can lead to unanticipated human error through what we call "Normative reliance" on the tool (node 15). By "normative" we mean it fits a "normatively correct", rational decision making process. This can take, at least, two different forms:

- Based on their experience with a highly sensitive tool, operators correctly use prompts as a sign of possible missed targets. This can lead to "Raised Diagnostic Threshold" (link to node 4) and eventually to increased operator FN rate (node 1) in the following way. If the tool is useful, it causes an increase of correct "alarm responses" but it may also increase the number of false alarm responses (human FPs). Operators know that too high an "alarm response rate" is unacceptable; for instance, too many false recalls may make a cancer screening program unable to cope with the true cases. Therefore, raising the operator's own threshold is a reasonable reaction, irrespective of whether it is intentional or not. However it may overcompensate, or at least make the operator miss some targets that s/he would not have missed without the tool, although overall s/he misses fewer with the tool.

- Many of the prompts are spurious, so operators correctly learn to associate "no prompt" with likely absence of target (node 17). This can lead to reduced data search (node 2). As a result, given a FN from the tool, the user's normative reliance on the tool will lead him/her to miss the target (node 1). A "rational" user will be especially likely to reduce the search in the light of absence of prompts if detailed analysis of every prompt is too demanding and, especially, if it is practically infeasible.

The association between absence of prompts and absence of target can lead to a different, less "rational", path, involving *trust* (node 11), an "affective" (rather than cognitive) state, which may be affected by experience of reliability, but also by many other factors, and may be far stronger or far weaker than warranted by experience. Here we envisage complacency, represented by "Abdicating responsibility to tool" (node 10) as the result of a person's "negotiation" between the trust s/he has in her/his own abilities (node 13) and her/his trust in the tool. Expert operators often have beliefs about what tasks they are good at and what tasks they are less competent at [37]. If the user trusts the tool more than her/himself for a particular task, s/he will be more likely to over-rely on it (i.e., relinquishing responsibility to automation). Various (non exhaustive) links in the graph indicate the various factors or mechanisms that may affect trust.

There are also situations when people abdicate responsibility to the tool even if they do not trust it. For example, just the fact that the operator knows that computer support is available could in itself lead to complacency (links from node 14, "Availability of the computer tool" *per se*, to node 10), in a process equivalent to what some psychologists term "social loafing": when people work with other people, diffusion of responsibility often takes place [43, 44]. Importantly, specific situations with high degrees of uncertainty (node 21), especially when other more reliable sources of information are missing (node 23), may make operators vulnerable and cause them to rely on computer support more than they would normally do, even if they do not trust its reliability. We found evidence for this in our study of CAD use with difficult-to-detect cancers.

Node 14 designates other ways in which the "Presence of the Tool" *per se* (no matter how reliable) can also contribute to human error without over-reliance or complacency. For instance, the need to examine and process the tool's output may in itself increase time pressure (node 9) and cognitive load (node 5).

For the sake of brevity, we leave out of this exposition a few of the nodes and links in the graph, which we believe are self-explanatory.

5   Discussion

5.1   Uses of This Approach

The main purpose of the diagram in Fig 1 is to assist a designer or assessor in identi-fying the causal chains leading to undesired effects. A designer can try to interrupt the chain by appropriate design decisions. The fact that the graph represents multiple interacting causal chains should help against tunnel vision, i.e., focusing on one obvious concern while ignoring others. For instance, a designer might try to counter-act factor 2 in the graph, assuming it is mainly caused by factor 17, via procedural restrictions, such as requiring that the user reach a provisional decision and take re-sponsibility for it (e.g. by recording it in a log) before seeing the tool's prompts. But this remedy might not work against factor 2, or might even make it worse if mandat-ing this more complex procedure exacerbates factor 9; or if, despite factor 2 being alleviated or eliminated, the main (neglected) mechanism through which the tool causes certain extra false negative decisions is factor 4.

So far we have talked about the need for completeness in analyses. In designing a human-computer system, it would be good to focus on those possible causal chains that will be important in a specific system and context of operation. For this kind of optimisation, one needs empirical observations in the environment of use, if feasible. To help when these observations are not available, further research should try to iden-tify general rules for forecasting the relative importance of the different mechanisms in a future system and environment of use. Last, system designers may wish to incor-porate in the design degrees of "tuneability" for the parameters (of the algorithms in the tool, the procedure for using it, etc.) to allow adjustments in operation, so as to achieve good trade-offs between positive and negative effects.

5.2   Limitations, Quantitative Aspects

We highlight next some problems that this descriptive approach does not address. Quantitative trade-offs may be necessary in design. The relative importance of the various causal mechanisms in the graph will vary between systems, between users in the same system and between demands. This is because the parameters of human reactions to cues and prompts may well vary between categories of demands, just as those of the tool's reactions do (e.g., being better at detecting and prompting certain kinds of cues than others). Especially with increasing experience, a user might, for instance, learn to trust a computer's prompts highly for certain types of demand, an only little for others. A support tool may have a positive effect on the reactions of certain population of users to most demands, but still have a detrimental effect on some categories of demands for a subset of those users. These factors may require designers to consider quantitative trade-offs, and to assess the effects of uncertainties about the environment of use of an alerting tool.

We modelled in [40] the cumulative effect of these different reaction patterns, to quantitatively identify possible design trade-offs, showing that complex effects are possible.

Depending on the trade-offs made by designers and their effects on various classes of demand (and the frequencies of these classes of demands), a tool designed to help might have a damaging effect (aggregated over the whole population of users and distribution of demands). Much more commonly, improving the aggregated dependability of the socio-technical system requires consideration of the various design trade-offs affecting the overall FN and FP rates for all classes of demands. For instance, if factor 4 in the graph causes, on average, operators to end up with a few more false negatives on a difficult but rare class of demands, while allowing them to reduce false negatives – without an excessive increase in false positives – on a more common class of demands, the net effect may be beneficial. A possible complication is that of errors causing different degrees of loss depending on the class of demands: in the above example, if FNs on the class of "difficult" demands tended to cause more serious consequences, using the tool might increase the overall amount of loss caused by the decisions compared to the unaided user. Even with a tool whose aggregated effect is unambiguously positive, its potential for increasing human FNs on specific classes of demands may cause concerns. For example, for a medical decision aid, the net effect may be a transfer of risk from certain patients to others: introducing the aid might reduce risk for the average patient and yet increase risk for the average patient from a certain age or ethnic group. Or the aid may have the effect of improving the performance of most doctors but making it worse for some specific doctors.

6 Conclusions

With reference to a category of computer-assisted human tasks, we have highlighted a variety of alternative mechanisms that could lead to omission errors by the computer assisted operators. We have shown that errors that are often ascribed to "complacency" or "over-reliance" on computers, can actually be caused by other mechanisms, in fact even when the operators do *not* trust the automated tool.

The various mechanisms are interrelated in complex ways, so that the presence and characteristics of the alerting tool may affect the FN rate in more than one way. If a designer focused on only part of the graph in our Fig. 1, trying to "cut" one of the edges so as to defeat one of these damaging mechanisms, succeeding might not bring any benefit because, in the system, the predominant damaging mechanism may be another one.

So, when designing a tool and the human-computer system to include it, it is certainly important to be aware of the risk of complacency (e.g. by prescribing appropriate training or procedures), but this may not be enough. In particular, we have shown that some of these error mechanisms may be an inherent part of the human cognitive apparatus for reacting to cues and alarms, so they cannot be effectively shut off. A proper design of the human-machine system would look for the best trade-off between the positive and negative effects, rather than assuming that negative effects can be completely eliminated; and evaluators and adopters, when assessing a design, need to be aware of these various facets of the effects of a tool.

The graph presented in Fig. 1, based on our deductions from empirical work and from prior literature, is likely to be incomplete; but it indicates a useful way towards more explicit and complete ways of considering error causes when designing human-computer systems.

Acknowledgments. This work was supported in part by the U.K. Engineering and Physical Sciences Research Council via project INDEED, "Interdisciplinary Design and Evaluation of Dependability" (EP/E000517/1) and by the European Union's Framework Programme 6 via the ReSIST Network of Excellence, contract IST-4-026764-NOE.

References

1. Bainbridge, L.: Ironies of Automation. Automatica 19, 775–779 (1983)
2. Sorkin, R.D., Woods, D.D.: Systems with human monitors: A signal detection analysis. Human-Computer Interaction 1, 49–75 (1985)
3. Hawley, J.K.: Looking Back at 20 Years of MANPRINT on Patriot: Observations and Lessons. Report ARL-SR-0158, U.S. Army Research Laboratory (2007)
4. Bisantz, A.M., Seong, Y.: Assessment of operator trust in and utilization of automated decision-aids under different framing conditions. International Journal of Industrial Ergonomics 28(2), 85–97 (2001)
5. Dzindolet, M.T., Peterson, S.A., Pomranky, R.A., Pierce, L.G., Beck, H.P.: The role of trust in automation reliance. International Journal of Human-Computer Studies 58(6), 697–718 (2003)
6. Muir, B.M.: Trust between humans and machines, and the design of decision aids. International Journal of Man-Machine Studies 27, 527–539 (1987)
7. Azar, B.: Danger of automation: It makes us complacent. APA monitor 29(7), 3 (1998)
8. Singh, I.L., Molloy, R., Parasuraman, R.: Automation-induced "complacency": development of the complacency-potential rating scale. International Journal of Aviation Psychology 3, 111–122 (1993)
9. Wiener, E.L.: Complacency: is the term useful for air safety. In: 26th Corporate Aviation Safety Seminar, pp. 116–125. Flight Safety Foundation, Inc. (1981)
10. Parasuraman, R., Riley, V.: Humans and automation: Use, misuse, disuse, abuse. Hum. Factors 39, 230–253 (1997)
11. Wickens, C., Dixon, S., Goh, J., Hammer, B.: Pilot Dependence on Imperfect Diagnostic Automation in Simulated UAV Flights: An Attentional Visual Scanning Analysis. In: Proceedings of the 13th International Symposium on Aviation Psychology (2005)
12. Cummings, M.L.: Automation bias in intelligent time critical decision support systems. In: AIAA 1st Intelligent Systems Technical Conference, AIAA 2004 (2004)
13. Skitka, L.J., Mosier, K., Burdick, M.D.: Does automation bias decision making? International Journal of Human-Computer Studies 51(5), 991–1006 (1999)
14. Meyer, J.: Conceptual issues in the study of dynamic hazard warnings. Human Factors 46(2), 196–204 (2004)
15. Mosier, K.L., Skitka, L.J., Heers, S., Burdick, M.: Automation bias: Decision making and performance in high-tech cockpits. International Journal of Aviation Psychology 8(1), 47–63 (1998)
16. Prinzel, L.J., De Vries, H., Freeman, F.G., Mikulka, P.: Examination of Automation-Induced Complacency and Individual Difference Variates. Technical Memorandum No. TM-2001-211413, NASA Langley Research Center, Hampton, VA (2001)
17. Skitka, L.J., Mosier, K., Burdick, M.D.: Accountability and automation bias. International Journal of Human-Computer Studies 52(4), 701–717 (2000)

18. Meyer, J., Feinshreiber, L., Parmet, Y.: Levels of automation in a simulated failure detection task. In: IEEE International Conference on Systems, Man and Cybernetics 2003, pp. 2101–2106 (2003)
19. Meyer, J.: Effects of warning validity and proximity on responses to warnings. Hum. Factors 43, 563–572 (2001)
20. Singh, I.L., Molloy, R., Parasuraman, R.: Automation-induced monitoring inefficiency: role of display location. International Journal of Human-Computer Studies 46(1), 17–30 (1997)
21. Bahner, J.E., Huper, A.-D., Manzey, D.: Misuse of automated decision aids: Complacency, automation bias and the impact of training experience. Int. J. Human-Computer Studies 66, 688–699 (2008)
22. Moray, N.: Monitoring, complacency, scepticism and eutactic behaviour. International Journal of Industrial Ergonomics 31(3), 175–178 (2003)
23. Wickens, C.D., Dixon, S.R.: Is there a Magic Number 7 (to the Minus 1)? The Benefits of Imperfect Diagnostic Automation: A Synthesis of the Literature, University of Illinois at Urbana-Champaign, Savoy, Illinois, pp. 1–11 (2005)
24. Dassonville, I., Jolly, D., Desodt, A.M.: Trust between man and machine in a teleoperation system. Reliability Engineering & System Safety (Safety of Robotic Systems) 53(3), 319–325 (1996)
25. Lee, J.D., Moray, N.: Trust, self-confidence, and operators' adaptation to automation. International Journal of Human-Computer Studies 40, 153–184 (1994)
26. Lee, J.D., See, K.A.: Trust in computer technology. Designing for appropriate reliance. Human Factors, 50–80 (2003)
27. Muir, B.M.: Trust in automation: Part I. Theoretical issues in the study of trust and human intervention in automated systems. Ergonomics 37, 1905–1922 (1994)
28. Muir, B.M., Moray, N.: Trust in automation: Part II. Experimental studies of trust and human intervention in a process control simulation. Ergonomics 39, 429–460 (1996)
29. Tan, G., Lewandowsky, S.: A comparison of operator trust in humans versus machines. In: Presentation of First International Cyberspace Conference on Ergonomics (1996)
30. de Vries, P., Midden, C., Bouwhuis, D.: The effects of errors on system trust, self-confidence, and the allocation of control in route planning. International Journal of Human-Computer Studies 58(6), 719–735 (2003)
31. Dzindolet, M.T., Pierce, L.G., Beck, H.P., Dawe, L.A.: The perceived utility of human and automated aids in a visual detection task. Human Factors 44(1), 79–94 (2002)
32. Parasuraman, R., Molloy, R., Singh, I.L.: Performance consequences of automation-induced "complacency". International Journal of Aviation Psychology 3, 1–23 (1993)
33. Bliss, J.P., Acton, S.A.: Alarm mistrust in automobiles: how collision alarm reliability affects driving. Applied Ergonomics 34(6), 499–509 (2003)
34. Parasuraman, R., Miller, C.A.: Trust and etiquette in high-criticality automated systems. Communications of the ACM 47(4), 51–55 (2004)
35. Alberdi, E., Povyakalo, A.A., Strigini, L., Ayton, P.: Effects of incorrect CAD output on human decision making in mammography. Acad. Radiol. 11(8), 909–918 (2004)
36. Alberdi, E., Povyakalo, A.A., Strigini, L., Ayton, P., Given-Wilson, R.: CAD in mammography: lesion-level versus case-level analysis of the effects of prompts on human decisions. Journal of Computer Assisted Radiology and Surgery 3(1-2), 115–122 (2008)
37. Alberdi, E., Povyakalo, A.A., Strigini, L., Ayton, P., Hartswood, M., Procter, R., Slack, R.: Use of computer-aided detection (CAD) tools in screening mammography: a multidisciplinary investigation. Br. J. Radiol. 78(suppl_1), S31–S40 (2005)

38. Povyakalo, A.A., Alberdi, E., Strigini, L., Ayton, P.: Evaluating 'Human + Advisory computer' systems: A case study. In: HCI 2004,18th British HCI Group Annual Conference, British HCI Group, pp. 93–96 (2004)
39. Povyakalo, A.A., Alberdi, E., Strigini, L., Ayton, P.: Divergent effects of computer prompting on the sensitivity of mammogram readers, Technical Report, Centre for Software Reliability, City University, London, UK (2006)
40. Strigini, L., Povyakalo, A.A., Alberdi, E.: Human-machine diversity in the use of computerised advisory systems: a case study. In: 2003 Int. Conf. on Dependable Systems and Networks (DSN 2003). IEEE, Los Alamitos (2003)
41. Hartswood, M., Procter, R., Rouncefield, M., Slack, R., Soutter, J., Voss, A.: 'Repairing' the Machine: A Case Study of the Evaluation of Computer-Aided Detection Tools in Breast Screening. In: Eighth European Conference on Computer Supported Cooperative Work, ECSCW 2003 (2003)
42. Pritchett, A.R., Vandor, B., Edwards, K.: Testing and implementing cockpit alerting systems. Reliability Engineering & System Safety 75(2), 193–206 (2002)
43. Karau, S.J., Williams, K.D.: Social loafing: a meta-analytic review and theoretical integration. Journal of Personality and Social Psychology 65, 681–706 (1993)
44. Latanedo, B., Williams, K., Harkins, S.: Many hands make light the work: the causes and consequences of social loafing. Journal of Personality and Social Psychology 37, 822–832 (1979)

Safety-Related Application Conditions –
A Balance between Safety Relevance and Handicaps for Applications

Friedemann Bitsch[1], Ulrich Feucht[2], and Huw Gough[2]

[1] Informatik Consulting Systems AG, Sonnenbergstr. 13, D-70184 Stuttgart, Germany
friedemann.bitsch@ics-ag.de
[2] Thales Rail Signalling Solutions GmbH, Lorenzstraße 10, D-70435 Stuttgart, Germany
{ulrich.feucht,huw-michael.gough}@thalesgroup.com

Abstract. Railway standards prescribe the use of Safety-related Application Conditions (SACs). SACs are demands to be observed when using a safety related system or a sub-system. The use of SACs can, however, easily be associated with difficulties. SACs of sub-systems can imply high efforts regarding their fulfillment at system level. Furthermore, SACs at sub-system level may become very obstructive for the user of the sub-system, if the safe application on system level has strong restrictions. Additionally, a large number of SACs may be very difficult to manage. In this way, SACs may obstruct the introduction of a system or a sub-system into the field. Particular hazards could arise from SACs, if they are formulated ambiguously, so that the originally intended safety-related measures are not taken at all. This paper presents the objectives and benefits of SACs and depicts difficulties and challenges associated with the use of SACs. The paper not only explains what should be the SAC content but also the quality criteria, the conditions for SAC creation and SAC fulfillment are described. The SAC management process introduced at Thales Rail Signalling Solutions GmbH is outlined. On the one hand, this process shall support the quality of SACs and on the other hand reduce the effort for SAC creation, fulfillment and evidence.

Keywords: Safety-related Application Conditions, SAC quality, conditions for defining SACs, process for defining and complying with SACs.

1 Introduction

Safety cases for safety-related railway control systems must be created for safety-related items[1]. A majority of the argumentation in the safety case is directed towards the internal attributes of the item. Moreover, also hazards are identified which cannot be covered by the internal attributes of the item itself, but rather through the adherence to certain requirements during the usage of the item in the intended superior

---

[1] The term "item" is used in this paper as an umbrella term for a system, a subsystem, a product or a component. A system can include several subsystems which can include several products. A product can be constructed from several components.

B. Buth, G. Rabe, T. Seyfarth (Eds.): SAFECOMP 2009, LNCS 5775, pp. 32–45, 2009.
© Springer-Verlag Berlin Heidelberg 2009

context. These requirements are Safety-related Application Conditions (SACs). They must be documented in the item safety case and handed over to the responsibility of the user of the item. The superior context means either the application by an end user or the application in the development on a superior level (compare with the levels described in section 2 and Fig. 1). SACs document the conditions which must be followed during the usage of the item in a superior context due to safety-related reasons, so that hazards are avoided. The adherence to conditions remains the responsibility of the user. However, it is safety critical if SACs are not fulfilled by the user e.g. because of communication problems about the content of the SAC or because the user does not perceive why the instruction of the SAC is necessary for safety.

An example of non-compliance with a safety-related regulation is explained in the judgment [2] for the Transrapid accident in Emsland, Germany in 2006. According to [2] the regulation of the manufacturing company was not fulfilled which defined that the electronic route gate has to be set obligatory in case of shunting operations. [2] explains that this was not implemented in the operating rules.

It is often possible to decide whether a SAC which has been formulated can be solved by avoiding the SAC altogether if measures are designed within the boundaries of the item itself, otherwise the decision is made to make development improvements on superior system level. Such SACs which could have been avoided, can implicate high efforts at fulfillment on superior system level. Avoidable SACs also may be unneeded and unreasonable demands for appliers when the required safe application of a system or product is very extensive, highly restrictive, if the SACs are difficult to interpret or if the amount of SACs is unmanageably large. In this way SACs may obstruct the introduction of a product in the market. SACs without real safety character complicate and handicap the application of the item unnecessarily.

Therefore approaches are necessary which support the creation of SACs with clear and precise description of their content and clearness about their safety relevance, the decision in which cases SACs are necessary and in which other cases SACs should be avoided and the compliancy with SACs without high efforts.

In section 2 the benefit of SACs is pointed out and a definition for SACs is given. Requirements of safety standards and related works for the SAC topic are explained in section 3. On that basis challenges and risks with SACs are handled in section 4 and needs for creating, complying with and demonstrating SACs are derived. In the sections 5 and 6 criteria for SAC creation and quality are introduced. Processes for defining and handling SACs are presented in section 7. Important issues for SAC quality and efficient handling with SACs are summarized in section 8.

2   Meaning and Purpose of SACs

2.1   Benefits of SACs

Before it is defined what SACs exactly are the question shall be pursued for what SACs are useful and necessary. SACs involve several benefits in the Product Life Cycle. SACs assure safe operation of products by prescribing demands, which ensure the safe deployment of a system. SACs are important to give users clear safety-relevant instructions. Consequently, SACs are necessary for safety. They are prescribed compellingly

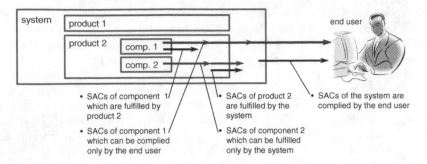

Fig. 1. Examples on which levels SACs are forwarded for fulfillment

by the railway standard EN50129 [1]. SACs can clarify safety responsibilities when using a system or a product in the phases after the development and the safety case have been completed, e.g. who of the end users has which safety responsibility. SACs clarify which safety responsibilities the maintenance staff, the rail traffic controller and the operating company have. SACs from subordinate items can clarify which safety responsibilities are on component, on product and on system levels. In Fig. 1 examples are given on which levels SACs could be forwarded to superior levels.

A typical example of a SAC which has to be fulfilled at development of a superior item, here a generic platform: *The application must ensure that a restart is possible only after the hardware has been reset. Reasoning: A soft reset is not sufficient for a safe restart. As the generic platform is designed the hardware has to be reset for a safe restart. It is the task of the application development to ensure this.*

A typical example of a SAC for an end user for any device is: *At least once within 12 months, the maintenance engineers have to check the device outputs with a certain test program. Reasoning: The calculated hazard rates are valid, only if the user complies with the Failure Detection Time of 12 months for the output circuits.*

Furthermore SACs can also be contributions to an economical development. SACs can allow the deployment of an item by definition of rules for safe application also with inexpensive design decisions. This is the case if easily to fulfill SACs can be defined instead of cost-intensive complex design solutions which are hard to realize.

2.2 Definition of SACs

SACs can be defined as followed which complies also EN50129 [1]. SACs are:

- regulations, that must be observed during the usage of an item in a superior context due to safety reasons,
- regulations, whose compliance lies in the responsibility of the user and
- regulations, which can avoid hazards, that are not covered through internal characteristics of the item itself, but which can be covered through the adherence of external measures or conditions during the usage of the item.

An example of a SAC is: *A point has to be switched once in 12 months.* The superior context for this example is the application of the point by the railway operator. The hazard is that the point switch is not in the correct position when it is run over because of an undetected failure in the switchover circuit. For avoidance of the hazard the external measure is the passing of the point in the test cycle of 12 months.

3 Related Works and State of the Art

A well-known accident which demonstrates the meaning of SACs is the Chernobyl disaster in 1986. This accident and the consequences of violating safety rules (SACs) for end users have been analyzed in detail in [3]. In this context psychological factors for violating safety rules are in focus and have been investigated in detail.

According to [3] an essential part of the accident causes were human failures. But "everything the [plant] operators did they did consciously and apparently with complete conviction that they were acting properly". [4] explains: "The plant operators, [...] however, thought in terms of linear networks of causation rather than considering potential side effects of their decisions and actions" . To handle these kinds of problems the consideration of safety regulations is absolute necessary. The human errors of Chernobyl were the consequences of the contempt of safety related regulations.

One reason for violation of safety rules according to [3] is that safety reasons for the rule are unclear for the operators. Furthermore, safety rules often bring a special effort for application. Therefore the violation of rules can lead to a simplified application. If a safety rule has been violated sometimes without any negative consequences then the tendency is in succession that the rule would be violated regularly. Then actions are based on own estimation of the situation. But this is hazardous because the user does not know the internal system states and the side effects.

IEC 61508 [5] only requires mandatorily that there must be operational and maintenance instructions to avoid mistakes during operation and maintenance procedures. In addition it is stated that all instructions must be easily understood. Explicit requirements for instructions related to safety are missing.

However in the railway standard EN50129 [1] SACs creation and compliance is prescribed compellingly. But there is little guidance related to handling and quality of SACs. The meaning of SACs is explained and it is prescribed in which parts of the safety case SACs have to be handled. SACs are defined as rules, conditions and constraints which shall be observed in the application of the system/sub-system/equipment. SACs from the current item to the superior items are part of the current item Technical Safety Report. Beside possible general topics the following specific topics are named and explained which shall be addressed in SACs: Sub-system/equipment configuration and system build, operation and maintenance, operational safety monitoring and decommissioning and disposal. In "Part 5" of the Safety Case with the topic "Related Safety Cases" it shall be demonstrated that all the safety-related application conditions specified in each of the related sub-system/equipment Safety Cases are either fulfilled, or carried forward into the safety-related application conditions of the item under consideration.

[6] describes a concept, which divides a safety case into modular safety cases according to modular architecture designs. Safety case 'contracts' are used to record the interdependencies that exist between safety case modules – e.g. to show how the claims of one module support the arguments of another. Safety contracts constrain

the interactions that occur between objects, and hence can ensure system behavior is safe. These contracts are broken down into individual requirements placed on the parts of the system. In difference to safety contracts SACs as a rule are directed bottom-up in a system architecture, i.e. an item addresses rules for a safety-related correct application to the superior architectural level.

As explained in section 7 a related topic is the specification, the fulfillment and the evidence of safety requirements. According to [1] safety requirements specifications contain functional safety requirements and systematic and random failure integrity requirements. Functional safety requirements concern all safety relevant control and monitoring functions of the system. Failure integrity requirements are the requirements regarding systematic and random failures.

Safety requirements are as other requirements part of requirements engineering. According to IEEE requirements engineering has to be divided into requirements elicitation, requirements analysis, requirements specification and requirements validation [7]. [5] gives criteria fort he quality of safety requirements. They have to be clear, precise, unambiguous, verifiable, testable, maintainable and feasible; and written to aid comprehension by those who are likely to utilize the information.

Generally there are two strategies to fulfill safety requirements [8], p. 398. The first strategy is to avoid safety critical faults and failures. The second strategy is the avoidance of hazardous consequences from faults and failures. The fulfillment of functional safety requirements is demonstrated by requirements tracing, verification of the several development phases, testing and validation. The compliance with random failure integrity requirements (quantitative safety targets) is shown by hazard analyses. The fulfillment of systematic failure integrity requirements is based on the evidence that adequate means of quality and safety management have been performed and that techniques and measures have been used to reach the necessary level of confidence in the development (Safety Integrity Level) [1] [9].

In comparison to conventional safety requirements the peculiarity of SACs is their origin and the kind of addressees. The origin of SACs are item safety cases. SACs are relevant for other development projects or the users of the customers. They are directed bottom-up to the superior architectural levels while conventional safety requirements concern top-down relations.

4   What Is Necessary for Defining and Handling SACs?

4.1   Challenges and Risks with SACs

Beside the benefits of SACs problems have to be considered which may arise in connection with SACs. Furthermore at SAC formulation and handling the purpose of SACs can be missed if some difficulties with SACs are not dealt with and are not avoided. A consequence could be that the SACs are only handicaps in the development of the concerned items instead of being useful for safe application. In the following those problems and difficulties are listed:

- Poor comprehensibility of SACs for the user.
- Declaration of SACs, which in fact are no SACs. This could lead to a large quantity of unnecessary SACs. That would be hardly manageable and could lead to the possibility of individual SACs not being taken seriously.
- Declaration of SACs that could have been avoided during product development.
- Missing or late information about SACs which must be fulfilled.
- High time investment for the proof of compliancy with SACs.
- Unrealizable SACs for the user, so that SACs counteract against the introduction of a product in the market.
- SACs as unreasonable demands for appliers, when the required safe application of a system or product is very expensive, very complex or highly restricted.
- Uncertainties: At what time do SACs arise in the Development Life Cycle? When are SACs necessary? In which documents should SACs be located and verified? How are SACs fulfilled? Who is jointly responsible for the compliancy and its proof?
- SACs that seem to be fulfilled but are not e.g. because they are ambiguous or misinterpreted or the compliance with the SACs or the evidence has been insufficient.

Challenges bring also the different view points and objectives of the different roles involved in the SAC topic and there are role specific thinking pitfalls. E.g. a safety manager may tend to the view that many SACs increase the safety of the item. With this point of view it can easily be overseen that there could be avoidable SACs which make the amount of SACs unmanageable (see explanation of avoidable SACs in section 1). E.g. a product responsible person easily tends to the view point that SACs are unreasonable demands for the clients. Here, the problem could be missing SACs which would be safety critical. A third view e.g. is this of the project which focuses on efforts and costs. It might seem to be more comfortable to define a SAC which has to be solved in the project of the superior item instead of solving the issues within the own project by technical measures. But it has to be considered, also, that often it is easier to solve safety issues in the own project than in the project of the superior item.

These kinds of problems arise if the conditions are not specified in which cases SACs have to be defined and what the quality criteria of the SACs of an item are.

4.2 Demands for Defining and Handling SACs

The problems and difficulties listed in the last section already lead to needs related to defining and handling SACs. The described different objectives of the different roles in projects can be useful for SAC quality, if there are defined rules for SAC formulation. SAC rules for compliancy must also be available. Rules have to be laid down for: Which aspects are SACs and which will not? What are SAC quality criteria? What are the processes of SAC formulation, compliance and demonstration of SAC fulfillment? Who is responsible for what in these processes? How shall SACs and their compliance be documented? When shall SACs be fulfilled? What is important to achieve efficiency? For Thales Rail Signalling Solutions GmbH these demands have lead to the development and introduction of a process instruction which is the basis for this paper.

5 Conditions for Defining SACs

In EN50129 [1] SACs are prescribed between items with separate Safety Cases. But if for a compound system only one safety case is used, then there could be the problem that the safety responsibilities between the items are unclear in detail. For that reason, it is meaningful that the SAC principles are used, this is also true for a compound system using only one Safety Case.

In the following, criteria are listed, stating in which cases SACs must be formulated. Criterion 1 must always be fulfilled together with criterion 2, 3 or 4.

1. Safety risk for non-compliance with an application instruction

A SAC must be created if the reasoning in the safety case or in corresponding documents is dependent upon the compliancy with certain safety rules. If the safety-related argumentation of the safety case requires certain activities of users then these activities will have to be described in SACs. Precondition for a SAC is that the internal attributes of the item are not sufficient for safety argumentation. A SAC should be defined, only if the hazard for which the SAC is a countermeasure for has not already been mitigated by another measure.

A SAC must be formulated if a safety risk occurs as a result of a regulation being ignored by the user, stipulated in a handbook (e.g. Operation Manual or Maintenance Handbook). The evaluation of the risk may result directly from the standards (e.g. demands for channel separation), or the gravity and the frequency of the particular case must be evaluated. In the best case, the degree of risk of the event which requires certain application rules should be examined within the scope of a hazard analysis. SACs should only be generated if the safety aim would fail without it.

2. SACs are reasonable demands for the appliers

SACs often mean that during the application of the considered item, special expenditures or special restrictions are necessary (examples for special expenditures: maintenance expenditures or development expenditures in the project of the superior item; examples for special restrictions: project planning restrictions and operation constraints). If such application expenditures or restrictions are to be avoided, then on the one hand higher development expenditures can be implicated for the own item. For example, there might be application cases which are not required by the customer but which are safety critical and must be excluded by certain SACs (e.g. the use of an interface for a safety related purpose). On the other hand also the benefits have to be considered, which SACs can have in the total Product Life Cycle.

For example, if a generic platform has a watch dog timer for which it is unknown and un-probable that any application will ever use this timer, a reasonable SAC would be: *The safety analysis shall be extended, if the watch dog timer of the hardware is used for safety related functions.* But if it is not expensive to involve this topic also in the generic safety analysis, then the SAC can be avoided.

SACs similar to all other requirements have implications on expenditures concerning realization and proof. Therefore, on the one hand it has to be checked, if a planned SAC is acceptable and reasonable for the user. On the other hand SACs can enable concept and design decisions, which altogether allow an economic development or deployment of a system if the SACs are reasonable for the users.

SACs are only useful if benefits in the whole Product Life Cycle justify the acceptance of special application expenditures and application restrictions. The result could be that SACs must be avoided by changes or extensions of the item. In other cases SACs can avoid extensive analyses in projects of superior items. E.g. a SAC which specifies that an item is not usable for open networks according to EN50159-2, avoids analyses on higher levels if the item is usable for open networks. Such SACs, which are justified in the item concept or design, can be avoided by early planning, about which SACs are necessary, compare with section 6. The requirements and the architecture of the considered item can be changed most easily at an early phase.

3. Eliminating defects in the scope of a project is no longer possible
The formulation of a SAC to bypass defects in the considered item is only acceptable if a change of the item is no longer possible within the scope of the project and an emergency solution (workaround) is reasonable. A precondition is of course that the defect can be adequately bypassed with the issue of a SAC. In this case, an entry in the defect management system is always required. As long as this entry exists, the issued SAC is necessary.

Such SACs can be avoided through careful planning early enough in the project, about which SACs are required, see last but one point in section 6.

4. Acceptance of SACs
If a SAC is addressed to a superior item, in which the requirements specification is already completed, then the SAC has to be placed there in form of a change request, compare with section 7.2. For such change requests, a voting process is required if the SACs in the superior project can still be fulfilled or if it is easier to avoid them in the original project. E.g. there can be the case that a superior item could have already been approved and a new release would be possible, only with very high effort. Consequently, the acceptance of a SAC is a condition of SAC creation.

6   Quality Criteria for SACs

The following items lists and explains criteria for the quality of SACs:

SAC character
A SAC must have SAC eligibility and fulfill criteria listed in section 5.

User addressing
The author of a SAC must always take care to whom the SAC should be addressed to. The phrasing must be correspondingly chosen and the user (according to the listed addressees in section 7.1) must always be explicitly named in the SAC. He must be able to understand and apply the SAC.

Context independent comprehensiveness
A SAC must be able to be understood from the SAC addressees, without the reader having to know the source document from which the SAC has been derived (e.g. a Technical Safety Report). Therefore the SAC must be formulated in such a way to allow the user to understand and fulfill the SAC.

Explanations
Explanations about a SAC are important in addition to the formulation of the SAC:

- *Background information:* Background information is useful for the context independent comprehensiveness. A SAC must be described so that it can be understood without special knowledge of the project in which the SAC was issued, even with or without explanations.
- *Cause and source document:* Even after, e.g. personnel fluctuations, it must be clear why the particular SAC was required. E.g. the safety manager of the next product release must know, what was the cause, origin and what the source document for the SAC is or from which SACs from a subordinate item did the SAC derive from (traceability).
- *Hazard / safety reference:* There must always be a comprehensive safety reference in the SAC. This reference should be clarified through explanatory notes or through a link to the hazard logbook or to the document where the reference is stated. It must be clear what hazard will be avoided through the SAC. Example:
  - *SAC-Formulation:* "If the system is in regular operation the diagnosis device must not be plugged in the diagnosis interface."
  - *Explanation:* „The maintenance staff has to observe that the safe operation is not guaranteed in case of diagnosis. If the diagnosis interface is used, there will be no channel independence of the system which is a basic safety principal of the system."
- *Relation to the defect management system:* For SACs that have been defined because certain product faults could not be corrected, due to hard project constraints (this kind of SACs should be avoided), there must be a reference to the defect management system. It must be clear which defects must be corrected in a consecutive release, so that the SACs will be corrected and thus, made irrelevant.

Feasibility
The demands that are set in the SACs must be able to be realized by the addressed users. The requirements must always be in the responsibility of the addressed user, so that he can fulfill the requirements according to the means available to him and the knowledge that is expected of him. Often, feasibility can be improved, if it is clear for the creator of a SAC, how the SAC can be fulfilled in general. If the SAC creator already records such hints, the expenditures of SAC handling could be reduced.

No overlaps between SACs
Overlaps between SACs must be avoided. This is why it must be checked in the SAC formulation process, if the topic has been covered already through existing SACs.

SAC amount
The amount of SACs is dependent upon the type of considered item. Generic items require typically a larger number of SACs than application specific items. However, it must be made sure that only necessary SACs are defined:

- A large amount of SACs is difficult to manage during the development of superior systems, so that the effort for compliancy proof is too large and difficult to control.
- A large number of SACs has the danger that the important SACs are lost in the bulk and are not taken seriously enough. If SACs are incomprehensive and there

are too many (unnecessary) SACs then nothing will be taken into consideration anymore!

• A large number of SACs delays the entry of the product into the market.

A sensible amount of SACs can be obtained by paying attention to the listed conditions for SAC formulation, listed in section 5. All SACs written according to the criteria mentioned in section 2.2 have SAC justification. SACs as a temporary means (workaround) for product defects should be avoided. The requirement for the limitation on the amount of SACs should not lead to important SACs being omitted and not defined. If the amount is too large however, the project must examine, which SACs could be avoided through improvements to the item. For understandability and for traceability of SACs it can be useful to define several smaller but understandable SACs, rather than having one extensive SAC. The number of SACs increases on the one hand but on the other hand, smaller SACs are easier to be fulfilled.

Earliest possible definition and distribution of SACs
An earliest possible definition of SACs is useful for different reasons:

• *Avoiding SACs:* If SACs are defined already in early development stages of an item it can be decided easier if the SAC can be withdrawn by changes in the concept, the specifications or the design of the item.
• *Complying with SACs in other projects:* Normally, SACs are embedded in the development process of concerned projects by taking them over as safety requirements (compare with section 7.2). Therefore SACs should be recognized already in the requirement phase of the respective project. It is inevitable that in the case of projects running in parallel those SACs or SAC concepts are made known to the other projects as early as possible. Then potential users in the other projects may react easier and quicker. This can also be reached by involving potential users in SAC consolidations (compare with section 7.1). If SACs are forwarded to superior projects after the requirements phase has been finished, then these SACs can be introduced in the respective project only by using change requests.

Compliancy with guidelines for the structure and description of SACs
SACs should be described, named and structured in a uniform manner. This can be set by company guidelines. Also a SAC should be recognized through a uniform layout.

7 Procedures for SAC Formulation and Handling

7.1 SAC Formulation

Fig. 2 gives an overview on possible procedures for SAC creation. To ensure that SACs have safety relevance a SAC draft shall be defined, only if a respective hazard has been defined for which it is not possible or sensible to counteract with item internal measures. The SACs are collected by the safety manager. In the best case a database is used for SAC storage, compare with the benefits explained in section 7.2.

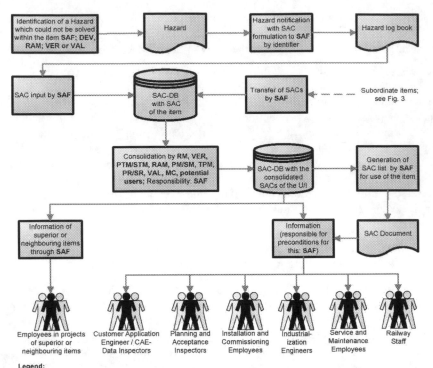

Legend:
DEV: Developer; MC: Manual Creator; PM/SM: Product/System Manager; PR/SR: Product/System Responsible; PRS/SRS: Product/System Requirements Specification; PTM/STM: Product/System Test Manager; RAM: RAM-Manager; RM: Requirements Manager; SAC-DB: SAC Data Base; SAF: Safety Manager; TPM: Technical Project Manager; VAL: Validator; VER: Verifier

Fig. 2. Process overview for SAC creation

As explained in section 4.1 the consideration of the different role specific views is important for SAC quality. All relevant roles (compare with Fig. 2) must be involved in this process. Known potential users who will have to comply with the SACs e.g. in the development of the superior system should also be involved. They can give important feedback on unambiguity and feasibility. In this way the consolidation of SACs is essential for SAC quality.

At consolidation the fulfillment of the quality criteria introduced in section 6 has to be checked. The consolidation is especially necessary for clarity, feasibility and identification of contradictions and overlaps. Here also the question should be treated if there are possibilities to avoid the SACs by realization of internal measures.

The SACs identification and creation should be done as soon as possible in a project (compare with section 6) e.g. either during development of the Safety Concept or while performing the Preliminary Hazard Analysis. But generally at anytime during a project, SACs are possible, e.g. even during the creation of the validation report.

The product of the described process is the SAC document, compare also with section 7.2. It must be part of the Technical Safety Report according to EN50129 [1]. It can be administered as a separate document and must contain all SACs of the considered item. As a consequence it is regulated unambiguously, where SACs of an item can be found exclusively.

The first version of the SAC document should be created with the Technical Safety Report because it is strongly related to the argumentation in this document. Furthermore the SACs must be available in a form that they can be transferred into the user handbooks. The end version of the SAC document must be created after completion of the validation report and together with finalization of the Safety Case. Fig. 2 lists also all potential kinds of SAC users who have to be informed about the SACs.

7.2 Compliance with and Evidence of SACs of Subordinated Items

For an item, it must be specified which SACs of other items are relevant and have to be fulfilled. It is obvious to specify this in the Safety Concept, System Concept or in the Preliminary Architecture document.

It can be very time consuming if the SACs in all their origin documents have to be searched for and gathered. If all SACs of one item are listed in its SAC document then it is not necessary to go through all documents where SACs could be specified and there is no uncertainty if all relevant SACs have been found. Another important step is to use a database over the SACs of all items as it is depicted in Fig. 2 and Fig. 3. Then the SACs can be simply queried from the SAC database and time and costs can be saved.

In EN50129 [1], complying with SACs is separated from fulfilling safety requirements. But a separated treatment in projects with different responsibilities for evidence of compliancy leads to additional project efforts. Therefore, if possible, SACs from subordinate items are usually taken over as safety requirements, forming a basis for verifications, being considered in test cases and being treated in the validation, compare with Fig. 3. Consequently, the techniques and measures, according to EN50128 [9] and EN50129 [1], to be used for the compliancy with SACs are the same as for safety requirements. They must always be determined project specifically.

If additional SACs from subordinate items appear after requirements specification has been finished, the safety manager must introduce the SACs to the project as a change request. Then, it has to be discussed, if it is easier to add a safety requirement in the affected project or if it is easier to avoid the SAC by concept or design changes in the source project, compare with section 5.

According to EN50129 [1] the safety management has to describe the relationship to the subordinate safety cases, which is normally in the document "Related Safety Cases", part 5 of the safety case. In this document the safety management confirms the process of SAC compliance with references to verification and validation reports. Also it has to be judged if all SACs of subordinate items have been fulfilled and proved or forwarded to a further level. SACs that could not be fulfilled within the scope of the own development project, but that are directed to the superior application level (compare with Fig. 2 and Fig. 3) must be passed on. Part 5 of the safety case contains a list of these SACs.

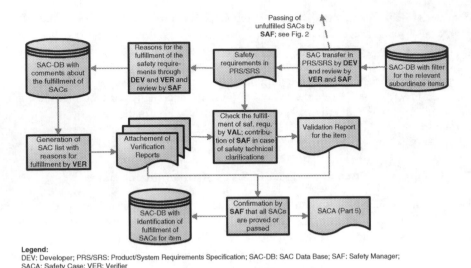

Fig. 3. Process overview about the handling of SACs from subordinate items

The proof must be justified for every SAC which has been identified as fulfilled. This can be achieved through:

- Reference to requirements specification with corresponding safety requirements and argumentations in a verification report.
- If the above point is not possible, a direct argumentative reason and, if required, a reference to safety analysis, to test results or to other documents is possible. A testable SAC must, however, be covered with a test case at all means.
- It is possible that SACs from subordinate items are only valid under certain preconditions or only for a certain context (e.g. customer specific, only valid for certain hardware or only for certain configurations). If these preconditions are not fulfilled, the SAC is not applicable and can be set as fulfilled.
- It can be reasoned, that another solution has been realized than this one which has been required in the SAC. Precondition in this case is that the solution is sufficient to reach the safety targets.

The decisive element for efficiency of SAC compliance and evidence is the quality of the SACs. If time has been invested in the quality of the SACs, then this would have a favorable effect. In addition the systematic cooperation between the roles involved with clear responsibilities is essential for this efficiency.

8   Conclusions

This paper addresses benefits and challenges of SACs. SACs are the necessary means if hazards cannot be avoided by internal attributes of a item itself, but through the adherence of certain regulations during the usage of the item in the intended superior context. We analyzed what are difficulties of formulating SACs, complying with

SACs and providing evidence of the compliance with SACs. The paper describes what is essential for SAC quality and for efficient handling of SACs:

- Rules have been introduced which define what are SACs and also what are not SACs. These should lead to a manageable amount of SACs which are taken seriously for safety. SACs always must have relevance for safety. Whenever a SAC is defined then the relation to a hazard has also to be specified.
- We defined quality criteria for SACs. A good quality of SACs simplifies and supports compliancy with SACs and its evidence. Therefore the SAC quality support to achieve the safety targets.
- We proposed a management process for formulating SACs, compliance with SACs and evidence of fulfilling SACs.
  - The creation of the SACs in early development phases is essential. It gives opportunity to avoid SACs and to react in time on SACs in affected projects.
  - Consolidation is fundamental to check the compliance with the quality criteria.
  - The SAC document and the use of a SAC database are important for a clear SAC storage and management so that efforts can be saved for gathering SACs. Clearly defined processes and responsibilities for SAC creation and handling of SACs on the one hand support the fulfillment of time and budget requirements. On the other hand it is important for safety as the amount of SACs must remain manageable and that the SACs give clear safety instructions.

The result is a process instruction which affects many other processes in the system life cycle and which therefore is complex. To support the handling and the compliance of this process instruction trainings are established.

References

1. CENELEC: Railway applications – Communication, signalling and processing systems – Safety related electronic systems for signalling, EN50129:2003-05-07 (2003)
2. Reuters: Geldstrafen im Transrapid-Prozess verhängt, 2008-05-23 (2008)
3. Dörner, D.: The Logic of Failure: Why Things Go Wrong and What We Can Do To Make Them Right. Metropolitan Books. Henry Holt and Co., New York (1996)
4. Hewison, N.S.: Book Review: The Logic of Failure: Why Things Go Wrong and What We Can Do To Make Them Right. Group Facilitation: A Research and Applications Journal 3, 86–89 (spring 2001)
5. International Electrotechnical Commission: Functional Safety of Electrical/Electronic/ Programmable Electronic Safety Related Systems, IEC 61508. Geneva, Switzerland (2000)
6. Bate, I., Bates, S., Hawkins, R., Kelly, T., McDermid, J.: Safety case architectures to complement a contract-based approach to designing safe systems. In: 21st International System Safety Conference, System Safety Society (2003)
7. Abran, A., Moore, J.W. (eds.): SWEBOK: Guide to the Software Engineering Body of Knowledge. IEEE Computer Society, Los Alamitos (2004)
8. Lauber, R., Göhner, P.: Prozessautomatisierung II. Springer, Heidelberg (1999)
9. CENELEC: Railway applications – Communications, signalling and processing systems – Software for railway control and protection systems, EN50128:2001-05-15 (2001)

Probability of Failure on Demand – The Why and the How

Jens Braband[1], Rüdiger vom Hövel[2], and Hendrik Schäbe[2]

[1] Siemens AG, Industry Sector, Mobility Division, Rail Automation,
Research & Development, I MO RA R&D R, Ackerstr. 22,
38126 Brunswick, Germany
[2] TÜV Rheinland InterTraffic GmbH, Assessment & Certification Rail, Am Grauen Stein,
51105 Cologne, Germany

Abstract. In the paper, we will study the PFD and its connection with the probability of failure per hour and failure rates of equipment using very simple models. We describe the philosophies that are standing behind the PFD and the THR. A comparison shows, how the philosophies are connected and which connections between PFH and PFD are implied. Depending on additional parameters, there can be deviations between safety integrity levels that are derived on the basis of the PFD and the PFH. Problems are discussed, which can arise when working with the PFD. We describe, how PFD and PFH in IEC 61508 are connected with the THR defined in the standard EN 50129.

We discuss arguments that show, why care is needed when using the PFD. Moreover, we present a reasoning, why a probability of failure on demand (PFD) might be misleading.

Keywords: Probability of failure on demand, rate of dangerous failures, safety integrity level.

1 The Problem

The standard IEC 61508 defines the following numerical characteristics per safety integrity level:

- PFD, average probability of failure to perform its design function on demand [1] (average probability of dangerous failure on demand of the safety function according to [2]), i.e. the probability of unavailability of the safety function leading to dangerous consequences
- PFH, the probability of a dangerous failure per hour (average frequency of dangerous failure of the safety function), which, until now, has been referred to as a failure rate. According to the most recent proposal [2] of IEC 61508, this is now interpreted as a frequency.

The numerical requirements are applied for the low-demand mode of operation (probability of failure on demand) and the high-demand or continuous mode of operation (probability of failure per hour), i.e. for continuous-run systems.

B. Buth, G. Rabe, T. Seyfarth (Eds.): SAFECOMP 2009, LNCS 5775, pp. 46–54, 2009.
© Springer-Verlag Berlin Heidelberg 2009

In many cases, analogous systems are used as well in continuous (in the standard called "high demand mode") as well as in demand mode (in the standards called "low demand mode"). Therefore, both concepts must be consistent. Note that, the terms in the standard (high demand mode and low demand mode) are misleading.

In EN 50129 [3], only one numerical characteristic is defined per safety integrity level. This is

- tolerable hazard rate per hour and function (THR).

In some cases, there are different approaches in both standards and differences in the various language versions. In addition to these differences, for the user the question arises why PFD (average probability of failure to perform its design function on demand) is not used in EN 50129 any more. Note that, in earlier draft versions of EN 50126 and EN 50129, PFD was still defined and used. A simple answer to this question would be the explanation that all control command and signalling systems in railway systems are continuously used or used according to high demand rates. This argument holds mainly true, but distracts attention from a deeper view of the PFD approach, its problems and its background.

Another formal but substantial difference is that EN 50126 considers a system function, whereas IE 61508 distinguishes the following equipment (see Figure 1):

- the equipment / machine itself, carrying out a certain task (Equipment Under Control (EUC))
- the EUC control system, which controls the EUC
- the programmable electronic system (PES), which is responsible for the safety of the EUC and the EUC operating device.

IEC 61508 has its origin in process industry. Traditionally, only the PES is considered there, whereas in railway technology the entire system is in focus.

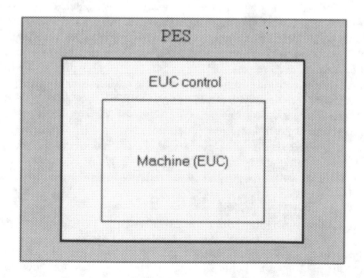

Fig. 1. System definition according to IEC 61508

When considering the low-demand mode of operation, it is assumed that the EUC and the EUC control device have a certain level of dependability. The PES then has only to intervene in cases where the EUC and the EUC control device are outside their normal functioning areas. For the high-demand or continuous mode of operation, it is assumed that a dangerous failure of the PES immediately leads to a dangerous failure of the system.

In this paper, we will study the THR and the PFD. We will show how they are interrelated and which problems can arise from the use of both these approaches.

Note that, software failures are treated as by IEC 61508: it is assumed that the necessary measures in software engineering have been taken, so that software failures can be neglected, compared with random hardware failures. Moreover, we only use constant failure rates of hardware, in order not to complicate the model.

This instruction file for Word users (there is a separate instruction file for LaTeX users) may be used as a template. Kindly send the final and checked Word and PDF files of your paper to the Contact Volume Editor. This is usually one of the organizers of the conference. You should make sure that the Word and the PDF files are identical and correct and that only one version of your paper is sent. It is not possible to update files at a later stage. Please note that we do not need the printed paper.

We would like to draw your attention to the fact that it is not possible to modify a paper in any way, once it has been published. This applies to both the printed book and the online version of the publication. Every detail, including the order of the names of the authors, should be checked before the paper is sent to the Volume Editors.

2 Risk

Safety-related systems are necessary to reduce risk. Safety analyses are carried out to determine risk and risk reduction achieved by safety-related systems.

Risk is usually given as damage (e.g. number of fatalities, injuries, material losses) per time unit [4 – 13]. To be precise, an event rate is given per severity class (e.g. single fatality), i.e. an average number of events per time unit. According to EN 50129, this can also be the probability of an event, "the combination of the frequency, or probability, and the consequence of a specified hazardous event".

This risk must be compared with the THR and the PFD. In both cases, the underlying concepts are different.

In order to simplify the following considerations, we restrict ourselves to the individual risk, i.e. the risk of a single, arbitrary but fixed individual. Furthermore, we restrict considerations to the risk of fatality of this individual. In order to better show the main relations, we will use a simplified formula for computation of the risk, compared with [14].

2.1 Risk Reduction According to the Philosophy of the THR

As a starting point, a safety system is taken, e.g. an interlocking. The system is operating continuously. Dangerous failures occur with a certain rate that must be smaller than the THR, e.g. a dangerous failure can be the composition of an inadmissible route in the interlocking. Here, no difference is made between the EUC, the EUC control device and the PES, i.e. the THR applies to the entire technical system.

A dangerous failure does not always lead to an accident, since other compensating measures (e.g. attention of the locomotive driver) or circumstances (e.g. there are no crossing trains at the moment) prevent an accident or reduce accident severity so that no fatalities occur. Let the probability that these other factors cannot prevent the accident be p_A, provided the conditions leading to the accident occurred.. Moreover, let p_I denote the probability that the considered individual is killed in the accident, provided the accident happened. Both probabilities are conditional probabilities. Then we have

$$IR = THR * p_A * p_I .\qquad(1)$$

In this philosophy, the safety-related system generates the dangerous events that can lead to the death of the considered individual under certain circumstances.

2.2   Risk Reduction According to the Philosophy of the PFD

Here, the safety-related system has a supervisory function. The safety-related system has to act only in cases where potentially dangerous events occur. This means that only the PES is considered. The demand for the PES is due to the failures of other components of the system, e.g. the EUC or the EUC control device. The demand rate is denoted by λ.

Only when the safety-related system fails in a demand situation, the individual is in danger. The coinciding rate is $\lambda * PFD$.

With this rate, at the output of the safety-related system, a dangerous failure occurs. The individual risk is then

$$IR = \lambda * PFD * p_A * p_I ,\qquad(2)$$

taking into account other measures and circumstances that might prevent the fatal accident.

2.3   Comparison of the Philosophies

The safety-related system is used in order to reduce the individual risk (IR), so that it does not exceed the admissible (tolerable) value of the individual risk (TIR), , i.e. the following requirement has to be fulfilled::

$$IR \leq TIR .\qquad(3)$$

For both philosophies, we derive from (1), (2) and (3) the following conditions

$$IR = THR * p_A * p_I \leq TIR\qquad(4)$$

for the THR philosophy and

$$IR = \lambda * PFD * p_A * p_I \leq TIR\qquad(5)$$

for the PFD philosophy. We then arrive at the requirements for the THR and the PFD, respectively

$$THR \leq TIR /(p_A * p_I) , \qquad (6)$$

$$PFD \leq TIR /(p_A * p_I * \lambda) . \qquad (7)$$

It is obvious that the requirement for the PFD depends directly on the intensity of requests for the supervisory function induced by other parts of the safety-related system, the EUC or the EUC control device. If the intensity of the requests changes with time, the requirement for the PFD would also change, leading to a changed safety integrity level.

In the THR philosophy, this connection does not exist. Changes of the implementation conditions influence probabilities p_A and p_I. However, this additional influence is present in both models.

Since both considerations – although different – apply to the same system, the individual risk must be the same, provided the same technical solutions have been applied. Therefore, we deduce

$$THR = \lambda * PFD . \qquad (8)$$

The THR is the THR of the entire system. Confusion might arise, since IEC 61508 considers only the PES so that the PFH for systems in continuous mode is related to the PES only.

2.4 Relation between the PFD and the PFH

The PFH is usually obtained when the system is analysed with the help of FMECA and the fault tree and after having distinguished the failure modes into dangerous and safe, detectable and non-detectable ones. This applies to the entity PES, too.

The PFD value is then computed from the PFH value. Two simple cases exist:

a) System (PES) with regular proof test

Assume the system is regularly checked with time interval τ. Assume further that, at the end of the interval and only then all dangerous failures are detected completely.
We then have

$$PFD = PFH * \tau/2 , \qquad (9)$$

where the requests to the system have been assumed as uniformly distributed in the proof test interval, giving mean time $\tau/2$ of the request.

b) System (PES) with permanent test and maintenance

Assume that the system is permanently tested and maintained, if necessary. Let the critical time (time at risk) be the time that elapses between testing and completion of the maintenance action that restores the system to a state as good as new. Again, this time is denoted by τ. Alternatively, τ can denote the time from the last test until the system is brought into a safe state for cases where the system is switched off, when a dangerous failure is detected. Equation (9) still holds. However, τ has another meaning.

If the failures cannot be detected completely, the PFD is not a constant but increases with time t:

$$PFD = PFH_d * \tau/2 + PFH_u * t . \tag{10}$$

Here, PFH_d denotes the rate of detectable failures and PFH_u denotes the rate of undetectable failures.

It can be observed that the PFD, which is important for determination of the safety integrity level, depends on proof test intervals and reaction times.

We may notice that the PFD in addition depends on the time in service for systems, where not all failures are detectable (see (10). The average probability which is mentioned in the standard IEC 61508 is then

$$PFD = PFH_d * \tau /2 + PFH_u * T/2 . \tag{11}$$

where T is the lifetime of the system, i.e. the PFD depends on the lifetime and on proof test interval τ.

2.5 Relation between the PFD / PFH and the THR

For the low-demand mode of operation, it can be derived from (8) and (9)

$$THR = \lambda * PFD = \lambda * PFH_{PES} * \tau/2 , \tag{12}$$

and for the continuous-demand mode of operation, there is

$$THR = PFH_{entire \ system} . \tag{13}$$

This relation has been proven formally in [15] with the help of Markov models.

2.6 Relation between the PFD and PFH in the Table of IEC 61508

The numerical values for the PFH and PFD as given in IEC 61508 (Part 1, Section 7.6.2.9) are related by a factor of 10,000, i.e. the value for τ is 20,000 h, which is about two years. This holds only if all dangerous failures are detected and removed.

If dangerous failures cannot be detected and removed, the lifetime should be about 20,000 h. Depending on fault detection coverage, combinations can be possible. The relation then becomes more complicated. This shows that defining a system with the low-demand mode of operation as a system with not more than one request per year is at least problematic. Thus, a correct and logical relation of both tables for the PFH and PFD cannot be given.

2.7 Problems with the PFD

We can conclude the following:

- A PFH can be derived directly by analysis as FMECA und the fault tree and by distinguishing dangerous and safe failures. For the PFD, an additional step is necessary.
- The PFD derived by this procedure depends on other parameters such as the proof test interval.
- The PFD that must be achieved by the system (PES) depends on the demand rate of the system.

- The relation between the PFD and the PFH as given in IEC 61508 lacks a sufficient logic.
- When considering the entire system which is the important point for safety considerations, a THR can be derived. This characteristic is identical with the PFH for systems with continuous demand.

Hence, when using the PFD, care is needed with the problems mentioned above. Moreover, the safety integrity level can change when parameters that influence the PFD are changed. This has implications on measures against systematic failures, too.

EN 50129 does not use a PFD and protects its user from problems arising from the factors mentioned above.

3 An Alternative Approach

The discussion above leads directly to the question of whether the approaches represented by the target failure measures PFD, PFH and THR can be harmonised. An initial idea has already been presented [16], which is developed here in more detail.

The basic observation is that all the target failure measures have relatively little meaning for the practitioner or user who usually simply asks the question: "How long will it take until the system fails for the first time?". Another observation is that, for him, the mathematics of fault trees or Markov models are usually too intricate and it is often desired to have a target failure measure which can be calculated much more easily.

This immediately leads to a simpler measure which is similar to the "Mean Time To (First) Failure" (MTTF) in reliability theory, namely the "Mean Time To (First) Hazard" (MTTH), which can be defined by the simple Markov model in Figure 2.

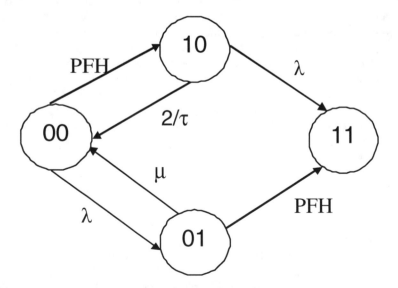

Fig. 2. Simple alternative Markov model

Table 1. Alternative SIL table

SIL	MTTH
4	> 10,000 years
3	> 1,000 years
2	> 100 years
1	> 10 years

The parameters and states in Figure 2 have the following interpretation:

λ	failure rate of the EUC and the EUC control system
μ	restoration rate of the EUC and the EUC control system
PFH	failure rate of the safety system
τ	proof-test interval of the safety system
00	no failure
01	demand
10	failure of the safety system
11	failure of the safety system during a demand

In this model (starting in state 00), either the PES may fail (transition to 10) or a demand may occur (transition to 01). If, in the first case, a demand occurs before failure of the PES is detected (transition to 11), then a hazard occurs. Alternatively, the PES may fail while the demand is still active. The model is stopped in the absorbing state as we are only interested in the initial transition from 00 to 11.

This approach has the advantage that it is not necessary to define different modes of operation and thus the problems with the distinction of the modes and different SIL tables are not present in this approach. Table 1 gives the unique SIL table which also relates better to real-life operating experience.

Last but not least, also the determination of the target measure is much easier, as, according to an approach by Birolini [17], the MTTH can be calculated as a solution of a set of linear equations (see (14-16) and the final result can even be given directly. So, not even a tool is necessary but a pocket calculator suffices.

$$MTTH = \frac{1}{\lambda + PFH} + \frac{\lambda}{\lambda + PFH} MTTH_{01} + \frac{PFH}{\lambda + PFH} MTTH_{10} \tag{14}$$

$$MTTH_{01} = \frac{1}{\mu + PFH} + \frac{\mu}{\mu + PFH} MTTH \tag{15}$$

$$MTTH_{10} = \frac{1}{\lambda + \frac{2}{\tau}} + \frac{\frac{2}{\tau}}{\lambda + \frac{2}{\tau}} MTTH \tag{16}$$

4 Conclusion

When considering the PFD and the PFH as defined in IEC 61508 and the THR as defined in EN 50129, the authors have found arguments that special care has to be taken when working with the PFD. The PFD is not present any more in EN 50129 and the other CENELEC railway standards. This is appreciated and makes the use of these standards simpler.

In addition, an alternative approach is presented which harmonises the different target failure measures and makes the necessary calculations much simpler.

References

1. IEC 61508-1 Functional safety of electrical / electronic / programmable electronic safety-related systems – Part 1: General requirements, 1st edn. (1998)
2. IEC 61508-1 Functional safety of electrical / electronic / programmable electronic safety-related systems, Part 1: General requirements, Committee Draft For Vote (CDV) (2008)
3. EN 50129 Railway applications – Communication, signalling and processing systems – Safety-related electronic systems for signalling (2003)
4. JAR 25 Large Aeroplanes
5. Kafka, P.: How safe is safe enough? – An unresolved issue for all technologies, Safety and Reliability. In: Schueller, G.I., Kafka, P. (eds.), vol. 1, pp. 385–390. Balkema, Rotterdam (1999)
6. Kuhlmann, A.: Introduction to Safety Science. Springer, New York (1986)
7. Saint-Onge, D.: Environmental Cleanup: What is Acceptable Risk, TriMediaConsultants, http://www.trimediaconsultants.com/risk.pdf
8. Skjong, R., Eknes, M.: Economic activity and societal risk acceptance. In: Zio, E., Demichela, M., Piccinini, N. (eds.) ESREL 2001 Towards a safer world, vol. 1, pp. 109–116. Politecnico die Torino, Torino (2001)
9. Schäbe, H.: Different Approaches for Determination of Tolerable Hazard Rates. In: Zio, E., Demichela, M., Piccinini, N. (eds.) ESREL 2001 Towards a safer world, vol. 1, pp. 435–442. Politecnico die Torino, Torino (2001)
10. Schäbe, H.: The Safety Philosophy behind the CENELEC Railway Standards. In: Decision Making and risk management, Proceedings of the conference ESREL 2002, Lyon, March 19 – 21, pp. 788–790 (2002)
11. Schäbe, H.: Apportionment of safety integrity levels in complex electronically controlled systems. In: Bedford, T., van Gelder, P.H.A.J.M. (eds.) Safety & Reliability – ESREL 2003, vol. 2, pp. 1395–1400. Balkema, Lisse (2003)
12. Schäbe, H., Wigger, P.: Experience with SIL Allocation in Railway Applications. In: Proceedings of the 4th International Symposium "Programmable Electronic Systems in Safety Related Applications", TÜV, Cologne, May 3 – 4 (2000)
13. Vatn, J.A.: Discussion of the Acceptable Risk Problem. Reliability Engineering and System Safety 61, 11–19 (1998)
14. Braband, J.: Risikoanalysen in der Eisenbahn-Automatisierung. Eurailpress (2005)
15. Braband, J.: Ein Ansatz zur Vereinheitlichung der Betriebsarten und Sicherheitsziele nach IEC 61508. In: Schnieder, E. (ed.) Entwurf komplexer Automatisierungssysteme, Proceedings EKA 2006, Brunswick, pp. 153–160 (2006)
16. Braband, J.: Safety Analysis based on IEC 61508: Lessons Learned and the Way Forward, Invited Talk. In: SAFECOMP 2006, Gdansk (2006)
17. Birolini, S.: Reliability Engineering. Springer, Berlin (2007)

Establishing the Correlation between Complexity and a Reliability Metric for Software Digital I&C-Systems

John Eidar Simensen[1], Christian Gerst[2], Bjørn Axel Gran[1], Josef Märtz[2], and Horst Miedl[2]

[1] Institute for energy technology, NO-1751 Halden, Norway
{John.Eidar.Simensen,Bjorn.Axel.Gran}@hrp.no
[2] Institute for Safety Technology GmbH, D-85748 Garching near Munchen, Germany
{Christian.Gerst,Josef.Maertz,Horst.Miedl}@istec.grs.de

Abstract. Faults introduced in design or during implementation might be prevented by design validation and by evaluation during implementation. There are numerous methods available for validating and evaluating software. Expert judgment is a much used approach to identify problematic areas in design or target challenges related to implementation. ISTec and IFE cooperate on a project on automated complexity measurements of software of digital instrumentation and control (I&C) systems. Metrics measured from the function blocks and logic diagrams specifying I&C-systems are used as input to a Bayesian Belief Net describing correlation between inputs and a complexity metric. By applying expert judgment in the algorithms for the automatic complexity evaluation, expert judgment is applied to entire software systems. The results from this approach can be used to identify parts of software which from a complexity viewpoint is eligible for closer inspection. In this paper we describe the approach in detail as well as plans for testing the approach.

1 Introduction

In software, possible faults to the system are introduced during the design phase or are due to erroneous usage. Unlike hardware systems, where e.g. the aging of components can cause a failure, software systems have faults inherent from their construction. If a software is fault-free after being designed and implemented, it is fault free during its entire life cycle, or as stated in [1]; all software failures are due to design faults. Designing fault-free software is considered difficult and proving that the software actually is fault-free is even more challenging. There are several methods available for the assessment of software [2], e.g. Fault Tree Analysis (FTA) and Failure Mode, Effect and Criticality Analysis (FMECA). An approach which is becoming more common is expert judgment. Expert judgment is defined as the consultation of one or more experts [3]. An expert expresses his belief in a system according to available information. Such information can be

B. Buth, G. Rabe, T. Seyfarth (Eds.): SAFECOMP 2009, LNCS 5775, pp. 55–66, 2009.

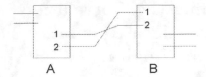

Fig. 1. Erroneously coupled function blocks

anything from user manuals and information on development tools and methods, to detailed specification about the system like e.g. its source code or logic diagrams specifying the system. Function blocks and logic diagrams are often used to specify the functionality of both analogue and digital instrumentation and control (I&C) systems. In many cases the number of logic diagrams specifying such systems is high and for an expert it is very difficult to assess most, yet alone all of these diagrams.

The purpose of the approach is to create a connection between system information and a reliability metric. To alleviate the amount of work for the expert, we present an approach for creating a connection between available system information and a reliability metric through the use of a Bayesian Belief Net (BBN) [4]. The choice of a BBN approach is also chosen due to long research interest on the applicability of BBN's at IFE [5][6][7][8]. The BBN is created on basis of the metrics available from the function blocks and the logic diagrams, and their combination in the BBN is decided using experts. The BBN is then adjusted on a smaller set of logic diagrams before the logic diagrams of an I&C system is evaluated by the BBN. The reliability metric can be used to indicate which LDs qualify for a closer inspection. In the following we give two examples on the difficulty of assessing LDs as a motivation for the automated complexity evaluation of digital I&C systems.

Two equal function blocks, A and B, consisting of two input signals and two output signals is shown in Figure 1. The output from block A is crossed erroneously to the input of block B. If the two signals 1 and 2 are of the same type the erroneous coupling is possible. In this very simple example the erroneous coupling is easy to identify.

Figure 2 shows an excerpt of an LD consisting of two types of seemingly similar, but different, function blocks. All input and output signals to the function blocks are of the same type. However, input signals going into function blocks of type B should be switched so that the output signals from the previous blocks are input correctly. Imagine an logic diagram with a large number of function blocks of the two types, e.g. in a ratio 70% A and 30% B. Manual verification of such a logic diagram is difficult and with a large number of diagrams to verify for experts, choosing the most important is a problem.

This paper is structured as followed. Chapter 2 describes the different subpackages of the project and introduction to how complexity measurement of function blocks and logic diagrams is performed in the project is given. In chapter 3 different possible approaches are suggested and reasons for using BBN in the approach are given. The construction of the BBN and its structure can be

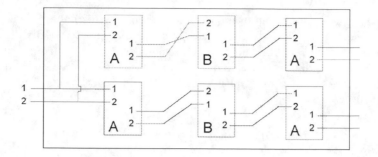

Fig. 2. Example of a Logic Diagram which can be difficult to assess

found in chapter 4. In chapter 5 the session were experts assigned conditional probabilities to the BBN nodes is described. In addition the plan for validating the BBN is suggested. Discussions on the approach and the case can be found in chapter 6. Chapter 7 contains a quick overview of the project and suggestions for further work.

2   Background

The work presented in this paper is part of a joint project on complexity[1] measurement of software in digital I&C-systems between the Institute for Safety Technology in Germany and the Institute for energy technology in Norway. The two institutes have been cooperating on several projects for many years, e.g. the VeNuS-project (Procedure for the efficient demonstration of usability and safety of computerised control systems) and the PODS-project [9] (Project On Diversity of Software). The project Complexity Measurement of Software Digital I&C-Systems is divided in four work-packages (WP), where:

- WP-1 is a methodology for automated complexity measurement of LDs. The outcome or result of the automated complexity measurement is represented in a complexity vector for each LD.
- WP-2 is dedicated to an automated complexity measurement tool consisting of an extractor and an evaluator. The extractor extracts complexity-relevant information from a database containing LDs and the evaluator generates a complexity-vector for each LD based on data mined with the extractor.
- WP-3 deals with the evaluation of the complexity measurements of LDs, evaluated on size and range of complexity-relevant items of a prototype-system. These items are found in tables generated by the extractor from WP-2.
- WP-4, for an which approach is suggested in this paper, is to develop a method to establish a correlation between complexity and reliability for LDs.

---

[1] By complexity we refer to the degree of difficulty involved in predicting the properties of a system when the properties of the induvidual parts of the system are known.

Work package 4, for which an approach is presented in this paper, utilizes complexity measurements from the first three packages as input to a BBN describing the correlation to a reliability metric. The suggested concept is that the BBN will single out logic diagrams which deviate in complexity and qualifies for closer inspection. More detailed information regarding the first three packages can be found in [10].

2.1 Complexity Measurement of Function Blocks and Logic Diagrams

Function blocks (FBs) constitute a set of software functions implemented in a high level, standardized programming language and represent some elementary function such as [10]:

- Logic or arithmetic functions, e.g. AND-, OR-, ADD-, XOR-gates.
- Basic I&C functions, e.g. an interpolation curve.
- Specific functions, e.g. ramp generator or sorter.

FBs can be defined as atomic software components [12] in a modern digital I&C-System and are implemented as modules of a software library. The functionality of a I&C-System can be implemented by combining different FBs. A FB is represented in a function block diagram and is defined as a graphical programming language standard in the international standard IEC 61131. A combination of FBs representing some I&C functionality is here referred to as a Logic Diagram (LD).

Complexity measurement of FBs and LDs is performed on two levels [10]. First, evaluation and measurement of the FBs is performed. The FBs form the basis for the evaluation of the LDs. The evaluation of the FBs outputs a matrix describing the complexity of each FB in the library. Second, evaluation and measurement of the LDs is performed. This evaluation takes into account the FBs represented in the specific LD and their belonging complexity matrices from the FB evaluation. In the following the FB evaluation and the LD evaluation is described in more detail.

2.2 Complexity Evaluation of the Function Blocks

The complexity measurement of the FBs is based on two approaches, white-box view and black-box view, depending on which information is available. E.g. when the source code of a FB is known, i.e. the provider of a digital I&C-System has made the code available, we have a white-box view. A white-box view presents the possibility to perform statistical analysis and extract metrics for the source code representing the FB. Measures available from a white-box view can be seen in Table 1. On the other hand, when such code is not made available by the system providers, we have a black-box view. Since source code is unavailable in the black-box view, other sources of information on the FBs e.g. product specifications and user manuals are taken into consideration instead. Information measures in a black-box view is given in Table 2.

Table 1. White-Box View Measures [10]

Volume Measures	Number of basic blocks
	Average length of basics blocks
	Lines of code
	Procedure entry- and exit-points
Control Organization Measures	McCabe's cyclomatic complexity
	Nesting Depth
	Reducibility
	Linear code sequence and jump (LCSAJ)
Data Organization Measures	Information Fan-in
	Information Fan-Out
	Parameters

Table 2. Black-Box View Measures [10]

Signals	Number and type of signals
Parameters	Number of parameters
	Type of parameters
Failure handling and status processing of signals	Failure propagation
	Failure barriers
	Signal status
Internal status	Internal memories
	Return codes
Resources needed	Time
	Memory

The I&C functionality is designed on basis of the available FBs. The higher the complexity of a FB is, the higher is the probability of erroneous implementation of the I&C function, due to e.g. erroneous usage of the FB or misinterpretation of the manual.

2.3 Complexity Evaluation of the Logic Diagrams

From the first three work packages of the complexity measurement project [10] at ISTec, the complexity of an LD is divided in three; basic counting metrics extracted from the graphic representation of the LD, variability features impacting the complexity, and metrics describing the interconnection complexity of the FBs of digital I&C-Systems. The counting metrics consists of basic counting size characteristics e.g. lines of code, number of operands etc. The variability features represent the flexibility or changeability of the FBs, e.g. number of internal states or changeable parameters. The interconnection complexity consists of two parts where one describes how an FB, or a set of FBs, produce more than one output signal, and the second part describes how an input signal is utilized by one or more FBs. A special metric $V(LD)$ was created for the representation of the two types of interconnection complexity.

2.4   Available Sources of Information

Detailed information regarding the FBs and the complexity measurements of the LD is preserved in a vector consisting of the following:

- The number of function blocks.
- Complexity of the function blocks.
- Number of input signals.
- Number of output signals.
- Interconnection complexity V(LD) of the function blocks.
- Number of changeable parameters.
- Number of internal memories (internal states).

These 7 metrics serves as the input to the Bayesian Belief Net providing a correlation to a reliability metric for the LD.

3   Approach

The purpose of the approach is to create a link between available system information and a reliability metric. The aim is not to find the true reliability of a system but rather use the reliability metric as a mean or a tool for adjusting the analysis work. The methods for identifying and collecting system information was described in Chapter 2 and they are performed in the three first work packages of the project. For the creation of a connection between the input and the reliability metric there are several viable approaches.

A neural network [11] is a traditional solution which is well documented as a successful decision engine. With a large set of training data the accuracy of a neural net is hard to match. Unfortunately, in our case the size of available training data is small and the black box attributes of a neural net is a problem for evaluation.

Expert judgment is another approach to decide the information to reliability metric connection. For each LD an expert can decide the corresponding reliability metric. As earlier stated this is time consuming work. With the large number of LDs available this approach is not good. With the size of the input information available in this project, and similarly so with most digital I&C-Systems specified using LDs, neural nets nor expert judgment are good methods for our approach.

The Bayesian belief net [4][6] approach has been selected because its modeling is divided into two distinct parts; the modeling of the node connections and the modeling of the dependencies. Describing the target system is straightforward when assigning subparts of the system as distinct nodes before describing the relationship between these system parts using conditional dependencies. More importantly it is possible to decompose a system using intermediate nodes to better describe the functionality of the system parts and the relationship between them. Compared to a neural net, a BBN is transparent and its contents can be described and altered in detail. This is a great benefit when the aim is to include expert judgment in the BBN.

4   Building the BBN

The construction of the BBN is done in two parts where one is selecting the nodes and the second is the selection of conditional probability tables (CPTs). In this chapter the process of selecting and grouping of nodes performed in the BBN is explained. The process consisted of two steps, where experts on BBNs, FBs and LDs decided the grouping of the available input metrics in the first step and decided the relationship between the input combinations in the second. The aim was to combine all relevant information, i.e. the input metrics, into the net.

The available input metrics (as mentioned in Chapter 2.4) were combined in three branches in the BBN, each using different input metrics in their top nodes and eventually, through a series of intermediate nodes, end in one leaf node describing the reliability metric. The experts decided the combination of inputs into the intermediate nodes.

4.1   Nodes in the BBN

The experts grouped the different input nodes together to form intermediate nodes. The input nodes considered the most important by the experts are presented first and their respective branch is explained before presenting the next branch. Figure 3 shows the BBN.

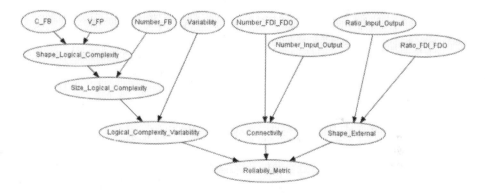

Fig. 3. Overview of the nodes in the BBN

The first branch. The input nodes *C_FB* (Complexity of the FB) and *V_FB* (Interconnection complexity of the FB) were connected by the experts into an intermediate node representing the shape of the logical complexity. This intermediate node represents complexity on a FB level. When the intermediate node *Shape_Logical_Complexity* was combined with the number of FBs it resulted in a new intermediate node named *Size_Logical_Complexity*. This intermediate node represents complexity on a both the FB and the LD level. The experts connected *Size_Logical_Complexity* with the node *Variability* to express complexity variability of the FBs and the LD in the intermediate node

Logical_Complexity_Variability. The first branch is from the last intermediate node connected to the node representing the reliability metric, namely *Reliability_Metric*.

The second branch represents the connectivity within the LD. The first input node, *Number_FDI_FDO*, represents the number of connected LDs to the input and number of connected LDs to the output of the LD. The second input node, *Number_Input_Output*, is the total inputs and outputs to the LD. The two input nodes were joined by the experts in the intermediate node *Connectivity* which represents the number of connected inputs and outputs to the LD in total, and the number of other LDs connected. The intermediate node *Connectivity* was connected to the reliability metric node.

The third branch represents the external shape of the LD. The external shape of an LD represents the connections to and from the LD and indicates how dependent the LD is on other LDs. It also gives an indication as to which degree one or more other LDs are affected by the current. The first input node, *Ratio_Input_Output*, is the ratio between all inputs and outputs to the LD The second input node, *Ratio_FDI_FDO*, represents the ratio number of connected LDs to the input and number of connected LDs to the output of the LD. The input nodes representing the ratio were combined in the intermediate node *Shape_external* which in turn was connected to the reliability metric node.

5   Assigning Conditional Probability Tables and Validating the BBN

In this chapter the process establishing the CPTs is explained and the plans for validating the BBN are presented. The process of creating all the CPTs is ongoing work.

5.1   Conditional Probability Tables

Assigning the CPTs was done in a session where experts expressed how they believed different nodes should be coupled, how the nodes would relate to each other and how this in turn would impact the complexity metric node. Rather than coming up with complete CPTs directly, the session was structured so that the experts decided the CPT framework through the use of numbers, lead words and color maps; the CPTs were decided indirectly. Some benefits from this approach were that the experts were able to express their beliefs about the entire BBN. Detailed discussions on the CPTs were avoided and simplification of the node relations ensured that the experts had an easier time understanding each other. Based on the results from the session, the initial CPTs will be created and adjusted using a subset of 20 LDs.

An example from the session can be seen in Figure 4. Here the size of the logical complexity is given as the combination of the shape of the logical complexity (Shape_LC) and the number of FBs. The Shape_LC was divided in three

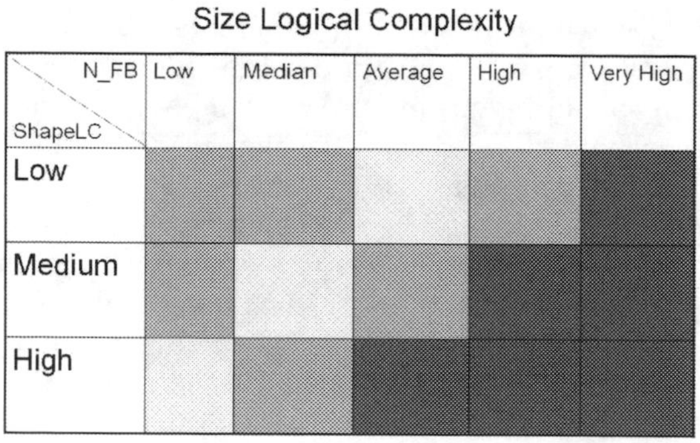

Size Logical Complexity

N_FB ShapeLC	Low	Median	Average	High	Very High
Low					
Medium					
High					

Fig. 4. Size of the logical complexity, grouped using the colors: green, yellow, orange, red, purple

categories (Low, Medium and High) and the number of FBs divided in five categories (Low, Median, Average, High and Very High). The experts decided on which fields should indicate the same complexity. A color map spanning from green to purple shows which fields that are grouped together and how complex a combination of Shape_LC and number of FBs is.

5.2 Validating the BBN

For validating the BBN it is planned to use a set of 20 LDs. These LDs will be used as input in the BBN to adjust the net and update the priori distribution. Which LDs to use is decided by an expert where the aim us to represent a broad specter of different LDs and FBs. There is a total of 1067 FBs in the system and the highest number of FBs in a LD is 265. The median number of FBs in a LD is between 4 to 8 and since the number of FBs is not evenly spread, but appearing in 5 groups (approx: 6, 20, 50, 100, 500 FBs in an LD), we believe 20 LDs should be sufficient for the validation of the net provided LDs from all 5 groups are represented. This work is ongoing.

6 Discussion

The discussion is divided in three parts. The first part address the available input metrics. The second part discuss the layout of the BBN and the motivation for our BBN structure. In the third part the applicability of the approach to other problems is discussed.

6.1 Input Parameters

The seven input parameters given in chapter 2 is well documented in the three first work packages of the project. One question is if there are more metrics available that better suited for evaluating complexity of FBs and LDs. For example, a

metric identifying LDs that are different but contain the same FDs could be useful for identifying erroneous implementation directly. Another question relates
to how much detail should be included. An example is information regarding
different pedigrees; should knowledge on developer information, e.g. tools used
in design or the qualification and experience of the designers, be included in the
BBN as well? Would such information contribute with meaningful information
when compared to the three types of metrics (counting, variability and interconnection) already available? For this project we believe the identified metrics
should be sufficient to differ between LDs of different complexity. Moreover, the
experts did not request additional metrics when making decisions on the BBN,
which indicates that the available metrics were suitable.

6.2   Node Combination and the BBN

The arrangement of the BBN nodes is very much dependent on the experts. Input
nodes are provided, but their combination and their importance are targets for
discussion. The same applies to the intermediate nodes in the net. The main
argument for deciding the layout and combination of nodes is that it should be
explainable and make sense. In that manner we are confident in our selection
of the intermediate nodes in particular. We also believe that by combining few
inputs to an intermediate node we are able to keep the net simple enough for
the experts to express their beliefs confidently.

It is obvious that different nets can be argued for but this is one of the features
of BBN. Our goal is to have a net which is easily explainable and provides
reasonable output values. We believe the first goal is already covered by the fact
that the experts were able to communicate their ideas and beliefs about the
BBN quite easily in a short amount of time. The second goal is subject of more
work as the creation of CPTs is still in progress and the evaluation of the BBN
has not yet commenced.

6.3   Applying the BBN to Other Problems

The change from analogue systems to digital systems is becomming more usual,
e.g. changing analogue power range monitoring system (PRM) with a digital
PRM. Both implementations serve the same function and although their implementation may differ there are similarities in their inputs and their outputs. An
interesting question in this situation is if analogue and digital systems performing the same job have the same complexity? How about the reliability metric;
is one approach more reliable than the other? Experts will most certainly differ
in their opinions. Given that both digital and analogue systems can be specified
graphically in a similar fashion it should be possible to apply the method to
analogue systems as well.

Are there other uses for the approach suggested in this paper? E.g. can the
approach be used for all state diagrams, control flow diagrams or static analysis
in general? Graphical system specifications are in theory accepted in in the
automated complexity measurement and evaluation approach suggested in this

paper. However, there would be a need to come up with new metrics for each type of diagram and to have the building blocks (e.g. FB) available in a library. The same applies for the combination of inputs and the selection of nodes in the BBN; experts will possibly be required to assess each system based on their specification to come up with the framework for the CPTs. At the moment we are not able to say something definitive about this methods applicability to other systems and specifications as the work is ongoing.

7   Conclusion

In this paper an approach for the complexity measurement of digital I&C-Systems was presented. The approach utilizes metrics extracted from FBs and LDs specifying a digital I&C-System to find a correlation between complexity and a reliability.

A case was presented where inputs, based on metrics available from a set of FBs and LDs specifying a digital I&C-System, were combined by experts in a BBN to express a relationship between complexity of a logic diagram and a reliability metric for that diagram. In the project, data from system specification have been extracted and complexity calculation for the metrics has been performed. A meeting with experts was facilitated for the creation of a Bayesian Belief Net connecting complexity with a reliability metric.

Further work includes finishing the CPTs of the BBN based on a meeting already held with the expert. The validation of the BBN is then performed before the BBN is used to evaluate the digital I&C-System. Results from this automated evaluation will be compared to manual expert judgment on the digital I&C-System performed separately.

References

1. Fenton, N., Littlewood, B., Neil, M., Strigini, L., Sutcliffe, A., Wright, D.: Assessing Dependability of Safety Critical Systems using Diverse Evidence. In: IEEE Proceedings Software Engineering, vol. 145(1), pp. 35–39 (1998)
2. Dahll, G.: Safety Assessment of Software Based Systems. In: SAFECOMP - The International Conference on Computer Safety, Reliability and Security, pp. 14–24. Springer, Heidelberg (1997)
3. Boehm, B.W.: Software engineering economics. IEEE Transitional on Software Engineering 10(1), 7–19 (1984)
4. Jensen, F.: An Introduction to Bayesian Network. UCL Press, University College London (1996)
5. Gran, B.A., Dahll, G., Eisinger, S., Lund, E.J., Norstrm, J.G., Strocka, P., Ystanes, B.J.: Estimating Dependability of Programmable Systems Using BBNs. In: Koornneef, F., van der Meulen, M.J.P. (eds.) SAFECOMP 2000. LNCS, vol. 1943, pp. 309–320. Springer, Heidelberg (2000)
6. Gran, B.A.: The use of Bayesian Belief Networks for combining disparate sources of information in the safety assessment of software based systems. Thesis 2002:35, NTNU, Trondheim, Norway (2002)

7. Gran, B.A.: Use of Bayesian Belief Networks when Combining Disparate Sources of Information in the Safety Assessment of Software Based Systems. International Journal of Systems Science 33(6), 529–542 (2002)
8. Gran, B.A., Helminen, A.: A Bayesian Belief Network for Reliability Assessment. In: Voges, U. (ed.) SAFECOMP 2001. LNCS, vol. 2187, pp. 35–45. Springer, Heidelberg (2001)
9. Bishop, P.G., Esp, D.G., Barnes, M., Humphreys, P., Dahll, G.: PODSA project on diverse software. IEEE Trans. Softw. Eng. 12(9), 929–940 (1986)
10. Märtz, J., Lindner, A., Miedl, H.: Complexity Measurement of Software in Digital I&C-Systems. In: Sixth American Nuclear Society Int. Topic Meeting on Nuclear Plant Instrumentation, Control, and Human-Machine Interface Technologies. NPIC&HMIT 2009, Knoxville Tennessee (2009)m American Nuclear Society, La-Grange Park (2009)
11. Lyu, M.R.: Handbook of Software Reliability Engineering, pp. 699–705. IEEE Computer Society Press, McGraw-Hill (1996)
12. Lyu, M.R.: Handbook of Software Reliability Engineering, pp. 41–43. IEEE Computer Society Press, McGraw-Hill (1996)

Exploring Network Security in PROFIsafe

Johan Åkerberg[1] and Mats Björkman[2]

[1] ABB AB, Corporate Research, 721 78 Västerås, Sweden
johan.akerberg@se.abb.com
[2] Mälardalens University, Academy of Innovation, Design, and Technology
P.O. Box 883 Västerås, Sweden
mats.bjorkman@mdh.se

Abstract. Safety critical systems are used to reduce the probability of failure that could cause danger to person, equipment or environment. The increasing level of vertical and horizontal integration increases the security risks in automation. Since the risk of security attacks can not be treated as negligible anymore, there is a need to investigate possible security attacks on safety critical communication.

In this paper we show that it is possible to attack PROFIsafe and change the safety-related process data without any of the safety measures in the protocol detecting the attack. As a countermeasure to network security attacks, the concept of security modules in combination with PROFIsafe will reduce the risk of security attacks, and is in line with the security concept *defense-in-depth*.

1 Introduction

In process automation, automation equipment is normally located within locked buildings were only authorized personnel may enter. The plant or fieldbus networks carrying information of production speed, quality, quantity as well as individual commands and feedback from actuators and sensors belong to closed networks, without any connections outside the physical building. New technological advancements in for example condition monitoring, wireless communication, and industrial Ethernet in combination with the demand of horizontal and vertical integration to master the complexities in production [1], increase the risk of security attacks on automation systems. An example of vertical integration is when a route is opened from the upper layer systems to access web servers in field devices. Wireless bridges, interlocking, or distributed control are some examples where horizontal integration is utilized in the plants. The previously hierarchical and natural borders are gradually disappearing due to horizontal and vertical integration and it is not that easy anymore to state that the risks of security attacks on automation systems are negligible. From the IT domain we know about viruses and Trojans that cause a great deal of efforts and problems. Consider a scenario with a virus residing on a PC belonging to an automation system, that instead of sending e-mails, is sending altered telegrams to affect the plant production and availability.

B. Buth, G. Rabe, T. Seyfarth (Eds.): SAFECOMP 2009, LNCS 5775, pp. 67–80, 2009.
© Springer-Verlag Berlin Heidelberg 2009

Some of the most important security concerns are [2][3][4]:

- *Confidentiality*, only authorized entities may read confidential data
- *Integrity*, unauthorized entities may not change data without detection
- *Availability*, the services should be available when needed
- *Authentication*, confirmation that an entity is what is claims to be.

The state-of-the-art in automation security is to use perimeter defense, firewalls, to restrict incoming and outgoing messages to the networks. This can be done in multiple layers, to protect even a single production cell with a firewall [5]. Within the network, protected by the same perimeter defense, communication is based on trust and nodes can communicate with each other without any restrictions. To communicate between network borders, the use of virtual private networks (VPNs) are recommended. How will laptops being moved on the networks for maintenance and tuning with various on-board wireless radios, or wireless sensor networks at fieldbus level, affect security? Using wireless radio communication could compromise security as malicious attackers can use the wireless radio communication to access the local networks. Focusing at the communication closest to the process, some Ethernet based fieldbus protocols are not even using layer 3 communication and cannot easily be protected by VPNs. This might implicate problems with horizontal and vertical integration since firewalls cannot be used in such cases and there is a trade off between horizontal and vertical integration versus security.

From the railway domain, especially in railway signaling, where communication cannot always be transmitted on trusted networks, measures must be taken to ensure authorization, integrity and even confidentiality of messages. As there are existing standards to cover safety-relevant communication on non-trusted networks in the railway domain, those standards will be used as reference when appropriate. This paper focuses on the security aspects of safety-relevant communication using PROFIsafe [6].

The main contributions in this paper are summarized as follows:

- It is shown that it is possible to take control over PROFIsafe nodes
- It is shown that attacks can be done without any of the peers detecting the attack
- The concept of *security modules* can be used to retrofit security to PROFIsafe when using PROFINET IO

The paper is structured as follows. In Section 2 related work is presented, Section 3 introduces PROFIsafe and in Section 4 the attack scenario and results are presented. In Section 5 network security countermeasures are introduced and finally in Section 6 conclusions are presented.

2   Related Work

The security threats to automation systems have been researched as well as evaluation of existing IT security solutions to automation networks and are summarized in [2][4][7]. In [2] and [4] existing IT security protocols, such as

Transport Layer Security and Secure Sockets Layer (TLS and SSL), and IPsec, are summarized and evaluated for use in the automation domain.

Different attempts and methods to attack PROFINET IO nodes were executed in [8] without success. The authors claimed that if standard Ethernet switches are used, it should be possible to deploy a successful man-in-the-middle attack, where an attacker can get in a position between the nodes, relaying and manipulating messages. In [9] it is shown that it is possible to deploy a successful man-in-the-middle attack on PROFINET IO and the concept of *security modules* is introduced to deal with authentication and integrity of PROFINET IO real-time communication.

A Denial-of-Service (DoS) attack, draining network and CPU resources to reduce the availability or deny service completely, is a non-trivial security threat that can not be prevented with cryptography. A generic approach to deal with DoS attacks in automation systems is presented in [10].

Since the encryption keys have to be exchanged at some point in time they might be exposed, and the weakest point of encryption and integrity is normally not the algorithms themselves, but the way the "secret keys" are distributed. Such key distribution schemes are an even bigger challenge to implement in existing systems than to find resources for executing the security algorithms. One such key distribution scheme has been presented for building automation in [11].

A Virtual Automation Network (VAN) [12][13][14] is a heterogeneous network consisting of wired and wireless Local Area Networks, the Internet and wired and/or wireless communication systems. VAN is not a new set of protocols; it aims at reusing as much as possible from the LAN, WAN and industrial communication. The aim of VAN is to transfer data through a heterogeneous network, through an end-to-end communication path, in the context of an automation application.

3   Basics of PROFIsafe

PROFIsafe is one out of four safety protocols described in the IEC 61784-3 standard [15]. PROFIsafe or functional safety communication profile 3/1 (FSCP 3/1) as it is referred to in the standard [6] can be used with both PROFIBUS and PROFINET. There are two versions of PROFIsafe, V1 that was originally designed to run on PROFIBUS and V2 is the extended version to handle communication on Ethernet and the extended functionality provided by PROFINET compared to PROFIBUS [16].

3.1   Black Channel

PROFIsafe's way of safety communication is based on the experience from the railway signaling domain and is documented in IEC 62280-1 [17] and IEC 62280-2 [18]. Safe applications and standard applications can share the same standard PROFINET IO communication system, the *black channel*, at the same

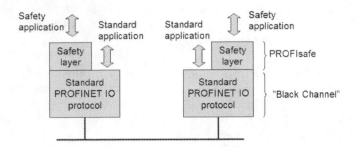

Fig. 1. The Black Channel principle, where safety-related and non safety-related communication co-exist on the same standard transmission system, which is excluded from functional safety certification

time. The safe transmission function comprises all measures to deterministically discover all possible faults and hazards that could be infiltrated by the black channel, or to keep the residual error probability under a certain limit [6]. Including

- random malfunctions, for example due to electromagnetic interference (EMI) impact on the transmission channel
- failures and faults on the standard transmission hardware
- systematic malfunctions of components within the standards hardware and software

Using the black channel, PROFIsafe perform safe communication by using

- a standard transmission system and
- an additional safety transmission protocol on top of the standard transmission system

and is illustrated in Fig. 1.

The black channel principle limits the certification effort to the safe transmission functions and the standard transmission system can be excluded from certification[6]. PROFIsafe is approved to apply on black channels with a bit error probability up to 10^{-2} [6].

3.2   Safety Measures of PROFIsafe

The selection of the generic safety measures in IEC 61784-3, section 5.5 is required for PROFIsafe [6]. The safety measures shall be processed and monitored within one safety unit. Table 1 describes possible communication error types as described in IEC 61784-3.

PROFIsafe specifies four different safety measures out of the total 8 specified in IEC 61784-3 [6]. Table 2 describes the safety measures and their coverage to master communication errors [6].

Table 1. Description of possible communication errors [15]

Error Type	Description
Corruption	Messages may be corrupted due to errors within a bus participant, due to errors on the transmission medium, or due to message interference
Unintended repetition	Due to an error, fault or interference, old not updated messages are repeated at an incorrect point in time
Unacceptable delay	Messages may be delayed beyond their permitted arrival time window, for example due to errors in the transmission medium, congested lines, interference, or due to bus participants sending messages in such manner that services are delayed or denied (for example FIFOs in switches, bridges, routers)
Incorrect sequence	Due to an error, fault or interference, the predefined sequence (for example natural numbers, time references) associated with messages from a particular source is incorrect
Loss	Due to an error, fault or interference, a message is not received or not acknowledged
Insertion	Due to a fault or interference, a message is inserted that relates to an unexpected or unknown source entity
Masquerade	Due to a fault or interference, a message is inserted that relates to an apparently valid source entity, so a non-safety relevant message may be received by a safety relevant participant, which then treats it as safety relevant
Addressing	Due to a fault or interference, a safety relevant message is sent to the wrong safety relevant participant, which then treats reception as correct.

Table 2. Deployed measures in PROFIsafe to master errors [6]

Communication error	Safety measures			
	(Virtual) Consecutive Number [1]	Timeout with receipt [2]	Codename for sender and receiver [3]	Data consistency check [4]
Corruption				x
Unintended repetition	x			
Incorrect sequence	x			
Loss	x	x		
Unacceptable delay		x		
Insertion	x	x	x	
Masquerade		x	x	x
Addressing			x	
Revolving memory failures within switches	x			

[1] Instance of "sequence number" of IEC 61784-3.
[2] Instance of "time expectation" and "feedback message" of IEC 61784-3.
[3] Instance of "connection authentication" of IEC 61784-3.
[4] Instance of "data integrity assurance" of IEC 61784-3.

3.3   PROFIsafe Container Structure

In Fig. 2 one single PROFIsafe container is illustrated that contains the safety-related IO data and an additional safety code (status / control byte). A PROFI-NET IO real-time frame may contain more than one PROFIsafe container, for example in the case of a modular IO device with several safety modules.

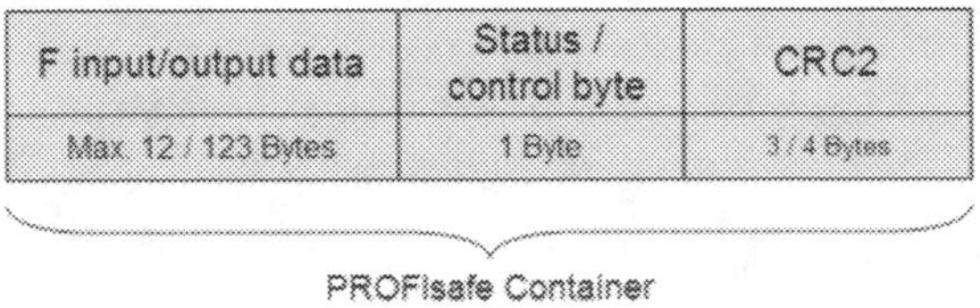

F input/output data	Status / control byte	CRC2
Max. 12 / 123 Bytes	1 Byte	3 / 4 Bytes

PROFIsafe Container

Fig. 2. A single PROFIsafe container

PROFIsafe uses several different CRCs to protect the integrity of safety-related messages, therefore CRCs with different numbers appear to differentiate them. The different CRCs are described Section 3.4. Factory automation and process automation have different requirements on number of IO and type of IO. Factory automation deals with binary IO processed at a very high speed and process automation normally deals with longer IO values as well (bit, integer, floating point), that take more processing time. PROFIsafe supports two different safety-related input/output data lengths that require CRC protection of different complexity to fulfill Safety Integrity Level 3 (SIL3) [19] requirements with an error probability requirement of $< 10^{-9}$ [6]. The choice between the two operational modes is done in the application relation creation phase by safety parameterization

- safety IO data up to 12 bytes together with a 24 bit CRC2 or
- safety IO data up to 123 bytes together with a 32 bit CRC2

The safety-related IO data of a safe node is collected in the safety payload data unit (PDU), and the data type coding corresponds to PROFINET IO. In the case of a few safety-related IO data up to 12 bytes the 24 bit CRC2 option shall be chosen for performance reasons. There are modular devices, beside compact devices, with safety and standard I/O units and sub-addresses. A PROFINET IO head station (Device Access Point) is considered to be part of the "Black Channel" and is used to agree upon the structure of a PROFINET IO message with several safety containers via start-up parameterization. One safety container corresponds to one subslot in PROFINET IO.

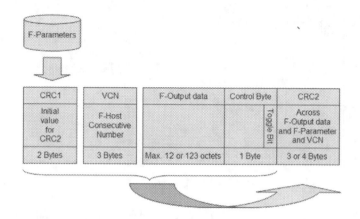

Fig. 3. CRC2 generation

3.4   Consistency Check of PROFIsafe Container

When the safety parameters have been transferred to the safe device, the safe host and safe device/module produces a 2 byte CRC1 signature [6] over the safety parameters. The CRC1 signature, safe IO data, Status or Control byte and the corresponding Consecutive Number are used to produce the CRC2 signature as illustrated in Fig 3. The CRC1 signature provides the initial value for CRC2 calculation that is transferred cyclically, thus limiting the CRC calculation for each cyclic PROFIsafe container to CRC2.

3.5   Virtual Consecutive Number

The consecutive number is used as a measure to deal with some of the possible communication errors, illustrated in Tab. 2. It is also used to monitor the propagation delay between transmission and reception. A 24 bit counter is used for consecutive numbering, thus the consecutive number counts in a cyclic mode from 1...FF FF FFh wrapping over to 1 at the end [6]. The consecutive number 0 is reserved for error conditions and synchronization of the VCNs.

The consecutive number is called Virtual Consecutive Number (VCN), since it is not visible in the safety PDU. The mechanism uses 24 bit counters located in the safety host and safety device and the Toggle Bit within the Status Byte and the Control Byte increment the counters synchronously. Figure 4 illustrates the VCN mechanism. To verify the correctness and to synchronize the two independent counters, the consecutive number is included in the CRC2 calculation that is transmitted with each safety PDU (Fig. 3).

The transmitted part of the VCN is reduced to a Toggle Bit which indicates an increment of the local counter. The counters within the safe host and safe device are incremented at each edge of the Toggle Bits. In case of a detected error the consecutive number will be reset to zero in both safe host and safe device [6]. Figure 4 illustrates the mechanism.

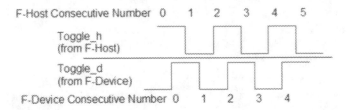

Fig. 4. The Toggle Bit function

4   Security Attack on PROFIsafe

The hypothesis used to deploy a successful security attack on PROFIsafe is that it will succeed if and only if the CRC2 is correctly recalculated after changes in safety-related IO data within the timing constraints of the protocol. To be able to recalculate CRC2, and bypass the data consistency check, the following information have to be obtained

- The current VCN
- The codename for the sender and receiver
- The actual set of safety parameters

The CRC1 is calculated over the codename for the sender and receiver and the actual set of safety parameters. It is known that the CRC1 will not change during the lifetime of the session. This knowledge will simplify the attempts to bypass the data consistency check later on. What is left before a security attack can be deployed is information on

- The current VCN
- The CRC1 that is static over the session lifetime

Next section will describe how to obtain the VCN and the CRC1.

4.1   Breaking the Code

By receiving one safety container, and applying brute force to calculate all valid combinations of CRC1 and VCN that generates the same CRC2 as in the received message, a set of possible CRC1 will be obtained. With the knowledge of that the CRC1 is static over the session lifetime, the remaining combinations can be reduced down to the CRC1 that is in use. This has to be done in an iterative process that terminates when the correct CRC1 has been found. CRC1 and VCN pairs can be eliminated if the next frame generates a VCN that is smaller than the previous frame. This can be done as the standard specifies that the VCN shall increase monotonically and wrap around at FF FF FFh to 1 and the CRC1 is static over the session lifetime.

Algorithm 1 will terminate with the correct CRC1, or in very seldom cases it will terminate with no CRC1 at all, if the VCN did wrap around during steps 3-11. The purpose of the research is not to find optimal algorithms, but to investigate the possibilities of security attacks on safety protocols. Thus the algorithm will not be refined any further.

Algorithm 1. Retrieving the $CRC1$ and VCN

1: Receive a safety container
2: Calculate and store all permutations of VCN and $CRC1$ that generate the same $CRC2$ as the received safety container in step 1
3: **repeat**
4:     Receive another safety container
5:     **for all** stored permutations of $CRC1$ and VCN from step 2 **do**
6:         Calculate $CRC2$ of safety container from step 4 with stored permutation of $CRC1$ and VCN
7:         **if** calculated $CRC2 =$ received $CRC2$ and $VCN <$ previous VCN **then**
8:             Discard the permutation as a possible candidate
9:         **end if**
10:    **end for**
11: **until** one or zero valid permutations of $CRC1$ and VCN remain

---

When the CRC1 and the latest VCN has been obtained, it should be possible to bypass the safety measures of PROFIsafe according to the hypothesis if the safety frame can be changed within given time constraints.

4.2 Attacking PROFIsafe Containers

The remaining challenge is to find the actual VCN very fast for all received safety containers. When the VCN has been obtained for the actual safety container, the safety-related IO has to be changed and the CRC2 has to recalculated. It is known that the VCN will increase monotonically at a rate depending on the bus period time, host and device period time executing the safety layer. If the attacking application is fast and can receive all safety containers, the VCN would not update for each and every frame received, thus relaxing the computational efforts to derive the VCN in "real-time".

A reasonable approach would be to start with the latest known VCN and recalculate the CRC2. If the CRC2 is not the same as the received one, continue by increasing the VCN until a match is found. The proof-of-concept implementation shows that this approach is fast and accurate. An alternative solution would be to increase the VCN when the toggle bit changes and reset it to zero in case of errors reported by the status bits in the control or status byte of the safety container. The advantage of the previous method is that the CRC1 and VCN will be validated for each frame, before they are used, to avoid wrong CRC2 calculation and thus detection by the safety nodes.

4.3 Test Setup

As PROFIsafe is designed and approved according to the *Black Channel* principle, it is independent of the transmission system used. The test setup is simplified but still relevant due to the Black Channel concept. For sake of simplicity the test is not performed on an industrial fieldbus like PROFINET IO, and the safety containers are transported directly on TCP/IP. It has been shown in [9] that it is possible to deploy a successful man-in-the-middle attack on PROFINET IO therefore PROFIsafe implementations for PROFINET IO has been used throughout the tests.

The test setup contains three applications that can be distributed freely over an Ethernet network.

1. *PROFIsafe host*, implements a PROFIsafe host according to IEC 61784-3-3.
2. *PROFIsafe device*, uses a SIL 3 certified PROFIsafe device implementation for PROFINET IO.
3. *PROFIsafe simulator*, application that can capture and influence the traffic sent between the PROFIsafe host and PROFIsafe device. Also implements the algorithms described in Section 4.1-4.2.

The PROFIsafe host and PROFIsafe device are exchanging safety containers at a relative fast rate of 5 ms, PROFINET IO is carrying data at a rate of 10 ms-100 ms. The communication is parameterized to use 32 bit CRC2 with CRC1 as start value.

4.4   Attack Results

The fist step was to find the value of CRC1 with brute force. Step 2 in Section 4.1 takes almost 11 hours on a 2 GHz laptop. In addition it takes approximately two minutes to eliminate the "wrong" CRC1 values and terminate with the correct value of CRC1. The algorithm and the implementation can most probably be optimized for shorter run time, but the most important result is that it is possible to derive the correct CRC1 value and the corresponding VCN within a reasonable time frame.

With the CRC1 and VCN value, the modification of the safety containers can begin. Safety containers in both directions are modified according to the algorithm described in Section 4.2. The algorithm works very well and the safety-relevant data can be changed in both directions without neither the PROFIsafe host nor the PROFIsafe device detecting any abnormalities. The safety layers carry on as usual, but forward wrong information to the application layers.

The most difficult part is to find the CRC1 and VCN out of a safety container. However, 11 hours of brute force is a long time to derive them, but it could have taken much longer time since the VCN is limited to 24 bits. The limitation of 24 bits is due to reasonable testing times during safety certification, as the wrap-around of VCN from FF FF FFh to 1 is part of a test case [6]. Ironically this reduction also reduces the time to derive the CRC1 and VCN out of a security container. On the other hand, the CRC1 is static during the lifetime of the session, which could last for years, and secondly attackers have probably much time to spend and will most probable refine the method and implementation for shorter run-time.

While running simulations in the PROFIsafe simulator to statistically drop and/or change safety-related packets without recalculating the CRC2, some interesting findings were made. In the case packets are dropped, the PROFIsafe implementation do not end up in fail-safe mode, setting the outputs in a safe state. This can be the case if a safety container is dropped due to a detected CRC error caused by EMI influence. When safety containers are intentionally changed, the PROFIsafe implementations enter fail-safe directly. This can be the case of an undetected error due to EMI influence or malfunctioning hardware. This is also safe and sound, we do not want to run the safety critical process with detected errors. The PROFIsafe standard states that all detected CRC2 errors, even if it is a duplicate of a previously received correct safety container, should trigger fail-safe mode. The reason for this statement is that the most probable cause is due to problems in the underlying transmission system, hardware or software, has been detected as sabotage is not assumed. Still safe and sound, but what if the safety container was intentionally changed by a malicious attacker? The system will end up in fail-safe mode, the staff has to investigate what has happened, probably not find any errors and reset the safety system. This means that by very simple means it is possible to affect the availability of the system, in case of a unsuccessful security attack. Or simply that this is the intention, to spuriously change safety containers. This will cause a great deal of headache, loss of production and in the end, reduced income.

5   Network Security Countermeasures

The safety measures from Tab. 2 from IEC 61784-3-3 are derived from IEC 62280-2, and are almost identical except that the cryptographic techniques are left out. However, it is written in IEC 61784-3-3, section 7.3.7, that sabotage is not assumed when using the CRC2 to ensure authentication. As a measure against masquerade, the source and destination relationship is included in the CRC1 signature that is used to calculate the CRC2 signature for message integrity.

The integrity of the messages have to be protected by Message Authentication Codes (MAC), also referred as cryptographic checksums, to secure integrity and authentication in case of threats from malicious attackers. The goal with a message authentication code MAC, given a plaintext message P and a secret key K, is that it should be exceedingly difficult to generate a valid pair $(P', MAC_K(P'))$, where P' is an altered plaintext message, even after eavesdropping one valid pair $(P, MAC_K(P))$. CRCs do not have this property, and that is the main reason that this kind of attack is possible.

According to IEC 62280-1 a proper CRC is sufficient if the risk of unauthorized access is considered negligible [17]. If the risks could not be considered negligible, cryptographic techniques have to be used instead of CRC signatures [18]. Usually when the safety-related transmission system uses a public network, radio transmission system, or a transmission system with connections to public networks, malicious attacks cannot be ruled out [18].

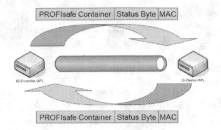

Fig. 5. Using security modules to protect the integrity and authentication of PROFIsafe containers, transmitted with PROFINET IO, when risk of malicious attacks cannot be treated as negligible

According to IEC 61784-3-3 it is required to use encryption and authentication if there are security threats when using wireless communication [6]. The use of WLAN and Bluetooth and how to configure the wireless access points are described in details in [6]. In addition the PROFINET IO security concept is based on the concept of "trusted zones", where each zone is protected by a perimeter defense. Within this zone, communication is based on trust and all nodes can communicate with each other freely without restrictions [20].

As we have shown in the previous sections, it is possible to deploy a man-in-the-middle attack on the network and alter safety-relevant data without detection. Security is a broad topic, ranging from physical security, device security to network security. Even if device security, preventing unauthorized access to the device, is addressed it would still be possible to deploy a man-in-the-middle attack. The other way around, only protecting the safety-related data with cryptographic checksums would not help either, as an unauthorized person can gain access to the device and change safety-related data before the cryptographic checksum is calculated. With this in mind we propose using the concept of *security modules* [9], a security software layer where the PROFINET IO real-time data is protected by a MAC, as a countermeasure to deal with integrity and authentication in the context of network security.

Using for example IPsec with PROFINET IO is not always possible, as PROFINET IO real-time frames do not always use layer 3 for the sake of processing speed, predictability and jitter. The security modules can be used with or without layer 3, i.e. IP, as the message authentication codes are calculated and verified at application level, thus providing end-to-end security. The concept of security modules is in line with both IEC 62280-2 and the principle of the black channel, and is possible to retrofit on PROFINET IO without any changes in the standards, transmission system or re-certification with respect to functional safety and IEC 61508. An alternative would be to exchange the CRC algorithm used in PROFIsafe to calculate CRC2 with a MAC instead to achieve authentication and integrity of the PROFIsafe containers directly. The drawback would be that then you always have security countermeasures even if there are no significant threats, aside from changes in the PROFIsafe standard and re-certification of the safety implementation.

By using the security modules, the system will not end up in fail-safe mode in the case of altered content in the PROFIsafe container, since such failures and/or modifications will be discarded by the security layer, as discussed in section 4.4. This is a positive side effect that will contribute to the overall availability.

6 Conclusions

As we show in this paper, it is possible to attack SIL3 certified implementations of the PROFIsafe safety protocol without being detected. In this particular case, network security was not even addressed, as sabotage is not assumed. Not surprisingly, n-programming, redundant hardware, hardware or software voting to mention some safety techniques, will not help much in the case of single path communication in an environment with malicious attackers.

The result is surprising, that it is possible to bypass all the safety measures, with quite simple techniques. One must not forget, physical access to the network is a precondition, and the probability of succeeding this kind of attack in practice is not significant. However, we recommend shifting focus from for example robustness testing of nodes to deal with network security on embedded systems. The consequences of man-in-the-middle attacks on safety-critical systems can be enormous compared to an denial-of-service attack, as DoS attack will trigger the safety-critical system to fail-safe mode. We also believe the same argumentation holds for non safety-critical systems as well. However, security is not better than the weakest link and security has to be addressed in several ways. We believe that it is easier to deploy a man-in-the-middle attack as we show in this paper, compared to trying to access the internal buffers holding the safety-relevant data in the embedded systems from the network.

In Section 5 we propose and discuss the concept of *security modules*, a security software layer, to retrofit security in PROFINET IO and PROFIsafe without any changes in the transmission system or standards. If the risk of security threats is not negligible, security modules can be used to add a security layer between PROFINET IO and PROFIsafe to reduce the possibilities of security attacks, and increase the overall availability. In addition for the studied system, the security modules will not forward safety containers that indicate compromised integrity, thus not putting the system in fail-safe mode due to spurious attacks on safety containers.

References

1. Sirkka, L., Jämsä, J.: Future trends in process automation. Annual Reviews in Control 31, 211–220 (2007)
2. Dzung, D., Naedele, M., Von Hoff, T., Crevatin, M.: Security for industrial communication systems. Proceedings of the IEEE 93(6), 1152–1177 (2005)
3. Tanenbaum, A.S.: Computer Networks, 4th edn. Pearson Education International, London (2003)

4. Treytl, A., Sauter, T., Schwaiger, C.: Security measures for industrial fieldbus systems - state of the art and solutions for ip-based approaches. In: IEEE International Workshop on Factory Communication Systems, September 2004, pp. 201–209 (2004)
5. Harada, M.: Security management of factory automation. In: SICE, 2007 Annual Conference, September 2007, pp. 2914–2917 (2007)
6. IEC: IEC 61784-3-3. Industrial communication networks - Profiles - Part 3-3: Functional safety fieldbuses - Additional specifications for CPF 3. International Electrotechnical Commission (2007)
7. Treytl, A., Sauter, T., Schwaiger, C.: Security measures in automation systems-a practice-oriented approach. In: 10th IEEE Conference on Emerging Technologies and Factory Automation, September 2005, vol. 2, p. 9 (2005)
8. Baud, M., Felser, M.: Profinet io-device emulator based on the man-in-the-middle attack. In: 11th IEEE Conference on Emerging Technologies and Factory Automation, pp. 437–440 (2006)
9. Åkerberg, J., Björkman, M.: Exploring security in profinet io. 33rd Annual IEEE International Computer Software and Applications Conference (2009) (in press)
10. Granzer, W., Reinisch, C., Kastner, W.: Denial-of-service in automation systems. In: 13th IEEE Conference on Emerging Technologies and Factory Automation, pp. 468–471 (2008)
11. Granzer, W., Reinisch, C., Kastner, W.: Key Set Management in Networked Building Automation Systems using Multiple Key Servers. In: Proc. 7th IEEE International Workshop on Factory Communication Systems (WFCS 2008), May 2008, pp. 205–214 (2008)
12. Neumann, P.: Virtual automation network - reality or dream. In: IEEE International Conference on Industrial Technology, December 2003, vol. 2, pp. 994–999 (2003)
13. Neumann, P.: Communication in industrial automation-what is going on? Control Engineering Practice 15, 1332–1347 (2006)
14. Neumann, P., Poeschmann, A., Messerschmidt, R.: Architectural concept of virtual automation networks. In: IFAC World Congress (2008)
15. IEC: IEC 61784-3. Industrial communication networks - Profiles - Part 3: Functional safety fieldbuses - General rules and profile definitions. International Electrotechnical Commission (2007)
16. PNO: PROFIsafe - Profile for Safety Technology on PROFIBUS DP and PROFINET IO. Version 2.0. Order No: 3.192. PROFIBUS Nutzerorganisation e.V. (2005)
17. IEC: IEC 62280-1. Railway applications - Communication, signaling and processing systems - Part 1: Safety-related communication in closed transmission systems. International Electrotechnical Commission (2002)
18. IEC: IEC 62280-2. Railway applications - Communication, signaling and processing systems - Part 2: Safety-related communication in open transmission systems. International Electrotechnical Commission (2002)
19. IEC: IEC 61508. Functional safety of electrical/electronic/programmable electronic safety-related systems - Part 1: General requirements. International Electrotechnical Commission (1998)
20. PNO: PROFINET Security Guideline, Version 1.0. PROFIBUS Neutzerorganisation e.V. (2005)

Modelling Critical Infrastructures in Presence of Lack of Data with Simulated Annealing – Like Algorithms

Vincenzo Fioriti[1], Silvia Ruzzante[2], Elisa Castorini[1], A. Di Pietro[1],
and Alberto Tofani[1]

[1] ENEA, Centro Ricerche Casaccia, Via Anguillarese 301, S. Maria di Galeria,
00123 Roma, Italy
[2] ENEA, Centro Ricerche Portici, Via Vecchio Macello
00122 Napoli, Italy
(vincenzo.fioriti,silvia.ruzzante,elisa.castorini,
antonio.dipietro,alberto.tofani)@enea.it

Abstract. We propose a method to analyze inter-dependencies of technological networks and infrastructures when dealing with few available data or missing data. We suggest a simple inclusive index for inter-dependencies and note that even introducing broad simplifications, it is not possible to provide enough information to whatever analysis framework. Hence we resort to a Simulated Annealing–like algorithm (SAFE) to calculate the most probable cascading failure scenarios following a given unfavourable event in the network, compatibly with the previously known data. SAFE gives an exact definition of the otherwise vague notion of criticality and individuates the "critical" links/nodes. Moreover, a uniform probability distribution is used to approximate the unknown or missing data in order to cope with the recent finding that Critical Infrastructures such as the power system exhibit the self-organizing criticality phenomenon. A toy example based on a real topology is given; SAFE proves to be a reasonably fast, accurate and computationally simple evaluation tool in presence of more than 50% missing data.

Keywords: interdependencies, simulated annealing, Critical Infrastructures.

PACS number(s): 9.75.Fb - Structures and organization in complex systems.

1 Introduction

The study of the technological networks (energy, transportation, communication, oil, gas, water, finance and ICT infrastructures) is showing a huge interest, because of its deep implications with safety and economics. These networks constitute the basis of the modern society, but they are threatened by unfavourable events, attacks and cascading failures. Many efforts have been spent in the last years to gasp a deeper understanding of the relations among these networks, efforts that require an interdisciplinary nature of the research in the fields of physics, reliability, statistics, applied mathematics Ref.[1], [5], [6], [7], [8], [10]. Central to our problem are the inter-dependencies among the elements of the networks, present in all the well-known four

B. Buth, G. Rabe, T. Seyfarth (Eds.): SAFECOMP 2009, LNCS 5775, pp. 81–88, 2009.

"dimensions" defined by Rinaldi Ref.[9]. Describing the inter-dependencies is a difficult task: not only at least four "dimensions" (physical, geographic, cyber, logical) are
to be taken into consideration, but are present feedbacks, feedforwards, non-physical
paths, a variety of dynamical modifications, non-linear relations among components,
time delays, different temporal scales ranging from milliseconds to years, granularity
levels, stochastic events. Moreover, the online monitoring is a prohibitive task: lack of
sensors, low sampling, disturbances, multidimensional data. Even in the most fortu-
nate cases, in the real world it is not possible to provide enough data for each infrastructure or device, i.e. we do face the problem of missing data Ref.[11].

2 Simulated Annealing and Graphs

The problem of missing data affects different disciplines and several approaches are
been proposed to deal with it. Ref.[9] deals with missing data related to HIV sero-
prevalence data from an antenatal study survey performed in 2001.The problem is
coped with different methods: random forests, autoassociative neural networks with genetic algorithm, autoassociative neuro-fuzzy configurations, and two random forest and
neural network based hybrids. Ref.[10] compares two approaches, max expectation algorithm and the auto-associative neural networks and genetic algorithm combination,
with respect to the problem of missing data evaluation in different application fields (industrial power plant, industrial winding process, and HIV sero-prevalence survey data).
In order to deal with the missing data problem, we propose a variant of Simulated Annealing (SA) Ref.[11] that is a random-search technique which exploits an analogy between the cooling of a material to a state of minimum energy (the annealing process)
and the search for a minimum in a more general system. SA behavior is similar to a ball
that can bounce over mountains from valley to valley. The initial temperature is so high
that the ball can bounce overcoming several mountains. As the temperature decreases,
bounces become more and more low and the ball can be trapped in a small set of valleys
(states to be explored). Probabilistic methods establish to stay in a new lower valley or
to bounce out of it. It has been proved that by carefully controlling the cooling of the
temperature, SA can find the global minimum. Although the SA algorithm avoids becoming trapped in local minima a lot of parameters have to be set in a suitable way.

3 Modelling the Inter-dependency

Dependence should be primary intended as a causal relation between two entities; here
we will focus on nodes of an oriented graph (network). A qualitative good definition is
the Rinaldi's one: "Dependency is a linkage between two infrastructure through which
the state of one influences or is correlated to the state of the other" Ref.[8]. Deciding the
direction of the dependence is usually a hard problem, but in the technological networks
is a good practice Ref.[8] to find out only the clearly oriented dependencies. In our
framework this is not a limitation. If we can observe input-output data, dependencies are
naturally defined. Otherwise it makes no sense assessing a probable hidden dependence
that acts on the unrecheable/unossevable parts of the system (node). Actually, we should
consider the inter-dependency meaning one or more nodes react to inputs by means of a
direct feedback reducing every inter-dependence to simple dependences. A dependence

between two nodes will be a link on the graph and characterized by direction, position, strength. In our framework the strength is a generic index of the functionality of the node derived directly from sensors: if a device or an element or a group of them is correctly working the operator will have an "on" signal. Summing up the signals it is easy to get a percentage of the overall functionality of the node transmitted as a causal action to other nodes (time delays were not considered in this simulation, as an extension to the time dependent case is straightforward). Consider our toy example (Table 1), a network of 11 nodes and 18 links where any known (monitored) node (4, 5, 7, 11, 12) has 100 on/off (1, 0) sensors :

Table 1. Nodes are indicated in the rows, sensors are indicated in the columns. "Functionality" is to be understood as operational capacity and "sensors" are SCADA equipments.

	1	2	3............99	100	Functionality
1	1	1	1......................1	1	100%
2	1	1	1......................1	1	100%
3	1	1	1......................1	1	100%
4	1	1	1..................1	1	100%
5	1	1	1 1	1	100%
6	1	1	1.................... .1	1	100%
7	1	1	1 1	1	100%
8	1	1	1......................1	1	100%
9	1	1	1......................1	1	100%
10	1	1	1......................1	1	100%
11	1	1	1 1	1	100%
12	0	1	00..................0	0	1%

Thus the % functionality is immediately derived; of course this procedure is very rough, nevertheless, often it is an handy way to earn a low cost picture of a network.

3.1 Description of the SAFE Algorithm

In the real world we have to face a dramatic shortage of information and data because either stakeholders are not willing to divulge their industrial secrets, sensors are not as many as needed, maybe ICT links are not online, and so on. To cope with these missing data we propose the SAFE algorithm to provide a number of cascading scenarios compatibly with the known data, minimizing the simulation error. To fix ideas we apply SAFE to a toy example, let's say we have the graph of Fig. 1 (representing a real topology of a technological network), knowing *a priori* the functionality values of some links (6 out of 18):

$$
\begin{aligned}
\text{Link } 4\_1 &= 100\,\% \\
\text{link } 5\_4 &= 100\,\% \\
\text{link } 5\_6 &= 100\,\% \\
\text{link } 7\_4 &= 100\,\% \\
\text{link } 11\_12 &= 100\,\% \\
\text{link } 12\_5 &= 1\,\%
\end{aligned}
\tag{4.1}
$$

and their transition rules (in order to simplify the work we consider the same transition rule for every node as the three state threshold 4.3). Each node gives a constraint to the simulation:

$$
y_j = TRSH \left(\sum (y_i)/n \right)
\tag{4.2}
$$

where y_i is the generic functionality value in input to node j, n is the number of inputs to j, *TRSH* is a threshold rule (see Fig. 2):

$$
\begin{aligned}
&\text{if } \sum (y_i)/n > 85 & &\text{then } y_j \,\epsilon[90, 100]\,, \\
&\text{if } 10 < \sum (y_i)/n < 85 & &\text{then } y_j \,\epsilon[40, 90]\,, \\
&\text{if } \sum (y_i)/n < 10 & &\text{then } y_j \,\epsilon[0, 10],
\end{aligned}
\tag{4.3}
$$

with y_j chosen randomly or according to some statistics. The threshold function *TRSH* is useful to simulate a non linear behaviour or a node which is partially operating but not completely out of work, as usually happens in the real world (the numerical parameters have to be chosen by experience and statistics).

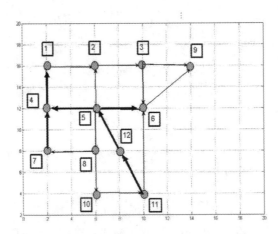

Fig. 1. Bold arrows (11_12, 12_5, 5_6, 5_4, 7_4, 4_1) indicate known functionality data

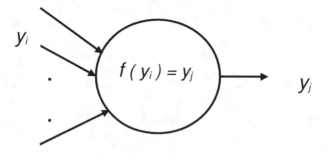

Fig. 2. y_i are the functionality values in input to the node j. $f(y_i) = TRSH\ (\ \sum y_i\ /\ n\ )$ simulates the nonlinear behaviour of the node.

The same procedure is used backward to evaluate y_i, till a known link value is reached. Now we have a weighted graph whose values depend partially from constraints, partially were previously known and the remaining are completely unknown. The first two data sets represent a target vector v to be compared with corresponding randomly generated values c from a uniform distribution. Therefore the missing data are estimated minimizing an error function $\mathcal{E}err$:

$$\mathcal{E}err\ =\ \sum{}_i (v_i - c_i)\ \leftrightarrow\ Gh \qquad i=1,2,\dots n \tag{4.4}$$

in presence of (4.3) constraints related to the subgraph Gh of G (G: N nodes, M links).

Actually, this is a brute force attempt to produce scenarios which minimize the error $\mathcal{E}err$ and clearly it is the most time-consuming calculation of the algorithm. Note that we use an uniform distribution to generate the missing data to approximate extreme failures (i.e. very low functionality values) at the same probability level with respect to the supposed more frequent failures (i.e. average functionality values) in order to consider recent findings. In fact, Carreras et alt. Ref.[2], [4], [12], [13], [15] have shown that as a consequence of the self-organizing criticality phenomenon (SOC), large failures in the power systems are not as rare as supposed a few years ago, instead they appear to follow a "fat tail" probability distribution Ref[14], a mark of the power law. If this is the case, the right side events (the extreme events) on the probability distribution function will be much more frequent with respect to the usual standard distributions. Clear evidences have been provided at least for large power systems outages in the USA (reports from other countries are known, see Ref.[16]); the ubiquity of power laws is a strong clue that the same situation is actually present also in other technological networks. Finally, we associate at every scenario a global error $\mathcal{E}err$, ranking it accordingly to the descending error. Establishing a desired error level, we iterate the algorithm until we get a number of scenarios below the desired error. Then we simply extract links that most frequently show a failure, i.e. links below 30% of functionality (this percentage is not significant). Some of these links may be present in every scenario among those showing the lower errors. Since the values of these links are the most probable and are *always* present in the most probable scenarios, they should be regarded as "critical" links. Moreover, if the departing and entering links from/to a node are failed links, then the node is a "critical" node. In this approach to the definition of criticality the impact plays no role, nevertheless it would be easy to associate an impact parameter to nodes or links and rank them this way, but here we prefer to stress the topological point of view. In our example of Fig 1 an initial failure is detected on link 12_5 with a functionality reduced to 1%, while the other known links (5_4, 4_1, 7_4, 5_6, 11_12) are at 100% functionality, which means we supposed to know 6 out of 18 links. As said, a link whose functionality value is below the 30% level is considered in failure, at least partially. *It may be argued that these values are non-stationary i.e. they do vary over time; however, to face this problem the most important component and devices (and only them) could be real-time updated in order to provide node/links with reliable data. Clearly, the SAFE algorithm supports the online mode depending on the available computer power (in any case, the actual Simulated Annealing algorithm would request a much larger computing effort).*

3.2 Results

In Figures 3, 4, 5 are depicted the best, average and worst scenario, with probability 0.67, 0.57, 0.40. They are evaluated as the most probable scenarios and suggest that the critical links are 5_8 and 11_6, (12_5 is the initiating failure) and the critical nodes are 8, 10, 11.

In fact, these links are always present in the three cases:

$$\begin{aligned}
&12\_5, \ \ 5\_8 &&&&(4.5)\\
&12\_5, \ \ 5\_8 &&& 11\_6 \\
&12\_5, \ \ 5\_8, \ \ 8\_10, \ \ 10\_11, \ \ 11\_6
\end{aligned}$$

The algorithm was iterated for 35000 cycles until the desired (78%) ε_{err} level was reached.

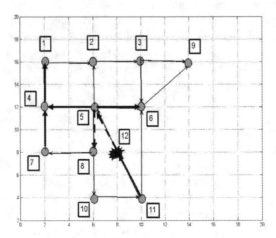

Fig. 3. The best case scenario. The initiating event is on the link 12_5 (node 12), dotted arrows indicate estimated failed links (functionality value below 30%).

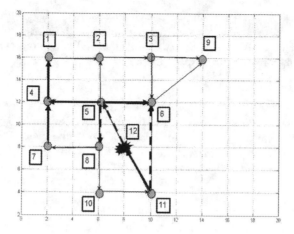

Fig. 4. The average case scenario. Dotted arrows indicate estimated failed links.

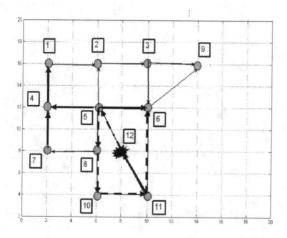

Fig. 5. The worst case scenario. Dotted arrows indicate estimated failed links.

4 Conclusions

The study of technological networks in the real world is hindered by the unavailable information about components, devices or the whole infrastructure. Even under the most favourable circumstances is not possible to monitor each important part of the infrastructures, or maybe it is too expensive. However, in some cases we are not interested in a deep understanding or a complete description of the situation, it would suffice an analysis of the most probable cascading failure scenarios. For these cases we propose a general functionality index as a suitable tool to collect and synthesize all available information according to a simple procedure, but again we have to face the lack of data problem. Hence we suggest the simulated annealing-like algorithm SAFE to evaluate scenarios congruent with the previously known data. Critical nodes of the graph are defined as those that are the most frequent in the most probable scenarios and are easily detected from SAFE. Although the SAFE random search requires a heavy calculation, efforts with respect to the classical SA are reduced so that an online implementation is feasible even for large ($N \geq 1000$) graphs.

Acknowledgements. Authors gratefully acknowledge S. Bologna, E. Ciancamerla, G. D'Agostino, G. Dipoppa, A. Fioriti, M. Minichino, V. Rosato, N. Sigismondi, K. Ykeda, M. Ruscitti, for useful discussions. One of the Authors (V. F.) was supported by the UE JLS EPCIP founded MIA Project.

References

1. Barabasi, A., Albert, R.: Emergence of scaling in random networks. Science 286 (1999)
2. Carreras, A., Dobson, A.: Evidence of self organized criticality in power systems. In: Hawaii International Conference on System Science (2001)
3. Carreras, A., Dobson, A.: Critical points in an electric power transmission model for cascading failure. Chaos 12, 985–992 (2002)
4. http://www.spectrum.ieee.org/print/4195
5. Ahmed, W., Sheta, A.: Optimization of electric power distribution using hybrid simulate annealing approach. Am. J. App. Sci. 5, 559–564 (2008)
6. Strogatz, S.: Exploring complex networks. Nature 3, 410–412 (2001)
7. Zio, E.: From complexity to reliability efficiency. Int. J. Critical Infrastructures 3, 3–31 (2007)
8. Wu, W.: Nonlinear system theory: another look at dependence. PNAS 102 (2005)
9. Rinaldi, J., et al.: Identifying critical infrastructure interdependencies. IEEE Control System Magazine 21, 337–351 (2001)
10. Rosas-Casals, R.: Topological vulnerability of the EU power grid, DELIS-TR-437, EU Integrated Project (2006)
11. Nelwamondo, V., Marwala, T.: Teciques for handling missing data. Int. J. Inn, Comp. 4, 1426–1507 (2008)
12. Carreras, B., et al.: Evidence of self-organizing criticality in a time series of electric power system blackouts. IEEE Trans. Circ. Sys. 51(9), 1733 (2004)
13. Carreras, A., Dobson, A.: Critical points in an electric power transmission model for cascading failure. Chaos 12, 985–992 (2002)
14. http://www.spectrum.ieee.org/print/4195
15. Carreras, B., et al.: Evidence of self-organizing criticality in a time series of electric power system blackouts. IEEE Trans. Circ. Sys. 51(9), 1733 (2004)
16. http://www.dcs.gla.ac.uk/johnson/papers/blackout_comparison/Johnson_Power.pdf

Environment Characterization and System Modeling Approach for the Quantitative Evaluation of Security

Geraldine Vache

CNRS; LAAS; Université de Toulouse - 7, Avenue du colonel Roche, F-31077 Toulouse, France
Université de Toulouse ; UPS, INSA, INP ; LAAS ; F-31077 Toulouse, France
gvache@laas.fr

Abstract. This article aims at proposing a new approach for the quantitative evaluation of information system security. Our approach focuses on system vulnerabilities caused by design and implementation errors and studies how system environment, considering such vulnerabilities, may endanger the system. The two main contributions of this paper are: 1) the identification of the environmental factors which influence the security system state; 2) the development a Stochastic Activity Network model taking into account the system and these environmental factors. Measures resulting from our modeling are aimed at helping the system designers in the assessment of vulnerability exploitation risks.

1 Introduction

Making an information system secure is a very hard work: since 2006, more than 7000 vulnerabilities have been published every year. In front of such a danger, evaluating information system security appears to be necessary in order to analyse and prevent risks. Our approach focuses on this issue and aims at producing quantitative security measures to assess the level of risk faced by an operational system considering an evolving environment. To this purpose, we first identify environmental factors that have an influence on the system vulnerability exploitation process: 1) the vulnerability life cycle events; 2) the attacker population behaviour; 3) the system administrator's behaviour. We study the evolution of these factors and model them and their interactions with the system, to evaluate their consequences on the system security.

This paper is structured as follows: Section 2 presents related work about security evaluation and introduces our approach. Section 3 describes our modeling approach in details and presents the first results obtained. Section 4 presents the main conclusions and some perspectives for future work.

2 Related Work

First approaches for the security evaluation of information systems appeared in the 80's with the development security evaluation criteria such the TCSEC [1], the ITSEC [2] and more recently the Common Criteria [3]. These criteria have given rise to the

B. Buth, G. Rabe, T. Seyfarth (Eds.): SAFECOMP 2009, LNCS 5775, pp. 89–102, 2009.

ISO 27000 standards [4,5]. They define security levels, guidelines and processes to support the assessment, during the design, of the level of protection provided by an information system to cope with vulnerabilities and security related risks. The security levels defined in these criteria are considered as qualitative, in spite of the not well-defined boundary between quantitative and qualitative measure in security[1]. Indeed, the ISO 27000 standards define security level classes, depending on the functionalities implemented in the system and the level of rigour and formalisation of the development processes, that are mostly considered as qualitative measures. Moreover, these security evaluation criteria are not well suited for the evaluation of security risks considering a changing environment: the evaluation processes are too complicated and take too much time to be run regularly during the operational life of the system.

Considering these problems, alternative approaches have been proposed to make quantitative security assessment feasible during the operational life of the system. In 1993, [8] argues that security can be evaluated in terms of effort, without proposing a measure and a practical model for assessing security. During the same year, [9,10] presented the privilege graph model. Based on the identification and analysis of a known vulnerabilities set of the system, the privilege graph highlights the different paths of vulnerability exploitation an attacker may use to reach security target. The privilege graph is a state-based model where arcs model vulnerability exploitation, and a weight is assigned to each arc to quantify the effort needed to exploit the vulnerability. These weights are used to evaluate a quantitative measure corresponding to the Mean Effort To security Failure, which is aimed at characterizing the capacity of the system to resist to attacks [11].

The attack graph formalism is described in [12]: each state in the graph represents the privilege owned by the attacker and also the attacker's knowledge and system environment state. In fact, any change brings the system in a new state even if privileges owned by the attacker are still the same. Studies to generate and reduce similar attack graphs are presented in [12-14]. The attack tree is another formalism used for example in [15]: an exploitability measure presented there weights each arc of the attack tree. The final measure is an exploitability measure taking the whole attack tree into account. These formalisms focus on the attack cost but quantify it objectively is an hard work.

Another measure called "Time To Compromise", was presented in [16], based on three different processes corresponding to three attack situations: 1) the attacker knows at least one vulnerability giving the wanted privileges and there is at least one known exploit; 2) there is at least one known vulnerability giving the privileges the attacker wants and the attacker does not know any successful exploit for the vulnerability; 3) the attacker is continuously looking for new vulnerabilities and new exploits. Processes 1 and 2 are exclusive and concern the exploitation of already known vulnerabilities. Process 2 is executed only if process 1 ends without success and if process 1 initial conditions are not valid anymore. Process 3 is executed in background of processes 1 and 2. The measure "Time To Compromise" results of this modeling and depends on probabilities of process occurrences and the time needed by the attacker to be successful for each process. Knowing how many vulnerabilities are

---

[1] In fact different considerations are made about quantitative and qualitative measure definitions, as discussed in [6,7].

present in the studied system is necessary for the evaluation of this measure. Moreover, the measure is valid considering only one attacker.

These quantitative approaches provide security measures for systems in operation and are considering an important factor of the environment: the attacker. However, the attacker is not the only environmental factor that may influence the system security. Indeed, three complementary metrics, presented in [17], take into account several environmental factors: 1) a *base metric* that is focused on the needed access rights to exploit the vulnerability and on the impact on confidentiality, integrity and availability; 2) a *time metric* that is focused on exploit and patch existence; 3) an *environment metric* that is focused on computer system neighbourhood having the same vulnerability. It also takes into account the measurement of damage on system environment. Numerical equations are provided to compute quantitative values for the proposed metrics, however it is not explained how the parameters involved in these equations can be estimated. These quantitative metrics aim at quantifying security in operational system life and take into account the system environment as a static factor: the environment influence is considered but changes that may happen are not taken into account.

The modeling approach and the results presented in this paper are aimed at addressing these issues. Indeed, we consider that the likelihood of an attack against a system exploiting a vulnerability is not constant in time: the likelihood that an attacker chooses to exploit a new vulnerability for which a patch does not exist yet may be higher than the likelihood that an attacker tries to exploit an old patched vulnerability, under the condition that the attacker has sufficient knowledge or an easy way to do it. So, one vulnerability and its effects on the system depend on the environment evolution, as presented in the next section.

3 Approach Description

In the previous section, we highlighted the high influence of environment evolution we want to take into account in our approach. Our purpose is to be able to 1) produce quantitative measures taking into account a more complex and realistic system environment; 2) study how a change in the environment may change the security of the system, evaluating the evolution of the likelihood for a system to be secure or compromised. Of course, environnement may change considering particular systems as military or bank systems. We do not pretend to consider all information systems but choose too focus on mass-market information systems. In this section, we focus on identifying important environmental factors and we study how these factors interact with the information system and with themselves. Secondly, we describe the consequences of these interactions and present details of our modeling. Finally, the third part analyses the obtained measures.

3.1 Environment Study

To study the environment evolution and its influence on the system, a first step is to identify important evolving factors of the environment that have a significant influence on the system, and then to define their influences on the system and their interdependencies.

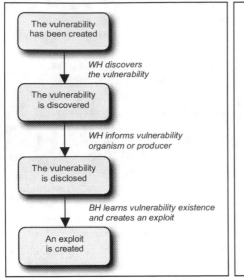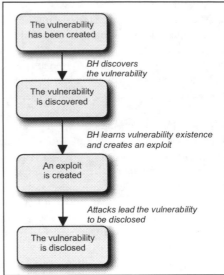

Scenario 1 : the vulnerability is discovered by a non malicious person

Scenario 2 : the vulnerability is discovered by a malicious person

Fig. 1. Influence between vulnerability life cycle and exploit creation

Let us first consider the risk induced by the presence of one vulnerability. The first element to be analyzed concerns the vulnerability life cycle that defines the set of important events that may occur and bring a change. As discussed in [18,19], we can take into account three main events: 1) the **vulnerability discovery**; 2) the **vulnerability disclosure**; 3) the **vulnerability patch publication**. The vulnerability discovery event occurs when somebody notices the vulnerability being in a component already available for sale or download. The vulnerability may be discovered by *malicious* or *non malicious people*. The vulnerability disclosure event is the official disclosure of the vulnerability by the component producer or by security alert and vulnerability publication centres like CVE [20] or Security Focus [21]. Other definitions of vulnerability disclosure are more restrictive: for example, [18] argues that vulnerability databases are not official sources for vulnerability disclosure. The last event of vulnerability life cycle is the vulnerability patch publication. When this event occurs, it is possible to remove the vulnerability from the system or to mask it. These events of the vulnerability life cycle have a direct influence on the system but also on another environmental factor: the existence of an *exploit*. As defined into [22], an exploit is a script, a software, a mechanism or other technique in which a vulnerability is used to realize an attack or a part of attack. The creation of an exploit by the attacker population is an important event that may occur only if a competent attacker knows that the vulnerability exists. Before the creation of the exploit, we suppose that only few attackers know about the vulnerability and have sufficient knowledge to be able to compromise the system exploiting the vulnerability. To simplify our approach, we make the assumption that the system may be compromised through one vulnerability only if an exploit is available. In this way, we focus on the biggest proportion of attacker population. The event of exploit creation is also influenced by the vulnerability life cycle: there will be much more attackers knowing about the vulnerability after the vulnerability disclosure. Thus, 1) more competent attackers will be able to create an exploit if none is available; 2) more attackers will know about the vulnerability and try to exploit it. Moreover, depending on the origin of the discovery (malicious or non malicious people), different scenarios can be observed from the vulnerability discovery to the exploit creation (see Figure 1). Attackers – or malicious people – are denoted by BH (meaning "Black Hats"). Non malicious people are denoted by WH (meaning "White Hats").

In the first described scenario, the vulnerability is discovered by a non malicious person. This one will inform the system producer or a vulnerability repository centre that the vulnerability exists. So, the vulnerability will be disclosed, making the attacker population aware of the existence of the vulnerability. In this way, attackers may create an exploit for this vulnerability. In the second scenario, the vulnerability is discovered by a malicious source. The vulnerability existence will be known only by the attacker population until an exploit is created, as attacks using the exploit will cause the vulnerability disclosure event.

The last environmental factor that is investigated in our approach is the administrator's awareness about information system security. This parameter is central in our approach. Indeed, whether the administrator is aware about security risks or not, may have high consequences for the system: the vulnerability patch publication is not enough to protect the system against attacks, the patch needs to be installed on the system in order to prevent the vulnerability exploitation. We consider the administrator as a third significant environmental factor in our approach. We know that the impact of the administrator's behaviour on the security of the system depends on the vulnerability life cycle: even if the administrator is very cautious, he cannot do anything as long as the vulnerability patch does not exist. Considering that the security risks faced by the system are depending on the vulnerability life cycle, [23] notices that the system is in the most serious danger between the vulnerability discovery and the vulnerability disclosure, as people are not aware of the vulnerability existence. However, [24] shows that many attacks occur just after the vulnerability disclosure. We are inclined to follow this interpretation: when many people know that the vulnerability exists, many attackers know about it as well. However, considering this environment study and this trend, we assume that the system is in very high danger between the disclosure of the vulnerability and the application of the corresponding patch. We call this time interval between vulnerability disclosure and patch installation "high risk zone" (see Figure 2). Let us denote T_{HR} this interval which can be measured as $T_{HR} = (t_c - t_p) + (t_{app} - t_c)$ where t_p, t_c and t_{app} are respectively dates of

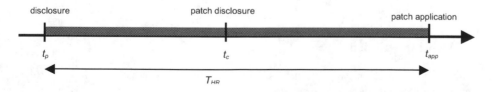

Fig. 2. High Risk Zone definition

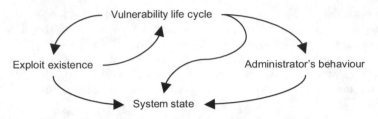

Fig. 3. Environmental factors' influence

vulnerability disclosure, vulnerability patch publication and patch application. This measure highlights the time period in which the system is in high danger taking into account system environment.

Let us consider as an example the Slammer worm vulnerability: the vulnerability and the patch were disclosed in the same time [25], July 24th, 2002. However, the Slammer worm epidemic began on January 25th, 2003, i.e. 185 days after [26]. An information system with an administrator aware about security who had applied the vulnerability patch was safe ($T_{HR} = 0$ day). In the other case of administrators who did not apply the patch, the T_{HR} was positive and often higher than 185 days. Many information systems were in this case and so were infected. This example shows the importance of administrator's security awareness. Of course, the patch application is not as simple that it seems to be described here: the patch installation via an software update for example may bring uncompatibility between systems components or install other vulnerabilities.

We sum up the system environmental factors we consider and their mutual influences in Figure 3. An arrow means that the destination factor is influenced by the origin factorLet us consider as an example the Slammer worm vulnerability: the vulnerability and the patch were disclosed in the same time [25], July 24th, 2002. However, the Slammer worm epidemic began on January 25th, 2003, i.e. 185 days after [26]. An information system with an administrator aware about security who had applied the vulnerability patch was safe ($T_{HR} = 0$ day). In the other case of administrators who did not apply the patch, the T_{HR} was positive and often higher than 185 days. Many information systems were in this case and so were infected. This example shows the importance of administrator's security awareness.

We sum up the system environmental factors we consider and their mutual influences in Figure 3. An arrow means that the destination factor is influenced by the origin factor

In the next section, we present our modeling approach of the system and the environmental factors we introduced here: the vulnerability life cycle, the exploit existence and the administrator's security awareness.

3.2 Model Description

In the previous section, we presented several environmental factors we have to take into account in our approach. In this section, we present a modeling approach aimed at the description of the system state evolution taking into account the environmental factors. Then, the model obtained can be used to evaluate quantitative measures characterizing the probabilities associated to the different states of the system. Our modeling approach is decomposed into two main steps: the first one consists in modeling the system and the environmental factors in the presence of one vulnerability. This modeling is a revised version of the one presented in [27]. We call that part of modeling *a pattern*. The second part addresses the modeling of multiple vulnerabilities; it describes how patterns interact with each other and identifies the dependencies between them.

The modeling is based on Stochastic Activity Networks [28] as this formalism can be easily used to describe the evolution of the system state and to express event occurrence conditions considering different types of stochastic distributions. SAN are composed of four modeling elements: 1) *places*: they contain one or more tokens and model the system and environment states; 2) *activities*: they model events that have an effect on the system or its environment; they can follow probabilistic or deterministic laws; 3) *input gates*: they contain activity firing conditions; it is possible to define predicates specifying the conditions to be satisfied for the firing of the activity, depending e.g. on the marking of some places; 4) *output gates*: they can be used to specify the consequences of an activity firing on the marking of the SAN places.In the next section, we describe our SAN modeling for one single vulnerability.

3.2.1 Single Vulnerability Model

We present how we model the system and environment states, considering one vulnerability. We create two pattern models, considering the two scenarios we described in the previous section depending on whether the vulnerability is discovered by an attacker or by a non malicious person   (see Figure 4 et 5). This single vulnerability pattern is composed of three main parts: at the top of the pattern, we model the vulnerability life cycle; just below, we model the attackers and the exploit creation; the rest of the model describes the different states of the system including the administrator's behaviour considering these two environmental factors. In this section, we describe the pattern model more in details, beginning by the vulnerability life cycle.

3.2.1.1 Vulnerability Lifecycle Modeling. First, we model the three main events of the vulnerability life cycle that may influence the system state. Three activities {discovery, disclosure, patch} model the three events of vulnerability discovery, vulnerability disclosure and vulnerability patch publication. States between these events are modeled by a set of four places {Ve, Vd, Vp, Vc} defined as follows: 1) Ve (meaning "existence") models the system state in which the vulnerability exists but has not yet been discovered; 2) Vd (meaning "discovery") models the system state in which the vulnerability has been discovered but has not been disclosed yet; 3) Vp (meaning "publication") models the system state in which the vulnerability has been discovered and disclosed but there is no patch available yet; 4) Vc (meaning "correction") models the system state in which the vulnerability has been discovered, disclosed and there is a patch available.

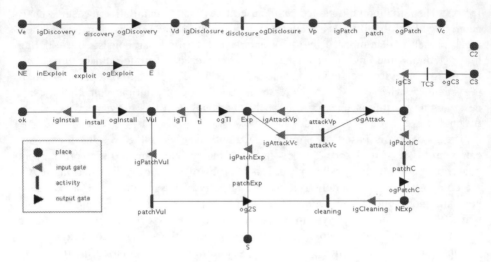

Fig. 4. Pattern SAN modeling with non malicious discovery

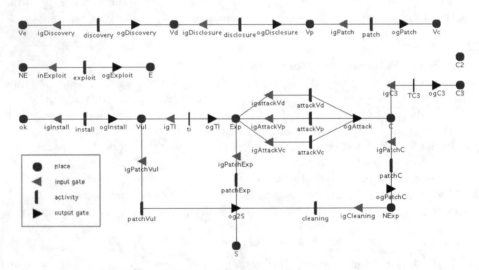

Fig. 5. Pattern SAN modeling with malicious discovery

3.2.1.2 Attackers and Exploit Creation Modeling. The exploit creation is modeled by an activity with different conditions reflecting the mutual influence between exploit creation and vulnerability disclosure, with respect to the two scenarios described in Section 2. So, the activity exploit shown in Figure 4 models exploit creation after vulnerability disclosure and the activity exploit in the Figure 5 models exploit creation before vulnerability disclosure. Like input and output conditions, parameters of the activity are also different. Indeed, the disclosure of the vulnerability will increase the likelihood that attacker population creates an exploit as much more attackers are able to know the vulnerability. The existence or the non existence of exploit are modeled by two places named respectively E (meaning "exploit") and NE (meaning "no exploit"). We noticed in the previous section the mutual influence between the vulnerability life cycle and the exploit existence depending on whether the origin of the vulnerability discovery is malicious or non malicious. Thus, we designed two basic patterns corresponding to the scenarios we described; they are shown in Figures 4 and 5. In the first pattern, Figure 4, we describe the scenario in which a non malicious person discovers the vulnerability. So, the exploit cannot appear before the vulnerability disclosure. This condition is included in the input gate inExploit. In the second scenario, Figure 5, we describe the scenario in which a malicious person discovers the vulnerability. In this case, the vulnerability disclosure coincides with the exploit creation. This condition is included in the input gate igDisclosure.

3.2.1.3 Administrator's Behaviour and Systems States Modeling. The third factor of the environment, the administrator's behaviour, is modeled in the system states themselves. Before the system is vulnerable, i.e. contains the vulnerable component, the system is in the state ok in which it is not in danger. The activity Install models the vulnerable component installation. So, the system becomes vulnerable, as it is modeled by the place Vul. Once the system is vulnerable, the system becomes exploitable as soon as an exploit exists (state modeled by the place E). This event is modeled by the instantaneous activity ti, conditions for the firing of this activity are defined in the input gate igTI: the existence of the exploit and the vulnerable state of the system are necessary conditions for the system to become exploitable. This exploitable state is modeled by the place Exp. The use of the exploit by an attacker on the system may be successful and this action is modeled by three activities {attackVd, attackVp, attackVc} corresponding to an attack event during the different phases of the vulnerability life cycle. We have to notice that the activity attackVd does not exist if we consider the first scenario in which the vulnerability is discovered by a non malicious person (see Figure 4). As a result of such attack, the system is compromised through the vulnerability exploitation, modeled by a place C. The two places C2 and C3 are related to the compromised state. Their role in the model is explained in next section. From this compromised state, only the vulnerability patch application by the administrator brings the system to another state, provided that, the vulnerability patch is available. This action is modeled by the activity patchC: it means that the vulnerability has been patched and cannot be exploited again. However, the system is not secure yet as the damage caused by the intrusion have not been fixed. This transient state is modeled by the place Nexp. From this state, the administrator has to clean the system, that brings it in the secure state S. However, the vulnerability patch application is an action from the administrator that may occur as soon as the patch is available and so before a vulnerability exploitation. The patch application may occur in two more different situations: 1) the system is only vulnerable – there is no exploit available yet; 2) the system is in the state exploitable but has not been the target of an attack. In these two cases, the system becomes secure (state S).

The two basic patterns presented in Figures 4 and 5, corresponding to the two scenarios described in the previous section, allow us to model the system and its environment behaviour with respect to one vulnerability. However, the system state does not depend on the presence of only one vulnerability. The modeling of multiple vulnerabilities is addressed in section 3.2.2.

3.2.2 Modeling of Mutiple Vulnerabilities

The modeling of several vulnerabilities could be done by considering several patterns running in parallel, each one associated to a vulnerability. In the SAN model, each single vulnerability pattern is modeled as a submodel. All patterns are composed using the JOIN operator to create the system model. As one event occurring in a pattern may have consequences on the system and on the other patterns running at the same time, studying dependencies between patterns is necessary. The modeling of such dependencies is facilitated by the use of shared places between the submodels (patterns) associated to the concerned vulnerabilities.

The first aspects we study are the consequences on a system induced by the exploitation of one vulnerability in a pattern. First, the exploited vulnerability may have more or less serious consequences on the system. That means that many functionalities of the system may become unavailable leading to the impossibility: 1) for the administrator to perform some of the actions (patch application, vulnerable component installation, system cleaning), and 2) for the attacker population to perform an attack. Thus, we define three degrees of compromised state seriousness: C1) the exploitation of the vulnerability has no effect on other vulnerability patterns; C2) only the application of the patch corresponding to the exploited vulnerability is possible; all other activities are blocked until the patch is applied; C3) the system is down: in every pattern, the administrator and attackers actions cannot be performed. The compromised state becomes absorbing. Each vulnerability is assigned a seriousness degree that induces vulnerability exploitation consequences.

To model these dependencies in the SAN, two places called C2 and C3 are added and shared by every running pattern (see Figures 4 and 5). The seriousness degree C1 having no consequences on other running patterns, we do not add one C1 shared place. For example, an exploitation of C3 seriousness degree vulnerability increases the marking of place C3 of one token, as it is illustrated by Figures 4 and 5, which describes a C3 seriousness vulnerability. The place C3 marking is monitored in each input gate of activities modeling an human action on the system. The same principle is applied for vulnerabilities of C2 seriousness degree. These shared places allow us to control the impact of a vulnerability exploitation on other vulnerability patterns.

Vulnerability exploitation is not the only situation in which we have to consider dependencies between patterns. Indeed, a vulnerability patch application may lead the administrator to update all the system, and so to apply patches corresponding to other vulnerabilities. We distinguish two administrator's behaviours: 1) if the administrator is aware about security issues, a patch application may induce a general security update for the system; all vulnerability patches available will be applied; 2) the administrator is not aware about security issues and applies only the patch corresponding to the vulnerability. We can assign different probabilities corresponding to the likelihood of occurrence of each of these administrator behaviours. These probabilities may be influenced by the context of the vulnerability patch application according to the existence or the non existence of the exploit.

3.3 Numerical Analysis

To illustrate our modeling approach, we considered the example of the vulnerability exploited by the Slammer worm. The measure we study in this example is the probability for the system to be in a compromised state considering different administrator's behaviours. This example has two purposes: 1) to validate our approach considering the well known Slammer worm epidemic; 2) to produce a usable security measure. Thus, it is necessary to assign parameters and distributions for our model. The next subsection (3.3.1) outlines the probability distributions and the parameters considered in this example. The second subsection analyses our results.

3.3.1 Parameters Description

We describe here the probability distributions and the numerical parameters used in the model for the study of the Slammer worm vulnerability. First, we study the modeling of the first environmental factor: the vulnerability life cycle. As we knew the life cycle of the vulnerability, we chose an exponential distribution with very high rate to model the vulnerability patch publication event, as the vulnerability disclosure and the patch publication have been made at the same time [29]. The parameters applied are shown in the table 1 below. The considered unit of time is the day.

The second environmental factor is the attacker population. [18] shows that the exploit creation may occur according to a Pareto probabilistic distribution. However, knowing the exact date of Slammer worm creation, we modeled the worm creation event by a deterministically. To model system attacks, we assume exponential probabilistic distributions. This choice was motivated by the need of having a density function with a high decrease and not by the need of the memory less property of this density distribution. The data published in [29,30] help us to calculate the attack rate. Nevertheless, the SAN model developed in our study can be run using other types of distributions.

Table 1. Experiment parameters definition

Activity	Distribution	Parameter	Value
discovery	Exponential	Rate	100 days^{-1}
disclosure	Exponential	Rate	100 days^{-1}
patch	Exponential	Rate	1000 days^{-1}
Exploit	Deterministic	Instant	185 days
Install	Exponential	Rate	1000 days^{-1}
patchVul	Normal	Mean (α_{Vul})	10 ⇨ 300 days
		Variance	0.5 days^2
patchExp	Normal	Mean (α_{Exp})	5 ⇨ 150 days
		Variance	0.5 days^2
patchC	Normal	Mean(α_C)	0.1 ⇨ 3 days
		Variance	0,5 days^2
attackVp	Exponential	Rate	23.4 days^{-1}
attackVc	Exponential	Rate	23.4 days^{-1}
Cleaning	Exponential	Rate	1 day^{-1}

The last part of the model is the system state considering the administrator's behaviour. This is the environmental factor we vary, to show its influence on the system security. The administrator's behaviour has an influence on two kinds of events in the presence of the vulnerability: 1) the vulnerability component installation; 2) the vulnerability patch application. The vulnerability component installation is modeled by an exponential distribution with a high rate. The administrator's behaviour is especially an important factor considering the time to vulnerability patch application. We model this behaviour according to a normal distribution. We define the mean time parameter considering the three different system state circumstances: 1) the system is vulnerable; 2) the system is exploitable; 3) the system is compromised. These three mean time parameters are called α_{Vul}, α_{Exp}, α_C and correspond respectively to these three circumstances and describe a particular administrator's behaviour. We defined 30 experiments corresponding to different possible administrator's behaviours. For each experiment, the correspondence between the parameters is as follows: $\alpha_{Vul} = 2.\alpha_{Exp} = 100.\alpha_C$.

3.3.2 Sensitivity Analysis

The model presented in section 3.2 allows us to quantify the probabilities associated to different states of the system. For the example, we evaluated the probability to have the system compromised by the Slammer worm, denoted as $P_C(t)$. To this purpose, we used Mobiüs tool simulation [31]. The results are given in Figure 6. They show the high influence of the administrator's behaviour on the probability of vulnerability exploitation. The more the administrator is aware of information system security issues, the less is the probability of vulnerability exploitation. The curves follow the trend describing the real Slammer epidemic: before the 185th day, the probability for the system to be compromised is null. Once the worm has been created, the probability to be in the compromised state increases quickly as soon as the worm exists, before decreasing gradually. This result is positive because our model reflects the observed trends. Moreover, the sensitivity experiments considering different values for the parameters α_{Vul}, α_{Exp} and α_C show the high influence of the administrator's behaviour: until the experiment 17, the probability of vulnerability exploitation is null, that means that the security awareness is sufficient to reduce the security risk induced by the Slammer worm. From the experiment 17, the security awareness of the administrator is not sufficient to protect the system. From this experiment, the less is the administrator's security awareness, the more is the probability for the system to be compromised, as it is shown by experiment 18 to 30. We verify that the probability to have a secure system increases with the administrator's security awareness.

This study may help to evaluate if the administrator's behaviour is corresponding to the security level the system needs. For example, the graph shows that a behaviour described by the experiment 18 ($\alpha_{Vul} = 180$, $\alpha_{Exp} = 90$, $\alpha_C = 1,8$) is sufficient to maintain exploitation vulnerability probability under 30%. From this study, the administrator may choose a behaviour considering the security level needed to be kept in from of a such danger.

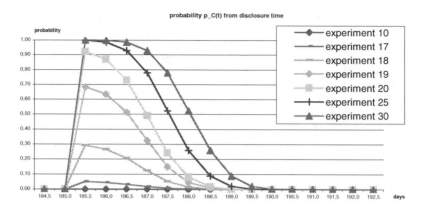

Fig. 6. Evolution of likelihood of vulnerability exploitation from disclosure time

4 Conclusion and Perspectives

Our approach aims at modeling dependencies between several important environmental factors to highlight system security risks. Our modeling allows us to quantify the probability that a system is compromised related to administrator's behaviour. So far, we have illustrated our approach considering the case of a single vulnerability. The analysis of an example taking into account multiple vulnerabilities is currently under investigation. Taking into account several vulnerabilities and considering the severity damage of vulnerability exploitation may be useful to risk management. Moreover, we plan to do a vulnerability classification to provide more generic parameters patterns. Such an approach may allow to study the tradeoff between the security level of the system and the security monitoring cost required to achieve this level.

Our modeling provides quantitative time measures to answer questions such as: how much time before having a likelihood of vulnerability exploitation higher than 80%? However, at this stage, the evaluation is not done with respect to specific security attributes (e.g., confidentiality, integrity, availability). This aspect will be studied in future work to complete our approach.

Acknowledgments. This work is partially funded by the European Commission through the ReSIST Network of Excellence (IST-4-026764-NOE). My special thanks go to my adviser Jean-Claude Laprie for his contributions and constructive feedbacks on this work. Also I would like to thank Vincent Nicomette and Mohamed Kaâniche for their help and their comments on the preliminary versions of this paper.

References

[1] U.S. Department of Defence Trusted Computer Security Evaluation Criteria (1985)
[2] European Communities, Information Technology Security Evaluation Criteria (1991)
[3] Common Criteria for Information Technology Security Evaluation (1996)
[4] ISO/IEC 27001:2005, Requirements for Information security management systems (2005)
[5] ISO/IEC 27002:2005, Code of practice for information security management (2005)

[6] Jaquith, A.: Security metrics-Replacing fear, uncertainty, and doubt. Addison Wesley Professional, Reading (2007)
[7] Laprie, J., Arlat, J., Blanquart, J., Costes, A., Deswarte, Y., Fabre, J., Guillermain, H., Kaâniche, M., Kanoun, K., Mazet, C., Powell, D., Rabéjac, C., Thévenod, P.: Guide de la Sûreté de Fonctionnement, Cépaduès (1995)
[8] Brocklehurst, S., Littlewood, B., Olovsson, T., Jonsson, E.: On measurement of operational security. Aerospace and Electronic Systems Magazine, IEEE 9, 7–16 (1994)
[9] Dacier, M.: Vers une évaluation quantitative de la sécurité informatique, Thèse de doctorat LAAS-CNRS (1994) (in french)
[10] Dacier, M., Deswarte, Y., Kaâniche, M.: Quantitative assessment of operational security: models and tools. CNRS-LAAS (1996)
[11] Ortalo, R., Deswarte, Y., Kaaniche, M.: Experimenting with quantitative evaluation tools for monitoring operational security. IEEE Transactions on Software Engineering 25, 633–650 (1999)
[12] Sheyner, O.M.: Scenario Graphs and Attack Graphs, PhD Thesis, Carnegie Mellon University, Pittsburgh, PA (2004)
[13] Jha, S., Sheyner, O., Wing, J.: Two formal analyses of attack graphs. In: Proceedings of 15th IEEE Computer Security Foundations Workshop, 2002, pp. 49–63 (2002)
[14] Swiler, L., Phillips, C., Ellis, D., Chakerian, S.: Computer-attack graph generation tool. In: Proceedings of DARPA Information Survivability Conference & Exposition II, DISCEX 2001, vol. 2, pp. 307–321 (2001)
[15] Balzarotti, D., Monga, M., Sicari, S.: Assessing the risk of using vulnerable component, Quality of Protection, pp. 65–77. Springer, Heidelberg (2006)
[16] McQueen, M.A., Boyer, W.F., Flynn, M.A., Beitel, G.A.: Time-to-Compromise model for cyber risk reduction estimation, Quality of Protection, pp. 49–64. Springer, Heidelberg (2006)
[17] Mell, P., Scarfone, K., Romanovsky, S.: CVSS v2 Complete Documentation. ccvs (June 2007)
[18] Frei, S., May, M., Fiedler, U., Plattner, B.: Large-scale vulnerability analysis. In: Proceedings of the 2006 SIGCOMM workshop on Large-scale attack defense, Pisa, Italy, pp. 131–138. ACM, New York (2006)
[19] Jones, J.R.: Estimating Software Vulnerabilities. IEEE Security and Privacy 5, 28–32 (2007)
[20] CVE - Common Vulnerabilities and Exposures (CVE), http://cve.mitre.org/
[21] SecurityFocus, http://www.securityfocus.org
[22] MAFTIA Consortium, Conceptual Model and Architecture of MAFTIA, MAFTIA (Malicious and Accidental Fault Tolerance for Internet Applications) project deliverable D21, LAAS-CNRS Report 03011 (1993)
[23] Frei, S.: 0-day patch - Exposing vendors (In)security Performance, Amsterdam, NL
[24] Fischbach, N.: Le cycle de vie d'une vulnérabilité (2003) (in french)
[25] Microsoft Security Bulletin MS02-039
[26] Computer Security Research - McAfee Avert Labs Blog
[27] Vache, G.: Towards Information System Security Metrics. In: Proceedings of Seventh European Dependable Computing Conference, Kaunas, Lithuania, pp. 41–44 (2008)
[28] Sanders, W.H., Meyer, J.F.: Stochastic Activity Networks: Formal definitions and concepts. Lectures on Formal Methods and Performance Analysis, pp. 315–343. Springer, Heidelberg (2001)
[29] Moore, D., Paxson, V., Savage, S., Shannon, C., Staniford, S., Weaver, N.: Inside the Slammer worm. Security & Privacy 1, 33–39 (2003)
[30] The Spread of the Sapphire/Slammer Worm, http://www.caida.org/publications/papers/2003/sapphire/sapphire.html
[31] The Mobiüs Tool, http://www.mobius.uiuc.edu/

Experiences with the Certification of a Generic Functional Safety Management Structure According to IEC 61508

Carlos G. Bilich and Zaijun Hu

Industrial Software Technologies, ABB AG
Corporate Research Center Germany,
Wallstadter Str. 59, 68526 Ladenburg, Germany
{carlos.bilich,zaijun.hu}@de.abb.com

Abstract. This article summarizes the experiences undergone while supporting ABB Business Units (BUs) in achieving functional safety certification according to IEC 61508 for their safety related products. Being part of a large global organization, ABB BUs enjoy certain freedom in the way they implement their product development process both for hardware and software. Many times these processes are inherited from long standing and successful development tradition from companies that have been later incorporated by ABB. Given so, when faced to the increased demand of IEC 61508 compliant products, the BUs find themselves implementing IEC 61508 and adapting their development processes from scratch for each new product. As a consequence, there are many different ways throughout the organization of implementing similar artifacts with the same scope (i.e. templates, lifecycles, reports, etc.). Since the BUs have recognized that this is clearly not efficient for redundancy, repetition, and finally costs reasons we have undertaken the task of creating a generic process to be used as framework for developing safety compliant products according to IEC 61508 that can be reused for different products across BUs. The requirements of this framework are that it has to be easier to use than the original standard; self-contained (i.e. no need to look up information over the original standard), flexible (i.e. applicable for different kind of products across different BUs); be certifiable by any major certification body; coupled with ABB's stage-gate business decision model; and most importantly: be attractive to BUs so that it can be widely adopted throughouto the organization. In order to satisfy those requirements we have developed a method and a set of components that we call "Safety Add-on", to create and manage functional safety design and development activities according to IEC 61508. The Functional Safety Management module of the Safety Add-on has been certified by TÜV Rheinland and is being successfully used by several BUs across ABB.

Keywords: Functional Safety, IEC 61508, reusable components.

1 Introduction

It has been recognized for some time already that safety critical control systems in process and machine automation is a high growth market with no signs of slowdown

B. Buth, G. Rabe, T. Seyfarth (Eds.): SAFECOMP 2009, LNCS 5775, pp. 103–117, 2009.
© Springer-Verlag Berlin Heidelberg 2009

in the short to medium term [1]. Accompanying this trend is also the increasing demand for certified products according to IEC 61508 [2]. IEC 61508 is one popular, voluntary but nevertheless largely accepted international standard covering the functional safety aspects of electrical, electronic and programmable electronic safety-related systems (E/E/PES). IEC 61508 is a complex standard of around 870 pages divided in 7 parts, covering hardware, software and containing several hundreds of prescriptive measures organized in 4 different Safety Integrity Levels (SIL) with state-of-the-art ideas and concepts which are the result of many years of research and discussions. As a consequence, complying with IEC 61508 is always an arduous task even for the most experienced practitioner.

On the other hand, being part of a large global organization, ABB Business Units (BUs) enjoy certain freedom in the way they implement their product development process both for hardware and software. Many times these processes are inherited from long standing and successful development tradition from companies that have been later incorporated by ABB. Given so, when faced with the increasing demand of IEC 61508 compliant products, the BUs often find themselves implementing IEC 61508 and adapting their development processes from scratch for each new product. As a consequence, there are many different ways throughout the organization of implementing similar things in scope (e.g. templates, lifecycles, reports and checklists inter alia). Several BUs have soon recognized this approach as clearly not efficient for the redundancy and repeated work that it generates, which ends up impacting cost as well as quality and time to market. After design and/or development of a product comes the certification which is typically done by a recognized certification body such as SIRA, TÜV, UL and alike. During this stage, the certification body analyzes carefully all the information submitted questioning it or asking for clarification in case of inconsistencies with respect to the claimed standard or safety integrity level. This process tends to be lengthy, even when the certification body was involved early in the design and/or development phase, so it is always desirable to shorten it as much as possible.

This paper summarizes the experiences undergone while supporting some ABB Business Units (BUs) in achieving functional safety certification according to IEC 61508 for several of their safety-related products. The rest of the article is organized as follows: section 2 describes the solution approach starting with the requirements and continuing with the concept design, development, integration with ABB's Business Decision Model (BDM) and certification as a mean of validation of the approach against the requirements of the standard. Finally, section 3 highlights the technical accomplishments and conclusions.

2 Solution Approach

First of all it becomes necessary to distinguish among different certification schemes used inside ABB. The first scheme is the *product certification*, whose objective is the certification of a specific product or solution. In order to qualify for certification, the product's development team shall provide evidence in functional safety management (FSM), personal competence and bring forward a meaningful safety case for the product among other things. This certification model is the most-expensive however the most flexible one. The second scheme is the *process certification* in which the target is to certify the functional safety management system (FSMS) by itself. The certified FSMS will then be used not for a specific product but for safety-related development in general across one BU. Thirdly comes the *organization certification* whose focus is an entire organization (e.g. ABB Oil & Gas [3]) which typically integrates the products of several BUs. Under this schema organizations need to demonstrate their functional safety capability [4]. The organizational certification is only valid for the certified organization while the process certification is not organization-specific.

The approach that will be described in this article focuses on product certification.

2.1 Major Requirements

As described before, the main driver behind the development of this framework was **reusability** of the elements or artifacts generated during the development of safety-related products according to IEC 61508 (e.g. templates, lifecycles, reports, checklists, etc.). However as we went along we discovered other requirements that are equally important to achieve success:

Simplicity: The framework should be easier to use than the original IEC 61508 standard, especially with respect to the selection and evaluation of safety integrity measures. From the certification point of view, the framework shall be as simple as possible but not simpler, so that there are just enough claimable safety arguments to facilitate the certification process.

Self-containment: The framework shall contain all the information necessary to drive autonomously the specification, design, development, implementation and test phases of a safety-related product so that the IEC 61508 standard documents are only required for consultation in case of outliers that fall outside the scope of the framework.

Flexibility/Adaptability: The framework shall be suitable for usage among different safety-related products and adaptable to potentially different development processes found across BUs.

Scalability: The framework shall be suitable for development of safety-related products of varying complexity, ranging from simple (e.g. contactors) to complex products (e.g. Robots). Also it is desirable to come up with a future-proof structure that can later incorporate other functional safety standards without difficulties (e.g. IEC 62061, ISO 13849-1, etc.).

Certifiable: The generic framework shall be certified by a recognized certification body as being suitable for safety-related product developments up to and including SIL3.

Minimum deployment impact: The safety development process included in the framework shall be compatible and synchronized with ABB's BDM and introduce none or minimum overhead to the current BU's product development practices. No changes to the current quality management system (QMS) shall be required to use the framework. Interfaces with quality management and project management models shall be clearly defined in order to avoid overlaps between activities.

Many of the requirements stated above are meant to make the framework "attractive" to the BUs in order to assure its wide adoption and consequent added value.

Standards can hardly be used "as is" in practice, therefore there is typically a facilitator in charge of joining together the rigidity of the standard with the realities of the daily praxis. The role of the facilitator is usually played by a safety consultant, either internal or external to the organization. Our goal with a framework with the characteristics stated before is to eliminate or reduce to a minimum the need of the BUs to turn to a human consultant to play the facilitator in their safety-related developments. The framework shall provide the means to achieve same levels of safety and development effectiveness while reducing time and cost.

2.2 Overall Concept Design

In order to tackle the described problem and satisfy the requirements stated before, we envisioned a framework that works as a safety complement to the current ABB BDM, therefore it was named: "*Safety Add-on*" for shortness [5]. As shown in Fig. 1, the Safety Add-on is organized in four components also named "add-ons" due to the fact that they can be used altogether or independently adding-on safety capabilities to already existing artifacts.

The scope of the *FSM Add-on* is to organize the functional safety development process. It shall contain the specification of accountability of the related producer in implementation of functional safety.

The scope of the *Template Add-on* is to aid in arguing about functional safety and contains a predefined set of document templates that help to deliver claimable evidence for the implemented functional safety. It shall also provide the related information or suggestion on the required approaches for documentation, semi-formal description, and verification and validation procedures. Templates can be structured based on the pre-defined phases. A structured specification for the safety requirements is assured by means of a meta-model for specifying safety functions and safety integrity requirements. The meta-model shall include descriptions of a safety function, a requirement, inputs, outputs, pre- and post-conditions, non-functional constraints, technical constraints, safety integrity parameters, failure behavior, etc. For the safety concept and design description the approaches recommended by IEEE 1471 shall be observed. Different viewpoints and views such as logical, process, deployment, and composition [6], [7], [8]; are also being taking into account for the design of this add-on.

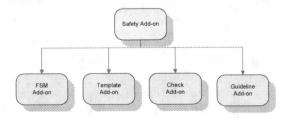

Fig. 1. Key components of the Safety Add-on

The *Check Add-on* is intended to assure compliance with the chosen functional safety standard. It is a review support element covering all the lifecycles phases to ensure that the artifacts created deliver the required evidence. It supports simple and formal review (e.g. Fagan inspections [9]).

Finally the *Guideline Add-on* is to provide best practices support by means of a module that collects and shares them. It shall include guidelines for software failure analysis, UML usage, requirements specification, lessons-learned from functional tests, etc. It shall support the addition of custom rules, policies and recommendations which are part of a company's specific policies and procedures.

Specifically referring to IEC 61508, the first and most critical step for compliance is to establish a meaningful Functional Safety Management (FSM) Plan [10], and so it made sense to begin also in this direction the development of the Safety Add-on. The rest of the article is therefore concerned with the development of the FSM Add-on.

2.3   Development Process of the FSM Add-on

In setting up a process to develop the FSM Add-on we faced the following constraints: there should be one FSM Add-on component that shall be of use for diverse products across different business units but we shall go thru the certification process only once due to limited resources; the timeframe for coming up with a certifiable reusable component was less than 1 year; leverage BUs' interests as much as possible while enforcing the requirements of the standard. This last constraint is very hard because usually BUs' interests and functional safety requirements go in opposite

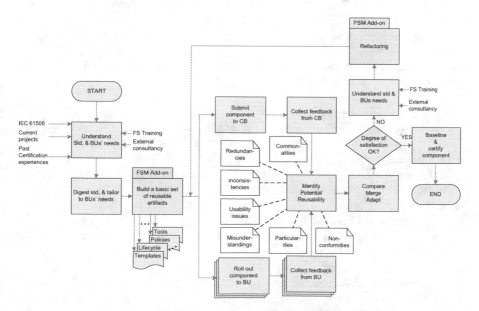

Fig. 2. Iterative development process for the FSM Add-on. It starts with an understanding phase that includes an early prototype which is then successively refined several times until it satisfies both the BUs' needs and IEC 61508 (BU: Business Unite, CB: Certification Body; FSM: Functional Safety Management).

directions (e.g. cost reduction vs. redundancy) therefore finding a solution with such constraints can be a tricky process that if not controlled can diverge consuming many iterations and resources. In order to satisfy the requirements under these constraints an iterative process was used where the final FSM Add-on component was obtained after a number of successive refinements. Fig. 2 shows an overview of the whole process.

To deal with the complexities and intricacies of IEC 61508 the first step was to work together closely with one major internationally accredited Certification Body (CB) gaining a disentangled understanding of the FSM requirements as stated in the standard. A key factor to understand the degree of rigor of certain requirements was to bring in previous functional safety certification experiences at this stage. Analyzing and confronting them, we found out that the understanding of some requirements can slightly vary form CB to CB, and this would affect the degree of rigor or the effectiveness of the implemented solution. Therefore, even tough we worked with only one CB, we leveraged our experience to manage the degree of rigor in order to maximize the chances that the solutions and criteria that forms the content of the FSM Add-on can also be accepted by other CBs as well. Apart from that, this stage was enriched with trainings on functional safety according to IEC 61508.

The understanding gained was then applied to digest and tailor the standard according to what our experience shows the BUs need. Throughout the process, as many reusable parts as possible were considered and so an early version of the FSM Add-on specifically optimized and tailored to ABB's E/E/PESs product portfolio was put together. The structure of this early prototype of the FSM Add-on included the following topics: policies; roles and training; organizational structure; E/E/PES and software lifecycles and their associated safety integrity measures; configuration management; development tools used; change control procedures; document list; and verification and validation plan.

Having reached this point, in order to continue, we had the following possible curses of action, each one with its own advantages and disadvantages:

1. Submit this early version to the CB and continue to do so with its successive refinements until the final component get certified and only then roll it out to BUs
2. Try first this early version out on one selected product, collect feedback, and then submit a refined version to the CB.
3. Roll it out to as many products as possible, collect feedback, and then apply for certification.
4. Apply for certification and in parallel roll it out to as many products as possible while concurrently reconcile the feedback obtained from the BUs and the CB, then put together a new version and re-submit it both to the CB and the BUs again in an iterative manner.

Given the constraints mentioned above, the last approach was undertaken. Compared with well known software development paradigms, we considered the first three approaches to be somewhat too "waterfalling" whereas the last to be more "agile". In the first case, according to our past experience, we felt that spending too much time working alone with the CB is not worth the effort because this isolation away from the BUs has the risk to bias the results towards aspects that have little relevance or even hinder the daily praxis. This would have undermined the applicability of the FSM Add-on on the field, thus loosing an opportunity for its wide adoption among BUs. The second approach has the opposite effect, i.e. the results could have been too much "BU biased". This could have caused delays later in the certification process as many aspects would have required substantial rework and adaptation. Finally, we think that the third approach would have made things worse, as simple including more products without incorporating iterative CB feedback would have only exacerbated the bias mentioned in the previous case.

The chosen approach abstracts and generalizes from a normal product certification procedure. The usual practice for the certification of one single product is to go thru a number of development–CB revision iterations until a certificate that the product satisfies the requirements of the standard is granted. We followed a similar approach but with many instantiations of the FSM Add-on, one for every selected product. Then we interfaced with the CB at each revision step generalizing the results collected from all the running instances of the FSM Add-on. When processing the feedback coming from the BUs instances, we tried to identify the constituents of a functional safety management plan that exhibit high degree of acceptance and reusability across BUs. (e.g. lifecycle phases, policies, tools, roles and training needs inter alia). We classified and grouped our findings in the following sets or categories:

- Commonalities
- Particularities
- Usability issues
- Redundancies
- Inconsistencies
- Misunderstandings
- Non-conformities

Commonalities emerged as the obvious candidates for being reused. We found commonalities in trivial things such as the way the documents are organized (e.g. headers and footers, details like Id, version, revision history, etc) or definitions, abbreviations and acronyms, as well as other more substantial things like usage workflows (i.e. the order in which the different parts of the plan were instantiated); policies (e.g. relation to ISO 9001, security policy, archiving policy, etc); roles (e.g. safety manager, safety assessor); lifecycle phases; tool rating (e.g. which type of tools are recommended or required for which SIL) among others.

The *particularities* include those things that were retained too project specific and therefore shall be described at instantiation time. Such things include the contents of the project and organization chart; the particular tools that will be actually used; the actual topics and schedule of the training courses; the names of the staff; the justification of the roles; the actual inputs and outputs of each safety lifecycle phase (although suggestions were made in form of templates).

Usability issues were detected for example when the users worked with the safety integrity measures suggested by the standard. The tabular form arrangement provided by IEC 61508 was cumbersome for many people especially when there is a need to lookup for cross references in other parts of the standard or in other tables. Grouping similar information, outlining and guiding the usage with comments were some techniques used to improve the usability of the component.

Redundancies. Many have recognized that IEC 61508 has considerable overlap, repetition and some degree of ambiguity (e.g. [11] and [12] inter alia). It is our experience that, being a generic standard, IEC 61508 leaves much to the discretion and interpretation of the user, and this characteristic tends to create some redundancies when the standard is being practiced that, when not revealed and removed, could mislead the development team. Specifically regarding the functional safety management plan, we found very often the definition of redundant roles, policies (e.g. between safety audits and safety assessments), plans (e.g. during the allocation of safety integrity measures during V&V planning and later in the lifecycle), among others.

Inconsistencies within a FSM plan occur due to the fact that IEC 61508 is quite complex, long and generic. Therefore it may be the case that several people work drafting different parts of the FSM plan. Due to the "generality" mentioned above, different people –when not adequately coordinated–, can interpret and write down sections that could potentially be inconsistent at later stage. It is our experience that such inconsistencies tend to be subtle, not easily noticed during FSM review meetings but nevertheless enough to puzzle, for example, the development or the verification team at a later time, or even worse, be detected during certification. Poor coordination

Table 1. Overview of the main findings encountered while analyzing the feedback collected from several instances of the FSM ran across different business units within ABB

Category	Feature / issue	Solution approach
Commonalities	High reuse potential (e.g. generic policies; lifecycle phases; roles; etc.).	Generalization, abstraction, "templatization".
Particularities	Project specifics.	Selectable controls (e.g. check boxes); Text placeholders; customization/instantiation/adaptation guidelines.
Usability issues	Cumbersome navigation thru information (e.g. information search across multiple cross-indexed tables).	Grouping; outlining; guidance comments, hyperlinks; automation (e.g. programming).
Redundancies	Overlapping, repetition, ambiguity.	Removal and/or consolidation of redundant information.
Inconsistencies	Dissimilar interpretation of similar concepts.	Thorough descriptions.
Misunderstandings	Requirement misinterpretation.	Re-stating or re-phrasing using IEC 61508 experts (e.g. certification authority); enlightening guidelines.
Non-conformities	Some customizations in disagreement with IEC 61508	Avoidance measures like contextual help; predefined text; etc.

is not that infrequent in project management; therefore whenever possible inconsistencies were detected in practice, they were clarified (e.g. describing concepts in greater detail) during the design stage of the FSM Add-on so that the risk of inconsistencies arising during instantiation is minimized.

Misunderstanding shall be interpreted here as some requirements of the standard being interpreted wrongly. Whenever that was repeatedly detected, we worked together with the CB to re-state the requirements such that they can be clearly understood by the BUs. Also when re-phrasing or re-stating alone was not enough, we tried to design enlightening guidelines to improve the understanding. The guideline however has to be as generic as possible so that it can be understood and followed by potentially different BUs and applicable to different projects of varying complexity.

Non-conformities comprise all those cases in which it was detected that the instantiated copies of the FSM Add-on were customized in disagreement with the requirements of IEC 61508. The reason for the non-conformity was discussed with the BU and the CB and a generic solution was elaborated to avoid it from happening again (e.g. templates, guided placeholders, contextual help, predefined layouts for documents, etc.). Table 1 shows an overview of the main findings encountered while analyzing the feedback collected from several instances of the FSM Add-on ran across different business units within ABB.

Using the previous classification we compared, merged and analyzed the results to evaluate the *degree of satisfaction* of the major requirements stated in section 2.1. We used the notion of "degree of satisfaction" because, being a generic component, the FSM Add-on cannot directly satisfy concrete requirements until it is instantiated for a particular product and this is explicitly noted in the certificate that was granted. But considering the cardinality of the previously given categories after each iteration we can assess if the degree of satisfaction is acceptable and whether to go for another refinement iteration or stop the process, baseline the component and apply for certification. Table 2 shows the criteria used to define an acceptable degree of satisfaction where n_i represents the cardinality of category number i.

Table 2. Criteria that define an acceptable degree of satisfaction of the major requirements imposed on the FSM Add-on

i	Category	Criteria	Comments
1	Commonalities	$n_1 \gg n_2$	
2	Particularities	$n_2 \ll n_1$	
3	Usability issues	$n_3 \le 5$	Only minor issues related mainly with intrinsic limitations of the implementation platform are tolerated. (e.g. Microsoft Excel poor for automatic table of contents generation). If the platform imposes a major or more than 5 minor usability issues it should be replaced by other more flexible platform.
4	Redundancies	$n_4 = 0$	
5	Inconsistencies	$n_5 = 0$	
6	Misunderstandings	$n_6 = 0$	
7	Non-conformities	$n_7 = 0$	

The maximum number of tolerated usability issues derives from our empirical observations on how the user reacts when s/he discovers that a certain limitation on the implementation platform constrains him/her to use the FSM Add-on in an unnatural or elaborated way. We noticed that when the user finds out more than 5 limitations s/he starts to argue about usability even if they are only minor issues.

When the BUs and the CB were both satisfied with the results and the above criteria have been met, the refinement process was stopped because the FSM Add-on has reached the necessary level of acceptance required to be certified and released for company wide usage. After that it went into maintenance mode, where company-wide feedback is collected for future versions.

2.4 Integration with ABB's Business Decision Model

Seamless integration with ABB's current BDM was a feature considered equally important for the CB, for us and for the BUs. In order to track and manage the phases of complex products development, organizations use detailed procedures that have been assembled into models. The models are different depending on the layer they are aiming to control. Often, organizations divide project controlling into a business decision layer and a project execution layer.

The project execution layer is typically controlled by some product development lifecycle model (PDLM). Some PDLMs widely used for software development are the Waterfall model, Spiral model, Agile model and the Unified Process. Due to the large variety of businesses and products within the ABB Group one cannot find one single development life cycle model which is actually being used company-wide. Through the years, each business unit adopted its own approach based not only on the type of product but also on several other factors like market type, country, early company know-how, past experiences, development team culture, etc.

At the business decision layer, business decision models (BDM) aim to facilitate the selection of products and projects for investment. A well known BDM is Cooper's Stage-Gate model [13], which consists of a number of different development stages separated by business decision gates. The activities performed at the stages are designed to provide the information required for the Gate. The gates are the decision points where the project's stakeholders decide about its future. ABB has its own harmonized company-wide BDM for R&D called "Gate Model". ABB's Gate Model builds upon Cooper's model and best practices derived from former, locally used decision models as well as shared experiences with other companies. The ABB Gate Model does not explicitly define any stages because it assumes that the underlying execution model already defines them. Therefore the ABB Gate Model is not thought to be used as an independent self-contained method but coupled with the PDLM that best suits the needs of the project at hand. This approach harmonizes well with specific company needs, and does not force the development team to use any prescribed development model but leave up to them the decision what is best suited for their way of working. Fig. 3 and Table 3 show the model and an overview of the gates.

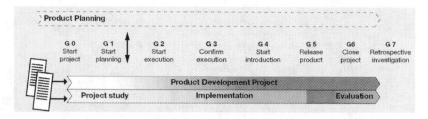

Fig. 3. The ABB Gate Model. Based on Cooper's stage-gate model, it has seven decision points and one additional checkpoint (G7) to consider the achievements of the projects and collect experience useful for process improvement (reproduced from [14]).

Table 3. Gates or decision points of the ABB Gate Model

Gate #	Name	Purpose
G0	Start Project (SP)	Agree to start the project. Typically, it evaluates a feasibility study or a project proposal including market analysis, competitors, intellectual property, product strategy, risks, needed resources and required technology.
G1	Start Project Planning (SPP)	Agree on project scope. An outlook is defined in terms of functions, features and quality as well as business constraints such as time to market.
G2	Start Execution (SE)	Agree on requirements and project plan. This gate assesses the required effort, time and cost, procedures for quality assurance, risk management, configuration management, etc.
G3	Confirm Execution (CE)	Confirm consensus about the proposed technical solution. This gate evaluates all technical solutions proposed and addresses all major risks.
G4	Product Introduction (PI)	Agree on the product's readiness for trial and market introduction. All functions and features should be implemented and the product should be ready for Beta or acceptance test and marketing.
G5	Product Release (PR)	Agree on release. A decision is made on whether the product is ready for release to the market or customer.
G6	Close Project (CP)	Agree on closing the project and handover the product to manufacturing and/or service for mass production and/or maintenance.
G7	Retrospective Investigation of Project (RIP)	Asses project results and evaluate its business success.

The integration with the ABB Gate Model was solved adapting the pre-gate milestone concept introduced by Wallin and Larsson [15], [16] originally thought for the integration of business and software development models. The concept dictates that all the outputs of the defined phases of the safety lifecycle must be mapped to a set of pre-gate milestones as shown in Fig. 4. In this way, for example, the FSM plan becomes itself a pre-gate milestone for G2. All pre-gate milestones must be delivered before a gate assessment. Therefore, it is before the gate assessment that related verifications required by the safety standards shall be performed.

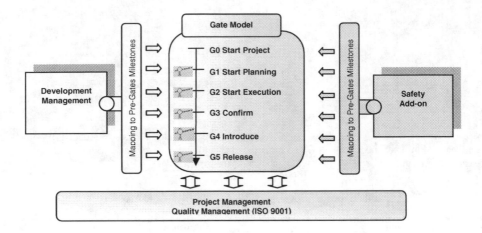

Fig. 4. Integration of the Safety Add-on using the Pre-gate milestone concept

2.5 Certification

The following criteria were used for the selection of a suitable certification body:

- international prestige
- years of experience in functional safety
- size of the functional safety team
- previous experiences and degree of appreciation within ABB
- level of expertise in safety-related software development process
- responsiveness
- location
- cost

After a careful evaluation of several major certification bodies, TÜV Rheinland Automation, Software and Information Technology group was chosen to act as the certification body for the FSM Add-on.

The certification of a generic structure not intended for any specific but for many and possible very diverse E/E/PES products was a challenging task for the CB as this is a novel idea where no previous experiences have been reported to the best of our knowledge. The main challenge for us was to convey the idea and for them to reach the same level of abstraction that we had in mind. Referring back to the process depicted in Fig. 2, it took in total 7 iterations and one year of work to complete a FSM Add-on version that can satisfy the requirements stated in section 2.1, the BUs' needs and the requisites of the CB altogether at the same time. The granted certificate is shown in Fig. 5.

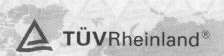

ZERTIFIKAT
CERTIFICATE

FUNCTIONAL **S**AFETY **M**ANAGEMENT
STRUCTURE
- IEC 61508 -

No.: 968/FSM 123.00/08

The Company

ABB AG
Forschungszentrum Deutschland
Industrial Software Systems
IIT Software Technologies (DECRC/I1)
Wallstadter Strasse 59
68526 Ladenburg
Germany

has created a project oriented Functional Safety Management Structure, namely "FSM Add On", which is intended to be applied for the realization of safety related products within ABB Corporate.

Scope is

IEC61508 (2000): E/E/PE- safety related System Realization

The main document of the FSM structure is the

Functional Safety Management Add On (Revision 21.x)

The structural requirements defined in the basic standard relating to the **Management of Functional Safety**, the **Documentation**, the **Functional Safety Assessment** as well as the **company specific Safety Lifecycle Phases** according to the scope of certification have been reviewed.

Object of the Scope of Certification is the realization of **E/E/PE-safety related systems**, including the **development of safety related Hardware** (E/E/PES safety lifecycle) and the **development of safety related Software** (Software safety lifecycle).

Safety related product realizations applying the "FSM Add ON" correctly and completely will comply with the requirements for Management of Functional Safety up to and including SIL Level 3.

The use of the "FSM Add On" will make the "ABB Gate Model" SIL compliant. Alternatively the "FSM Add On" can be used as a standalone framework for the Management of Functional Safety. The "FSM Add On" also comprises FSM Plan, V&V Plan with safety integrity measures, change control procedures, tool classification and document plan.

This certification does not replace the approval or certification of specific E/E/PE-safety related System Realizations.

TÜV Rheinland Industrie Service GmbH
Geschäftsfeld ASI
Automation, Software und Informationstechnologie
Am Grauen Stein, 51105 Köln
Postfach 91 09 51, 51101 Köln

Cologne, 2008-11-28

Dipl.-Ing. Heinz Gall, Certification Body for FSM-Systems

Further information referring to the scope of certification are published on http://www.tuvasi.com

Fig. 5. Certificate of compliance of the FSM Add-on with the requirements of IEC 61508 up to and including SIL 3

3 Conclusions

A SIL certification normally presupposes adjustments in the associated quality management system, technical development and project management to successfully meet the requirements imposed by the related safety standards. In addition, an individual and separate functional safety management system needs to be established for each individual project that strives for a product certification. Changes in the QMS and establishment of the related FSM are always associated with effort, time and resources, which force many development organizations to think about the profit of development of the safety-related products. With efficiency and effectiveness in mind we have developed a novel approach to assist and expedite the implementation of a FSM plan according to IEC 61508 which is reusable, adaptable, scalable, certified and can be used stand-alone or integrated with a business decisional model.

References

1. Exida.com LLC: Safety and Critical Control Systems in Process and Machine Automation. Market Report (2007)
2. Gall, H.: New Standards for Functional Safety Gain Acceptance. AutomationWorld.com (September 8, 2008)
3. ABB Oil & Gas Industry Portal, http://www.abb.com/oilandgas
4. Nunns, S.R., Prew, R.W.: Safe and sound Achieving organizational functional safety certification for IEC 61508 and IEC 61511. Special Report on Process Automation Services & Capabilities; ABB Review (April 2008)
5. Hu, Z., Bilich, C.: Safety Add-on – an Efficient Way to Make Development SIL-Compliant. In: 8th International Symposium Programmable Electronic Systems in Safety-Related Applications, Cologne, Germany (September 2-3, 2008)
6. Clements, P., Garlan, D., Little, R., Nord, R., Stafford, J.: Documenting software architectures: views and beyond. Addison-Wesley, Reading (2002)
7. Kruchten, P.: The Rational Unified Process: an Introduction, 2nd edn. Addison Wesley, Reading (2000)
8. Hofmeister, C., Nord, R.L., Soni, D.: Describing software architecture with UML. In: Proceedings of the 1st Working IFIP Conference on Software Architecture (WICSA), pp. 145–160. Kluwer Academic Publishers, Dordrecht (1999)
9. Fagan, M.E.: Advances in software inspections. IEEE Trans. Softw. Eng. 12(7), 744–751 (1986)
10. Gall, H.: Functional safety IEC 61508 / IEC 61511 the impact to certification and the user. In: IEEE/ACS International Conference on Computer Systems and Applications, 2008. AICCSA 2008, March 31-April 4, pp. 1027–1031 (2008)
11. Smith, D.J., Simpson, K.G.L.: Functional Safety: A Straightforward Guide to Applying IEC 61508 and Related Standards, 2nd edn. Butterworth Heinemann, Butterworths (2004)
12. Faller, R.: Project Experience with IEC 61508 and Its Consequences. In: Voges, U. (ed.) SAFECOMP 2001. LNCS, vol. 2187, pp. 200–214. Springer, Heidelberg (2001)
13. Cooper, R.G.: Winning at New Products, 3rd edn. Perseus Publishing, Cambridge (2001)

14. Larsson, S.B.M., Kolb, P.: Software process improvement at ABB. ABB Review (3), 10–14 (2001)
15. Wallin, C., Ekdahl, F., Larsson, S.: Integrating business and software development models. IEEE Software 19(6), 28–33 (2002)
16. Wallin, C., Larsson, S., Ekdahl, F., Crnkovic, I.: Combining models for business decisions and software development. In: Proceedings of 28th Euromicro Conference, 2002, pp. 266–271 (2002)

Analysing Dependability Case Arguments Using Quality Models

Michaela Huhn and Axel Zechner

Institute for Software Systems Engineering
Technische Universität Braunschweig
Braunschweig, Germany
{m.huhn,a.zechner}@tu-braunschweig.de

Abstract. The Goal Structuring Notation (GSN)[1] facilitates a clear presentation of the argument structure in dependability cases for dependable systems. However, assessment of an argument structure with respect to validity, sufficiency and consistency of argumentation and the provided evidence still strongly depends on individual, tacit expert knowledge. We propose a 2-phase analysis method for argument structures:

Firstly, syntactic completeness, consistency, and proper instantiation of argument patterns are examined using a UML profile for GSN and OCL constraints. For the second phase, we propose 2-dimensional quality models to assist the expert in explicitly judging on the conclusiveness of argumentation. A quality model explicitly represents the impact of *facts* on design activities and software-system's properties relevant for dependability. The impact value aggregates state-of-the-art knowledge and standard's recommendations. Missing, negative or conflicting impact indicates impairment of the argument either by revealing a gap in the line of arguments or incompatibilities or opposing principles between decisions or techniques in the process. We show first steps towards the integration of the analysis into model-based tool supported development.

Keywords: Safety Case, Dependability Case, Argument structures, Argument Assessment, Quality models, Model-based development.

1 Introduction

Dependability, safety, trust, and other high assurance properties of a system are usually demonstrated in so-called *dependability, assurance* or *safety cases*. Citing Bishop and Bloomfield - a (safety) case is "a documented body of evidence that provides a convincing and valid argument that a system is adequately safe for a given application in a given environment[2]. Assessing the line of arguments and the evidence provided in the dependability case is a task assigned to certification authorities by law (see e.g. EN50126 for the railway domain).

Dependability cases are provided by manufacturers and operating companies. They usually comprise large, complex argument structures on the development process, on system properties and environmental assumptions, and on operating procedures with multiple interdependencies and references to external documents

B. Buth, G. Rabe, T. Seyfarth (Eds.): SAFECOMP 2009, LNCS 5775, pp. 118–131, 2009.
© Springer-Verlag Berlin Heidelberg 2009

containing facts backing the evidence. As a major step towards a clear presentation of arguments, Kelly proposed the Goal Structuring Notation (GSN) [1]. However, judging conclusiveness of the argument structure and strength of evidence needs structured methods (1) to make the expert's assessment explicit and defensible and (2) to support communication on the findings to all stakeholders.

As a preparatory step to argument assessment, we propose structural wellformedness checks: Modelling an argument structure within a UML profile for GSN enables automated exploration by using static analysis techniques. Thus, syntactic rules and proper instantiation of argument patterns can be analysed.

The focus of this paper is set on a method to assess the conclusiveness of argumentation. The underlying rationale is transferred from activity-based quality models for software characteristics [3,4] like maintainability or architecture evaluation: Relevant *facts*, characterising the system or its environment, development or operation, are appraised with regard to their *effects* on *product-oriented*[1] *activities* undertaken to achieve and assure the requested system quality. An argument is confirmed, in case it is drawn upon activities positively supported by facts. Otherwise, the argument is marked as weak or even rebutted. We structure facts and activities in taxonomies adjusted to dependable systems. Fact and impact values reflect dependability-related aspects of the considered system. Thus, the method fosters systematic assessment of the following issues in the concrete system context: (1) Are the selected activities and techniques appropriate for their purposes and criticality level? (2) Is the portfolio of techniques sufficient and consistent? Does it conform to the relevant standards? (3) Have the selected activities the potential to constitute conclusive evidence for the dependability claims? If not, the causal entry in the quality model indicates a substantial reason for rejecting the argument and for improving the system or the case.

An indispensable further step is to appraise the evidence or external references of an argument structure. However, this part is not considered here.

2   Background

According to [5], dependability is an integrative concept composed of the attributes: *"availability: readiness for correct service; reliability: continuity of correct service; safety: absence of catastrophic consequences on the user(s) and the environment; confidentiality: absence of unauthorized disclosure of information; integrity: absence of improper system state alterations; maintainability; ability to undergo repairs and modification.* Such emergent system properties are usually demonstrated by argumentation in so-called dependability cases.

2.1   Goal Structuring Notation

The Goal Structuring Notation (GSN) by Kelly [1] is a widely accepted concept for concise, graphical presentation of safety cases (see Fig. 1). In principal, a

---

[1] "Product-oriented" focusses on artifacts, deliverables and operational actions that directly concern the system, and is meant in opposite to a process-centric view.

Fig. 1. Elements of the Goal Structuring Notation

goal structure shows how goals (claims about the system) are successively decomposed into sub-goals until claims are directly supported by available evidence (solutions). Basic argumentation elements are:

Goal represents a proposition for which evidence is to be provided.

Solution Evidence for a proposition is presented via a Solution element.

Context The Context element exposes the constraints of validity of a statement (e.g. to the system, operational environment, etc.).

Strategy Decomposing a proposition into subgoals is often ruled by a strategy. Relationships between entities are expressed as directed edges; the whole graph forms a *goal structure*. GSN is complemented with elements for *justification* and *assumption*. For premature argumentation, goals can be marked as *undeveloped*, and alternative lines of argumentation are denoted with a *choice* element.

2.2   Related Work

Various approaches to assess the conclusiveness of a dependability case argumentation have been discussed in the literature:

Structural correctness rules and patterns: Already in the original work on GSN, Kelly gives syntactic correctness rules for an argument structure. Additionally, Graydon, Kelly et al. list in [6,7,1] "success arguments" or "argument patterns" which describe generic strategies for engineering argumentations as abstract fragments of rationales. Such patterns of argumentation show up as result from surveying established safety cases in the engineering field. Mayo [8] proposed a framework for reviewing of GSN arguments containing logical argumentation patterns. Such inspection techniques capture the syntactic structure of a GSN argumentation, or the conclusiveness of local neighbourhoods of arguments elements with respect to logical fallacies and common engineering principles. By annotating a goal structure with this knowledge, an inspection can be performed automatically using static analysis techniques (see Sec. 3).

Quantitative approaches to confidence: To assess the compelling power of an argumentation several authors suggest quantitative reasoning based on credibility values assigned to individual argument elements and aggregation. Kelly and Wu [9] use Bayesian Belief Networks to deduce the confidence in a goal from credibility of its backing arguments. Cyra and Gorski [10] built a credibility value for a node by combining discrete values from a decision and a confidence scale. Starting the assessment from the leafs of an argument structure, credibility values for goals are aggregated by rules that account for the kind of reasoning from the premises (child nodes) to the conclusion (parent node).

In practice, assigning credibility values and weights quantifying a premise's impact on a goal is highly subjective. Within large argument structures, uncertainty often accumulates on the way to upper level goals expressing the significant dependability claims. Last but not least, in case assessment results in rejection, backtracking is restricted to pure figures but doesn't explain and direct the stakeholders to the critical issues that need to be clarified.

Software Quality Models and Safety Cases: In present standards like EN50128 or IEC61508, the impact of recommended activities and concrete methods on quality attributes specifically required for certain artefacts is not made explicit. In practise, this leads to non-uniform interpretations of *"what and how is safe enough"*. Annex C of the Committee Draft for Voting of IEC 61508-3:2008 attempts to remedy this. Thus, it contains a classifying quality model that explains how rigorously a class of methods is expected to contribute to specific software quality attributes considered relevant in a specific development phase.

Activity-based Quality Models: In the field of software-quality, quality models are established that hierarchically decompose key software characteristics into contributing factors. Deissenböck, Wagner et al. [3] observed that even the decomposition for key attributes like maintainability or usability is not agreed among the stakeholders and even worse, evaluation results are of little value for further development and evolution because clear indication of hot spots and directives for improvement are missing. Similar observations are independently reported by Salger et al. [4] on architecture evaluation of large systems. As a solution, Deissenböck, Wagner et al. proposed 2-dimensional quality matrices to describe the effect of relevant facts about the system on activities (see Fig. 4). The idea behind is that a desired quality becomes manifest in the stakeholder's activities performed on the system. Moreover, by presenting a taxonomy of facts and assigning an impact value, an evaluation becomes repeatable and defensible and directives for improvement are immediate, as shown in [3].

3   Structural Analysis

3.1   UML Profile for GSN

UML and SysML are widely accepted modelling languages and well-supported by development tools. To benefit from model-integration, we propose a UML-profile (see Fig. 2) for GSN. The profile constitutes the types of argumentation elements (*Goal, Solution*, etc.) of the GSN with *Stereotypes*. All types of elements inherit from *GSNElement* (not depicted), a common ancestor representing shared information properties like a short and a long description. The *Reason* element was introduced and stands for an implicit meta concept of *Justification* and *Assumption*. All relations of elements of a goal structure are semantically bound to the context of argumentation. The tagged values "AnnotatedElements" and "URI" allow for referring to UML-elements or external evidence.

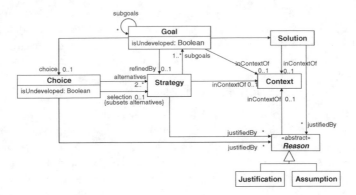

Fig. 2. Basic metamodel for the representation of goal structures

3.2   Structural Wellformedness

An argument structure has to obey certain rules: Each claim (Goal)
  - must either be directly backed by evidence (Solution),
  - or immediately refined by sub claims decomposing the higher level claim,
  - or, GSN-specifically, must be refined following a strategy which in turn must
    decompose into a set of goals.
  - No other type of element but a Goal may be the root of a goal structure.
Furthermore, claims, strategies, and evidence must form a directed acyclic graph,
otherwise some node refers to an antecedent claim as backing.

The rules concerning the relations between elements are encoded in the profile itself. The remaining rules and also constraints on relation-cardinalities have
been implemented using the Object Constraint Language (OCL) resulting in 19
formulas, e.g.: *The goal structure must not contain a cycle in argumentation.*

```
context Goal inv Goal_DAG: not
Goal.allInstances->iterate(e;
  r:Set(Goal)=self.subgoals | r->iterate(g:Goal; rs:Set(Goal)=r |
    rs->union(g.subgoals)->union(g.refinedBy.subgoals->flatten())
      ->union(g.choice.alternatives.subgoals->flatten())))->includes(self)
```

3.3   Argumentation Patterns

The second part of structural analysis is predicated on knowledge on well proven
argument patterns in the engineering domain. So-called "argument patterns"
[6,7,1] are made explicit by enhancing a GSN structure with explicit pattern
information. Examples for argumentation patterns are:

  - Functional Decomposition   - Diverse Argument
  - Hazard Directed argument   - Compliance
  - Use of Existing Evidence   - Formal Method
  - Safety Margin

To assure that a pattern is instantiated correctly, it has to be assured that there
exists a proper partial mapping of the goal structure to the pattern roles, i.e.
the elements in the pattern argumentation: (1) For each role there must exist

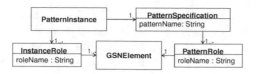

Fig. 3. Extensions of the GSN metamodel for pattern

at least one corresponding entity in the goal structure. (2) The relations of a pattern are represented properly in the goal structure. Requiring a one to one mapping of relations seems too restrictive. Thus, we demand a directed path between instance arguments being related in the pattern structure.

In order to represent argumentation patterns, we extend the profile for GSN (see Fig. 3) with concepts for pattern specification, pattern instance, pattern roles and refinement mapping that are adapted from the UML concept for *Collaborations* (c.f. [11]).The specification of a dependability argument pattern is realized as a fragment of a goal structure and modelled using the profile. The *PatternSpecification* represents the anchor element for a pattern specification. A *PatternRole* links a concrete GSN element (Goal, Solution, Strategy etc.), which inherits from *GSNElement*, to its specification tagged with its role name. Each instance of a pattern is indicated by a *PatternInstance* which is related to the corresponding pattern specification. The refinement mapping is realized by relating elements from *InstanceRoles* and *PatternRoles* with identical names.

Evaluation of correct instantiation is provided by OCL constraints in the profile: e.g., *checking for proper mapping of pattern roles to instances*

```
context PatternInstance inv:
self.patternSpecification.roleElements
  ->forAll(re|self.instanceElements->exists(ie|ie.gSNElement->notEmpty()
    and re.base_Comment.body=ie.base_Comment.body))
```

3.4 Tool Support

One of our objectives is to leverage a tight integration of model-based software development and dependability argumentation. We implemented tool support as a set of extensions to the Papyrus UML / Eclipse environment: (1) graphical and textual modelling of argumentation with clever import from MS Word, (2) an intelligent context-sensitive outline for concurrent development, maintenance, and assessment of software and argumentation, and (3) model-based structural analysis of argumentation structures based on the presented OCL constraints.

4   Conclusiveness of Argumentation

The previous section dealt with structural aspects of argumentation. To complement, this section will address the software engineering substance of argumentation in a case. A dependability case shall provide strong evidence that all risks are properly managed such that the system will deliver its service dependably.

Previous works on argument assessment (see Sec. 2.2) address knowledge on universal engineering principles or generic logical reasoning. But, they are unspecific to the application domain and require a per argument and per project expert's judgement on credibility. We aim at improving assessment of arguments by incorporating domain knowledge, making the assessment repeatable.

Assessors and authors of software dependability cases are experienced experts having a reasonable "feeling" of what is a good argument founded on best practices in software engineering. In part, domain-specific standards, e.g. IEC61508 or EN50128, reflect this knowledge and complement by lists of recommendations referring to specific process artefacts, engineering methods and technologies giving detailed information how to perform activities in a dependable system's life-cycle. From that observation and the literature [12] we conclude that an assessment of an argumentation shall be *activity-centric*, encompass a domain-specific viewpoint relying on profound engineering expertise: Are the selected activities and techniques appropriate for their purposes and criticality level? After confirming that *a sufficient set of adequate activities has been performed accurately (in development, evolution, or operation of the system)* we should look on the results of these activities in a further step. I.e., the evidence provided for the solution elements is appraised wrt. their validity and strength, e.g.: investigation of the identified risks, of the software architecture, of test reports, or other verification results. This step is out of the scope of this paper.

Our key idea of an activity-centric view on a dependability argument structure is (1) to associate a claim with those life-cycle activities it addresses and (2) to evaluate whether facts (how to derived them is explained in Sec. 4.2) have either supportive or prejudicial impact on the activities. Activities, facts and impact are presented in a 2-dimensional quality model described in Sec. 4.1. Selecting information from the quality model and interpreting the impact leads to a judgement on the compelling power of the line of arguments (see Sec. 4.3).

4.1   Quality Model for Dependability Argumentations

Quality Model. The quality model inspired from Deissenboeck et al. [3] aligns activities and facts on the system and the process along two dimensions: The first dimension lists facts that may be derived from evidence provided in the case, other information known in the system context, from standards or domain specific best practices. A *fact* describes a property of an artefact of investigation. A fact can be evaluated, that means it is assigned a value by appraisal. Depending on the kind of fact the value can be quantitative, i.e. a number, or qualitative. Qualitative values are further categorized in nominal values (e.g. existent, nonexistent) and ordinal values, which also offer an ordering (e.g. low, high).

Along the second dimension we align activities. An *activity* is carried out within the life-cycle, development, deployment, operation, maintenance and disposal of a system. Development activities are those executed to produce a system; deployment activities to install it; operation activities are performed with the system providing its functionality; maintenance activities to keep or restore system operation. The argument may require a certain performance-degree of

		Identify Tests	Plan Tests	Feasibility	Plan Impl.	Track Impl.	Detect Failure	Locate Error
Architecture	Environment Model	X	X					
	Behaviour Model	X	X	X		X		
	Interface Design				X			
Code	Data-Monitoring						X	X
	Control-Flow-Monit.						X	X
	Modularization					X		X
Modelling	Lang. Reduction					X		
Language	Access Control					X	X	
	Verif. Support					X	X	

Fig. 4. Simplified excerpt of an effect relation for dependability

activities which we will annotate as an attribute[2]. Thus, the performance-degree of activities has principal impact on what we understand as quality.

The connection between a fact and an activity is what we call *effect*. An effect describes the impact of an evaluated fact on the activity denoted as entry in the quality matrix. The fact's value has to be translated to the effect's domain, e.g. by a table. In general the domain of effect values is subdivided into positive, neutral and negative values. Here, the set of effect values is mostly an ordinal scale (e.g. $--, -, 0, +, ++$), which also expresses the strength of the effect. A positive effect value improves, a negative impairs the performance of an activity:

$$\text{Fact} \mid \text{Value} \xrightarrow{+/-\text{Strength}} \text{Activity}$$

The effect relation (translation table) encodes domain knowledge which is made explicit this way. Fig. 4 displays a conceptual sketch of an effect relation as a matrix; each cross "x" stands for a fact-to-effect-translation.

Basic evaluation. In the simplest case, assessment is performed only on arguments and evidence presented in the dependability case. The qualified activities are derived from the arguments and arranged along the activity-dimension, evidence along the facts-dimension. Filling the matrix yields a set of effects on each activity column. The goal is to detect inconsistencies and tacit trade-offs: Uniform negative impact corresponds to strong counter-evidence that the activity is performed adequately. Mixed directions of effects indicate implicit rebuttal of arguments. Even a uniform positive effect may be below the quality level required for some activity which alludes to lack of strength of backing arguments resulting in undercutting defeat. A conclusive argumentation solely relies on activities supported by uniform impact of evidence to the required quality level. Salger et al. employ in [4] a similar interpretation schema for architecture trade-off analysis. The interpretation contrasts the usual understanding of quality models allowing implicit trade-off and mutual compensation of arguments.
Example: Let us consider a part of argumentation for availability relying, inter alia, on quick detection and repair in case of runtime-errors (subgoal). The

---

[2] E.g. in *Functional safety (goal) is supported by a straight architectural design (strategy)* the strategy addresses the *architectural design* activity qualified as *straight*.

system is implemented with pre- and post-conditions for data-range checks to detect runtime errors yielding a fact [DataMonitoring | 100%Coverage]. A metrics suite evaluates the code [ModuleSize, avg. | 100 LoC]. In the quality model, a senior test expert recorded the effect of *Data Monitoring* and *Module Size* on *Detect Failure* and *Locate Error* activities. Evaluation of present data results in "++" on *Detect Failure*, but "−" on the *Locate Error* activity. Mixed effect directions occur: Although data-range errors can be detected quickly, the argumentation is seriously weakened by the fact of expected long repair times.

If we just want to evaluate whether an argument structure is acceptably conclusive in the presented universe of discourse, the current model representation would be sufficient. However, most dependability standards comprise recommendations on activities to be performed with a certain quality, in particular to achieve higher levels of dependability (so-called Safety Integrity Levels (SIL) in EN 50128). Thus, we enhance quality model with necessary activities and *requirements* to be fulfilled by the evidence on the facts' dimension.

Example: EN50128 declares design modularization as mandatory for all safety-critical software (SIL 1-4) to reduce effort for error-locating. If a system development aims at conformance to EN50128, *Locate Error* activity is added to the quality model (even if not mentioned in the case) and we impose a requirement that *at least* ++ for the activity *Locate Error* has to be contributed from a design fact about the module structure or size. Now, an acceptable argument needs backing evidence (facts) whose effect evaluates to ++.

A *requirement* can also be stated as minimum level of performance of an activity to achieve a desired quality. An argument is regarded sufficiently supported if one of the affecting facts establishes that level of performance at least.

Instead of building separate quality models for each standard and level of criticality level, we build *views* on a global quality model for different levels of criticality by simply adjusting the requirements accordingly. This way, we note a set of requirements on the quality matrix reflecting specific recommendations for instance *EN50128 (SIL 1-2) view*.

4.2   Criteria for Dependability

We propose a dependability taxonomy focussing on software development (see Fig. 4.2) as a guideline to derive the dimensions of facts and activities.

Life-cyle. The life-cycle of a software system forms a superordinate category of the taxonomy for dependability. Although dependability is a quality in use, a dependability case for a newly built system is justified nearly exclusively on evidence established in the development phase. Here we emphasize development phases: requirements, architecture, design, implementation, validation and verification and integration. System facts resulting from artefacts early in the life-cycle determine the quality of latter activities, e.g. encapsulation and coherence of functionality in design alleviates error locating during maintenance. The phases of a system's life-cycle incorporate in our quality model in two ways: (1) The

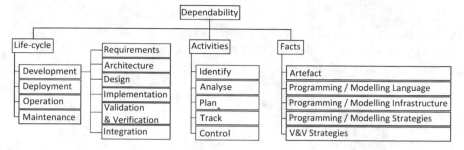

Fig. 5. Taxonomy of dependability criteria

life-cycle gives an order to facts and activities. (2) Phases and their results of development phases determine the possibility of effects.

Activities. In general, activities derive from the whole life-cycle of a system, including operation, but we focus on those activities related to software dependability [5]. We regard in detail the activities of dependability management to avoid the risk of systematic errors. Dependability management comprises abstract activities originating from SW risk management as presented in [13]:

Identify. Before addressing dependability issues, they are identified. Identification surfaces risks for dependability in the life-cycle of the software.

Analyse. Analysis serves to convert information about dependability risks into decision-making information. It provides the basis for the software designer to address the important issues.

Plan. Planning turns dependability risks into design and development decisions. Planning involves developing actions to address individual issues while maintaining a global view on systematic error avoidance.

Track. Tracking consists of monitoring the realization of actions to mitigate dependability risks.

Control. Control corrects for deviations from planned risk mitigation. Deviations originate from unforeseen problems within the advancing development.

The names of the abstract activities stand for categories of concrete activities of the life-cycle addressing problems of that certain phase.

Facts. The third category of our dependability taxonomy is dedicated to facts. Artefacts, modelling language, modelling infrastructure, modelling strategies and verification strategies serve as input for facts. Artefacts are documents, models and other products which are created during the development process. Facts from artefacts describe product-specific information and results from analyses, e.g. verification-results, preliminary analyses. The modelling language defines the representation and expressiveness of a model. Here we use modelling language for all kinds of representation formats of a system, e.g. UML, C++, flow charts, written text. Facts about model transformation, compilation, and testing are covered by modelling infrastructure. A modelling strategy imposes rules and guidelines on design and implementation. Verification and validation strategies prescribe how testing shall be realized. The facts about a system constitute the evidence necessary to argument in a dependability case.

This taxonomy classifies criteria which we consider relevant for dependability cases: activities to manage dependability, facts providing evidence and the life-cycle as a principle of order and influence. Those serve as the basis for deriving an instance of our quality model described in the previous section.

4.3   Assessment Procedure

Before assessment the underlying quality model has been stated, e.g. from an external or internal standard. The assessment is carried out in two phases:
1. Evaluate quality model
    (a) Go through the argument structure
    (b) Fill in the facts presented in the arguments.
    (c) Fill in the performed activities addressed in the arguments
    (d) Select the requirements view for the degree of dependability and strategy
    (e) Evaluate effects
2. Review potentially flawed arguments.

Argumentation to Model Input. To prepare assessment, the quality model has to be populated with activities and facts from the argumentation or a view, resp. The underlying reference model then yields a set of effects on each activity.

Evidence naturally is deduced from properties gained from the subject by investigation. The representation of evidence either is itself a value or can be evaluated to a value. The interpretation of evidence remains to the argument. Therefore, facts can be gained directly from the evidence.

As stated earlier, argumentation in a dependability case relies on the proper management of dependability risks. Hence, individual arguments are related to at least one of the category of activities: identify, analyse, plan, track, control. Regarding a instance of a quality model those activities are refined further. For our analysis, the assessor associates the argument to the concrete activity. That way, the evaluation of the impact on an activity is traceable to an argument.

Additional requirements rely on the evaluation strategy and form the dependability view which determines a requirement value for a particular activity.

Evaluation Strategies depend on the purpose of the assessment:

1. Evaluate consistency and expressiveness within argumentation. The evaluation is performed only on evidence and arguments presented in the case. This strategy yields whether the argumentation is consistent in itself.
2. Evaluate arguments against available evidence. In addition, all known facts represented in the quality model are considered. This strategy will additionally find possible counter-evidence neglected by the dependability case.
3. Check coverage of activities. A view representing recommendations for a certain criticality level in a norm is attached. The quality model probably highlights more activities than addressed by the arguments. The activities addressed in the case are compared to the view's activities. The results of the comparison enumerates missing activities related to a requirement.

N.b., negative findings in the evaluation only indicate a possible flaw in the presentation of arguments. Further interpretation is needed. Nevertheless, a negative evaluation directly points to a cause in terms of facts and activities:

Guided Review. Based on the evaluation, three steps are performed: (1) look for reasons explaining the impairment, (2) revaluate arguments, (3) create a report. The evaluation reports suspicious activities. The corresponding activities trace to arguments associated at population of the quality model. The assessor then looks for additional explanations putting even strong findings into a perspective: Often, contextual information defines and constrains the actual system requirements. Claims may be additionally supported by implicit or explicit assumptions and justifications. Some arguments may already suffice (e.g. mixed directions in weak effects, cumulative effect of weak facts) or are justified (e.g. by new evidence, not contained in facts or operational constraints). The assessor revaluates the arguments and facts regarding collected explanations. Revaluation results are captured in the review report. Repair activities can be planned.

5   Case Study

To demonstrate suitability of the approach we performed a case study from the rail automation domain. As system under design we considered an automatic train operation platform to improve safety in regional railways along the lines of German Zugleitbetrieb (ZLB) which is similar to track warrant control. The ZLB-Protection System (ZLB-PS) was designed as a close-to-reality industrial case study for research purposes during the ranTest[3] research project. ZLB-PS's major service is simplified interlocking. Dependability obviously is an issue.

System Facts. ZLB-PS was designed from scratch. The requirements are stated in a handbook for the operating procedure of ZLB. Behaviour of the route-allocation logic (40%) on the architectural level is modelled using the formal Scade-Language. However, the implementation is written in C++. All interface signatures were prescribed in the architecture specification and implemented accordingly (98%). Behaviour was verified by manual and unit-testing (60%; route-allocation logic: 100%). Data-Monitoring is realized by pre- and post-conditions (only 15% of functions). Modularization was monitored using a metrics-suite for function-code-size, parameter-count, etc. Only 10 classes have an explicit state variable which is checked in pre-conditions (control-flow-monitoring).

Assessment.   The assessment was performed on the dependability-subset of the argumentation which is presented as a goal structure (simplified extract in Fig.6(a)). We adopted the quality model to the EN50128. We extracted the facts and activities from the recommendations. Requirement levels were mapped from the level of recommendation (NR=not recommended, -, R, HR, M=Mandatory). Accordingly, SILs map to three views (SIL0, SIL1&2, SIL3&4). The resulting quality model is a matrix of 67 facts by 54 activities; most entries can be evaluated in check-list manner. Figures 4 and 6(b) show a very simplified portion of

---

[3] http://www.rantest.de

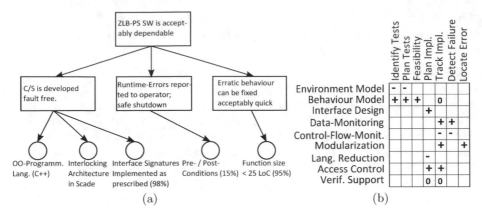

	Identify Tests	Plan Tests	Feasibility	Plan Impl.	Track Impl.	Detect Failure	Locate Error
Environment Model	-	-					
Behaviour Model	+	+	+		0		
Interface Design				+			
Data-Monitoring						+	+
Control-Flow-Monit.						-	-
Modularization					+		+
Lang. Reduction		-					
Access Control				+	+		
Verif. Support				0	0		

(a)   (b)

Fig. 6. Dependability argumentation (a) and evaluation results (b) of the ZLB-PS case study: facts aligned vertically, activities horizontally

the quality model as effect-relation and product evaluation. The evaluation was performed for view "SIL 1&2" relevant for ZLB-PS.

Results. Since student trainees designed, implemented and documented the ZLB-Protection system, it was no surprise to find flawed arguments. The assessment yielded severe inconsistencies (see Fig.6(b)) in the principal arguments for dependability management: A formal design model is of limited value without environment model. However, the simulation capabilities of the Scade model could be used to identify test-cases for unit-testing.

Discussion. The taxonomy (Sec. 4.2) of criteria turned out to be of great help for adopting the quality model. Facts from EN50128 could be extracted straight forward. Identifying the activities and assigning effect-values needed some interpretation and has yet to be confirmed by experts. The guide-words from the dependability-risk management served well. Quality evaluation could be performed by software engineers without problems. However, review and revaluation afforded expert-knowledge. An affiliated safety expert from industry appreciated the documentation of assessment that is a by-product of our method. However, the technical evaluation and assessment was experienced time-consuming. Computerized support and integration with existing tools would be a solution.

6 Conclusion

The paper introduced a new 2-phase method to assess GSN argument structures in dependability cases. Firstly, structural well-formedness constraints and proper pattern instantiation are automatically checked on a GSN structure. This part holds off logical fallacies and violations of common engineering principles.

Secondly, conclusiveness of argumentation is assessed. This method relies on an activity-based quality model that comprises the effect of facts on activities relevant in dependable system's development. The taxonomy of facts and activities as well as the effect relation makes domain specific expert knowledge explicit. The assessment may reveal inconsistent or insufficient argumentation or even neglected counter-evidence. Using specific views, the quality model is adopted and facilitates the assessment of conformance to a norm. Negative findings, i.e. a lack of confidence in the argumentation, can be retraced: The cause is given in terms of system or process facts that impair with their effects activities needed to achieve an acceptable dependability. The method yields a reason for rejecting an argumentation as well as a directive for improvement. In that, our approach complements quantitative approaches like [10]. In future work we aim at tool-support for guided assessment of argumentation.

Acknowledgements. This work was partially supported by Siemens Industry Sector Mobility Rail Automation. We are grateful to Stefan Gerken from Siemens and the anonymous reviewers for their helpful comments on earlier versions of this work.

References

1. Kelly, T.: Arguing Safety – A Systemic Approach to Managing Safety Cases. PhD thesis. University of York (1998)
2. Bishop, P., Bloomfield, R.: A methodology for safety case development. In: Safety-Critical Systems Symposium (SAFECOMP), pp. 194–203 (1998)
3. Deissenboeck, F., Wagner, S., Pizka, M., Teuchert, S., Girard, J.F.: An activity-based quality model for maintainability. In: Proceedings of the 23rd International Conference on Software Maintenance, ICSM 2007 (2007)
4. Salger, F., Bennicke, M., Engels, G., Lewerentz, C.: Comprehensive architecture evaluation and management in large software-systems. In: Becker, S., Plasil, F., Reussner, R. (eds.) QoSA 2008. LNCS, vol. 5281, pp. 205–219. Springer, Heidelberg (2008)
5. Avizienis, A., Laprie, J.C., Randell, B.: Fundamental concepts of dependability. Technical Report no. 01-145, UCLA, LAAS-CNRS, Univ. of Newcastle (2001)
6. Kelly, T.P., McDermid, J.A.: Safety case construction and reuse using patterns. In: Intl. Conf. on Computer Safety and Reliability (SAFECOMP), pp. 55–69 (1997)
7. Graydon, P., Knight, J.: Success arguments: Establishing confidence in software development. Technical Report CS-2008-10, University of Virginia (2008)
8. Mayo, P.R.: Structured safety case evaluation: A systematic approach to safety case review. In: Inst. of Engineering and Technology Intl. Conf. on System Safety, pp. 164–173 (2006)
9. Wu, W., Kelly, T.: Combining bayesian belief networks and the goal structuring notation to support architectural reasoning about safety. In: Saglietti, F., Oster, N. (eds.) SAFECOMP 2007. LNCS, vol. 4680, pp. 172–186. Springer, Heidelberg (2007)
10. Cyra, L., Gorski, J.: Expert assessment of arguments: A method and its experimental evaluation. In: Harrison, M.D., Sujan, M.-A. (eds.) SAFECOMP 2008. LNCS, vol. 5219, pp. 291–304. Springer, Heidelberg (2008)
11. OMG Object Management Group: Unified modeling language specification (2003)
12. Maibaum, T.S.E., Wassyng, A.: A product-focused approach to software certification. IEEE Computer 41(2), 91–93 (2008)
13. Carr, M., Kondra, S., Monarch, I., Ulrich, F., Walker, C.: Taxonomy-based risk identification. Technical Report CMU/SEI-93-TR-006, CMU/SEI (93)

Experience with Establishment of Reusable and Certifiable Safety Lifecycle Model within ABB

Zaijun Hu and Carlos G. Bilich

ABB Corporate Research Center, Wallstadter Strasse 59,
68526 Ladenburg, Germany
{zaijun.hu,carlos.bilich}@de.abb.com

Abstract. One basic requirement for a functional safety development project is to establish a SIL-compliant safety lifecycle model. For a company with a big family of safety-related products and a great number of development projects like ABB, it would be very time-consuming and cost-intensive for each safety development project to develop a safety lifecycle model. One approach for managing the corresponding costs and effort is to create a common lifecycle model that fulfills the SIL requirements and can be reused by safety-related projects. In this paper we are going to present such a common safety lifecycle model, its structure and components, and our experience on how to establish and apply it in safety-related product development projects. The paper analyzes the design constraints for the development of a common safety lifecycle model such as complexity, flexibility, simplicity, conformity and the safety integrity. It shows how these constraints drive the design of the safety lifecycle model to be developed. Our design concept, design considerations, development strategy, and our experience in establishing such a common safety lifecycle model will also be discussed in the paper.

Keywords: Safety Lifecycle, Management of Functional Safety, IEC 61508.

1 Introduction

IEC 61508 [1,2,3] requires a safety development project to specify and apply safety lifecycles (SLC). IEC 6508 specifies and recommends 3 safety lifecycles: the overall, E/E/PES and software safety lifecycles. To simplify the description we use the safety lifecycle model (SLCM) as an abbreviation for the related safety lifecycles that are needed in a safety development. This paper focuses on the E/E/PES and software safety lifecycle. A SLCM that a safety development uses provides a framework for specifying the management and technical activities to ensure the implementation of the required measures for risk reduction. Carefully and well-defined SLCM helps to establish repeatable and controllable management of functional safety for achieving the targeted safety integrity. However developing and maintaining the required SLCM are a time-consuming and effort-intensive activity. The overall costs even increase immensely if there are many safety development projects within a company and each project has to create its own SLCM. That is the situation that a global company like

B. Buth, G. Rabe, T. Seyfarth (Eds.): SAFECOMP 2009, LNCS 5775, pp. 132–144, 2009.
© Springer-Verlag Berlin Heidelberg 2009

ABB with huge number of product families and safety development projects needs to manage. To control the overall costs of the safety development within a company it is normally a good practice to define and specify a common SLCM or a few SLCMs, which can be customized and tailored for each safety development project. However such a kind of approach needs to manage diversity in the development environment and culture of different development project teams and different hardware and software complexity of different products. In this paper we are going to present our experience with such a kind of practice. The paper is organized as follows: chapter 2 presents the solution approach with our design considerations, key design constraints, the design concept, the development strategy and the framework of our SLCM. Chapter 3 gives an overview on how the design constraints are considered and implemented, while chapter 4 discusses our experience with the deployment of our SLCM. Chapter 5 gives the conclusion of the paper.

2 Solution Approach

As mentioned in the previous chapter our solution strategy to manage and control the related overall costs is to create a common and reusable safety lifecycle model that can be customized and tailored to a specific safety development project. The key success criteria for this solution strategy are reusability and low cost in the customization and tailoring.

2.1 Initial Consideration

Our first consideration was to check if we can simply use the E/E/PES and software safety lifecycles recommended by IEC 61508 as a common model. After comprehensive investigation we came to the following findings:

1. The SLCM recommended in IEC 61508 only defines the requirements on each phase. There are no clearly defined activities and approaches that are sufficiently concrete for execution. This fact leads to additional effort that a safety development project needs to specify the concrete activities and approaches to satisfy the related requirements if it directly uses the recommended lifecycles.
2. There are no recommended documentation approaches, which help to structure and describe the required safety evidences and then to provide them to the related certification body. Documentation is one of most time-consuming and effort-intensive activities in a safety development project.
3. There are no specified approaches or guidelines in IEC 61508 for integrating the SLCM of IEC 61508 into an existing development environment, which includes the existing development lifecycle, the quality management, the project management, and the supply management.
4. There are no clearly defined design elements for hardware and software development to manage complexity of a safety development project. Although system, subsystem, component and module are used in the SLCM, there is too much interpretation freedom, which leads to uncontrollable uncertainty and difficult in specifying the required outputs of each safety lifecycle phase.

5. There are no specified verification approaches for verifying the outputs of each safety lifecycle phase.
6. There is no framework in the SLCM of IEC 61508 to integrate the valuable best practice, experience, knowledge and pitfalls of previous safety development projects, which are an efficient way to reduce the related costs of a safety development.

Thus the direct application of the SLCM of IEC 61508 to a safety development project means a huge amount of additional work for a project team. It is also clear that those issues discussed above cannot be addressed by a common safety standard like IEC 61508 directly, because many of them are dependent on specific application domains and corresponding organizations and thus can only be treated by those organizations or the related project teams.

Based on those findings above we decided to design and create a common ABB SLCM for a group of ABB business units in order to avoid the costs and effort regarding the establishment of the required SLCM for the related development teams. Those organizations and development teams have similar product complexity and mainly develop E/E/PES products as components, which can be used in a safety application.

2.2 Key Design Constraints

The analysis of the findings of our investigation shows that the following design constraints will help to create an efficient and useful safety lifecycle model.

Simplicity, easy-to-use, adaptability, and complexity
Simplicity means that a SLCM shall be as simple as possible. That is very important for its successful use. Only in this way it can help to specify and structure the management and technical activities in an efficient way. A simple SLCM means simple and clear structure, simple phases, limited roles and activities.

Easy-to-use means that a SLCM shall be easy to customize and tailor. That is the key factor for a success of a SLC and also the added value for a common SLCM. High costs in customization and tailoring makes a common SLCM no sense. Easy-to-understand is another measure to ensure easy-to-use, i.e. a SLCM should be intuitive, self-explained. Furthermore it is important to help people to find the necessary information as quickly as possible, that means the related information should be structured in an integrated way so that searching for and browsering the related information become easier.

Adaptability means that a common SLCM shall be adaptable to different development complexity. This constraint is very important for ABB because ABB has a great number of products with different complexity. It is necessary to define the adaptation rules for those who are responsible for specifying the SLCM that is used in a safety development project.

Conformity
A common SLCM shall fulfill all necessary requirements of the safety standard (IEC 61508). Additionally it should be compliant with the E/E/PES and software safety lifecycles recommended in IEC 61508. It should show that the failure avoidance and

control measures recommended by IEC 61508 shall be considered as required for the safety integrity level to be achieved.

Safety evidence
A SLCM shall assist safety development teams to document the required safety evidences to the related certification body.

Management of functional safety (FSM)
A SLCM shall provide assistance to safety development teams in specifying the management and technical activities and in management of functional safety, including role allocation, functional safety planning, safety verification and validation, and safety assessment.

Applicability
A SLCM to be developed shall be applicable in ABB development and organizational environment. It shall also take the ABB application domains into account.

Integration
A SLCM should cover all requirements contained in IEC 61508. It should also provide a framework for integrating the collected best practices, experience, knowledge and guidelines. Furthermore it should cover the documentation and verification approaches. In addition, it shall be possible to integrate the SLCM to be developed into the ABB development environment, especially in ABB Gate process [7, 8].

2.3 Concept for Design

The design of the common SLCM began with answering the question on how to ensure conformance with IEC 61508. Although it is allowed to use a different safety lifecycle model from the one recommended by IEC 61508, all the objectives and requirements specified in IEC 61508 for the safety lifecycles shall be met. If we had designed a SLCM from scratch, we would have needed to define a SLCM architecture that systematically structured all the objectives and requirements from IEC 61508, including the safety integrity requirements. However, to reduce the related work on the one hand and ensure conformance with the safety standard on the other hand we decided to make use of the structure of the SLCM recommended by IEC 61508 and extended it by additional SLC components and mechanisms that promoted reusability, adaptability, and simplicity, ensured conformity and helped cost reduction and efficiency increase. The following figure illustrates the concept.

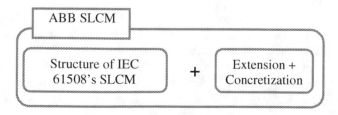

Fig. 1. Design Concept

2.4 Development Strategy

To address the design constraints we have selected several safety development projects with different hardware and software complexity in order to collect inputs, and to understand the related domains, the corresponding problems, needs and development environments. They are also used to verify our SLCM. In addition, we have used the functional safety initiative of the automation product division (one of five ABB divisions) as a platform to collect the related experience and knowledge in the safety development to ensure reusability of our SLCM. To guarantee the conformance we had our SLCM assessed by TÜV in the context of the certification of our FSM Add-on [6], which includes our SLCM. Fig. 2 illustrates our development strategy. As input for the development of our SLCM we also referred to different development lifecycle models such as V-model [12], RUP [11], Harmony [13] and the best practice, knowledge and experience [4,5,13,14].

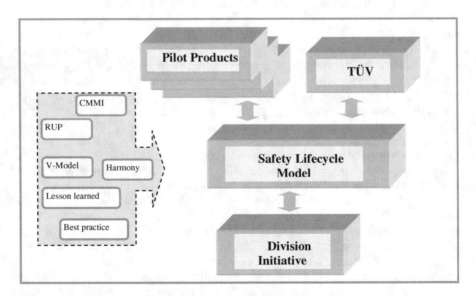

Fig. 2. Development Strategy

2.5 SLCM Framework

The design of the common SLCM to be developed shall take the design constraints into account. Based on the structure of the SLCM of IEC 61508, the following model framework for creating the common SLCM is constructed in order to structure and describe the SLC components and mechanisms of the common SLCM.

The SLCM framework includes not only the SLCM but also the functional safety management plan (FSM plan) and the product design model, which is used to describe the design structure of a product.

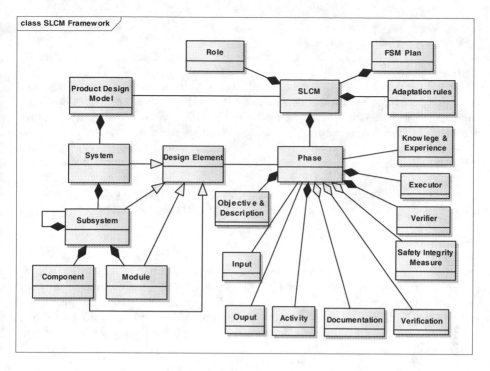

Fig. 3. SLCM Framework

Phase

A SLCM consists of a set of phases. As we built upon the structure of the SLCM recommended by IEC 61508 our SLCM has the same number of phases as the one from IEC 61508. Similar to IEC 61508 a phase of our SLCM has objectives, description, inputs, outputs and the related safety integrity measures for failure avoidance recommended by IEC 61508, which shall be selected or equivalently substituted according to the safety integrity level to be achieved. In addition, we added detailed activities, documentation, verification, verifier, executor and knowledge & Experience as extension to the related phases. Those additional SLC components are not included in the SLCM from IEC 61508, however they are necessary because a safety development team can save a lot of effort through such kind of support. In addition a phase is associated with the related design elements (as shown in Fig. 3), which help to manage the product complexity and to specify the outputs of that phase.

Input and output

Input stands for what kinds/types of input artifacts a phase needs for performing the defined activities while the output for what kinds/types of output artifacts that the phase shall generate after the defined activities are executed. The output artifacts of a phase can be input artifacts of the subsequent phase. A phase can have more than one input or output. For a specific safety development project it is necessary to specify inputs and outputs for a phase. To support the functional safety management it is helpful to provide a mechanism to specify concrete designation of input and output artifacts e.g. file name.

Activity
Activity specifies a set of actions that are needed to be performed during a phase. Differently from the SLCM recommended by IEC 61508, which specifies the related requirements that a safety development should satisfy, our SLCM defines activities that help a safety development to fulfill the requirements. With simplicity and applicability in mind, we try to define and describe the required activities in such a way that they shall not be misunderstood and misinterpreted. In many cases the sequence, in which the required actions are performed, is important. We give certain suggestion by numbering the activities. For those actions, which require particular knowledge and experience, we will give the related reference information for reference.

Documentation
Documentation stands for documentation approaches, which are used to generate the required artifacts as safety evidences. Documentation has direct impact on the assessability of artifacts. Good documentation helps to deliver sufficient and convincing evidences without too much effort. Our SLCM incorporates the documentation approaches by providing the related templates. In order to support the functional safety management our SLCM also provide mechanism to specify the designations of artifacts (e.g. file name).

Verification
Verification is required for safety development. It is helpful to give certain suggestions for verification approaches. Our SLCM incorporates the related verification approaches into each phase by referring the suggested verification approaches and review check lists for review.

Safety integrity measure
The safety integrity measure covers the measures that are required to fulfill the safety integrity requirements. Selection and implementation of the safety integration measures depends on the safety integrity level to be achieved. For us the question was how to structure and organize those failure avoidance measures and incorporate them into our SLCM. As our SLCM uses the same structure and phases as the one of IEC 61508, it is quite easy to realize the incorporation. All measures are associated to the same phases similar to the SLCM of IEC 61508. Incorporation of the failure avoidance measures into a SLCM makes it different from a normal development lifecycle model.

Knowledge and Experience
A phase is associated with knowledge and experience, which represent the best practices, the latest state of art or pitfalls and help the execution of the activities defined for the phase in more efficient and effective way. The knowledge and experience are collected from previous safety development projects or from research results. They are then analyzed and incorporated into our SLCM if they can help to increase development efficiency. Our SLCM incorporates the knowledge and experience into a

phase by either embedding or referring to them. Through this mechanism it is possible to continuously incorporate the new knowledge and experience into our SLCM. In this way we can ensure the sustainable improvement of our SLCM.

Verifier and Executor
The verifier, who is assigned to a phase, is responsible for verifying the output artifacts of the phase while the executor is responsible for the execution of the defined activities for that phase.

Product design model (PDM)
Our SLCM incorporates a product design model to manage different complexity. A product design model provides a design structure to decompose a product into parts. It is a very important method to ensure adaptability of our SLCM. The PDM of our SLCM has 4 design elements: system, subsystem, component and module. Table 1 gives definition of the four design elements.

Table 1. Design Elements of PDM	
System	System is a top-level design element, which consists of subsystems.
Subsystem	A system consists of a set of subsystems. A subsystem is composite hardware and software design element, which can be composed of further subsystems or components or modules. Examples for subsystems are power supply, input, output, logic unit, software, …
Component	A component is the smallest hardware design element whose further breakdown makes no sense in managing hardware complexity. Examples are resistors, capacitors, comparators, operational amplifiers, microcontroller, ASIC etc.
Module	A module is the smallest software design element whose further breakdown makes no sense in managing software complexity. Examples are scheduler, monitor, event handler, …

Fig. 4 illustrates the hardware part of the PDM of our SLCM with the key practices such as system criticality analysis, system FMEA (failure mode and effect analysis), component FMEA and fault insertion test, which are necessary for the safety development and will be assessed by certification bodies. The E/E/PES part of PDM has four levels: the top level for E/E/PES Safety Requirement Specification (E/E/PES SRS) and Validation, the architecture level including Architecture Design and Integration Testing, the detailed design level for Detailed Design and Subsystem Testing, and the implementation level. On the architecture level the system criticality analysis and system FMEA help to identify the safety-critical parts of a system and the potential failures that can be considered in the early phases of the SLCs while the component criticality analysis on the detailed design level tells which components are safety-critical and the component FMEA provides the basis for the quantitative calculation of the related data such as probability of failures per hours. Fig. 4 also

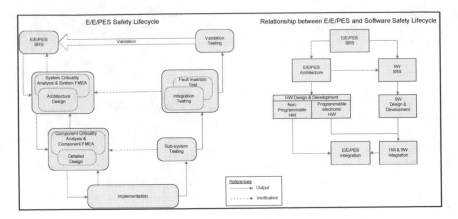

Fig. 4. E/E/PES part of PDM

illustrates the relationship between E/E/PES and software safety lifecycles where the software safety requirement specification (SW SRS) uses E/E/PES SRS and E/E/PES Architecture as input and the hardware and software integration is necessary.

Functional safety management (FSM) plan
In order for our SLCM to support management of functional safety management activities, we have incorporated our SLCM into the FSM plan. This greatly helps to specify the management and technical activities from the FSM point of view because you can directly define the inputs and outputs, assign the defined roles to persons, plan the required activities.

We also considered the solution where the FSM plan is separated from the SLCM. In this case a SLCM is created and documented in a so-called safety development handbook. The argument for this separation is that the SLCM is normally stable and has little change; therefore it is good to keep it in a separate document. Another argument is that if a modification is needed, it is only necessary to change the safety development handbook. All people using it will get the update. Our observation and experience shows that this solution has the following drawbacks

- It is quite difficult to use the same SLCM repeatedly from one project to another without any change. Normally a change or an adaptation, no matter if it is big or small, is necessary. In that case we will face the problem of documenting the adaptation and keeping the FSM plan consistent with the SLCM. That means additional effort.
- As the SLCM is used to specify the management and technical activities planned in the FSM plan, the person responsible for the FSM plan needs to search for the required information in the relevant chapters or sections of the document describing the SLCM and read it.
- The certification body needs to read two documents and check them for consistency. That is not good for accessibility.

Thus we decided to incorporate our SLCM into the FSM plan, which is provided as FSM Add-on (a kind of template) [6] to a safety development project. For a concrete development, the FSM Add-on will be instantiated. In this way we also solve the update problem.

Role
Our SLCM introduces roles: safety manager, safety assessor and audit, verifier, developer, project leader, configuration manager, and supplier.

Integration into existing development environment
One important issue in the design of our SLCM is the integration of the SLCM into the existing development environment. The success of using the SLCM depends how well it can be integrated into an existing development environment. ABB has a Gate process [7,8,9,10] as a business decision model for controlling a project execution from the business points of view. For the purpose of integration we use the concept – pre-gate milestone introduced in [7] and [8]. This concept was originally used to integrate a product development model and a business decision model. That means all outputs of the defined phases of the safety lifecycles for E/E/PES and software will be mapped to a set of so-called pre-gate milestones. The detail can be found in [6].

One important advantage of our SLCM is its integration, which includes integration of documentation, best practices and experience, verification approach, safety integrity measures and last but not least the integration mechanism by using pre-gate milestones.

3   Design Check

The design constraints drove the design our SLCM. In this chapter we are going to check if and how the design constraints are fulfilled. The following table gives the related overview.

Table 2. Design Check	
Design constraint	*Design measure*
Simplicity, easy to use, adaptability and complexity	• *Only necessary roles are defined for the SLCM. We try to keep the number of roles to minimum* • *Simple PDM, only 4 design elements are introduced* • *Simple definition of activities* • *Adaptation rules* • *Understandable and unambiguous definition of activities* • *Integration of all related information (knowledge and experience, documentation, verification, SLCM and FSM plan)*
Conformance	• *Use of the structure and phases of the SLCM of IEC 61508* • *Incorporation of the failure avoidance measures* • *The activities defined fulfill the requirements* • *Our SLCM is checked by TÜV in the context of the certification of FSM Add-on [6], which includes SLCM and FSM plan*

Table 2. (*continued*)	
Safety evidence	• *Document templates* • *Incorporation of documentation into SLCM*
Management of functional safety	• *Incorporation of our SLCM into the FSM plan, i.e. SLCM is part of the FSM plan. Our SLCM also supports definition of inputs and outputs, selection of failure avoidance measures, and selection of the documentation approaches*
Applicability	• *Select several products as pilot* • *Use the functional safety initiative of the automation product division as a platform*

4 Our Experience

We have selected a few safety development projects as pilot for using and verifying the developed SLCM. In selecting the safety development projects we considered the development complexity, project team size, competence of the project team regarding functional safety and application domains. The following table outlines our major findings.

Table 3. Our Experience	
Context and findings	*Descriptions*
Application domain	*Motor control, switchgear system, arc protection*
Development complexity	*Hardware: the number of the components on PC boards ranges from several hundreds to over thousand components* *Software: the line of code ranges from several 10k to over 100k*
Project team size	*6-15 persons*
SIL to be achieved	*1-3*
Competence of the project teams	*No experience with the safety development based on IEC 61508 in the past; however some of them have experience with safety development. Most of them got 1-2 days training regarding functional safety and workshops organized by a certified functional safety engineer*
Approach for deploying the SLCM	*For use or adaptation of the SLCM, workshops were organized where the project team members together with a person who had good knowledge of the developed SLCM. At the workshops it was discussed how to customize or tailor the SLCM*
Actions for deploying the SLCM	• *Adaptation of the PDM to reflect the development complexity. However in most cases there is no need to adapt the PDM. The design elements – system, subsystem, component and module are normally sufficient to address most design tasks.*

Table 3. (*continued*)	
	• *Adaptation of the phases of the SLCM to the specific development project. We normally experienced merging of phases. We observed that the hardware and software integration happened earlier than expected, even before the software integration. In many cases the software module test already required the software and hardware integration.* • *Adaptation of the defined activities for specific safety development projects. However the normal case was that there was little need to modify the defined activities.* • *Definition of the outputs and inputs* • *Mapping of outputs to the pre-gate milestones. Because the most projects used ABB Gate Model, thus such a mapping was not avoidable* • *Mapping of the outputs to the one of the existing development lifecycles. Some project teams also use their own development lifecycles; in those cases it is necessary to map the outputs of our SLCM to those of the existing development lifecycle.* • *Selection of the documentation approaches and the related templates* • *Selection of the failure avoidance measures based on the SIL to be achieved.*
Effort	*Adapting the SLCM normal needed several days. The effort heavily depended on the competence of the participating people. We have observed that most of the effort was spent on the selection and discussion of the failure avoidance measures, followed by adaptation of the phases, PDM and documentation approaches.*

5 Conclusions

In this paper we have presented our experience with development and use of a common SLCM for ABB. Our experience shows that a common SLCM will greatly reduce the overall costs of the safety development. It also helps to create the functional safety management plan more efficiently. As our SLCM is part of the FSM Add-on certified by TÜV, it also greatly helps the conformance of FSM with IEC 61598. Continuous collection of the best practice and improvement of the SLCM is an important way to ensure the long-term benefits of using a common SLCM.

References

1. IEC 61508 – Part 1: Functional safety of electrical/electronic/programmable electronic safety-related systems – General Requirements (1998)
2. IEC 61508 – Part 2: Functional safety of electrical/electronic/programmable electronic safety-related systems – Requirements for electrical/electronic/programmable electronic safety-related systems (2000)
3. IEC 61508 – Part 2: Functional safety of electrical/electronic/programmable electronic safety-related systems – Software requirements (1998)

4. Smith, D.J., Simpson, K.G.L.: Functional Safety: A Straightforward Guide to Applying IEC 61508 and Related Standards, 2nd edn. Butterworth Heinemann, Butterworths (2004)
5. Faller, R.: Project Experience with IEC 61508 and Its Consequences. In: Voges, U. (ed.) SAFECOMP 2001. LNCS, vol. 2187, pp. 200–214. Springer, Heidelberg (2001)
6. Hu, Z., Bilich, C.: Safety Add-on – an Efficient Way to Make Development SIL-Compliant. In: 8th International Symposium Programmable Electronic Systems in Safety-Related Applications, Cologne, Germany (September 2-3, 2008)
7. Hallqvist, S., Moström, J.: ABB Gate Model: A Process Management Model for Product Development in ABB, Master Thesis in Business Administration, Linköping University, Department of Management and Economics (2003)
8. Wallin, C., Larsson, S., Ekdahl, F., Crnkovic, I.: Combining models for business decisions and software development. In: Proceedings of 28th Euromicro Conference, 2002, pp. 266–271 (2002)
9. Wallin, C., Ekdahl, F., Larsson, S.: Integrating business and software development models. IEEE Software 19(6), 28–33 (2002)
10. Larsson, S., Kolb, P.: Software process improvement at ABB. ABB Review (3), 10–14 (2001)
11. Kruchten, P.: The Rational Unified Process: an Introduction, 2nd edn. Addison Wesley, Reading (2000)
12. V-Modell® XT, http://v-modell.iabg.de/
13. Douglass, B.: Real-Time UML Workshop for Embedded Systems. Elsevier Inc., Amsterdam (2007)
14. Borcsok, J., Schaefer, S.: Software development for safety-related systems. In: Second International Conference on Systems, ICONS 2007, April 22-28, pp. 37–37 (2007)

Automotive IT-Security as a Challenge: Basic Attacks from the Black Box Perspective on the Example of Privacy Threats

Tobias Hoppe, Stefan Kiltz, and Jana Dittmann

Research Group on Multimedia and Security
Otto-von-Guericke University of Magdeburg
Universitaetsplatz 2, 39106 Magdeburg, Germany
{tobias.hoppe,jana.dittmann,
stefan.kiltz}@iti.cs.uni-magdeburg.de

Abstract. Since automotive IT is becoming more and more powerful, the IT-security in this domain is an evolving area of research. In this paper we focus on the relevance of the black box perspective in the context of threat analyses for automotive IT systems and discuss typical starting points and implications of respective attacks. We put a special focus on potential privacy issues, which we expect to be of increasing relevance in future automotive systems. To motivate appropriate provision for privacy protection in future cars we discuss potential scenarios of privacy violations. To underline the relevance even today, we further present a novel attack on a recent gateway ECU enabling an attacker to sniff arbitrary internal communication even beyond subnetwork borders.

1 Introduction / Motivation

Looking at current trends in automotive IT, a clear trend of increasing complexity, connectivity, customisability and extendibility can be recognised. Dozens of electronic control units (ECUs) communicating via field bus networks implement a big part of modern car's functionalities. However, along with these improvements on automotive systems' capabilities, also the attention paid by unauthorised parties is on the increase. Also (or especially) in the automotive domain the spectrum of potential attackers is as multifaceted as their individual motivations (e.g. see [1]). To face these upcoming threats and provide a solid basis for future automotive applications, holistic concepts for IT-security in automotive systems are an emerging challenge of research.

Since especially in the automotive domain detailed technical specifications about the networked automotive IT systems are usually kept secret by the manufacturers, attackers often have to start with little detailed information. In this paper we discuss this black-box-perspective that is relevant to the majority of potential automotive attackers. We generalise typical approaches for attacks on automotive IT, e.g. in the shape of five basic attack principles and point out potential classes of attack implications having to be respected especially in the automotive domain.

B. Buth, G. Rabe, T. Seyfarth (Eds.): SAFECOMP 2009, LNCS 5775, pp. 145–158, 2009.

As an evolving aspect of automotive IT security we refer to threats to the increasing amount of privacy relevant data stored and processed by modern cars. We list current and oncoming examples for potentially privacy relevant data in cars and discuss potential implications of the personalisation trend in automotive IT.

To illustrate the state of the art and as a practical example for privacy-relevant automotive attacks already possible today we demonstrate an attack on a recent gateway ECU from a big international car producer. By only requiring access to the open On-Board Diagnostics (OBD) port in the car interior (i.e. without requiring intrusive actions like locating and hooking up bus wires), the attack on the gateway ECU bypasses the software-based network isolation and can enforce the leakage of arbitrary (potentially privacy relevant) internal communication to the outside. Firstly presented at the escar 2008 workshop, this attack is now publicly presented in this work.

In the following section 2, we point out the increasing need for privacy protecting measures in future IT security concepts. As a focus on current threats to automotive IT security, in section 3 we emphasise the relevance of the black box perspective for attackers in the automotive domain and discuss typical attacking principles and implications. Subsequently we introduce the practical black-box attack at the gateway ECU in section 4, discuss privacy preserving measures for future IT security concepts in section 5 and summarise the paper in section 6 with a final conclusion.

2   Increasing Attacks on Privacy Issues in the Automotive Domain

As a practice-oriented topic of IT-security that we expect to be of rising relevance in the automotive context, in this section we refer to the increasing amount of privacy relevant information (i.e. person-related or person-relatable data) stored and processed by modern cars. To sensitise the reader about the increasing relevance of this aspect of IT security, in subsection 2.1 current and oncoming examples for potentially privacy-relevant information in cars are identified. Subsequently, in subsection 2.2 we discuss the trend of the increasing individual-related processing and storage of data within automotive IT-systems. In two exemplary scenarios we discuss relevant parties potentially interested in exploiting privacy relevant data in automotive systems.

2.1   Examples for Privacy Related Data in Automotive IT Environments

Even current automotive systems store and process a lot of information which allow significant statements about the users, their habits and behaviour. We do not neglect the comfort offered this way to the users, but also potential threats of this trend have to be discussed increasingly, e.g. to also address privacy issues. Exemplary references to person related or person relatable data are listed in the following:

- Personalisation data (i.e. customer individual settings for vehicle applications)
  - Especially for comfort and infotainment applications, for example radio (e.g. individually programmable station lists, preferred tone colour for the sound system, etc.), navigation (user profiles e.g. containing presets for frequently used routes or routes recently taken), integrated hands-free phone systems (e.g. these often hold internal copies of the contact lists) or personal presets for climate / heating systems, windscreen wiper settings etc.

o Some manufacturers store a large part of such personal settings on a central device; on activation, it communicates these settings to the affected applications via the internal CAN (Controller Area Network) bus.

- Communication data
  o Due to the increasing connectivity of automotive IT and user-centred communication services, also potentially privacy-relevant connection information are increasingly processed and stored by automotive IT. For example these can be related to phone usage (e.g. contact lists, connection data of active or even previous in/outgoing calls), mobile Internet access (email contact lists, connection data, cached files etc.) or Car-to-Car/Infrastructure (person related or relatable data processed by future C2C/C2I systems).
- Indirect, personal characteristics
  o By a correlation of common internal status information (e.g. on the internal buses: diverse sensory input, current time, engine speed, GPS position etc.) often more significant personal characteristics can be inferred. Some examples are the personal driving style (temporary maximum speeds, acceleration/braking intensity and frequency, steering characteristics, etc.), covered distances (time, GPS coordinates, etc.), primary time of driving like common daytime, weekdays, etc., frequently visited locations / driven routes (time, GPS coordinates, etc.) or the presence / absence of further occupants (seat usage sensors, belt usage information, etc.).
- Personal data of future automotive applications
  o Due to the increasing provision of user-centred services in modern cars, the amount of stored and processed user-specific, personal information is expected to increase notably in the future. One example are biometric samples. These would have to be stored by potential future automotive biometrics systems for all registered users in order to provide services like automatic authentication [2].

As we discuss in the next subsection, some of these person-related of person-relatable information would already be of high interest to certain groups of people. Depending on the way the diverse information as listed above is stored and processed by the automotive IT system, attackers have to use different ways to collect it. We group the appearance of diverse kinds of data into two general classes:

- Accessible permanently (stored persistently, at least for some slot of time): Stored in the persistent memory of ECUs (today flash memory in most cases), some can be read out externally, for example the lists of error codes which can be retrieved and reset by diagnostics software. If not retrievable otherwise, physically intrusive actions (like directly reading out flash chips) might be required
- Observable live only (not stored persistently): Some live data can be found at the internal buses (status information like digitised sensor data that is usually transmitted periodically). Other data is only evident within the relevant ECUs in normal operation (i.e. not communicated by default). For maintenance, some ECUs allow such data to be monitored from the bus level on explicit request, e.g. using live data queries or calibration protocols like CCP/XCP. Otherwise physically intrusive action (like accessing open JTAG interfaces) might be required.

While already today first wireless connections from external devices to automotive IT networks are possible, threats of unauthorised accesses to privacy relevant data in automotive systems can be expected to increase even more in the future in face of the plans for external automotive communication on a grand scale. This motivates the need for privacy-preserving, holistic automotive security concepts in the context of oncoming C2C/C2I systems even more. Continuing our focus on potential future privacy threats, in subsection 2.2 we discuss scenarios of misuse of privacy-relevant, automotive data, the trend of increasing personalisation of automotive systems as well as potential future implications to their role in everyday life.

2.2 Personalisation and Privacy Threats – Exemplary Scenarios

Looking at automotive IT systems, a clear trend of personalisation can be noticed to increasingly customise them towards the users' needs. Future user-centred automotive IT environments might allow similar customisability as in today's PC domain and be equivalently be integrated in world wide communication networks. Users might be able use the automotive IT infrastructure for a considerable amount of personal activities (e.g., in current cars telephone contact lists can be managed) that today PC systems are used for. Just like desktop PCs today, automotive IT environments in ten years might also be regarded as integrated parts of their user's personal lifestyle.

Beside the positive effects regarding the increased comfort of such future cars, this trend would also increase the interest of third parties even more to access and evaluate the contained person related or relatable data. Consequently, the security and especially privacy aspects will have to be well protected in these complex systems.

We now discuss a few exemplary scenarios of misuse of privacy related data in automotive systems that some adversaries might be interested in even today.

Rental car agencies or *car-pools in bigger companies* might increasingly intend to generate user profiles to facilitate customer-dependent tariff models or to even ban unwanted users. E.g., they could analyse each user's personal manner of driving that influences issues like fine/accident risks or mechanical wear and tear by reading out sensitive data after each trip or by even attaching a data recorder to each car that constantly stores data snapshots like the intensity of acceleration, brake or steering inputs (this has already been used on a voluntary basis in insurance schemes such as MyRate[1]). Even GPS coordinates from the navigation system could be recorded to reconstruct the routes taken, e.g. to check if the user leaves the registered routes, frequently visits dangerous areas etc. Because the companies are the legal owner of the vehicle and already know the person to which such recorded person-relatable data belongs (due to the contract), the realisation of such privacy constraints is very likely.

In future, the interest of different parties in privacy relevant data in automotive systems might increase even more. For example biometric reference samples stored by future automotive biometric authentication systems would have to be especially protected to prevent potential adversaries from stealing these data. *Impersonators* might use this to generate faked biometric credentials for unauthorised access.

Also legal guidelines justify privacy protecting measures in future automotive IT-security concepts: In 2008, the Federal Constitutional Court of Germany constituted a civil right of the provision for confidentiality and integrity of IT-based systems (*"Grundrecht auf Gewährleistung der Vertraulichkeit und Integrität*

---

[1] See http://auto.progressive.com/progressive-car-insurance/myrate-default.aspx

informations-technischer Systeme"). This might increasingly also be relevant for cars as more and more powerful IT-based systems. However, such legal regulations might also affect more legitimate purposes of automotive data collection. E.g., the work of accident research teams[2] might be hindered, if they first had to ask the driver and/or vehicle owner for permission (who might be absent or not addressable because of injuries).

3   Respecting Automotive Attacks from the Black Box Perspective

The broad spectrum of automotive attackers can include all sorts of people with different skills and detail of knowledge and having a wide range of professions. A majority of the various attacks on automotive IT can be expected to be run by attackers from a black-box-perspective (e.g. see [3]). Independent from the level of his personal skills, the attacker usually does not have access to manufacturer-specific internal specifications. In this section we discuss this black-box-perspective by referring to common starting points for attacks at partially unknown automotive IT systems. We also address five basic attack principles and point out potential classes of attack implications having to be respected in the automotive domain.

Except for insiders, most automotive attackers have to face modern automotive IT systems from the black box perspective:

- They barely have detailed technical information accessible, e.g. underlying specifications of the manufacturer
- Consequently, they have no knowledge about detailed internal coherences
- A lot of information is obtained by trial-and-error
- Some attacker classes (like tuners) are highly interconnected and actively exchange their experiences and resources, often in public Internet forums
- Various attackers can browse such resources for useful information and documents

After these initial enquiries, these attackers often follow typical approaches and basic attack principles which we discuss in subsection 3.1.

3.1   Automotive Attacks: Common Starting Points and Basic Principles

Today, automotive attackers usually have physical access to the target system (or a system identical in construction). In isolated locations like their home garage they can invest (almost) arbitrary time for its analysis and for conceiving attacks. In face of the frequent lack of detailed information about the target's internals, black box attackers can start their examinations on specific components of its IT infrastructure which have a (more or less) open specification and compatible equipment available.

Such basic starting points can, for example, be found deep inside in the internals of a target ECU. Automotive devices often contain off-the-shelf chips for which useful resources are available on the Internet. One common example are data sheets by their manufacturers with detailed information like their pin assignments.

---

[2] E.g. in the German towns Hanover and Dresden [4] such mobile teams join specific accident scenes to collect relevant electronic data for the investigation of accident reasons in order to improve the vehicle and road safety in future.

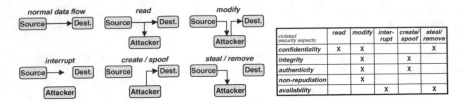

Fig. 1. Basic attack principles and violated security aspects

Another common starting point requiring less intrusive access are the automotive communication networks. Most manufacturers today install standardised field bus technology like CAN, LIN, MOST or FlexRay. Especially for the widely used CAN bus system, various hard and software equipment is available. Protocols like OBD have partly been standardised or reverse-engineered and cheap equipment is available for sale (often from independent vendors) for most car brands. The spectrum of equipment for analysing and interacting with automotive IT ranges from self-made equipment and free software to professional devices and commercial development suites. Locating internal bus circuits in cars is usually also no difficult task. Corresponding cables in the wiring harness are often apparent by their individual colour or can be determined on any attached ECU with reference to the pin assignments in the data sheets of the contained controller chips (see above).

After obtaining basic means of access, attackers can investigate the target system in a more structured way. They might be able to monitor or even generate bus communication on a raw data level even without any information about the manufacturer specific syntax of the active protocols. To gather more experiences about the observed system, five basic attack principles are common initial strategies. These deviations from the intended *normal data flow* are illustrated in Figure 1 with a listing of security aspects commonly violated by such attacks. An attacker might simply *read* (sniff) the transmitted information. Active intrusions occur if he would *modify* the data as a man in the middle, *interrupt* the transmission, *create / spoof* messages (on behalf of the original sender) or *steal / remove* transmitted data.

Wider attacks can often be interpreted as a combination. E.g., a *replay attack* consists of a basic *read* attack followed by some *create / spoof* activity. Beside on data transmissions, attackers can also apply them in offline states, e.g. on data sources or storage places; also combinations of these two approaches are conceivable.

3.2   The Potential Range of Automotive Attack Implications

Compared with attacks on desktop IT systems, violations of the IT security of automotive IT (being part of moving vehicles) can have more severe implications, including the reduction of the safety of the system, its occupants and environment.

Even if the reduction of safety might be no intended aim of the intrusive actors, such risks frequently arise due to the common lack of comprehension of the complex coherences within the overall system (which is partly also caused by the mentioned lack of commonly available technical specifications). We differentiate between two general classes of potential attack implications:

- **Functional implications:** Direct implications that the attack has on the function of the targeted component, service etc.. Usually identical to the desired attack result.
- **Structural implications:** Indirect implications that the attack (or its functional implications) has on the functionality of the overall system and its environment. Typically these have neither been expected nor desired by the attacker (and can therefore differ from his actual intentions) or are accepted carelessly.

To illustrate these issues, we now discuss two exemplary attacking scenarios:

Example 1: A car seller manipulates the mileage counter (possibly using professional equipment) to increase the resale value and the instrumentation presents a lower mileage (*functional implication*). Because the betrayed buyer supposedly relies on this false information a noncompliance with the service intervals can be expected resulting in higher wear and tear and, consequently, repair costs. Though not intended by the seller in his attack, he might have been unaware of these *structural implications* or just carelessly accepted them since they don't affect him personally.

Example 2: A hobby car tuner wants to unlock his TV system for the usage whilst driving ("TV in motion"). Depending on the implementation, the TV functionality might be linked to the condition that the hand brake is applied. By permanently short-cutting the corresponding signal wire to ground or by digitally setting/clearing the corresponding signal in the bus system, he might succeed in removing the TV restrictions (*functional implications*). However, under certain circumstances also other automotive devices might react on this faked input; for example, an unexpected activation of the steering lock whilst driving could pose severe safety risks not intended by the attacker (*structural implications*).

4 Enforcing Information Leakage Today: A Practical Attack

In this section we illustrate the black box perspective and the basic attack principles by presenting an information leakage attack on a central gateway ECU from a recent car series (built since 2005) of a big international manufacturer. It allows an attacker to bypass the software-based network isolation and to enforce the leakage of arbitrary (potentially privacy relevant) internal communication to the outside. The attack serves as a practical example for privacy-relevant attacks on automotive IT-networks that are already possible today (even from a black-box perspective) and exemplifies the increasing relevance of privacy threats to automotive IT.

4.1 Our Test Environment and Introduction of the Selected Attack Target

Figure 2 illustrates the generic bus topology of the target car from the perspective of the gateway ECU, that coordinates the communication of five CAN[5] (sub-)networks (i.e. only specific information is transmitted amongst them like the current speeds from the powertrain network that are to be displayed in the instrumentation). Beneath performance reasons, this filtering also provides a basic level of network security by dividing the entire network into several (functionally divided) subnetworks.

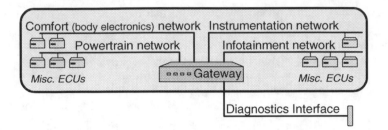

Fig. 2. The network topology from the gateway's perspective

As starting point we chose the open On-Board Diagnostics interface that is accessible from the car interior and directly connected to the gateway. Unlike first attacks we presented in the past, this attack requires no intrusive actions like hooking up any internal bus wires. By connecting to the CAN bus pins of the OBD II socket via a USB-to-CAN device we are able to receive existing and send own CAN messages. Due to its open accessibility, the diagnostics CAN subnetwork has to be isolated from the communication in the internal CAN subnetworks, which is also evident in the implementation of the tested gateway device: During normal operation, the regular internal communication is not visible from this position. Only when an attached diagnostics client runs a session, belonging messages can be recorded.

4.2 Analytically Examining the Gateway from the Black Box Perspective

To learn about the general properties of the gateway ECU and the potential of the Diagnostics Interface, this section introduces further black box examinations.

Because the sole application of the basic attack principle *read* from this position does usually not reveal any information we then additionally attached a commercial diagnostics solution. During regular diagnostics of arbitrary internal ECUs from the diagnostics product, we read out the communication in the diagnostics subnetwork for a subsequent analysis as a first result of, the basic attack principle *read*. Table 1 shows an excerpt of the CAN communication recorded after pushing the diagnostics software's button for the inspection of an exemplary ECU (located in the internal Comfort CAN subnetwork). Table 1 lists each message's timestamp, CAN-ID (an 11 bit identifier indicating its content type), the size of its payload (data length code / DLC) and the up to 8 bytes of payload itself as raw data bytes.

Table 1. CAN log excerpt of the beginning of a regular diagnostics session (basic *read* attack)

Timestamp	CAN-ID	DLC	Raw Data
147.818146	200	7	2C C0 00 10 00 03 01
147.824188	22C	7	00 D0 00 03 3D 03 01
147.842743	33D	6	A0 0F 8A FF 32 FF
147.844910	300	6	A1 0F 8A FF 4A FF
147.920792	33D	5	10 00 02 10 89
147.923233	300	1	B1
147.933578	300	5	10 00 02 50 89

Table 2. Analyses via a replay attack (a basic *create/spoof* attack using previously *read* data)

Timestamp	CAN-ID	DLC	Raw Data
134.876587	**200**	**7**	**2C C0 00 10 00 03 01**
134.883987	22C	7	00 D0 00 03 3D 03 01
134.984848	22C	7	00 D0 00 03 3D 03 01
135.084930	22C	7	00 D0 00 03 3D 03 01
135.184860	22C	7	00 D0 00 03 3D 03 01
135.284851	22C	7	00 D0 00 03 3D 03 01
135.384857	22C	7	00 D0 00 03 3D 03 01
135.484833	22C	7	00 D0 00 03 3D 03 01
135.584869	22C	7	00 D0 00 03 3D 03 01
135.685104	22C	7	00 D0 00 03 3D 03 01
135.785156	22C	7	00 D0 00 03 3D 03 01
135.885345	22C	7	00 D0 00 03 3D 03 01
135.984955	300	1	A8

Even without the specification of the underlying protocols, an attacker from the black box perspective can easily derive its rough functionality. A basic assumption might be, that the first message from Table 1 (ID 0x200) stems from the external tester, which initiates the session in the client role. This can be verified by applying the basic *create/spoof* attack principle as indicated by Table 2 (injected messages are indicated bold): after replaying the initially observed message onto the diagnostics CAN bus, the car replies by sending the second message (type 0x22C) 11 times and then stops communicating after a final message of type 0x300. This appears to be the system's reaction to our missing response after sending the initial message.

Also when choosing other ECUs in the diagnostics software, its initial message always uses CAN-ID 0x200; only the first payload byte is varying, which therefore seems to be some kind of unique identifier for the device queried. This device ID is then used by the gateway to select the correct internal subnetwork where this request is to be forwarded to. Once arrived there, the destination ECU replies with a message which is forwarded via the gateway ECU back to the diagnostics interface. The ID of this message (0x22C in Table 1) obviously depends on the device ID (0x2C) from the request and is different for each internal ECU (which we could verify by observing further diagnostics sessions).

As it can also be noticed in Table 1, after the exchange of the first two CAN messages (type 0x200 and 0x22C) the further communication exclusively uses CAN messages of the IDs 0x300 and 0x33D. Interestingly, exactly these two integer values can be found in Little Endian encoding located in the fifth and sixth byte of the aforementioned two initial CAN messages. This leads to the final assumption, that each session partner notifies the other one during this initialisation, for which CAN-ID it will be listening for the rest of the session.

However, up to this point the potential of an attacker with access to the restricted diagnostics interface does not exceed the options he would have anyway by directly using a diagnostics product, which is even more comfortable than struggling with the raw communication. The next subsection introduces the formation of an attack based on the knowledge obtained so far to exceed the limited scope of the intended diagnostics functionality.

4.3   Conceiving an Exemplary Black-Box Attack on the Gateway ECU

By *modifying* the previously *read* 0x200 initialisation message, we could practically verify our final assumption: After altering the fifth and sixth byte to an increased value of 0x301, an equivalent *create/spoof* attack results in the target ECU choosing this different CAN-ID for its reply during the diagnostics session (see Table 3).

Table 3. Influencing message ID usage (a basic *create/spoof* attack using *modified* data)

Timestamp	CAN-ID	DLC	Raw Data
20.362113	**200**	**7**	**2C C0 00 10 01 03 01**
20.371685	22C	7	00 D0 01 03 3D 03 01
...	...	...	...
21.372926	22C	7	00 D0 01 03 3D 03 01
21.472362	301	1	A8

To summarise: The gateway only forwards internal CAN messages to the open diagnostics CAN interface if they belong to active diagnostics sessions. Diagnostic testers outside the car are able to influence the CAN-ID used for the CAN messages to be sent back from the internal ECUs during the session. These observations might enable attackers to run information leakage attacks, depending on the implementation of the filter functions in the gateway ECU, which can follow two general approaches:

• *Static Filtering:* Certain ranges of CAN message IDs are reserved for the exclusive use during diagnostic sessions. The gateway could always let pass any messages with these CAN-IDs (in this case this might be 0x3**) between the internal CAN subnetworks and the diagnostics CAN without any further checks. To respect the isolation from the internal communication, it has to be ensured that these message types are not used by any internal devices for their regular internal communication.

• *Stateful Filtering:* The gateway ECU could also evaluate the session initialisation message pair and dynamically unlock only the two message IDs for passing during the length of the session.

Our gateway ECU implements a stateful approach, as another simple replay attack confirms: Any of the previous 0x300 messages manually replayed into the respective internal subnetwork does not get forwarded by the gateway to the diagnostics interface in the absence of an active session. Also without directly accessing internal networks, trying the following attack on suspicion would have confirmed this.

If the gateway ECU performs stateful filtering of diagnostics sessions, decisions about passing incoming CAN messages between an internal and the diagnostics CAN bus system are based on its current knowledge about active sessions. If it solely relies on the CAN message IDs announced for the usage during the session by both session partners, an attacker located at the open diagnostics interface could exploit this:

Again, he injects a session initialisation message with a forged ID for the response messages. But this time he selectively chooses an ID which is supposed to be already used within the target subnetwork for other CAN messages as part of the local internal communication. He does this based on the suspect that the gateway in this case can not distinguish between CAN messages belonging to the diagnostics session (as sent by the target ECU) and other CAN messages with the same ID (sent by any ECU within the target CAN subnetwork) and, consequently, will forward all these messages too for the length of the session.

Table 4. Basic information leakage attack (a basic create/spoof attack using modified data)

Timestamp	CAN-ID	DLC	Raw Data
17.327831	**200**	**7**	**2C C0 00 10 31 06 01**
17.333843	22C	7	00 D0 31 06 3D 03 01
17.433887	22C	7	00 D0 31 06 3D 03 01
17.534733	22C	7	00 D0 31 06 3D 03 01
17.634720	22C	7	00 D0 31 06 3D 03 01
17.734713	22C	7	00 D0 31 06 3D 03 01
17.834602	22C	7	00 D0 31 06 3D 03 01
17.934696	22C	7	00 D0 31 06 3D 03 01
18.034748	22C	7	00 D0 31 06 3D 03 01
18.135729	22C	7	00 D0 31 06 3D 03 01
18.141830	631	4	1E 1E 5F 1E
18.235039	22C	7	00 D0 31 06 3D 03 01
18.335571	22C	7	00 D0 31 06 3D 03 01
18.435036	631	1	A8

Table 4 shows a log of this *create/spoof* attack where the session initialisation message specifies the device ID of an ECU in the Comfort CAN subnetwork and a forged response message ID of 0x631. Obviously, at timestamp 18.141830 an eye-catching additional message of type 0x631 appears. This regular message has been sent by some ECU within the target subnetwork (i.e. the Comfort CAN) while the diagnostics session was active; the gateway could not keep it apart from CAN messages being authentic diagnostic reply from the target ECU and, consequently, illegitimately forwarded also this internal bus message to the outside. This way we practically demonstrate that an attacker can create a transparent channel from internal bus networks to the external, restricted diagnostics port. This allows him to read out arbitrary internal CAN communication by only sending a single CAN message.

4.4 Advancements of the Attack, Further Test Results and Final Remarks

For several tests with this information leakage attack we further extended its functionality and implemented a prototypical demonstrator as a virtual device within the automotive development, simulation and analysis environment CANoe [6] which is also widely used in the automotive industry. Figure 3 shows the graphical user interface (GUI) of the current implementation of our prototypical attack demonstrator. By specifying the CAN-ID of the message type to sniff and the target subnetwork that should be read from, this attack can be performed with a simple button click. The message ID and an appropriate device ID for the respective subnetwork are automatically inserted in the generated initialisation message of type 0x200 after pushing the "Start" button. The extended implementation additionally includes the support to keep the host session alive by sending additional idle-messages, which removes the limitation of the described attack to 1-2 seconds due to the session time-out. If sniffed messages arrive, these are logged and, at the same time, displayed in the bottom part of the user interface. Figure 3 shows an active attack on the message type 0x520 from the instrumentation CAN subnetwork. The sniffed messages for example contain the current mileage value (18123 km) as hexadecimal value (0x46CB) Little Endian encoded in its last 3 bytes (CB 46 00).

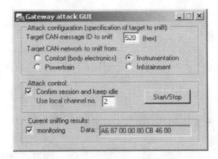

Fig. 3. Graphical user interface of the prototypical attack demonstrator

In additional tests we found another flaw that even increases the potential impact of this attack technique: The gateway does not only accept incoming diagnostics requests when arriving from the diagnostics port but also from any of the internal subnetworks, which bears additional security risks: Any, potentially infected, device within any CAN subnetwork could establish regular diagnostics sessions to any other ECU within the car and potentially perform malicious coding alterations like enabling or disabling certain features. Furthermore we could prove that using our attacking technique it could also read out arbitrary CAN communication from different internal CAN networks which might not be intended to be accessible from that location.

Furthermore, the described attacking technique also provides basic potential to indirectly *write* forged messages into internal networks exploiting the side-effect that the internal ECU will send at least one message with the CAN-ID controlled by the attacker (see Table 3). Such ambiguous messages might not only be misunderstood by the gateway but also by other ECUs. Beneath unintended malfunctions due to such misinterpreted communication (unintended, structural implications according to section 3.2), certain diagnostic response messages could possibly be provoked by an attacker to indirectly inject arbitrary bus messages into the target network.

Reviewing the results of our black box examinations, a more careful implementation of the gateway ECU could have prevented its easy success. Sound measures would have been the restriction of the CAN IDs to a reserved range not used by other internal ECUs and the rejection of diagnostics sessions from internal subnetworks. In future, wider security measures could improve gateway security even more, e.g. by content inspection techniques within automotive firewall or IDS [7] components. However, since direct access to internal bus systems (which is not even necessary for the presented attack) does also not mean much additional effort to an attacker, holistic measures for the IT security of future cars and their internal and external communication are inevitable in the long term. In section 5 we discuss basic approaches for the improvement of privacy protection in future automotive systems.

5 Privacy Preserving Measures for Future Automotive IT Security

When considering privacy preserving measures for the automotive domain, it helps to first estimate the suitability of established solutions from the desktop IT.

Common strategies are ***pseudonymisation*** or ***anonymisation*** techniques. Usually requiring little computing and storage overhead, they could be considered for automotive applications. However, most cars are usually expected to only have a very small number of entitled users, rendering these measures inappropriate in many cases, because the privacy relevant data obviously has to belong to some of the few users of the car. Nevertheless, these approaches can be reasonable for other applications like protecting privacy relevant data in the context of external C2C communication [8].

Another approach is the ***encryption*** of privacy relevant data during communication and storage. This usually requires a higher computational overhead, but is applicable in a much wider scope since it can principally be applied to any kind of data: while pseudonymisation or anonymisation approaches usually involve loss of information (the link to the identity), encrypted data can always be transferred back to the original form (i.e. decrypted by any authorised entity). This way, the entire bus communication could be secured by an additional encryption layer [9]. However, since especially in the automotive domain there is a high relevance of attackers with physical access, the keys have to be especially protected (e.g. in terms of processing and storage). One approach currently discussed to address this is the provision of trusted automotive hardware platforms based on an adaptation of Trusted Computing technology to the requirements of the automotive domain (see [1]).

Even given such secure hardware bases, future IT security concepts have to respect the entire automotive IT system in its environment in order to provide a holistic IT security supporting the multitude of various requirements. With reference to the diagnostics field addressed by this paper, the following exemplary requirements illustrate the complexity of potential automotive IT security policies: accesses to (wired or wireless) diagnostics interfaces by unauthorised persons should be prevented; registered car service stations are authorised, but may not access privacy relevant data; after an emergency case, only trusted and authenticated accident research teams may acquire the full data from the wreck. Future systems should also incorporate the possibility to completely erase privacy relevant data by the car owner. This will be important to heighten the acceptance of future automotive systems by potential users, who worry about potentially leaving incriminating evidence (like remaining records about maximum speeds and past driving times or routes).

6 Summary and Conclusion

In this paper we pointed out the special relevance of attacks from the black box perspective in the automotive domain and discussed common starting points and basic attack principles of such attackers. To reduce respective risks, automotive IT security is an emerging topic of research. With a focus on increasing threats to privacy related data we discussed examples such data in current and oncoming cars and referred to respective scenarios. We motivated the provision for privacy preserving measures as part of future, holistic automotive IT security concepts and practically demonstrated an information leakage attack to recent automotive IT, which empowers an attacker to read out arbitrary internal bus communication from the (usually restricted) diagnostics port via an enforced transparent channel. In face of wireless diagnostics solutions (e.g. over GSM [10]), attackers might manage to implement *remote* versions of similar attacks, if the wireless protocols are not secured well enough. We used this example to illustrate the black box perspective and its main steps with reference to the basic attack principles. We finally discussed basic approaches of privacy-preserving strategies in the context of automotive IT systems and their common environment.

As our practical demonstration showed, effective attacks on automotive IT can be conceived by ambitious attackers even without the underlying specifications available. The provision for holistic security concepts is one of the main challenges within automotive IT research. On a secure basis, several aspects of automotive IT security will have to be realised to be compatible with the multifaceted environments, use cases and technical progress during the life time of such future vehicular IT systems. The provision of privacy protecting measures to reduce the threats to the expected multitude of personal information stored and processed by future automotive IT systems is only one of these oncoming challenges.

Acknowledgements. The work described in this paper has been supported in part by the European Commission in the context of the programme *COMO - Competence in Mobility* (EU/EFRE) under Contract No. C(2007)5254. The research about basic attack strategies was additionally supported by the German BMBF (Project *ViER-forES*, No. 01IM08003). The information in this document is provided as is, and no guarantee or warranty is given or implied that the information is fit for any particular purpose. The user thereof uses the information at its sole risk and liability.

References

1. Wolf, M., Weimerskirch, A., Wollinger, T.: State of the Art: Embedding Security in Vehicles. EURASIP Journal on Embedded Systems 2007, Article ID 74706, 16 (2007)
2. Büker, U., Schmidt, R., Fahreridentifikation, B.: Automotive Security, VDI-Berichte Nr. 2016. In: Proceedings of the 23. VDI/VW Gemeinschaftstagung Automotive Security, Wolfsburg, Germany, November 27-28. VDI-Verlag (2007)
3. Hoppe, T., Dittmann, J.: Vortäuschen von Komponentenfunktionalität im Automobil: Safety- und Komfort-Implikationen durch Security-Verletzungen am Beispiel des Airbags. In: Sicherheit 2008; Sicherheit - Schutz und Zuverlässigkeit, Saarbrücken, Germany (2008)
4. VUFO-Verkehrsunfallforschung an der TU Dresden GmbH(January 2009), http://www.verkehrsunfallforschung.de/
5. BOSCH CAN (January 2009), http://www.can.bosch.com/
6. Vector Informatik CANoe (January 2009), http://www.vector.com/vi_canoe_de.html
7. Hoppe, T., Kiltz, S., Dittmann, J.: IDS als zukünftige Ergänzung automotiver IT-Sicherheit. In: Horster, P. (ed.) DACH Security 2008; Bestandsaufnahme, Konzepte, Anwendungen, Perspektiven; Syssec (2008)
8. Weyl, B.: Secure and Privacy-Preserving Car-to-X Applications: C2C-CC Baseline Concepts, escar – Embedded Security In Cars, Munich, Germany, November 6-7 (2007)
9. Wolf, M., Weimerskirch, A., Paar, C.: Sicherheit in automobilen Bussystemen, Automotive - Safety & Security 2004, Oktober 6-7. Universität Stuttgart (2004)
10. BMW Teleservice Diagnosis and Help (Teleservice of the BMW Connected Drive system) (January 2009), http://www.bmw.com/com/en/insights/technology/connecteddrive/bmw_teleservices_2.html

Safety Requirements for a Cooperative Traffic Management System: The Human Interface Perspective

Thomas Gruber, Egbert Althammer, and Erwin Schoitsch

Austrian Research Centers GmbH - ARC, Austria
{thomas.gruber,egbert.althammer,erwin.schoitsch}@arcs.ac.at

Abstract. Traffic management systems are complex networks integrating sensors, actors, communication on different levels and humans as active part, consisting of road-side infrastructure coupled with advanced driver assistance systems and on-board data collection facilities.

COOPERS[1] has the objective of co-operative traffic management by implementing intelligent services interfacing vehicles, drivers, road infrastructure and highway operators. These services have different levels of criticality and safety impact, and involve different types of smart systems and wireless communications. In the initial phase of the COOPERS project a RAMSS[2] analysis was carried out on road traffic scenarios, services and communications. The analysis yielded that the HMI (Human Machine Interface) is one of the major threats to reliability.

After a short overview on COOPERS and the RAMSS analysis, this paper describes the risks of the HMI and human factors in the specific situation of a driver and gives concrete recommendations for the OBU (On-Board Unit) user interface.

Keywords: RAMSS, dependability analysis, co-operative traffic management, traffic telematics, road safety, human factors, HMI dependability.

1 Improving Road Traffic Safety by a Co-operative Integrated Traffic Management System

In the sixth framework program of the European Commission, one of the thematic main lines deals with road traffic safety. Several projects funded by the 6th IST Framework Program address this topic, but COOPERS 1] takes a specific position with unique ways and methods to attain a safety improvement through an intelligent network which exploits existing technologies for co-operative services.

COOPERS prepares the way for improving road safety on motorways at an affordable cost. Based on existing technologies and infrastructure, the driver is provided with real-time data on the current traffic situation ahead (see 1]). In each car, a

---

[1] Research supported in part by COOPERS (Co-Operative Networks for Intelligent Road Safety, www.coopers-ip.eu), an integrated project funded by the EU within priority "Information Society Technologies (IST)" in the sixth EU framework programme (contract no. FP6-IST-4-026814).

[2] Acronym for Reliability, Availability, Maintainability, Safety and Security.

B. Buth, G. Rabe, T. Seyfarth (Eds.): SAFECOMP 2009, LNCS 5775, pp. 159–172, 2009.

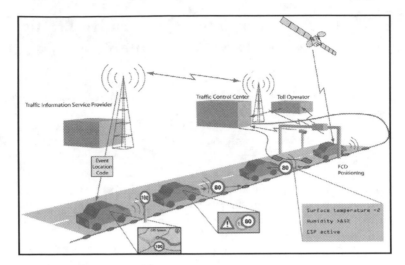

Fig. 1. Intelligent infrastructure and smart cars plus individual location based services – I2V and V2I communication

receiver for the I2V (infrastructure to vehicle) communication encapsulated in an OBU and a display offer information about accidents, traffic jams, road construction sites and other location and time related events. Only messages relevant for the driver on a particular segment are passed on. No irrelevant data about traffic congestions or accidents in remote areas of the country is shown like in traffic radio broadcasting services. The information is accurate and precise both in terms of location and time.

COOPERS started with an assessment of existing wireless, in-car and roadside technologies, of the possible safety improvement and a selection of services most appropriate for supporting the new approach like for instance "Accident warning", "Weather condition warning", "In-vehicle variable speed limit information" or "Recommended next link".

COOPERS services are expected to reduce the risk in road traffic from the current level to a significantly lower value, expressed by number and severity of accidents, injuries and fatalities counts. However, the implementation of a service may be faulty, and it is even possible that the driver is exposed to a higher risk by using the service than the risk without COOPERS. This may be caused, for instance, by dangerous reactions of the driver as a consequence of wrong or misinterpreted information, by degraded attention through distraction by the COOPERS display or through full reliance on the in reality possibly unreliable COOPERS services. Therefore a RAMSS analysis was performed in 2006 at an early stage of the project.

2   RAMSS Analysis for COOPERS

Methodology as well as the results of the COOPERS RAMS analysis are described in detail in 3] and 4], so here we give only a short abstract.

The RAMSS analysis was intended to give advice on how to construct COOPERS services, regarding their functional architecture as well as the selection of appropriate technologies. By introducing the services mentioned above a safety gain of the current road traffic situation is expected. It was clear that the quality aspect of safety played the major role and was therefore the main objective of our analysis.

From a technical point of view, all COOPERS services represent an information transfer through the signal flow path as depicted in Fig. 2, and it is evident that the availability of the single node functions and of each signal flow through the edges in the information flow path will play the key role.

Fig. 2. Signal flow path of the data

In any safety or reliability analysis the first step is to define the borders of the system and the undesired event. It had been decided early in the project that COOPERS services would NOT have direct influence on the car, so we defined that the car itself is not in the scope. As for the driver, we focused on granting positive preconditions for the correct perception of the COOPERS services. The proper reaction should be supported by creating conditions under which the driver is most likely to react correctly, while details should be investigated by driver behavior analyses in the final stage of the project - the COOPERS service demonstrations in six European countries. From the above defined scope of consideration follows that the unwanted event is the driver reacting in an inappropriate manner to a COOPERS service message, whether he does not receive or perceive the information generated by some sensor system or he is subjected to conditions which hamper him from reacting adequately.

We applied the generic safety standard EN ISO/IEC 61508 [2] to the signal path and interpreted the COOPERS services as safety functions. The safety standard prescribes measures and methods to reduce the risk from an unacceptably high level to one below the so-called "tolerable risk", which is typically in the magnitude of the natural risk to which a human is exposed without the system. For our specific case a modified risk reduction approach had to be chosen: In COOPERS, we start from a risk level which society already considers tolerable, and the services are expected to reduce the risk even further.

Consequently, the question arises why we investigate system safety whilst the risk *with* COOPERS is expected to be even below an already accepted level. Well, the reason is the validity of the assumption that COOPERS really reduces risk. The implementation may be faulty, services may show wrong or contradictory information, and - finally - drivers may disregard or misinterpret the warning messages or simply not understand them in terms of content, location and time.

As a first step a Preliminary Hazard Analysis (PHA) was performed to investigate the co-operative system with the intention to identify the hazards of road traffic. (Read more about the PHA method in [5].) It became clear that the main risks arise from stored kinetic energy (vehicle collisions) and we may neglect rarely emerging hazards like chemical energy from fuel transports and the like.

The second and much more detailed step was a HAZard and OPerability analysis (HAZOP). (A detailed description of this method can be found in [5], too.) Each node in the signal flow path (cf. Fig.2) was analyzed with respect to reliability and availability, and the risks associated with delayed and distorted messages were analyzed. Still there were no final decisions made about the technologies, but it was evident that all electronic components expose a reliability of at least one magnitude higher than the one of the nodes and paths with the lowest reliability and availability values: The wireless connection and the perception of the driver.

The comparably low reliability and availability of wireless data transfer was treated in several work packages of COOPERS. A parallel use of two diverse wireless channels was discussed but considered too expensive. Therefore, the services were designed fault-tolerant against temporary unavailability of wireless connections.

The driver is the other comparably unreliable node in the signal flow path; we therefore made an extensive analysis of the requirements to the human machine interface HMI, taking into account various aspects of human error. Below, this analysis will be described in detail.

3 Human Factors in COOPERS

3.1 Human Perception

Driving on a motorway is a highly complex task because of the large amount of information the driver has to face. Most information is visual input (like road vehicles, pedestrian, signs, passing scenery, map), some is auditory input (radio, talking, engine, wind noise, other cars), some is tactile input (vibrations, steering wheel, throttle control, brake control, acceleration, gearshift), and there is also some internal input (remembering directions, thoughts, plans). Thereby the human has to rely on limited resources like: perception, attention, and memory.

Human information processing can be modeled by four stages as depicted in Fig.3.

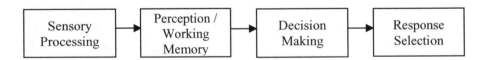

Fig. 3. Simple four-stage model of human information processing [6]

In each stage of this model specific tasks are carried out [7]:

1) **Sensory Processing**: Acquire information, detecting and registering sensations. The time of correct detection decreases with greater signal intensity (brightness, contrast, size, loudness, etc.) and is faster for auditory signals than for visual ones.

2) **Perception/Working Memory**: Analyze information and identify the situation; apply cognitive functions to the information; recognize the meaning of the sensation. Here the time increases with low signal probability, uncertainty (signal location, time or form), and surprise. Additionally when there

are multiple possible signals and responses, it is generally much slower than simple sensations.

3) **Decision Making**: Decide which response to make and program the movement. Response selection generally slows down under choice when there are multiple possible responses. Conversely, practice decreases the required time.

4) **Response Selection**: Execution of functions, choice of action or movement to be implemented. The more complex the movement, the longer the movement will take. Increased arousal and practice decrease movement time.

3.2 Human Error

3.2.1 Classification of Human Error
According to M. Green [8], three principal types of human errors can be distinguished:

1) **Perceptual Errors:** Critical information is below the threshold to be noticed, e.g. too dim, blinded by glare, low contrast, or the driver makes a perceptual misjudgment, regarding speed, distance or curve radius.

2) **Skill-based Errors:** Driver fails to attend or notice critical information, because his mental resources were focused elsewhere, misordering of steps in procedures, the manner or the technique one uses when driving a vehicle.

3) **Decision Errors:** These are procedural errors (misapplied or in inappropriate circumstances), poor choices (simply put, sometimes we chose well, and sometime we do not – or even do not chose at all), and problem solving errors, e. g. when the problem is not well understood, and formal procedures and response options are not available.

3.2.2 Unsafe Acts Caused by Humans
The three types of errors enumerated above match with those defined in the Human Factors Analysis and Classification System (HFACS), which is a general human error framework for classifying aviation accidents. It has been developed and used within the U.S. military, applied to commercial aviation accident records and proved to be a valuable tool in the civil aviation area. But it makes also sense to apply the classification scheme in other areas, like in COOPERS.

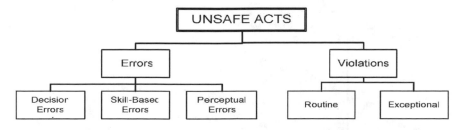

Fig. 4. Human Factors Analysis and Classification System (HFACS)

Apart from the three kinds of errors described above, the HFACS distinguishes two further types of unsafe acts, confer "Violations" in Fig. 4. In contrast to errors, violations represent the willful disobedience of the (legal) rules and (traffic) regulations.

1) **Routine Violations:** These are habitual by nature and are often tolerated by the authority (e.g. always driving 10 km/h faster than the legal speed limit), sometimes also known as "bending the rules".

2) **Exceptional Violations:** These are isolated deviations from rule-conformance; they do not necessarily characterize an individual's behavior and are generally not condoned by authority. The unexpected nature of exceptional violations makes them difficult to predict and manage. Therefore this type of violation was not considered further for COOPERS.

Within each of the four stages of the model of human information processing, errors can occur.

Other authors like Jens Rasmussen ([14], [15]) distinguish between different levels of human performance and correlate them to required attention and familiarity with the task, cf. Fig.5. It is evident that knowledge-based actions are associated with the highest error probability, but most actions required from a car driver are rule based like obeying traffic signs, or skill-based like changing the gears.

3.2.3 Human Error Probability
It is difficult to obtain valid reliability figures for humans because available data rarely stem from field experience but mostly from simulations and laboratory studies, which yield distorted results due to the artificial conditions under which they are measured.

Rasmussen gives a first clue about error probabilities for different kinds of actions, cf. Fig.5. But error probability depends also on factors like environmental conditions and workload. P. J. Comer and others (cf. [9]) investigated human error in the domain of petroleum platform workers; the error probability values he found depend on different types of human behavior under various conditions and are shown in **Table 1** above.

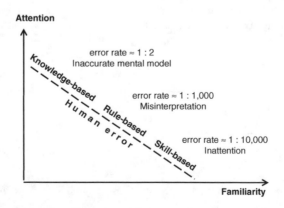

Fig. 5. Jens Rasmussen's human performance model

Table 1. Range of human error probability

Type of Human Behavior	Human Error Probability
Extraordinary errors – Those for which it is difficult to conceive how they could occur. Stress free, with powerful cues pointing to success.	10^{-5}
Error in regularly performed, commonplace, simple tasks with minimum stress.	10^{-4}
Errors on commission, such as pressing the wrong button or reading wrong display. Reasonably complex tasks, little time available, some cues necessary.	10^{-3}
Errors of omission where dependence is placed on situation cues and memory. Complex unfamiliar tasks with little feedback and some distraction.	10^{-2}
Highly complex task, considerably stress, little time available.	10^{-1}
Process involving creative thinking, unfamiliar, complex operations where time is short and stress is high.	$1 \ldots 10^{-1}$

Although this table was developed for a different industrial sector the behavior types match well with the situations of a driver in road traffic, and the values can therefore be used for assessing the significance of human error in vehicle based systems.

What can be clearly seen from the probability data in Table 1 is that there are external factors, which heavily influence the reliability of people. The environment, for example, affects the performance, which means for example that the human body performs best in a fairly restricted temperature range.

Table 2. Human error probability and stress [16]

Stress level	Increase of error probability	
	with experience	without experience
Very low (monotony)	* 1	* 2
optimal	* 1	* 1
high	* 2	* 4
extremely high	* 5	* 10

Stress and fatigue can further impair human behavior, which depend often on the risk taking attitude, tight economic or personal conditions like the pressure to meet a schedule. Table 2 gives factors by which error probability increases under stress conditions. Experienced people are less affected by stress, and interestingly extremely low stress, i.e. monotony, can even increase the error rate, at least for inexperienced persons.

4 COOPERS HMI Construction

Following the results of the RAMSS analysis, and considering the role which the driver plays with respect to his ability to perceive the information provided by COOPERS correctly and to be in a state to react properly, we had to pay special attention to the HMI. Therefore, a work group within the COOPERS development work package was installed in 2007 which discussed the HMI aspects applicable to the COOPERS OBU and finally formulated requirements for hardware as well as software, which are described in this paper.

4.1 RISKS in the HMI

In the specific environment and situation of the driver in a car, the HMI is inherently associated with a considerable number of risks:

- Delayed information
- Confusion through information overload
- Visibility issues like direct sunlight or glare
- Misunderstanding displayed information, e.g. due to language problems or unclear symbols
- Lack of clarity or ambiguity cause a slow understanding process distracting the driver from his primary task
- Non-intuitive interface causes difficult handling
- Driver distraction by other sources, e.g. video playing

All these risks hamper correct information perception, and they all may finally result in a wrong driver reaction. Impairments of the visual sense like short-sightedness and far-sightedness, glaucoma, cataract, colour-blindness or reduced range of visibility after a cerebral insult were not in our scope.

4.2 The Range of Human Visual Perception

Research at Fraunhofer FIRST in Berlin (cf. [11]) showed in which horizontal and vertical angles humans are able to recognize visually presented information.

It was no surprise that the recognition of text is limited to a very narrow angle of +/- 10° in vertical as well as horizontal direction. Apart from that, the eye must focus on the text in order to read it, which distracts the driver's attention from the road. The eye needs time for accommodating, then for reading the text and finally for focusing back on the road.

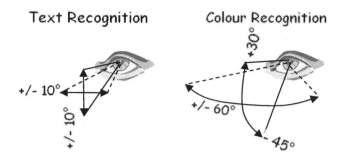

Fig. 6. Human ability to recognize text and color information

In contrast, the range of color recognition spans a much wider angle of +/- 60° horizontally and +30°/-45° vertically. Coloured elements placed in this visible field are discernable without loss of focus; so it is possible to focus on the traffic and at the same time to recognize the coloured information on the screen. And humans' visual perception is able to recognize colours within only 200-300ms.

The screen in a car is normally mounted on the dash board at a horizontal angle of 15-30° and at a vertical angle of approximately ±20°. The consequence on the COOPERS HMI was clear: Use colour symbols and not text.

4.3 European Standard for Automotive HMI Safety and Usability

Since the late 1990s, the European Commission has elaborated a recommendation for in-car information systems, which was issued in 2007 as "Commission Recommendation of 22 December 2006 on safe and efficient in-vehicle information and communication systems, see [13]. This recommendation is an update of the European Statement of Principles on Human Machine Interface (1999) and describes on a generic level how the service interaction with the driver shall be implemented; it suggests driver training and gives advice regarding user as well as installation manuals issues. The EU recommendation was a valuable source for many of the COOPERS HMI requirements.

4.4 COOPERS HMI Requirements

4.4.1 Overview
The following Fig. 7 gives a concise overview on which factors have to be considered when selecting properties for a display. Note that additional decisions had to be made for the keyboard, for the use of audio displays (sound), and for the possible use of haptic displays. Moreover, critical aspects of information presentation had to be considered.

4.4.2 Types of Displays
For COOPERS, several variants of displays were considered, based on the proposed devices for implementing the electronic in-car equipment:

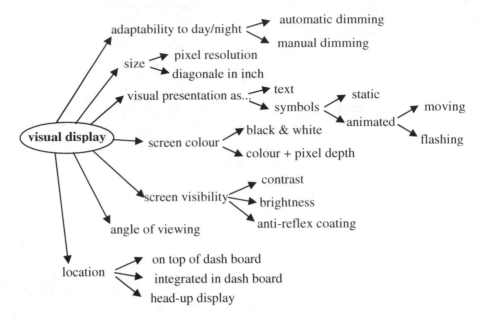

Fig. 7. Essential properties of visual displays

- Graphics display integrated in the OBU
- Graphics display integrated in the dashboard
- External graphics display
- Graphics head-up display integrated with the windscreen
- Alphanumeric display integrated in OBU.

Text displays were excluded, due to the narrow visibility angle as described in section 4.2, the longer time required to understand them, and also potential language problems. Head-up displays are costly and therefore not preferred. And a solution integrated in the dashboard behind the steering wheel was considered less desirable than a lateral location because research showed that it takes more time for accommodation to look down than to look aside. So the recommendation was finally an external graphics color display mounted on the dashboard in a lateral position.

4.4.3 Display Size

The ideal size is from 5" upwards, typical displays have a diagonal of between 5 and 7 inches. For nomadic devices like personal digital assistants (PDA) or enhanced mobile phones, 4" is also acceptable. There are larger displays with good usability, but when mounted on top of the dashboard they may hamper free sight through the windscreen. And at least in Sweden there are even legal restrictions with respect to the maximum size of on-top-of-dashboard mounted displays.

For the pixel resolution, a minimum of 320*240 is recommended.

4.4.4 Colour

Colour is clearly preferred to black and white displays as - on the one hand - traffic signs are usually in colour, and - on the other hand - research gave clear evidence that colour can be recognized in a very wide angle of view, cf. section 4.2. A restriction to a limited set of colours is a software question and had therefore no influence on the OBU hardware decision. Anyway, eight bit colour was considered adequate.

4.4.5 Symbols

Symbols are better than text as they are easier to understand. Text should preferably only be used for additional information. The symbols shall be identical with the national traffic signs displayed on VMS (variable message signs). The national set of signs displayed on the on-board unit shall be configurable. The European and many other states have adopted the catalogue of traffic signs contained in the "Vienna Convention on Road Signs and Signals" of 1968 [17]. This standard defines the shape and the content of traffic signs and leaves only little space for choosing between colour schemes or between slightly modified graphic symbol variants. At least the symbols for moving traffic, which are relevant to the COOPERS services, can be well recognized also by drivers with various kinds of colour-blindness.

Usually driver distraction should be minimized by use of static symbols. Animated symbols are reasonable only for urgent messages. If moving symbols are used the movement must be meaningful.

4.4.6 Aspects of Information Presentation

Different presentation of critical and non-critical messages is desirable; they can be distinguished by animation and audio information. The latter is highly recommended. Symbols for hazards shall be displayed twice as big as speed limit w. r. t. area of the bounding rectangle (1.41. times length and width).

Driver distraction is an issue; information overload must be avoided by prioritization if several messages have to be shown simultaneously. Symbols on the display shall never obscure one another, and their number shall be limited to a maximum of five. Derived from the Gestalt principles [12], the speed limit symbol shall always appear at the same fixed position, which must not be occupied by hazard warnings, and the space for hazard warnings shall not be occupied by a speed limit sign.

4.4.7 Visibility / Contrast in Sunlight and Night

Visibility and contrast in sunlight as well as night is an important issue. Many modern devices expose excellent image quality including adaptive abilities for various light situations. Standard VGA (Video Graphics Array) screens usually don't offer a comparably high quality. A relevant aspect is also the anti-reflex coating. COOEPRS partners made the experience that an experimental comparison of the brightness of different displays in direct sunlight is necessary as the numeric brightness values in a data sheets may be misleading.

Today only part of the displays has automatic dimming; the rest can be dimmed manually. Of course, the COOPERS software might control brightness using a separate light sensor. But for the COOPERS prototypes on the test sites high display quality and automatic dimming does not play such an important role as it will for future consumer versions. So we considered these properties for the COOPERS prototype OBU of minor relevance.

4.4.8 Input Devices

The following options were taken into consideration:

- touch screen
- hard keys
- remote control

For simple yes/no decisions hard buttons are as good as touch screens. For more complex decisions touch screens are recommended. For most COOPERS services there is not much input expected.

A remote control is considered not very practical as it may be displaced.

4.4.9 Displays, Sound

We can distinguish between different types of audio displays

- Independent external loudspeaker
- Loudspeaker coupled with car radio (mobile phone input via cable or Bluetooth)
- Shared use of car radio loudspeaker
- Independent headset

and different kinds of sound

- Beep tone
- Speech synthesizer

For critical information an audible message is highly recommended, but too much sound is nasty and causes the driver to turn off the loudspeaker. The decision between simple warning tones and speech generation is a software question and additionally a cost factor. Muting the car radio is recommended, the mobile phone input shall be used. A headset is not very practical.

4.4.10 Haptic Displays

Following types of haptic displays were considered:

- Actuator for haptic sensation, e.g. trembling steering wheel or seat
- Mechanical reaction of a car HMI component, e.g. accelerator pedal reaction

Haptic displays may distract the driver's attention because the reason of the haptic sensation is often not clear. A tremble may, for instance, be misinterpreted as a technical defect like a flat tire. For these reasons haptic displays are not recommended.

5 Conclusions and Future Work

In this paper, the basic principles of human perception and human error have been outlined shortly. Based on the COOPERS RAMSS analysis [3], the driver has been detected as one of the weakest links in the information flow chain. The risks in the OBU have been identified and analyzed, and finally a set of COOPERS HMI requirements has been elaborated.

The requirements outlined here have been implemented in the COOPERS OBU prototype and - as a next step - need to be validated. If the HMI really supports the driver in a satisfactory - and especially safe - manner will be investigated in the COOPERS demonstrations in 2009. These will be performed by COOPERS partners who are or have close relations to road operators in Austria, Belgium, France, Germany, Italy and the Netherlands. A specific service called "International service handover" will demonstrate the interoperability when driving across national borders, i.e. there is an information exchange between neighbouring road operators in order to grant seamless traffic information. Measurement of physiological parameters of the drivers as well as evaluation of questionnaires will eventually prove the quality of the requirements presented in this publication. Further work will be based on the results of the demonstrations.

Acknowledgments. The research for the COOPERS HMI requirements was collected in a special workgroup and would not have been possible without the valuable contributions of several project partners. I would like to express my gratefulness to all who contributed to this research, in particular

o   Anne Bolling, Selina Mårdh and Matthias Hjort of Statens väg- och transport-forskningsinstitutet in Linköping, Sweden
o   Birgit Kwella, Norbert Pieth and Matthias Schmidt of Fraunhofer-Gesellschaft zur Förderung der angewandten Forschung e.V. in Berlin, Germany,
o   Marianne Bezoen of ARS Traffic and Transport Technology B.V. in Leidschendam, The Netherlands,
o   and to Jörg Worschech who was that time with Efkon AG in Graz, Austria.

References

1. http://www.coopers.at
2. EN ISO/IEC 61508, Functional Safety of Electrical/Electronic/Programmable Electronic Systems, Part 1 – Part 7 (1998 – 2001)
3. Selhofer, A., Gruber, T.: COOPERS RAMS Analysis Safecomp (2007)
4. Gruber, T., Althammer, E.: Sicherheitsanforderungen und Validierung eines kooperativen integrierten Verkehrsmanagementsystems. In: Proceedings Informationstagung Mikroelektronik ME 2008, Vienna, pp. 320–326 (2008)
5. American Institute of Chemical Engineers, Center for Chemical Plant Safety. Guidelines for Hazard Evaluation Procedures. DC, American Institute of Chemical Engineers, Washington (1992)
6. Parasuraman, R., Sheridan, T.B., Wickens, C.D.: A model for types and levels of human interaction with automation. IEEE Transaction on Systems, Man, and Cybernetics A30(3), 286–295 (2000)
7. Green, M.: How Long Does It Take to Stop? Methodological Analysis of Driver Perception-Brake Times. IEEE Transportation Human Factors 2(3), 195–216 (2000)
8. Green, M., Senders, J.: Human Error in Road Accidents (2003), http://www.visualexpert.com/Resources/roadaccidents.html
9. Comer, P.J., Kirwan, B.J.: A Reliability Study of a Platform Blowdown System. In: Automation for Safety in Shipping and Offshore Petroleum Operations. Elsevier, Amsterdam (1986)

10. Nielsen, J.: Usability Engineering. Academic Press, London (1993)
11. Rettinger, C.: How to provide maximum possible guidance while driving; ITS in Europe, Hannover (June 2005)
12. Rock, L., Palmer, S.: The legacy of gestalt psychology. Scientific American 263, 84–90 (1990)
13. Commission Recommendation of 22 December 2006 on safe and efficient in-vehicle information and communication systems, update of the European Statement of Principles on human machine interface, 2007/78/EC
14. Rasmussen, J.: Human Errors. A taxonomy for Describing Human Malfunction in Industrial Installations. Journal of Occupational Accidents 4, 311–333 (1982)
15. Rasmussen, J.: Skills, Rules, and Knowledge; Signals, Signs, and Symbols, and Other Distinctions in Human Performance Models. IEEE Transactions on Systems, Man, and Cybernetics SMC-13(3) (May/June 1983)
16. Interdisziplinäres Zentrum für Verkehrswissenschaften, Universität Würzburg
17. Vienna Convention on Road Signs and Signals, United Nations (1968)

The COMPASS Approach: Correctness, Modelling and Performability of Aerospace Systems*

Marco Bozzano[1], Alessandro Cimatti[1], Joost-Pieter Katoen[2],
Viet Yen Nguyen[2], Thomas Noll[2], and Marco Roveri[1]

[1] Fondazione Bruno Kessler, Trento, Italy
Tel.: +39 0461 314367; Fax: +39 0461 302040
bozzano@fbk.eu
[2] Software Modeling and Verification Group, RWTH Aachen University, Germany

Abstract. We report on a model-based approach to system-software co-engineering which is tailored to the specific characteristics of critical on-board systems for the aerospace domain. The approach is supported by a System-Level Integrated Modeling (SLIM) Language by which engineers are provided with convenient ways to describe nominal hardware and software operation, (probabilistic) faults and their propagation, error recovery, and degraded modes of operation.

Correctness properties, safety guarantees, and performance and dependability requirements are given using property patterns which act as parameterized "templates" to the engineers and thus offer a comprehensible and easy-to-use framework for requirement specification. Instantiated properties are checked on the SLIM specification using state-of-the-art formal analysis techniques such as bounded SAT-based and symbolic model checking, and probabilistic variants thereof. The precise nature of these techniques together with the formal SLIM semantics yield a trustworthy modeling and analysis framework for system and software engineers supporting, among others, automated derivation of dynamic (i.e., randomly timed) fault trees, FMEA tables, assessment of FDIR, and automated derivation of observability requirements.

1 Introduction

The design of modern space missions and systems poses fierce challenges. On the one hand, the involved systems are clearly critical, and huge amounts of money are at stake. On the other hand, the design involves the integration of a large number of heterogeneous requirements (e.g. functional correctness, dependability, observability, performance), for which different teams are responsible, and that often do not communicate in the early stages of the process.

In this paper, we describe an integrated, model-based methodology for system-software co-engineering, which is tailored to the specific characteristics of critical on-board systems for the space domain. The approach covers modeling,

---

* Funded by ESA/ESTEC under Contract No. 21171/07/NL/JD.

B. Buth, G. Rabe, T. Seyfarth (Eds.): SAFECOMP 2009, LNCS 5775, pp. 173–186, 2009.

functional correctness, and performance analysis. In terms of modeling, the approach is based on a System-Level Integrated Modeling (SLIM) language. The SLIM language is inspired by the well-known AADL [30] and provides engineers with convenient ways to describe nominal hardware and software operation, hybridity, (probabilistic) faults and their propagation, error recovery, and degraded modes of operation.

A fundamental feature of the approach is model extension: starting from a nominal model of the system, and a set of possible faults, the extension operator is able to generate a comprehensive description combining both the nominal and the faulty behaviours of the model. The SLIM language also allows for a comprehensive representation of partial observability, necessary to describe the actual sensing capabilities at the disposal of an on-line monitoring system.

The SLIM language allows to describe discrete dynamics, real time, and continuous dynamics, both in a qualitative and in a probabilistic fashion. A formal semantics allows to precisely characterize the complete set of nominal and non-nominal behaviours of the model, and opens up the possibility to apply a wealth of formal verification techniques for various forms of analysis. These include symbolic model checking for functional verification and formal requirements analysis, FTA and FMEA, testability, and performance analysis.

The activity described in this paper is inspired by the COMPASS project[1] (Correctness, Modeling, and Performance of Aerospace Systems). The project is in response to an invitation to tender by the European Space Agency. The methodology described in this work is made practical by a comprehensive toolset, called the COMPASS toolset, based on state of the art tools in verification, such as NuSMV [26], FSAP [19], Sigref [31], and MRMC [25]. The toolset and the methodology are currently under industrial evaluation and will be applied to several case studies by a major industrial developer of aerospace systems.

The paper is structured as follows. In Section 2, we describe the features of the SLIM language. In Section 3, we discuss how the various analyses can be reduced to (qualitative and quantitative) problems in formal verification. In Section 4, we present the structure of the COMPASS toolset. Finally, in Section 5 we draw some conclusions and outline directions for future work.

2   The Modeling Language

The System-Level Integrated Modeling (SLIM) language [7] has been designed in order to provide a cohesive and uniform approach to model heterogeneous systems, consisting of software (e.g., processes and threads) and hardware (e.g., processors and buses) components, and their interactions. Furthermore, it has been designed with the following essential features in mind.

  – Modeling both the system's nominal and non-nominal behavior. To this aim, SLIM provides primitives to describe software and hardware faults, error propagation (that is, turning fault occurrences into failure events), sporadic

---

[1] http://compass.informatik.rwth-aachen.de

```
device Battery
  features
    empty: out event port;
    voltage: out data port real;
end Battery;

device implementation Battery.Imp
  subcomponents
    energy: data continuous initially 100.0;
  modes
    charged: initial mode
              while energy' = -0.01 and energy >= 20;
    depleted: mode
              while energy' = -0.015;
  transitions
    charged   -[when energy >= 15
                then voltage := f(energy)]-> charged;
    charged   -[empty when energy<20]->      depleted;
    depleted  -[then voltage := f(energy)]-> depleted;
end Battery.Imp;
```

Fig. 1. Specification of a Battery Component

(transient) and permanent faults, and degraded modes of operation (by mapping failures from architectural to service level).
- Modeling (partial) observability and observability requirements. These notions are essential to deal with diagnosability and Fault Detection, Isolation and Recovery (FDIR) analyses.
- Specifying timed and hybrid behavior. In particular, in order to analyze continuous physical systems such as mechanical and hydraulics, the SLIM language supports continuous real-valued variables with (linear) time-dependent dynamics.
- Modeling probabilistic and quantitative aspects, such as probabilistic faults and performability measures.

The characteristics listed above make SLIM an ideal language to specify and reason about the following system properties: functional correctness, in particular in case of degraded hardware operation; safety and dependability; diagnosability and FDIR; system performance and performability.

2.1   Specifying Nominal Behavior

A SLIM model is hierarchically organized into *components*, distinguished into software (processes, threads, data), hardware (processors, memories, devices, buses), and composite components. Components are defined by their *type* (specifying the functional interfaces as seen by the environment) and their *implementation*(representing the internal structure). The implementation part contains:

```
system Power
  features
    voltage: out data port real;
end Power;

system implementation Power.Imp
  subcomponents
    batt1: device Battery.Imp in modes (primary);
    batt2: device Battery.Imp in modes (backup);
  connections
    data port batt1.voltage -> voltage
      in modes (primary);
    data port batt2.voltage -> voltage
      in modes (backup);
  modes
    primary: initial mode;
    backup: mode;
  transitions
    primary -[batt1.empty]-> backup;
    backup  -[batt2.empty]-> primary;
end Power.Imp;
```

Fig. 2. The Complete Power System

the structure of the component as an assembly of subcomponents; the interaction through (event and data) port connections; the (physical) binding at runtime; the operational modes as an abstraction of the concrete component behavior, possibly representing different system configurations and connection topologies, with mode transitions which are spontaneous or triggered by events arriving at the ports; the timing and hybrid behavior of the component. The overall specification can be organized into *packages* to support modularity.

To give a more concrete idea, Fig. 1 shows an example specification of a simple battery device. Its type interface features two ports: an outgoing event port empty which indicates that the battery is about to become discharged, and an outgoing data port voltage which makes its current voltage level accessible to the environment.

The corresponding component implementation specifies the battery to be initially in the charged mode with an energy level of 100 (%). This level is continuously decreased by 1% per time unit (in Fig. 1, energy' denotes the first derivative of energy) until a threshold value of 20% is reached, upon which the battery changes to the depleted mode. This mode transition triggers the empty output event, and the loss rate of energy is increased to 1.5%. Moreover, the voltage value is regularly computed from the energy level (the corresponding function, f, is not detailed here) and automatically made accessible to the environment via the corresponding outgoing data port.

The next specification, presented in Fig. 2, shows the usage of the battery component in the context of a redundant power system. It contains two instances

```
error model BatteryFailure
  features
    normal: initial state;
    dead:    error    state;
end BatteryFailure;

error model implementation BatteryFailure.Imp
  events
    fault: error event occurrence poisson 0.001;
  transitions
    normal -[fault]-> dead;
end BatteryFailure.Imp;
```

Fig. 3. An Error Model

of the battery device, being respectively active in the `primary` and the `backup` mode. The mode switch that initiates reconfiguration is triggered by an `empty` event arriving from the battery that is currently active. Moreover the `voltage` information of the active battery is forwarded via an outgoing data port.

2.2   Specifying Faulty Behavior

Nominal component specifications can be extended by *error models* to support safety and dependability analyses. For the sake of modularity, nominal specifications, error specifications, and their mutual association are separated from each other.

Again, an error model is defined by its type, its implementation, and its effect. An error model *type* defines an interface in terms of error states and (incoming and outgoing) error propagations. Error states are employed to represent the current configuration of the component with respect to the occurrence of errors. Error propagations are used to exchange error information between components. An error model *implementation* provides the structural details of the error model. It is defined by a (probabilistic) machine over the error states declared in the error model type. Transitions between states can be triggered by error events, **reset** events, and error propagations. Error events are internal to the component; they reflect changes of the error state caused by local faults and repair operations, and they can be annotated with occurrence distributions to model probabilistic error behavior. Moreover, **reset** events can be sent from the nominal model to the error model of the same component, trying to repair a fault which has occurred. Outgoing error propagations report an error state to other components. If their error states are affected, the other components will have a corresponding incoming propagation. An error effect is specified by expressions that overload the nominal assignments when the error occurs. Fig. 3 presents a simple error model for the battery device. It introduces a probabilistic error event, `fault`, which is assumed to occur once every 1000 time units on average.

```
system PowerSystem
  features
    voltage: out data port real;
    alarm: out data port bool initially false observable;
end PowerSystem;

system implementation PowerSystem.Imp
  subcomponents
    pow: system Power.Imp;
  connections
    data port pow.voltage -> voltage;
  modes
    normal: initial mode;
    critical: mode;
  transitions
    normal -[when voltage < 4.5 then alarm:=true]-> critical;
    critical -[when voltage > 5.5 then alarm:=false]-> normal;
end PowerSystem.Imp;
```

Fig. 4. The Complete Power System with an Alarm

Whenever this happens, the error model changes into the dead state, that could for instance be associated with voltage being constantly 0.0.

2.3 Specifying Observability

In order to enable modeling of partial observability, the SLIM language allows the specifier to explicitly define the set of observables. For instance, in the battery example, we may assume that the output voltage of the power system is observable, whereas the internal status of the batteries and the occurrence of faults is not. Fig. 4 shows an example in which an alarm, modeled as an observable Boolean output signal, is raised whenever the voltage is lower than 4.5 volts. Once raised, the alarm is deactivated if the voltage increases to 5.5 volts.

2.4 Formal Semantics

To enable trustworthy modeling and analysis of systems, our SLIM language is equipped with a formal semantics (see [7]) that provides the interpretation of SLIM specifications in a precise and unambiguous manner. The semantics has been designed in such a way to conform to the environment described in [3], which encompasses different aspects of the development of reactive systems, from functional verification to safety analysis, dependability and diagnosability, within the framework of symbolic model checking.

The semantics of a nominal specification is defined on two levels, distinguishing between the local behavior of an active component and the interaction between active components via ports and connections. This interaction is highly dynamic as local transitions can cause subcomponents to become (in-)active, and can change the topology of event and data port connections. On the level of the formal model this means that both the activation status of components and their interconnection relation depend on the modes of the components.

When it comes to integrating faulty system behavior, first the association between nominal and error models has to be specified. In the example above, e.g., one would connect (every instance of) the `Battery` device to the `BatteryFailure` error model. The occurrence of an error event, or a propagation in an error model implementation, indicates a (local, respectively global) fault, and generally causes the transition to a new error state. *Failure effects* can be attached to error states in order to specify the impact of a fault to the nominal behavior of that component. Every such effect is defined by a list of assignments to the component's data elements that overrides the nominal transition effects in the presence of an error. In the case of the battery example, one could reset the `voltage` level to zero while being in error state `dead`.

The actual integration of the nominal and the error model, the so-called *(fault) model extension*, works similarly to the procedure described in [8]. It takes the nominal model and enriches it by the error model specification, thus producing an integrated model which represents both the nominal and the failure behavior. Informally, this model is obtained as follows. Its modes are pairs of nominal modes and error model states. The set of event ports is obtained by adding the error propagations to the original event ports, in order to represent the exchange of error information via propagations as event communication. Correspondingly, the set of event port connections has to be extended by propagation port connections. Finally, in the mode transition relation of the integrated model, all possible interleavings and interactions between the nominal and the error model have to be considered.

2.5   Comparison with AADL

The SLIM language covers a significant subset of AADL. Many features of AADL have been omitted (such as properties, extensions, prototypes, and flow specifications), and the set of available component categories has been reduced. Also some "mixed" concepts (such as **event data** ports or **in out** ports) have been omitted to simplify the implementation. There are, however, some extensions that have been introduced in our language to support the description of dynamic system behavior.

- Initialization values for data ports and data components have been added.
- To support mode history, **initial** and **activation** modes are distinguished. This allows to express that after a re-activation of a component due to a system reconfiguration, the component should resume its operation in the state in which it had previously been deactivated.
- Explicit binding relations between subcomponents (**stored in**, **running on**, **accesses**) have been introduced.
- To support the specification of timed and hybrid behavior, mode invariants (**while**), transition guards (**when**) and transition effects (**then**) have been added (similarly to the AADL Behavior Annex).

From the semantical perspective, as a difference with AADL, which supports asynchronous communication via event queues, the SLIM language is based on (possibly multi-way) *synchronous* event communication.

3   Analyzing System Specifications

In this section we discuss the main analysis capabilities of the COMPASS approach. The available functionalities are summarized by the use case diagram in Fig. 5.

3.1   Property Specification and Validation

Formal properties are increasingly being used to describe the qualitative and the quantitative requirements of electronic designs. These properties are used both for verification and as a means to describe the requirements for a system before it is built. The use of a formal language to state formal properties is a first and substantial step towards a high quality specification, as it makes subtle questions explicit that otherwise might be hidden in the ambiguity of natural language.

Within the COMPASS project, we use temporal logic properties to describe both the qualitative and the quantitative properties the system under analysis has to satisfy. Linear Temporal Logic (LTL) [28] and Computational Tree Logic [13] are used to express qualitative properties. Probabilistic Computation Tree Logic (PCTL) [21] and Continuous Stochastic Logic (CSL) [2] are used to express quantitative properties. The definition of properties from non expert users can be facilitated by the use of property patterns [17].

The COMPASS approach supports property validation, to check correctness and completeness of a set of properties [27]. First, it allows to check for *logical*

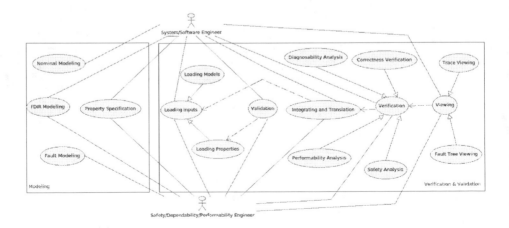

Fig. 5. Functionalities of the COMPASS approach

consistency. Logical consistency can be intuitively defined as "freedom from contradictions": in fact it is possible that two properties mandate mutually incompatible behaviors. Consistency checking of temporal properties can be carried out by dedicated formal verification algorithms [11].

Second, it is possible to check the set of properties is *strict enough* to rule out unwanted behavior and that it is *not too strict* to disallow for certain desirable behavior. Checking that the properties are not too strict amounts to verifying whether a set of conditions (also called a scenario) is possible, given the constraints imposed by the considered set of properties. If the scenario is possible, we obtain a behavior trace compatible with both the properties and the constraint describing the scenarios. Otherwise, we obtain a subset of the considered set of properties that prevents the scenario to happen. Checking that the properties are strict enough to rule out unwanted behavior amounts to verifying whether an expected property (describing the desired behaviors) is implied by the considered set of properties. This check is similar in spirit to model checking [15], with the considered set of properties playing the role of the model. When the property is not implied by the specification, a counterexample, witnessing the violation of the property, is produced.

3.2 Verification of Functional Properties

A SLIM model can be evaluated using model checking techniques, in order to guarantee that it satisfies the required functional properties. To this aim, the model can be translated into a Labeled Transition System (LTS) and exhaustively analyzed by the model checker to check whether the properties hold. If a property does not hold, a counterexample trace can be generated to show an execution trace of the model that violates the property. To cope with the state explosion problem, advanced techniques can be applied, in particular symbolic techniques based on Binary Decision Diagrams (BDD) [9] and SAT-based Bounded Model Checking [4,5,22,18] (BMC). Verification can also benefit from advanced techniques for compiling temporal properties into a symbolic LTS [12].

In order to deal with the timed and hybrid domain (i.e., SLIM models containing integers and reals), standard symbolic model checking techniques cannot be applied. The most noticeable approach is Counterexample Based Abstraction Refinement [14] (CEGAR). Here, a property is verified in an abstraction of the original model. If verification is not conclusive, the abstraction can be automatically refined, based on analysis of the trace generated by the model checker, and the verification process is iterated. Advanced techniques for computing and refining the abstraction include techniques based on the emerging technology of Satisfiability Modulo Theory (SMT) [10]. Similar techniques can also be exploited in BMC. All these techniques have been incorporated into the NuSMV [26] model checker.

3.3 Verification of Safety/Dependability Aspects

The COMPASS methodology can be used to produce artifacts and support activities that are specific of safety assessment, such as techniques for hazard analysis.

The use of formal techniques for such activities is relatively new. The COM-PASS methodology relies on the seminal work carried out within the ESACS[2] (Enhanced Safety Assessment for Complex Systems) and ISAAC[3] (Improvement of Safety Activities on Aeronautical Complex systems) projects, two European-Union-sponsored projects involving various research centers and industries from the avionics sector, and that resulted in the FSAP tool[19]. As advocated in [8], an essential step of the methodology is the decoupling between the nominal behavior and the faulty behavior of the system, that is realized by means of the model-extension step (cf. Section 2.4).

The COMPASS methodology supports two of the most popular hazard anal-ysis techniques, that is, Failure Mode and Effects Analysis (FMEA) and Fault Tree Analysis (FTA). FMEA uses an inductive approach; it starts by consid-ering the initiating causes of a given hazard, and traces them forward to the corresponding safety consequences. FTA, on the other hand, is a deductive tech-nique; it starts by considering an unintended behavior of the system at hand, and traces it, in a backward reasoning fashion, to the corresponding causes. The COMPASS methodology can automatically generate (dynamic) fault trees [16,24], given an extended model and a property representing the hazard. Fur-thermore, (dynamic) FMEA tables can be automatically generated, given a set of failure modes (more in general, a set of fault configurations, which may include combinations of different faults) and a set of properties. Finally, it is possible to compute a criticality measure, which combines probability of occurrence and severity of the consequences.

3.4   Diagnosability Analysis

The COMPASS toolset support diagnosability analysis and FDIR (Fault Detec-tion, Isolation and Recovery). These analyses are based on the notion of *observ-ables* in the input model. In particular, fault detection analysis checks whether an observation can be considered a *fault detection means* for a given fault, that is, every occurrence of the fault eventually causes the observable to be true. All such observables are reported as possible detection means. Fault isolation analy-sis generates fault isolation measures, namely, for each of the observables, it gen-erates a fault tree that contains the minimal explanations that are compatible with the observable being true (the fault tree contains one cut set consisting of a single fault, in case of perfect isolation). Finally, fault recovery verifies whether a user-defined recoverability property is satisfied. The COMPASS toolset can also check whether a system is diagnosable with respect to a diagnosability property, and synthesize a set of observables that ensure diagnosability.

3.5   Quantitative Analyses

To guarantee the required performance, a SLIM model can be evaluated using probabilistic model checking techniques [2]. Prior to this, the user has to specify

---

[2] http://www.esacs.org
[3] http://www.cert.fr/isaac

the formal performance requirements through PCTL or CSL properties: e.g. the system under degradation always has to recover within 40 time units with a probability of 0.98; or, that in the long run, the system will be down with a probability of 0.005. To check whether the SLIM model meets these requirements, it has to be transformed into its underlying Markov chain through probabilistic information captured by the occurrences definitions in the error models. The Markov Reward Model Checker [23] (MRMC) can then be used to evaluate whether the Markov chain meets the expressed performance requirements.

The same probabilistic model checking techniques are used for computing the probability of the top-level event in fault trees. They can be extended to computing probabilities for dynamic fault trees [6]. Akin to checking the correctness of FDIR measures, we use the same probabilistic techniques to evaluate FDIR performance. For example, in addition to checking whether a fault is detected or not, we compute the probability of detection; in case of fault recovery, we compute the probability that the system will recover from a fault.

Finally, it is possible to analyze the timing behaviour of a SLIM model, like for example whether the system will correctly reset a valve between 20 and 30 minutes. Clock invariants, constraints and resets expressed in the SLIM models are used for this. Drafting the transformations from these timing constructs to the underlying formal model, timed automata [1], is still work in progress.

4   Tool Support

The activities described in the previous sections are supported by an integrated platform, which incorporates extensions of existing tools in a uniform environment. Verification and validation functionalities of the toolset are based on symbolic model checking techniques. In particular, the tool set builds upon the NuSMV [26] symbolic model checker, the MRMC [25] probabilistic model checker, and the RAT [29] requirements analysis tool. The architecture of the tool set is shown in Fig. 6.

The toolset takes as input a model written in the SLIM language, and a set of property patterns [17,20]. It generates several artifacts as output, among them: traces resulting either from simulation of the SLIM specification or as counterexample for properties not satisfied by the specification; (probabilistic) Fault Trees and FMEA tables; diagnosability and performability measures.

In order to perform all the verification activities, the SLIM high-level specification is parsed and an internal representation of the input files and a symbol table are constructed. Depending on the specific verification task to be run, different transformations of the input files are then possible, and realized by the building blocks shown in Fig. 6. The ModelExtension block takes care of performing model extension, when required. It generates as output another SLIM model with probabilistic annotations (if any) that represent the faulty system. The Slim2SMV translator is used to translate a SLIM specification into a semantically-equivalent SMV file, which can be used for all NuSMV-based analyses, and to produce separate probabilistic information (if any). The safety analysis activities are performed by FSAP[19], which has been integrated within NuSMV. The SMV file

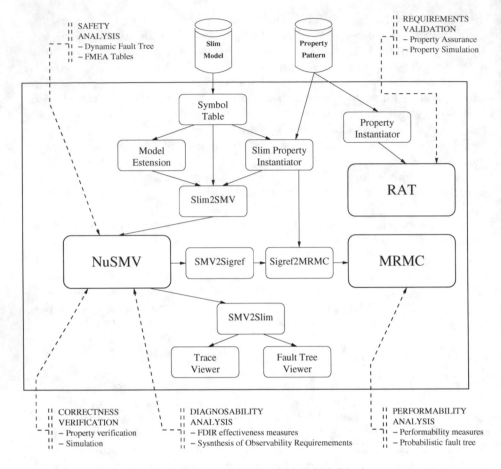

Fig. 6. Architecture of the COMPASS Platform

and the probabilistic information are used by the SMV2Sigref and Sigref2MRMC blocks, that collaborate to transform an SMV file into an equivalent input file for MRMC (the latter also contains probabilistic information), which can be used for all MRMC-based activities. Property patterns are used to create formal properties [17,20]. These properties are processed either by the Slim Property Instantiator, and then converted into SMV or MRMC format, or by the Property Instantiator, that transforms them into RAT format for requirements validation. Finally, the block SMV2Slim converts the results of the analyses back from the internal tools' format into SLIM format, which can be processed by the visualizers, namely graphical fault tree and trace viewers.

5   Conclusions and Future Work

In this paper, we presented a comprehensive, end to end methodology for the design of complex systems. The approach covers all possible user queries in a unique methodology, and it is formally well founded. It includes in a unique, clear formal framework, a number of analyses, and has a full-fledged support by the integration of several state of the art verification tools.

An industrial evaluation of the methodology on realistic case studies is currently ongoing within the COMPASS project. This will provide substantial insights on the applicability of the proposed methodology and the effectiveness of the tool chain. Of particular interest is the verification of reactive systems modeling continuous dynamics. In the future, we plan to systematically investigate the combination of symbolic model checking techniques for the effective construction of the state space to scale up quantitative and probabilistic analyses.

Acknowledgments

We wish to acknowledge and give special thanks to Benedikt Brütsch, Roberto Cavada, Christian Dehnert, Friedrich Gretz and Andrei Tchaltsev, that assisted us by programming a great part of the developed toolset and actively participated to the fruitful discussions that came along the way when we stumbled upon technical issues.

References

1. Audemard, G., Cimatti, A., Kornilowicz, A., Sebastiani, R.: Bounded Model Checking for Timed Systems. In: Peled, D.A., Vardi, M.Y. (eds.) FORTE 2002. LNCS, vol. 2529. Springer, Heidelberg (2002)
2. Baier, C., Haverkort, B., Hermanns, H., Katoen, J.-P.: Model-checking algorithms for continuous-time Markov chains. IEEE TSE 29(6), 524–541 (2003)
3. Bertoli, P., Bozzano, M., Cimatti, A.: A Symbolic Model Checking Framework for Safety Analysis, Diagnosis, and Synthesis. In: Edelkamp, S., Lomuscio, A. (eds.) MoChArt IV. LNCS (LNAI), vol. 4428, pp. 1–18. Springer, Heidelberg (2007)
4. Biere, A., Cimatti, A., Clarke, E., Zhu, Y.: Symbolic Model Checking without BDDs. In: Cleaveland, W.R. (ed.) TACAS 1999. LNCS, vol. 1579, pp. 193–207. Springer, Heidelberg (1999)
5. Biere, A., Heljanko, K., Junttila, T.A., Latvala, T., Schuppan, V.: Linear encodings of bounded LTL model checking. Logical Methods in Comp. Sc. 2(5) (2006)
6. Boudali, H., Crouzen, P., Stoelinga, M.: Dynamic fault tree analysis using input/output interactive Markov chains. In: DSN, pp. 708–717. IEEE, Los Alamitos (2007)
7. Bozzano, M., Cimatti, A., Nguyen, V.Y., Noll, T., Katoen, J.P., Roveri, M.: Codesign of Dependable Systems: A Component-Based Modeling Language. In: Proc. MEMOCODE 2009 (2009)
8. Bozzano, M., Villafiorita, A.: The FSAP/NuSMV-SA Safety Analysis Platform. International Journal on Software Tools for Technology Transfer 9(1), 5–24 (2007)
9. Bryant, R.: Symbolic Boolean Manipulation with Ordered Binary Decision Diagrams. ACM Computing Surveys 24(3), 293–318 (1992)
10. Cavada, R., Cimatti, A., Franzén, A., Kalyanasundaram, K., Roveri, M., Shyamasundar, R.K.: Computing Predicate Abstractions by Integrating BDDs and SMT Solvers. In: Proc. FMCAD, pp. 69–76. IEEE Computer Society, Los Alamitos (2007)

11. Cimatti, A., Roveri, M., Schuppan, V., Tonetta, S.: Boolean abstraction for temporal logic satisfiability. In: Damm, W., Hermanns, H. (eds.) CAV 2007. LNCS, vol. 4590, pp. 532–546. Springer, Heidelberg (2007)

12. Cimatti, A., Roveri, M., Tonetta, S.: Symbolic Compilation of PSL. IEEE Trans. on CAD of Integrated Circuits and Systems 27(10), 1737–1750 (2008)

13. Clarke, E., Emerson, E., Sistla, A.: Automatic verification of finite-state concurrent systems using temporal logic specifications. ACM Transactions on Programming Languages and Systems 8(2), 244–263 (1986)

14. Clarke, E., Grumberg, O., Jha, S., Lua, Y., Veith, H.: Counterexample-guided abstraction refinement for symbolic model checking. JACM, 752–794 (2003)

15. Clarke, E., Grumberg, O., Peled, D.: Model Checking. MIT Press, Cambridge (2000)

16. Dugan, J., Bavuso, S., Boyd, M.: Dynamic fault-tree models for fault-tolerant computer systems. IEEE Transactions on Reliability 41(3), 363–377 (1992)

17. Dwyer, M., Avrunin, G., Corbett, J.: Patterns in property specifications for finite-state verification. In: Proc. ICSE, pp. 411–420. IEEE, Los Alamitos (1999)

18. Eén, N., Sörensson, N.: Temporal induction by incremental SAT solving. Electronic Notes in Theoretical Computer Science 89(4) (2003)

19. The FSAP/NuSMV-SA platform, http://sra.itc.it/tools/FSAP

20. Grunske, L.: Specification patterns for probabilistic quality properties. In: ICSE 2008: Proceedings of the 30th international conference on Software engineering, pp. 31–40. ACM, New York (2008)

21. Hansson, H., Jonsson, B.: A logic for reasoning about time and reliability. Formal Aspects of Computing 6(5), 512–535 (1994)

22. Heljanko, K., Junttila, T.A., Latvala, T.: Incremental and complete bounded model checking for full PLTL. In: Etessami, K., Rajamani, S.K. (eds.) CAV 2005. LNCS, vol. 3576, pp. 98–111. Springer, Heidelberg (2005)

23. Katoen, J.-P., Khattri, M., Zapreev, I.: A Markov reward model checker. In: QEST, pp. 243–244. IEEE CS, Los Alamitos (2005)

24. Manian, R., Dugan, J., Coppit, D., Sullivan, K.: Combining Various Solution Techniques for Dynamic Fault Tree Analysis of Computer Systems. In: Proc. High-Assurance Systems Engineering Symposium (HASE 1998), pp. 21–28. IEEE Computer Society Press, Los Alamitos (1998)

25. The MRMC model checker, http://wwwhome.cs.utwente.nl/~zapreevis/mrmc/

26. The NuSMV model checker, http://nusmv.itc.it

27. Pill, I., Semprini, S., Cavada, R., Roveri, M., Bloem, R., Cimatti, A.: Formal analysis of hardware requirements. In: Proc. DAC, pp. 821–826. ACM, New York (2006)

28. Pnueli, A.: A temporal logic of concurrent programs. Th. Comp. Sc. 13, 45–60 (1981)

29. RAT: Requirements Analysis Tool, http://rat.itc.it

30. Architecture Analysis and Design Language (AADL) V2. SAE Draft Standard AS5506 V2, International Society of Automotive Engineers (March 2008)

31. Sigref — A Symbolic Bisimulation Tool, http://sigref.gforge.avacs.org/

Formal Verification of a Microkernel Used in Dependable Software Systems*

Christoph Baumann[1], Bernhard Beckert[2], Holger Blasum[3],
and Thorsten Bormer[2]

[1] Saarland University, Dept. of Computer Science, Saarbrücken, Germany
[2] University of Koblenz, Dept. of Computer Science, Germany
[3] SYSGO AG, Klein-Winternheim, Germany

Abstract. In recent years, deductive program verification has improved to a degree that makes it feasible for real-world programs. Following this observation, the main goal of the BMBF-supported Verisoft XT project is (a) the creation of methods and tools which allow the pervasive formal verification of integrated computer systems, and (b) the prototypical realization of four concrete, industrial application tasks.

In this paper, we report on the Verisoft XT subproject Avionics, where formal verification is being applied to a commercial embedded operating system. The goal is to use deductive techniques to verify functional correctness of the PikeOS system, which is a microkernel-based partitioning hypervisor.

We present our approach to verifying the microkernel's system calls, using a system call for changing the priority of threads as an example. In particular, (a) we give an overview of the tool chain and the verification methodology, (b) we explain the hardware model and how assembly semantics is specified so that functions whose implementation contain assembly can be verified, and (c) we describe the verification of the system call itself.

1 Introduction

Background. As correctness of the built-in operating system is a crucial requirement for the reliability of safety- and security-critical systems, the goal of the Verisoft XT (see http://www.verisoftxt.de/) Avionics subproject is to prove functional correctness of the microkernel in the partitioning hypervisor PikeOS, a commercial operating system for embedded systems [3].

For verification, we use tools like VCC (the Verifying C Compiler [7]) developed by Microsoft Research, which follows the verifying compiler paradigm, i.e., when all specifications and other required information have been added as annotations to the source code (which is the actual user effort required), the tool verifies the code automatically. First experiences with this verification paradigm and the new tool are described in this paper.

---

* Work partially funded by the German Federal Ministry of Education and Research (BMBF) in the framework of the Verisoft XT project under grant 01 IS 07 008. The responsibility for this article lies with the authors.

B. Buth, G. Rabe, T. Seyfarth (Eds.): SAFECOMP 2009, LNCS 5775, pp. 187–200, 2009.
© Springer-Verlag Berlin Heidelberg 2009

This Paper. In Section 2, we describe the PikeOS system and motivate why the particular system at hand is a suitable target for deductive program verification. Then, in Section 3, we give an overview of the tool chain and the verification methodology used in the Verisoft XT Avionics project.

The goal of the project is the full functional verification of all system calls of PikeOS (i.e., the functionality that the kernel provides to guest systems). In this paper, we present our approach to verifying system calls using a system call for changing the priority of threads as an example. While this particular call has a simple functionality, its execution spans all levels of the PikeOS microkernel, from hardware-related levels to high-level kernel functionality. Using this example, we first give a detailed account of how we handle (inline) assembly code blocks, which are needed to access hardware functionality that is not visible in plain C. We picture how the PowerPC assembly language semantics can be specified, such that its functionality and especially its interaction with the C state can be verified (Sect. 4). Then, in Section 5 we use the same example to show how the system call has been specified and proved to be functionally correct using the VCC tool.

The same approach is being applied to verify system calls with more complex functionality that still span the same levels in the kernel as a call with simple functionality.

Related Work. The Avionics subproject of Verisoft XT builds upon previous work in the precursor project Verisoft, where the pervasive verification of an academic microkernel written in the C0 dialect of C and running on verified DLX hardware was undertaken [11]. Within Verisoft XT, in another subproject, the European Microsoft Innovation Center, DFKI and Saarland Univ. are verifying Microsoft's Hyper-V hypervisor [5].

Related work in kernel verification was already done in the '70s and '80s in the projects UCLA Secure Unix and KIT and more recently at the Universities of Dresden and Nijmegen (VFiasco project) and in the EROS/Coyotos project. An overview and comparison of these and other related projects is given in [13]. A current project in kernel verification is L4.verified at NICTA (Australia) [14].

2   Features of the PikeOS Hypervisor

PikeOS (see http://www.pikeos.com/) consists of a microkernel acting as paravirtualizing hypervisor and a system software component. The PikeOS *kernel* is particularly tailored to the context of embedded systems, featuring real-time functionality and orthogonal partitioning of resources such as processor time, user address space memory and kernel resources. The PikeOS *system software* component is responsible for system configuration. Thus the allocation of resources can be bound at compile-time, for example to conform to partitioning requirements in an Integrated Modular Avionics [1,18] or in an automotive [17] virtualization context. At the kernel level, the mechanisms for communication between threads are IPC, events, and shared memory. High-level communication concepts such as Integrated Modular Avionics ARINC ports can be mapped onto

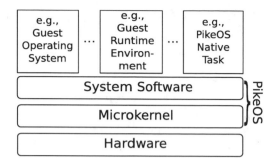

Fig. 1. Exemplary structure of a running PikeOS system

these kernel-level mechanisms. For a thorough discussion of PikeOS and its evolution, see [12]. For an exemplary deployment of a running PikeOS system see Fig. 1. For concrete examples we refer to [20], e.g. one can run a Linux system in one partition and (in avionics contexts) an ARINC-653 application or (in traffic control contexts) a POSIX or Java runtime-environment in another.

Most parts of the PikeOS kernel, especially those that are generic, are written in C, while other parts that are close to the hardware are necessarily implemented in assembly. PikeOS runs on many platforms, including x86, PowerPC, MIPS, and ARM among others and the exact amount of assembly depends on the architecture one works on. The verification target we have chosen for our project, is the PikeOS version for the PowerPC processor family, the OEA architecture, and the MPC5200 platform [10], a single processor setup. In this particular case, PowerPC assembly is about one tenth of the codebase.

3   Verification Methodology and Toolchain

The Verifying C Compiler. In the verifying compiler approach, to check whether a program to be verified performs according to its low-level formal specification, a logical formula is automatically generated from the source of the program and the specification. This formula, called *verification condition*, is rendered in predicate logic and has the property that, if it is valid, then the program is correct w.r.t. its specification. Finding a proof for the validity of this formula, which would serve as a witness for the correctness of the program, is then a task to be solved by a theorem proving system.

Within our Verisoft XT subproject, we use the Verifying C Compiler (VCC) developed by Microsoft Research [7]. VCC uses a specification language tailored to C, which allows a verification engineer to write the specification in a way close to the syntax and semantics of the programming language. In addition, this specification is transparent to the normal C compilation process.

In the case of VCC, the verification condition generation is preceded by an intermediate step, the compilation of the program into an imperative programming language called BoogiePL [9]. This representation is further transformed into first-order predicate logic formulas, which are in turn given to the automatic theorem prover Z3 [8] for verification.

The possible results Z3 may return are: (1) a proof for the validity of the formulas. (2) a counter-example. (3) Z3 runs out of resources (time or space). In Case (1) above, the program verification was successful. In Cases (2) and (3), the verification engineer has to analyze the problem and correct the error. In Case (3), he/she may also find that the program indeed satisfies the annotations. Then new annotations (stronger invariants, helpful lemmas, etc.) have to be added. This process is repeated until Z3 finds a proof.

Specification Language. Below, we give an overview of VCC's specification language, as far as necessary for the examples used throughout this paper.

Annotations, Implementation Variables and Ghost Variables. Annotations are written in the form `keyword`(block) where `keyword` gives the specification constraint to be enforced. In a block, the verification engineer writes (depending on the `keyword`) an expression or statements (statements again may contain expressions). Expressions are written in a C-like syntax and may use implementation variables. They also may use object variables that are not part of the implementation state (called "ghost variables"). Declarations of ghost variables are guarded by `spec()`, and statements changing values of ghost variables are guarded by `speconly()`. Expressions in annotations also may use implementation variables and ghost variables simultaneously. Note that annotations must not affect the actual behavior of the program.

Object Invariants and Ownership. One way to capture global properties of a software system is to define invariants for data structures (i.e., `struct`s in the case of C) used in the program. With VCC, such invariants can be given by annotating a `struct` with (arbitrarily many) `invariant` clauses. To enable modular reasoning about properties of complex data structures (e.g., pointer structures or nested `struct`s), and to capture relations between data structures, the concept of *ownership* between structured data is used (VCC's ownership model is an extension of the one used in the Spec# methodology [15]). Every `struct` has exactly one "owner" and can itself own arbitrarily many structures. At the top of the ownership hierarchy, `struct`s can be owned by executing threads. The ownership relation is provided explicitly in annotations by the verification engineer, and it reflects his/her abstract knowledge about the data structure and how it is used.

It would not be efficient to always check all invariants on all data structures. Hence, a data object can have two states, `open` and `closed`. The convention is that a thread only may change objects it owns and that it may force a check on all invariants by `wrapping` an object, that is by moving it from `open` to `closed`. Ignoring volatile variables, a property that VCC enforces in verification is that members of a closed `struct` cannot be modified by the program. In addition, if an object is closed, its invariants are guaranteed to hold. That is relevant in a concurrent setting when a context switch may occur.

Function Pre- and Postconditions. The specification of a C function in the sequential context can be seen as a contract between the caller of the function and the function itself and is given by pre- and postconditions. These are inserted between the function head and the function body. The precondition of a function is labeled with the keyword `requires`, and the postcondition is labeled with `ensures`. The keyword `result` represents the return value of the function. In the examples of the following sections, the reader will also encounter ownership relations asserted at the function level.

Further Specification Constructs. For convenience, `maintains` can be used for a property that a function both `requires` and `ensures`. `writes` can be used to denote the set of memory locations to which a function (at most) writes. `returns` is shorthand for `ensures` on a `result`. Objects that are typed and owned by the current thread are called `wrapped`, if they are closed and otherwise called `mutable` if they are open, which means that they may be modified. `keeps` denotes that an object owns a certain set of objects only (and nothing else).

Guidance for the Automatic Proving Engine. The verification engineer may have to give some hints to the prover: this is achieved by, e.g. `bv_lemma` for bitvector related lemmas or `assert` for intermediate assertions to be enforced. Such annotations are in some cases excluded from the listings for clarity.

4   Verification of Assembly Code and Low-Level Functions

Unlike ordinary C programs real-world microkernels contain a high percentage of assembly code. It may be found in separate assembly files (macro assembly) or be inlined into the C code using the `__asm__` keyword. Moreover, this code uses privileged mode instructions which are commonly neglected in formal definitions of instruction set semantics for user space programs [2,4]. Because of the ubiquity of assembly language in the near-hardware layers of PikeOS, we have to define a hardware model that allows verifying the functionality of machine instructions with VCC. In this paper we especially focus on the inline assembly portions, where C and hardware semantics are mixed and data is interchanged between the models. To our best knowledge only the Verisoft project [11,19] achieved substantial progress in this specific field. However our approach is different in that we chose an industrial microprocessor (Freescale MPC5200) as the target architecture and we employ a real-world optimizing compiler (GNU C compiler). Although we lack formal semantics for the latter one, in some places (e.g. inline assembly, memory and branch instructions) we have to simulate the behavior of the compiler assuming its correctness, e.g. its adherence to the ABI.

In the following, we introduce our approach to model the hardware and the semantics of assembly instructions. Furthermore we exemplify how this methodology is applied to actual PikeOS functions in the second part of this section.

4.1   Defining the Semantics of Privileged Mode PowerPC Assembly

We establish the semantics of assembly instructions as a transition relation in the set of hardware configurations. First we have to make an abstraction and identify the hardware components that must be represented. Then the effect of each PowerPC instruction can be stated by writing a specification function which reflects the corresponding impact on the hardware configuration.

Modeling Hardware Components in the Global PowerPC Ghost State.
The PowerPC core of the MPC5200 microprocessor comprises a variety of different components, such as general purpose registers (GPRs), special purpose registers and other user and system registers, caches, translation look-aside buffers (TLBs). Also the physical memory must be taken into consideration. When building a hardware model for a modern processor on the C level, several questions arise.

Where is the model defined and how does it interact with the kernel implementation? There are in fact several ways to implement the model and each has its assets and drawbacks. We decided to keep the whole hardware model in the specification-only ghost state. At first sight, with this approach one would face the problem to transfer data between the hardware ghost state and the C state, which VCC forbids. However, one can circumvent this issue via axiomatic specification functions that indirectly "assign" some value to a C variable by assuming their equality as a postcondition (cf. `PPC_assign` in Sect. 4.2).

Following these thoughts we defined the global hardware configuration `PPC_c` in ghost state, which then can be modified by assembly instructions only

As C code runs on the underlying hardware, how can these effects be captured? Basically this is impossible as there is no formal C and compiler semantics available to project the execution of C statements to the machine level. Hence we simply divide the hardware components into those that are not changed by C statements (like system and special purpose registers) and those that are affected by the execution of C (basically the user-visible registers). The former ones are comprised in the `PPC_c` structure while the latter ones only become visible as local variables in the context of assembly code. Such code is either encapsulated in external assembly functions or in inline assembly blocks which have their own interface with the C environment. Thus general purpose registers in the assembly context in general only depend on the effects of preceding C statements in a few defined cases (e.g. parameter passing). However, if the programmer applies knowledge about the C and compiler internals and assumes certain properties about globally invisible components, they must be initialized accordingly at the beginning of the assembly block, assuming compiler correctness.

How do we model caches, TLBs and the physical memory? In a single-processor setting caches and TLBs (which are in fact also just caches for page address translations) are invisible to the programmer under certain realistic assumptions. Therefore we do not need to model caches and TLBs. However, separate proofs to validate these claims are in order. As we are lacking a formal compiler semantics which would define the memory allocation of C variables and code, modeling the complete physical data and instruction memory is also impossible. Therefore memory does not belong to our global hardware model. For memory and branch instructions special measures are taken locally.

Specifying PowerPC Assembly Instructions. Based on the hardware component definitions we can specify the effect of the execution of assembly code. For each instruction we define a specification function which is equipped with pre- and postconditions that reflect the functionality of the particular instruction. For plain register transfer operations this is easy. E.g. there are privileged mode instructions mfmsr and mtmsr, which move GPR contents from resp. to the machine status register (MSR). An extract of the PPC_c definition and the specification function for mfmsr are given below:

```
1 spec( struct PPC_config_struct {        1 spec( void PPC_MFMSR(PPC_B32_t *dest)
2  // exemplary component:                2   maintains(wrapped(&PPC_c))
3  PPC_MSR_t msr; // Machine State Register 3   maintains(mutable(dest))
4  invariant(keeps(&msr)) // ownership inv. 4   writes(dest)
5 } PPC_c; )                               5   ensures( *dest == PPC_c.msr.reg ); )
```

The first two maintains-clauses refer to the memory resp. ownership-model of VCC. The writes-clause specifies that the destination register is written by the instruction. The last line states the postcondition of mfmsr. In this way, most of the PowerPC instructions can be handled. However, for memory and branch instructions there may be access to the kernel and user address spaces, which requires additional handling. How to model these instructions is outside the scope of this paper, though.

Assembly Code Translation. After having defined the hardware configuration and instruction semantics, the remaining question is how to integrate the hardware model into the PikeOS code. As VCC does not recognize assembly code, for verification these commands have to be replaced by the corresponding specification function calls, which then simulate the execution on the model. The assembly instructions can be translated to our specification functions automatically using a parser. Such a parser has already been created for x86 assembly code in the Verisoft XT Microsoft hypervisor (Hyper-V) subproject [16].

The methodology pictured above applies to both the simulation of macro assembly and that of inline assembly code. For the latter purpose additionally an interface between the local C variables and the general purpose registers has to be established. Their relation is specified in the PowerPC ABI [21] and compiler specifics concerning the syntax and semantics of an __asm__ statement. It is concealed which registers are chosen by the compiler to contain the respective data. However, it is not necessary to know the exact distribution of data over the registers. We can just choose any free registers which then have to be initialized with values of the corresponding variables and after execution of the inline assembly block the results are written back.

4.2 Verifying Low-Level PikeOS Functions

To demonstrate our methodology in more detail we will now apply it to two exemplary functions which are called from p4syscall_fast_set_prio, a PikeOS system call to be examined later on. The functions contain inline assembly code, which is translated according to the approach pointed out above. Then we can annotate and automatically verify the translated versions with VCC.

Translation of Inline Assembly Code. Firstly we look at the translation from (inline) assembly language to hardware model functions by examining the first auxiliary function, namely p4arch_disable_int. This function disables the signaling of external interrupts by clearing the corresponding EE bit in the CPU's machine status register (MSR, bit 16). It returns the old value of the MSR. See its code along with the translation result below.

```
1 static inline P4_cpureg_t
    p4arch_disable_int(void)
2 {
3   P4_cpureg_t ret;
4   P4_cpureg_t val;
5   __asm__ ("mfmsr %0" : "=r"(ret));
6   val = ret & ~MSR_EE;
7   __asm__ ("mtmsr %0" : : "r"(val) :
      "memory");
8   return ret;
9 }


1 static inline P4_cpureg_t
    p4arch_disable_int(void)
2 {
3   P4_cpureg_t ret;
4   P4_cpureg_t val;
```

```
5  // inline asm variables and initialization
6  spec(PPC_B32_t gpr[32];) // step 1
7  void * PPC_ret; // step 1

8  // start inline asm block
9  PPC_MFMSR(spec(&gpr[3])); // step 3
10 // end of block, assign return values
11 PPC_assign(spec(&PPC_ret,gpr[3]));//step2
12 ret = (P4_cpureg_t)PPC_ret; // step 2

13 val = ret & ~MSR_EE;

14 // start inline asm block, pass parameters
15 speconly(gpr[4] = val;) // step 2
16 PPC_MTMSR(spec(gpr[4])); // step 3

17 return ret;
18 }
```

The translation is done in three steps and above for each new line there is a label in which step it was produced. Old lines not resulting from the translation are printed in grayish color. Ghost code and ghost variable declarations are included using the **speconly** and **spec** keywords (Sect. 3). Functions and data belonging to the hardware model are indicated by the PPC_ prefix.

At first we define the local specification and temporary variables to establish the hardware context. The second step is only needed for inline assembly as we parse the syntax of the __asm__ statement and extract the corresponding pairs of register aliases and C variables. For each of them a free hardware register is determined according to the ABI and set to the value of the C variable it was allocated to. After the assembly block the results are written back to the variables when necessary. This is achieved by assigning the register values to an intermediate local variable using the specification function PPC_assign.

In the third step the assembly syntax is parsed and the commands are replaced by their hardware model counterparts. Note that the translated version of the code does not overwrite the original functions but is only visible to the compiler when the verification mode is enabled.

Annotation and Verification. Replacing the assembly commands by calls to their representative functions in the hardware model enables us to discuss the functionality of the code. The expected behavior of each function can now be specified by adding annotations and assertions to the code, which are then validated by VCC.

As an example for the verification of function-level annotations and to introduce the counterpart to `p4arch_disable_int`, we examine in the following the method `p4arch_restore_int` which restores the bit MSR.EE from a given value `msr`:

```
1 static inline void                       9  spec(PPC_B32_t gpr[32];)
    p4arch_restore_int(P4_cpureg_t msr)     10 void * PPC_ret;
2 {
3   unsigned ret;                           11 PPC_MFMSR(spec(&gpr[3]));
4   unsigned val;                           12 assert(gpr[3] ==
5   __asm__ ("mfmsr %0" : "=r"(ret));          (P4_cpureg_t)PPC_c.msr.reg);
6   val = ret | (msr & MSR_EE);
7   __asm__ ("mtmsr %0" : : "r"(val) :      13 PPC_assign(spec(&PPC_ret,gpr[3]));
    "memory");                              14 ret = (P4_cpureg_t)PPC_ret;
8 }
                                            15 val = ret | (msr & MSR_EE);

1 static inline void                        16 bv_lemma(forall(unsigned int x,y;
    p4arch_restore_int(P4_cpureg_t msr)     17   (GET_BE(x|(y & MSR_EE),16) ==
2   writes(&PPC_c)                               (GET_BE(x,16)|GET_BE(y,16)))));
3   maintains(wrapped(&PPC_c))              18 bv_lemma(forall(unsigned int x,y;
4   ensures(PPC_c.msr.fld.EE ==             19   (GET_BE(x|(y & MSR_EE),17) ==
    (old(PPC_c.msr.fld.EE)|GET_BE(msr,16)))      GET_BE(x,17))));
5   ensures(PPC_c.msr.fld.PR ==
    old(PPC_c.msr.fld.PR))                  20 speconly(gpr[4] = val;)
6 {                                         21 PPC_MTMSR(spec(gpr[4]));
7   unsigned ret;                           22 }
8   unsigned val;
```

For simplicity, here we concentrate on two properties of the function:
(1) The bit MSR.EE is set to the corresponding bit's value in parameter `msr`.
(2) All other MSR bits (e.g., the current privilege mode MSR.PR) are preserved.

The translated code is shown below with all necessary annotations above as well. The global hardware model is included in the **writes** clause as it is modified by the assembly portions. Using the macro GET_BE we access single bits of the `msr` parameter in big endian order. The **ensures** clauses specify properties of the function as a transition relation between the old (marked `old`) and new state of the data structures (PPC_c in this case). To ease proving the postcondition, intermediate asserts like in line 12 are helpful. Moreover non-linear arithmetic, such as bit vector operations are hard for automated provers. Here VCC offers an extended axiomatization via `bv_lemma`, which introduces and validates bit-vector-related lemmata where they are necessary to verify corresponding C code.

With the few additional assertions as "step stones" for the verification, VCC is able to prove the two postconditions of the function shown above in about 5 seconds on an AMD Athlon 64 X2 Dual Core 4000+ processor. Adding the postconditions and additional annotations for the other 15 relevant MSR bits increases verification time to roughly 9 seconds.

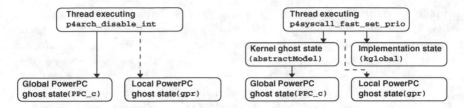

Fig. 2. Verification setups for the exemplarily low-level function `p4arch_disable_int` introduced in Section 4 *(left)* and the entire system call introduced in Section 5 *(right)*. Straight arrows indicate VCC ownership relations (Sect. 3), dashed arrows indicate implicit dependencies.

5   System Call Verification

Below, we show how to verify a PikeOS system call using the hardware model and specifications of low level kernel functions as presented in the previous section.

Verification Setup. Because system calls are at the user's interface to the kernel and the PikeOS system is multi-platform, the kernel's specification has to hide any PowerPC implementation details to ensure proper encapsulation. In our modeling this implies that the abstraction of the kernel's state in ghost state, specified as `abstractModel`, *owns* the PowerPC machine model `PPC_c` as formalized by the invariant `keeps(currentThread, &PPC_c)`. The complete ownership relations of our system call example are shown in the right part of Fig. 2.

```
1 spec( struct absModel_str {
2     bool interruptsEnabled;
3     invariant(interruptsEnabled == (PPC_c.msr.fld.EE == 1))
4     struct P4k_thrinfo_t *currentThread;
5     invariant(keeps(currentThread, &PPC_c))
6     invariant(currentThread != NULL && ...)
7 } abstractModel; )
```

The specifications of the C methods on the upper layers of the kernel, like system calls, can now be written in terms of the elements of the abstract model.

An Exemplary System Call. As a first target for verification we have chosen the system call `p4syscall_fast_set_prio`, which changes the priority of a thread. The parameter `newprio` of the system call may not exceed the user-configured *Maximum Controlled Priority* (MCP).

This call has a rather simple functionality, but it serves very well as an example because its execution spans all levels of the PikeOS microkernel, from high-level kernel functionality to hardware-related levels and the user-level interface (system calls are invoked via user interrupts). Systems calls with more complex functionality still span the same levels.

For verifying the `p4syscall_fast_set_prio` system call, two components of the abstract model are needed, namely `interruptsEnabled`, which indicates whether the system currently allows external interrupts to occur, and a pointer to the thread currently running in kernel mode that is given by `currentThread`. These two elements of the abstract model are related to the underlying hardware and hence its representation as the ghost structure `PPC_c`. This relation is explicitly stated as invariant (`keeps(...)`) of the `abstractModel` data structure.

Whether external interrupts are allowed or disallowed in the kernel is indicated by the field `PPC_c.msr.fld.EE` in the global ghost state model of the PowerPC hardware, as described in Section 4.2. In `abstractModel`, interrupts are defined to be enabled, iff this bit in the hardware model is set to 1, as stated by the invariant in line 3 of the specification of `absModel_str`.

We now consider the actual C and annotation code for the system call under consideration. Setting the new priority values in the data structures of the thread and, for the purpose of faster look-up, in a global info data structure of the kernel (called `kglobal`), is done by the helper function `p4_runner_changeprio`:

```
1  P4_prio_t p4_runner_changeprio(P4k_thrinfo_t *proc, P4_prio_t newprio)
2    writes(&abstractModel, &kglobal)
3    requires(proc == abstractModel.currentThread)
4    maintains(wrapped(&abstractModel) && wrapped(&kglobal))
5    ensures(proc->schedprio == newprio && ...)
6    returns(old(proc->userprio))
7  {
8    P4_prio_t oldprio; P4_cpureg_t oldstat;
9    unwrap(&abstractModel);
10   oldstat = p4arch_disable_int();
11   speconly(abstractModel.interruptsEnabled = 0;)
12   unwrap(proc);
13   oldprio = proc->userprio; proc->userprio = newprio; ...;
14   wrap(proc);
15   ... //update global kernel information
16   p4arch_restore_int(oldstat);
17   speconly(abstractModel.interruptsEnabled = PPC_c.msr.fld.EE;)
18   wrap(&abstractModel);
19   return oldprio;
20 }
```

Firstly, this function disables handling of external interrupts by calling the method `p4arch_disable_int` (line 10), so that from here on concurrency does not need to be considered. Before this, the struct `abstractModel` has to be unwrapped (line 9) because `p4arch_disable_int` writes to the struct `PPC_c`, which is owned by the `abstractModel`.

After `p4arch_disable_int` has set the EE bit of the MSR variable in `PPC_c` to 1, one invariant of `abstractModel` no longer holds. Before `abstractModel` can be wrapped again (line 18), that invariant has to be restored. This is achieved by updating the `interruptsEnabled` flag of `abstractModel` (line 17). After the interrupts are disabled, the different updates on the priority values of the thread and (left out for clarity in the code) kernel information data structure can be performed (lines 12–15). Restoring the interrupt-enabled state (lines 16–17) and returning the old priority of the thread complete this method.

Using VCC it is now possible to prove that the function satisfies its specification given in lines 2–6. For this, in fact, several intermediate assertions before and after calls to helper functions are necessary to let the verification system validate that certain properties have been preserved during method calls (we have omitted these "lemmas" for brevity).

Following our bottom-up approach, we arrive at **p4syscall_fast_set_prio** which calls **p4_runner_changeprio** (see above) among other functions. The implementation of the system call (not shown here), uses the helper methods **p4_runner**, which returns the thread data structure for the current thread, and **p4_runner_changeprio**, which changes the priority values of the thread. The method **p4_runner** is a wrapper for the function **p4arch_runner** which yields the address of the page to which the stack pointer points. The specification of **p4_runner** abstracts from the concrete return value of **p4arch_runner** and instead returns the ghost variable **abstractModel.currentThread**. This abstraction is valid as it is a system invariant that the stack pointer for the kernel stack always points to the page corresponding to the current thread. The thread data structure of the current thread is placed at the beginning of this particular page.

This, finally, allows us to verify the following method contract for our exemplary system call **p4syscall_fast_set_prio**:

```
1 P4_uint32_t p4syscall_fast_set_prio(P4_uint32_t prio)
2   writes(&abstractModel, &kglobal)
3   maintains(wrapped(&abstractModel) && wrapped(&kglobal))
4   ensures(prio <= abstractModel.currentThread->mcprio ?
5           abstractModel.currentThread->schedprio == prio && ...
6         : abstractModel.currentThread->schedprio ==
7           abstractModel.currentThread->mcprio && ... )
```

The postcondition of this method (**ensures** clause in lines 4–7) directly matches the informal specification in the kernel reference manual: "This function sets the current thread's priority to newprio. Invalid or too high priorities are limited to the caller's task MCP. Upon success, a call to this function returns the current thread's priority before setting it to newprio."

Besides this postcondition, the contract specifies that the method is (only) allowed to write to **abstractModel** and **kglobal** (line 2), and that these two data structures are required to be wrapped according to the ownership methodology of VCC before and after the call to the function, i.e., the thread that is currently executing the method is in possession of these data structures, all their non-volatile fields remain unchanged and all their invariants hold.

6   Conclusion

Verification Setup for a System Call. We have presented the use of deductive program verification in the Verisoft XT Avionics subproject. The formalization of PowerPC assembly language semantics enables us to verify kernel functionality spanning all levels of the PikeOS microkernel. In particular, we have shown how interrupts are disabled and then restored again to ensure that the bulk of the system call is in non-concurrent mode. The same approach can be applied to verify system calls with more complex functionality as these still span the same levels in the kernel as a call with simple functionality (this is ongoing work).

Future Work. It is current work to apply the verification approach presented in this paper to all the system calls and interrupt handlers of PikeOS to get a full functional verification of the kernel. In a next step, we will then consider the effects of concurrency when parts of the kernel are executed without disabling of interrupts. Support for verifying concurrency has recently been added to VCC by its developers [6].

Our bottom-up approach is complemented by top-down paper-and-pencil proofs of how partitioning requirements are reflected in the implementation.

Acknowledgments. We are very grateful to Sabine Schmaltz and Matthias Daum (Saarland Univ.) for help and many fruitful discussions, and to Markus Wagner (Univ. of Koblenz) for his work in Verisoft XT Avionics. We also thank Alexander Züpke, Jacques Brygier, Knut Degen, Tobias Stumpf, Stephan Wagner, Michael Werner (SYSGO AG), the Verisoft XT ES.1 group, Mark Hillebrand, Dirk Leinenbach (DFKI), Marko Wolf (escrypt) and the VCC research team at Microsoft Research (EMIC), in particular Markus Dahlweid, Michał Moskal, Thomas Santen, and Stephan Tobies, and the participants of the RTCA SC-205/EUROCAE WG-71 formal methods group meeting (Cologne, Feb 2009).

References

1. Airlines Electronic Engineering Committee. Avionics Application Software Standard Interface. Aeronautical Radio, Inc., 2551 Riva Road, Annapolis, MD 21401, ARINC specification 653 (1997)
2. Alglave, J., et al.: The semantics of Power and ARM multiprocessor machine code. In: DAMP 2009: Proceedings of the 4th Workshop on Declarative Aspects of Multicore Programming, Savannah, GA, USA, pp. 13–24. ACM, New York (2009)
3. Baumann, C., Beckert, B., Blasum, H., Bormer, T.: Better avionics software reliability by code verification. In: Proceedings, embedded world Conference, Nuremberg, Germany (2009)
4. Blazy, S., Dargaye, Z., Leroy, X.: Formal verification of a C compiler front-end. In: Misra, J., Nipkow, T., Sekerinski, E. (eds.) FM 2006. LNCS, vol. 4085, pp. 460–475. Springer, Heidelberg (2006)
5. Cohen, E., Dahlweid, M., Hillebrand, M., Leinenbach, D., Moskal, M., Santen, T., Schulte, W., Tobies, S.: VCC: A practical system for verifying concurrent C. In: Theorem Proving in Higher Order Logics (TPHOLs 2009), Munich, Germany. LNCS, vol. 5674. Springer, Heidelberg (to appear, 2009) (invited paper)
6. Cohen, E., Moskal, M., Schulte, W., Tobies, S.: A practical verification methodology for concurrent programs. Technical Report MSR-TR-2009-15, Microsoft Research (2009), http://research.microsoft.com/vcc
7. Dahlweid, M., Moskal, M., Santen, T., Tobies, S., Schulte, W.: VCC: Contract-based modular verification of concurrent C, http://research.microsoft.com/vcc
8. de Moura, L., Bjørner, N.: Z3: An efficient SMT solver. In: Ramakrishnan, C.R., Rehof, J. (eds.) TACAS 2008. LNCS, vol. 4963, pp. 337–340. Springer, Heidelberg (2008)
9. DeLine, R., Leino, K.R.M.: BoogiePL: A typed procedural language for checking object-oriented programs. Technical Report MSR-TR-2005-70, Microsoft Research (2005)

10. Freescale Semiconductor. MPC5200B User's Manual, Rev. 1.3 (September 2006), http://www.freescale.com/files/32bit/doc/ref_manual/MPC5200BUM.pdf
11. In der Rieden, T., Tsyban, A.: CVM: A verified framework for microkernel programmers. In: Huuck, R., Klein, G., Schlich, B. (eds.) 3rd International Workshop on Systems Software Verification (SSV 2008). ENTCS, vol. 217, pp. 151–168. Elsevier Science B.V, Amsterdam (2008)
12. Kaiser, R., Wagner, S.: Evolution of the PikeOS microkernel. In: Kuz, I., Petters, S.M. (eds.) MIKES: 1st International Workshop on Microkernels for Embedded Systems (2007), http://ertos.nicta.com.au/publications/papers/Kuz_Petters_07.pdf
13. Klein, G.: Operating system verification: An overview. Technical Report NRL-955, NICTA, Sydney, Australia (June 2008), http://wwwbroy.informatik.tu-muenchen.de/~kleing/papers/os-overview.pdf
14. Klein, G., Norrish, M., Elphinstone, K., Heiser, G.: Verifying a high-performance micro-kernel. In: Proceedings, 7th Annual High-Confidence Software and Systems Conf., Baltimore, USA (2007)
15. Leino, K.R.M., Müller, P.: Object invariants in dynamic contexts. In: Odersky, M. (ed.) ECOOP 2004. LNCS, vol. 3086, pp. 491–515. Springer, Heidelberg (2004)
16. Maus, S., Moskal, M., Schulte, W.: Vx86: x86 assembler simulated in C powered by automated theorem proving. In: Meseguer, J., Roşu, G. (eds.) AMAST 2008. LNCS, vol. 5140, pp. 284–298. Springer, Heidelberg (2008)
17. Pelzl, J., Wolf, M., Wollinger, T.: Virtualization technologies for cars: Solutions to increase safety and security of vehicular ECUs. In: Proceedings, embedded world Conference, Nuremberg, Germany (2009)
18. Radio Technical Commission for Aeronautics. Integrated Modular Avionics (IMA) Development Guidance and Certification Considerations. DO-297. Radio Technical Commission for Aeronautics (RTCA), Inc., 1828 L Street NW, Suite 805, Washington, D.C. 20036 (November 2005)
19. Starostin, A., Tsyban, A.: Correct microkernel primitives. In: Huuck, R., Klein, G., Schlich, B. (eds.) 3rd International Workshop on Systems Software Verification (SSV 2008). ENTCS, vol. 217, pp. 169–185. Elsevier Science B. V, Amsterdam (2008)
20. SYSGO AG press releases. PikeOS selected for traffic control system (August 07, 2007), Flight management system will run on SYSGO's PikeOS in the DIANA project (July 17, 2008), AIRBUS selects SYSGO's PikeOS as DO-178B reference platform for the A350 XWB (November 18, 2008), Rheinmetall selects DO178B certifiable PikeOS from SYSGO for A400M project (December 10, 2008), http://www.sysgo.com
21. Zucker, S., Karhi, K.: System V Application Binary Interface: PowerPC Processor Supplement. SunSoft, Mountain View, CA, USA, 802-3334-10 edn. (September 1995), http://refspecs.freestandards.org/elf/elfspec_ppc.pdf

Issues in Tool Qualification for Safety-Critical Hardware: What Formal Approaches Can and Cannot Do

Brian Butka[1], Janusz Zalewski[2], and Andrew J. Kornecki[3]

[1] Electrical Engineering, Embry Riddle Aeronautical Univ., Daytona Beach, FL 32114 USA
butkab@erau.edu
[2] Computer Science, Florida Gulf Coast University, Fort Meyers, FL 33965 USA
zalewski@fgcu.edu
[3] Computer&Software Engineering, Embry-Riddle Aeronautical Univ.,
Daytona Beach, FL 32114 USA
kornecka@erau.edu

Abstract. Technology has improved to the point that system designers have the ability to trade-off implementing complex functions in either hardware or software. However, clear distinctions exist in the design tools. This paper examines what is unique to hardware design, areas where formal methods can be applied to advantage in hardware design and how errors can exist in the hardware even if formal methods are used to prove the design is correct.

Keywords: Tool Qualification, HDL, PLD, Hardware Design, Safety-Critical Systems, Formal Methods.

1 Introduction

Safety-critical applications, such as a modern aircraft use not only increasing numbers of microprocessors and microcontrollers but also dedicated hardware to process the growing amounts of data needed to control the flight and related systems, and monitor their status. Rapid progress of digital technology in the last 25 years can be shown on example from Airbus industries: the increase of number of digital units from 70 to 300, number of transistors from 10^5 to 10^8, and number of gates per chip from ten to 600 thousand [1]. Recent proliferation of custom micro-coded components changed the market and the ways how the industry operates. These complex programmable electronic components are not only programmed using conventional programming languages but their logic designs are also developed by writing code in a Hardware Description Language (HDL) such as VHDL, Verilog, or SystemC. The two distinctive categories of modern electronic components are programmable logic devices (PLD) and application specific integrated circuits (ASIC). PLD is purchased as standard electronic parts and then altered (or programmed) to perform specific function. ASIC is developed using an expensive process of fabrication with the design embedded in the layers of silicon. Once manufactured, ASIC cannot be re-programmed and

B. Buth, G. Rabe, T. Seyfarth (Eds.): SAFECOMP 2009, LNCS 5775, pp. 201–214, 2009.
© Springer-Verlag Berlin Heidelberg 2009

thus it is not a PLD – although the original program for ASIC is developed in HDL, in the same manner as for PLD. The primary and most popular PLD components type are field programmable gate arrays (FPGA), often treated as a separate category. The scope of this research has been limited to tools supporting development of FPGA that have been used, or have a potential to be used, in airborne applications.

Most of these devices can be configured to implement a particular design by downloading a sequence of bits. In that sense, a circuit implemented on programmable logic device is literally software. Software tools are used to simulate the logic, synthesize the circuit, and create the placement and routing for the electronic elements and their connections in preparation for the final implementation, i.e., programming the logic devices, which used to be conventionally called "burning into the logic." The development of hardware relies significantly on the quality of tools, which translate the software artifacts from one form to another. Both software and hardware use extensively very complex tools, i.e., integrated programming environments taking the project from its conceptual stage into the final product. Thus, the quality of such tools is essential for the proper operation of respective products in the real-life environment, especially in safety-critical systems, where computer systems may cause unintended harm to human life or property.

The objective of this work is to analyze the use of software tools in hardware development for safety-critical systems, from the perspective of potential application of formal approaches to improve product quality. The rest of the paper is structured as follows. Section 2 sets the stage for the analysis, providing an overview of a design flow for PLD components, with emphasis on design verification. Section 3 outlines the potential impact of tool quality on product safety, and Section 4 discusses specific hardware issues that can still remain unresolved after formal verification of the design.

2   PLD Design Flow and Formal Approaches

A generic PLD design flow is shown in figure 1. The PLD design process begins by describing the hardware functionality in an HDL. The HDL code can then be simulated to verify correct function at the behavioral level. The synthesis process converts the high-level HDL code into a netlist of interconnected logic functions. The place and route process fits the netlist to the vendor specific hardware architecture of the PLD. The synthesis and place and route processes provide opportunities for errors to be introduced to a logically correct HDL description of a design. In the rest of this section, we review the formal approaches addressing some of these problems from the tools perspective, as well as outline an engineering view based on practical experience with similar issues.

2.1   Review of the Use of Formal Approaches in Hardware Design Tools

A thorough review of literature for the last decade, or so, reveals a number of attempts to formalize reasoning about hardware design, for example [2], with very few of them related to tools. A handful of selected papers are mentioned below, in chronological order. For the purpose of this discussion, we follow the definition of a formal method as given by the NASA Langley Formal Methods Group:

"Formal Methods" refers to mathematically rigorous techniques and tools for the specification, design and verification of software and hardware systems. The phrase "mathematically rigorous" means that the specifications used in formal methods are well-formed statements in a mathematical logic and that the formal verifications are rigorous deductions in that logic (i.e. each step follows from a rule of inference and hence can be checked by a mechanical process.) (http://shemesh.larc.nasa.gov/fm/fm-what.html)

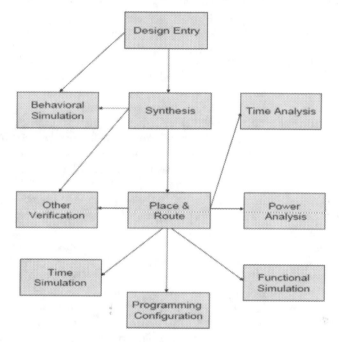

Fig. 1. A generic PLD design flow

In an overview paper [3] Kern and Greenstreet identify two main aspects of the application of formal methods in a hardware design process: (a) the formal framework used to specify desired properties of a design, and (b) the verification techniques and tools used to reason about the relationship between a specification and a corresponding implementation. They survey a variety of frameworks and techniques proposed in the literature as applied to actual designs. The specification frameworks include temporal logic, predicate logic, regular languages, abstraction and refinement. The verification techniques include model checking, automata-theoretic techniques, automated theorem proving, and approaches that integrate the above methods. The paper presents a selection of case studies where formal methods were applied to industrial-scale designs, such as microprocessors, floating-point hardware, protocols, memory subsystems, and communications hardware.

Only relatively recently authors of papers on formal methods began considering tools supporting these approaches. A handful of related papers are discussed below. Turner and He [4] investigate specification, verification and test generation for synchronous and asynchronous circuits. Their approach is based on temporal ordering specification using Digital Logic In LOTOS (DILL). The paper defines relations for strong conformance to verify a design specification against a high-level specification, and describes tools for automated testing and verification of conformance between an implementation and its specification.

Aljer and Devienne [5] consider the use of a formal specification language as the foundation of real validation process. They propose architecture based upon stepwise refinement of a formal model to achieve controllable implementation. Partitioning, fault tolerance, and system management are seen as particular cases of refinement in order to conceptualize systems correct by proven construction. The methodology based on the refinement paradigm is described. To prove this approach, the B-HDL tool based on a combination of VHDL and B method formal language has been developed.

Nehme and Lundqvist [6] describe a framework combining software tools for application verification and hardware platforms for execution and real-time monitoring. The tool translates safety critical VHDL code into a formal representation in a form of finite state machine (FSM) model. Formal techniques can then be applied on FSM representation to verify properties such as liveness and deadlock and to validate that the timing constraints of the original system are met. Three aspects of the tool implementation are discussed: transformation of source code into an intermediate representation, verification of real-time properties, and some tool-related implementation issues.

Dajani-Brown et al. [7] focus on the use of SCADE (Safety Critical Application Development Environment) and its formal verification component, the Design Verifier, to assess the design correctness of a sensor voter algorithm used for management of three redundant sensors. The algorithm, captured as a Simulink diagram, takes input from three sensors and computes an output signal and a hardware flag indicating correctness of the output. Since synthesis of a correct environment for analysis of the voter's normal and off-normal behavior is a key factor when applying formal verification tools, this paper is focused on: 1) approaches used for modeling the voter's environment; and 2) the strengths and shortcomings of such approaches when applied to the discussed problem.

Hilton in his thesis [8] proposes a process for developing a system incorporating both software and PLD, suitable for safety critical systems of the highest levels of integrity. This process incorporates the use of Synchronous Receptive Process Theory as a semantic basis for specifying and proving properties of programs executing on PLD, and extends the use of SPARK Ada to cover the interface between software and programmable logic. The author claims that the demonstrated methods are not only feasible but also scale up to realistic system sizes, allowing development of such safety-critical software-hardware systems to the levels required by current system safety standards.

Finally, with the emergence of the FAA endorsed document DO-254 "Design Assurance Guidance for Airborne Electronic Hardware" [9], more papers began to appear that discuss not only tool support for formal approaches, but also compliance with the DO-254 standard. This is where initial discussions of product or process certification and tool qualification begin to take place.

Dallacherie et al. [10] look at a static formal approach that may be used, in combination with requirements traceability features, in the design and verification of hardware controllers to support such protocols as ARINC 429, ARINC 629, MIL-STD-1553B, etc., with respect to compliance with DO-254. The paper describes the application of a formal tool in the design and verification of airborne electronic hardware developed in a DO-254 context. imPROVE-HDL tool is a formal property checker that complements simulation in performing exhaustive debugging of VHDL/Verilog Register-Transfer-Level hardware models of complex avionics protocol controllers without the need to create testbenches. Another tool, Reqtify, is used to track the requirements and produce coverage reports throughout the verification process. The authors claim that using imPROVE-HDL coupled with Reqtify, avionics hardware designers are assured that their bus controllers meet the most stringent safety guidelines outlined in DO-254.

Karlsson and Forsberg [11] discuss the additional strategies identified in RTCA DO-254 for the highest levels of design assurance (A and B). In particular, the use of formal property specification language (PSL) in combination with dynamic (simulation) and static (formal) verification methods for programmed logic devices are addressed. Using these methods, a design assurance strategy for complex programmable airborne electronics compliant with the guidelines of RTCA DO-254 is suggested. The proposed strategy is a semi-formal solution, a hybrid of static and dynamic assertion based verification. The functional specification can be used for both documentation of requirements and verification of the design's compliance. It is possible to tightly connect documents and reviews to present a complete and consistent design/verification flow.

As shown above, formal approaches have some demonstrated successes in hardware design; however, the essence of formal methods is that they require a perfect model of the physical system. Thus, due to the complexity of actual systems, formal approaches can be only used in parts of the design process. Typically, formal methods are used early in the development life cycle substituting formal abstraction for a complete physical model. Subsequent refinement is then used to map forward requirements to the later stages of the life cycle.

2.2 Engineering Approach to PLD Design Verification

Simulation, which requires the generation of appropriate test vectors, is an accepted traditional method for functional verification during the design creation phase. Verification of the hardware using simulation may consist of both directed test vectors and randomly generated vectors. This method has been considered adequate to verify that the design specified in HDL Register Transfer Language (RTL) performs the intended function at the behavioral level. Verification of million-gate designs at the gate level requires that transitions on every gate be tracked, resulting in runtime of weeks for substantial million-gate designs.

Since an RTL design can be implemented in a variety of ways on the gate level, the number of test vectors grows exponentially during verification. Any unintended effect of synthesis or timing optimization can insert a design error affecting a part of the circuit, and thus manifest itself with a few combinations of values on the inputs.

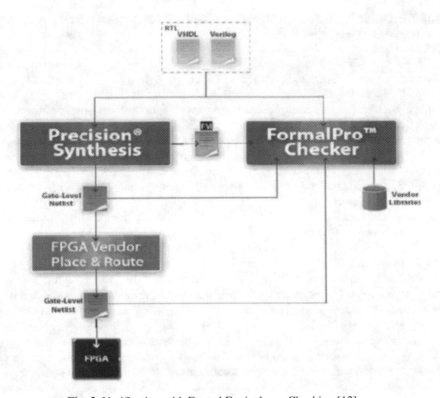

Fig. 2. Verification with Formal Equivalence Checking [12]

To guarantee detection of such an error with gate-level simulation, every possible combination of inputs must be applied, resulting in an infeasible size of test vector being required to ensure 100% error coverage. One solution to this problem could be the utilization of formal methods. The approach used is based on rigorous verification of RTL as an input artifact, while showing that the transition to the gate level is consistent, correct, and does not change the semantic properties of the original input artifact.

One such approach is an equivalence checker, which uses static verification techniques to prove that the RTL and gate-level representations of digital design are an exact functional match. Full verification at the gate-level simulation for modern million-gate designs is infeasible. A formal checker (figure 2 [12]) uses a formal verification interface file (FVI) as a basis for comparison with gate-level netlists generated as a result of the first synthesis and subsequent place-and-route processes. FVI is a readable text file including setup information with file names, paths, constraints, and name matching. If the equivalency of these representations is assured, it can be assumed the final design is consistent with the original design intent.

Assuming that the original RTL representation (in VHDL or Verilog) verified by extensive simulations is functionally correct, equivalence checking is an acceptable solution, since it ensures that transformations throughout the design flow comply with the original functionality. However, equivalence checking does not replace timing analysis. Static and dynamic timing analysis tools should still be used to confirm gate-level timing.

Despite the obvious advantages of the formal equivalence checking approach, there are limitations. Formal tools appear to provide the ultimate assurance of design correctness. At the end of a run, the program provides counter-examples for each specified property specified by developer which were found not valid. Every property is 100% covered. But the Achilles heel of the process is determining how completely the set of properties covers the design intent. This requires "human-in-the-loop" - the skill of experienced designers.

There are numerous safety issues for designers to consider during the synthesis and place and route processes of a hardware design. The related potential errors are often caused by unexpected optimizations occurring during the tool-driven synthesis process. Because these errors occur while translating from the HDL description to the hardware implementation, the resulting design may be faulty even though the HDL implementation has been proven to be correct. In the next section, we take a closer look at the issues relevant to tool use in the design synthesis process.

3 Safety Issues

The case studies have been developed based on the expressed concerns of the airborne systems developers and certifying authorities with the reference to tools used for FPGA development under the FAA mandated RTCA DO-254 guidelines [9]. Largely, these concerns are relevant to development of all safety-critical and real-time systems. The approach was that the tools will be used in worst-case least-likely use scenarios, to test the bounds of the tools' capability. The black box design entered into the tool shall have a one-to-one mapping trace to the black box operation that is finally implemented. To facilitate design independence, case studies are very simple cases exploring specific attributes of a tool. This method has been selected over a large elaborate design to avoid unnecessary issues related to flaw in the design itself. The case studies address timing constraints, power integrity, and undefined input/output states. Additionally, the research explored issues of differences between behavioral simulation and implemented circuit behavior as well as tool awareness of circuit implementation on a faulty hardware.

3.1 Background

The design synthesis process is highly customizable and varies significantly from tool vendor to vendor. The variety of options and configurations make it difficult for an inexperienced designer to know exactly what the default synthesis settings are. Certain functions of synthesis, such as VHDL interpretation, are standardized by IEEE [13]. However, non-standard optimization techniques constitute the trade secret and are considered a competitive advantage of a given vendor. The tool user or designer often does not know the details of synthesis algorithms and thus is not aware of how the tool works. The magnitude of change of the intended design in the synthesis process and thus the impact on the final design may not be precisely known. The impact of the change depends upon the intricacies of the actual logic design, the selected tool used for synthesis, and the tool's current settings. Regrettably, synthesis is not a standardized process; each vendor's tool is different. The differences are only known by a comparison of input versus output of different tools. Due to obvious reasons dealing with intellectual property and competitive advantage, it is not easy to publicize what synthesis algorithms are or what specific methods and techniques are used for simplification and optimization.

Creation of a placed and routable circuit from the HDL code that meets the performance goals is accomplished by merging logical synthesis and physical implementation technologies. When such created designs cannot meet their realistic timing objectives, the solution is to use more traditional design methodologies. The intricacies of logical and physical synthesis are closely guarded intellectual property of specific tool vendors. The general underlying background is well known, but the specifics of algorithms are not.

Safety is obviously an overall system property depending on behavior of hardware circuit as well as software that are developed to monitor and control the system. The issues discussed in the following sections have clearly impact of the ultimate safety of the system. The confusion between what the designer think the circuit (or the algorithm) will do versus what the actual physical circuit (or the running program) does is the main reason for potential safety violation.

3.2 Synthesis Issue #1 - Getting Less Than Expected

The default configuration for almost all FPGA design tools is that all of the compiler and synthesis optimizations are enabled. This can lead to unexpected implementations. For instance, to reduce a design's sensitivity to single event upsets (SEU) errors a designer may write HDL code to specify a triple redundant module as shown in figure 3(A). However, the synthesis tool may determine that most of the hardware is redundant and implement the system as shown in figure 3(B). The independent multipliers were identified as redundant and optimized away during synthesis.

3.3 Synthesis Issue #2 - Getting More Than Expected

In order to meet timing, the synthesis tool will sometimes create redundant hardware to improve timing in what is called flip-flop replication. This can produce problems,

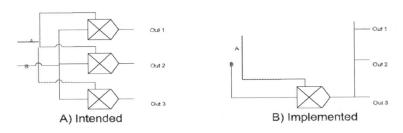

Fig. 3. Triple Redundant Module with Three Multipliers

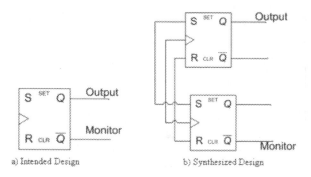

Fig. 4. Flip-Flop Replication

particularly in systems where part of the circuit is monitoring the performance of another circuit. In designs that are intended to be tolerant of SEU, it is common to monitor that a critical flip-flop's outputs are logical opposites of each other under all conditions. Consider the circuit of figure 4(a) where the Output and the Monitor are always logically opposite. A logically equivalent implementation that could be generated by the synthesizer to meet timing constraints is presented in 4(b). In such a solution, a single event upset of the top flip-flop will not affect the monitor output. However, the resulting circuit does not guarantee that Output and Monitor are logical opposites, which defeats the purpose of the monitor output.

3.4 Synthesis Issue #3 - Hardware That Is Non-functional in Normal Operation

The triple redundant module and metastability examples take place when design optimizations are applied during synthesis. Typically, the software tool would not generate explicit warnings that the optimization had been used. The additional circuitry should not be active during the normal operation. Therefore this error may not be detectable during hardware validation since validation is performed using working hardware. The only methods of verifying correct operation of this circuitry is via simulation of the HDL. Since we cannot independently verify the operation of this circuitry in the hardware, the gate-level implementation must be verified. Formal methods offer the most appealing solution to this problem.

Since the above problems are caused by the synthesizer performing optimizations, we could turn off all synthesizer optimizations. Occasionally it can be a feasible solution. However, in most cases it is difficult to meet the timing and the chip area constraints without optimizations. An experienced designer would recognize such issues and configure the synthesizer optimizations appropriately. It is still difficult to assess if the designer has handled all possible areas of concern. There is evident need for a testing/design process where the experience of both the design and verification teams is considered in determining the level and rigor of verification that must be demonstrated.

4 Hardware Specific Issues

Even if a design has been formally verified by a tool of respective pedigree, it is still possible for hardware circuits to produce incorrect results. The hardware-related issues can be broadly classified as timing, signal, and power integrity issues.

4.1 Timing Issues

Perhaps the most difficult aspect in verifying the correctness of hardware is that even minor changes in the timing can produce major differences in the logical operation of a circuit. Consider a bus of many bits that instantaneously transitions from all of the bits being zero (0) to all of the bits being one (1). Due to differences in the routing and random variations in the devices, some bits will transition faster than others. This results in a period of time where some of the bits are stable and some of the bits are still transitioning. During this period, the data on the bus is invalid. Accurate simulation of this timing variation requires knowledge of the exact placement and routing of the devices. Any simulation not incorporating timing data from the place-and-route process will not be able to see these differences. In addition, since the simulation timing step size is typically much larger than the timing differences, the timing differences will not show up in the simulation output. Designers must always be aware of the limits of the simulation.

It is possible to minimize the timing variations caused by routing differences by placing timing constraints on the design tools. However, there is always a timing variation due to random device variations and these effects are rarely (if ever) included in logic simulator models. Even when the simulations show that the data is always valid, random device variations guarantee there are periods where the data on the bus is invalid. The design tools cannot change the physics. Designs must be tolerant of the fact that there are always periods when the data on any bus is invalid.

4.1.1 Synchronous Design

To overcome the problem of not knowing when the data is valid, almost all hardware designs use a synchronous design with a clock. In this design style, the data is valid for some time before the clock edge (setup time) and for some time after the clock (hold time). The clock signal is generated from a master source and then distributed throughout the device. Special care must be taken so that the clock arrives to all devices in the device at the same time. Delivery of the clock to different devices at different times is known as clock skew. FPGAs contain a limited number of specialized trees that can be used to minimize clock skew. Although the design tool attempts to recognize clock trees, the design must often explicitly declare these trees so that the synthesis tool will correctly accommodate them. The clock trees are often heavily loaded, driving many devices while the data lines often only drive a single device. This means the data is often naturally too fast and that the synthesis tool must incorporate delays to allow the device to meet timing. These delays are often created by inserting additional buffers in the data signal path or by artificially loading the data, without notifying the designer. Speed differences between the clock and the data path may result in the failures due to the data arriving too soon or too late. These failures are particularly sensitive to variations in temperature and voltage and often are concealed in simulation.

4.1.2 Synchronous Design -- Multiple Clock Domains

Ideally, a design will have only a single master clock. Unfortunately, modern designs commonly require several independent clocks used within a single system. When signals move from one clock domain to another, special circuits and analyses are required. Correct operation of circuits crossing clock domain boundaries cannot be guaranteed by simulation because the timing between different clock domains can vary arbitrarily which would require an infinite number of simulations. Special design techniques are used to allow signals to cross between clock domains and designers must insert them where needed.

4.1.3 Asynchronous Designs

The most risky of all design styles is asynchronous design, where inputs and/or outputs are allowed to vary without respect to any clock. Modern designs use increasing number of clocks. Asynchronous circuits are subject to a condition called "metastability," in which signals transition from one value to another via quasi-stable states exhibiting an intermittent failure. Neither simulation (testing logic function) nor static timing analysis (testing single clock domain) can detect such failure.

A typical example of such a situation is when the clock and data inputs of a flip-flop change values at approximately the same time. This leads to the flip-flop output oscillating and not settling to a value within the appropriate delay window. It happens when there is communication between discrete systems using different clocks.

Experienced designers mitigate the event by adding synchronization between clock domains and isolating the "metastable" output to reduce propagation effects. This state introduces a delay which varies depending on the exact timing of the inputs. This delay can only be analyzed statistically. We cannot prevent an error from happening; we can only bind its probability. Although most designers avoid asynchronous design, there are cases where such solution is required. An example would be a reset path that must operate, even if the synchronizing clock is not present.

4.2 Signal Issues

4.2.1 Combinational Feedback and Quasi-digital Circuits

PLDs provide the user with the ability to configure the device a nearly infinite number of ways. This flexibility can allow the designer to implement unexpected configurations. For instance, it is possible to configure an odd number of inverter gates into a circuit known as a ring oscillator. Inverters 1, 2, and 3 form the oscillator while inverter 4 converts the analog sine wave back to a square wave (figure 5). This configuration has an output, but no inputs, and the timing is determined by the speed of the inverters and is not synchronized to any clock. This makes the ring oscillator very sensitive to temperature variations and this configuration is often used as a temperature sensor. When the hardware is operating as a ring oscillator, the signals do not switch between normal digital signal levels. The oscillator is essentially an analog device using the gain present in the logic gates to produce oscillations. Most HDL simulators assume only digital logic and are unable to correctly simulate this simple

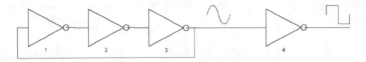

Fig. 5. Ring Oscillator

analog configuration. Many design tools prevent the user from implementing a combinational feedback configuration such as a ring oscillator. To guarantee the correctness of the tools, we must restrict the designer's ability to produce problematic configurations.

4.2.2   Undefined States and Constant Signals

FPGAs may contain large numbers of states which are defined as "don't care" for certain modes of operation. Many inputs and internal variables are often defined as constants. Different synthesis tools handle the "don't care" states and constants quite differently. This makes formal verification a very user intensive process requiring manual customization of the verification tool.

4.3   Power Issues

4.3.1   Power-Up and Reset

When an FPGA or ASIC is either powered up or comes out of reset, there is often a period of time when the device outputs are unpredictable. The performance of a component during power-up is difficult to predict, as there are often multiple power supplies to the part which will turn on in an uncontrolled fashion. If the output drivers receive power before the internal logic, all of the glitches produced by the internal logic can be sent through the outputs to other devices in the system. Even a normal reset can contain internal race conditions that can produce periods where the outputs are unstable. The Wide-Field Infrared Explorer (WIRE) spacecraft was lost when the FPGA produced unexpected outputs during power-up. The unexpected output resulted in the system reset process not completing, which lead to the early firing of a pyrotechnic device and ultimately to the failure of the mission [14].

4.3.2   Signal and Power Integrity Errors

Single ended signaling is often used on aircraft to reduce the weight of the wiring. In single-ended signaling, inputs and outputs (I/O) share a common power and ground connection. If all of the I/O connected to the common power supply or ground change state simultaneously, a large spike in current will occur. Any parasitic inductances in the power supply and ground distribution network will have voltages induced across them which are proportional to the derivative of the current. These induced voltages are known as supply/ground bounce and can be large enough to lead to erroneous circuit operation.

Noise can also be introduced into the system via crosstalk between signals. Crosstalk coupling is primarily a function of the total inductance of the current path. This inductance is a function of the distance between the ground (GND) and supply voltage (VDD) pins to the signal pin. Signal pins farther away from a GND or VDD pin are more susceptible to noise. This problem is exacerbated when a large number of I/O in the region switch simultaneously.

5   Conclusions

Technology has improved to the point that system designers have the ability to trade-off implementing complex functions in either hardware or software. However in the design tool world there are clear distinctions between software and hardware tools. One of the major concerns in any hardware design is assuring that the hardware correctly implements the HDL description. As the synthesis and place and route process proceeds the architecture used to implement any given HDL description can be changed to optimize the design for area, power, or timing. The synthesis tool views all of the implementations as logically equivalent, but they may not be equivalent in the eyes of the designer. Formal tools and specifically equivalence checking approach seem to be an excellent method to guarantee that the designer's intent has been translated to the physical hardware. While both verification of models and hardware synthesis have been successfully applied in industrial practice, there are several caveats in practice when physical components come in play. The issues are not due to the incorrectness of neither formal analyses nor errors in the synthesizers, but the inadequacy of the analyzed models and the not-so-simple internal conditions and related synthesizers' construction.

Formal methods must never give us a false sense of confidence. Despite the best design and verification efforts the hardware may still produce unexpected results. These errors can be due to noise, supply bounce, timing issues, or even cosmic radiation. It should be noted that specialized design tool suites to address all of the above error conditions exist. The tradeoffs between the costs and benefits of using these tools must be investigated for each design. Despite all of the design tools available, the most important component of any safety-critical design is an experienced designer with the experience and ability to differentiate between what issues are critical and what issues are negligible. It should be also noted that a rigorous process and safety culture promoted by appropriate guidance in regulated industries (e.g. FAA in aviation, FDA in the medical domain) is an integral element to improve safety.

Acknowledgements. The presented work was supported in part by the Aviation Airworthiness Center of Excellence under contract DTFACT-07-C-00010 sponsored by the FAA. Findings contained herein are not necessarily those of the FAA.

References

1. Pampagnin, P., Menis, J.F.: DO254-ED80 for High Performance and High Reliable Electronic Components, Internal Paper, Barco-Siles S.A., Peynier, France (2007)
2. Bernardo, M., Cimatti, A. (eds.): SFM 2006. LNCS, vol. 3965. Springer, Heidelberg (2006)
3. Kern, C., Greenstreet, M.R.: Formal Verification in Hardware Design: A Survey. ACM Trans. on Design Automation of Electronic Systems 4(2), 123–193 (1999)

4. Turner, K.J., He, J.: Formally-based Design Evaluation. In: Margaria, T., Melham, T.F. (eds.) CHARME 2001. LNCS, vol. 2144, pp. 104–109. Springer, Heidelberg (2001)
5. Aljer, A., Devienne, P.: Co-design and Refinement for Safety Critical Systems. In: Proc. DFT 2004, 19th IEEE International Symposium on Defect and Fault Tolerance in VLSI Systems, pp. 78–86. IEEE, Los Alamitos (2004)
6. Nehme, C., Lundqvist, K.: A Tool for Translating VHDL to Finite State Machines. In: Proc. DACS 2003, 22nd Digital Avionics Systems Conference, October 12-16, vol. 1, pp. 3.B.6-1-7 (2003)
7. Dajani-Brown, S., Cofer, D., Bouali, A.: Formal Verification of an Avionics Sensor Voter Using SCADE. In: Lakhnech, Y., Yovine, S. (eds.) FORMATS 2004 and FTRTFT 2004. LNCS, vol. 3253, pp. 5–20. Springer, Heidelberg (2004)
8. Hilton, A.J.: High-Integrity Hardware-Software Codesign, Ph.D. Thesis, The Open University (April 2004)
9. DO-254, Design Assurance Guidance for Airborne Electronic Hardware, RTCA Inc., Washington, DC (April 19, 2000)
10. Dellacherie, S., Burgaud, L., di Crescenzo, P.: imPROVE–HDL: A DO-254 Formal Property Checker Used for Design and Verification of Avionics Protocol Controllers. In: Proc. DACS 2003, 22nd Digital Avionics Systems Conference, Indianapolis, Ind., October 12-16, vol. 1, pp. 1.A.1-1.1-8 (2003)
11. Karlsson, K., Forsberg, H.: Emerging Verification Methods for Complex Hardware in Avionics. In: Proc. DASC 2005, 24th Digital Avionics Systems Conference, October 30 - November 3, vol. 1, pp. 6.B.1 - 61-12 (2005)
12. Henson, J.: Equivalence Checking for FPGA Design, White Paper, Mentor Graphics Corp., Wilsonville, Ore. (May 2007)
13. IEEE Std 1076-2002, Standard VHDL Language Reference Manual, The Institute of Electrical and Electronics Engineers, New York (2002)
14. Bridgford, B., Carmichael, C., Tseng, C.W.: Single-Event Upset Mitigation Selection Guide, Application Note XAPP987, Xilinx Inc., San Jose, Calif. (March 2008)

Probabilistic Failure Propagation and Transformation Analysis

Xiaocheng Ge, Richard F. Paige, and John A. McDermid

Department of Computer Science, University of York, UK
{xchge,paige,jam}@cs.york.ac.uk

Abstract. A key concern in safety engineering is understanding the overall emergent failure behaviour of a system, i.e., behaviour exhibited by the system that is outside its specification of acceptable behaviour. A system can exhibit failure behaviour in many ways, including that from failures of individual or a small number of components. It is important for safety engineers to understand how *system* failure behaviour relates to failures exhibited by individual components. In this paper, we propose a safety analysis technique, *failure propagation and transformation analysis* (FPTA), which automatically and quantitatively analyses failures based on a model of failure logic. The technique integrates previous work on automated failure analysis with probabilistic model checking supported by the PRISM tool. We demonstrate the technique and tool on a small, yet realistic safety-related application.

Keywords: failure, safety analysis, probabilistic analysis, component-based system.

1 Introduction

Modern systems, comprising hardware and software components, are becoming increasingly complex. The design and development of these complex systems is challenging, because engineers need to deal with many functional and non-functional requirements (e.g., safety, availability, and reliability requirements), while keeping development cost low, and the engineering life-cycle as short and manageable as possible.

Component-based software development has emerged as a promising approach to developing complex systems, via an approach of composing smaller, independently developed components into larger assemblies. This approach offers means to increase software reuse, achieve higher flexibility and deliver shorter time-to-market by reusing existing component, such as off-the-shelf components. Component-based software development is realised in a number of different ways, e.g., through model-based development or service-oriented computing.

Safety critical systems, like many other domains, may benefit from the flexibility offered by component-based software development. However, to be applicable to safety critical systems, component-based development must directly support modelling and analysis of key non-functional concerns, such as availability, reliability, and the overall failure behaviour of the system, in order to deliver a

B. Buth, G. Rabe, T. Seyfarth (Eds.): SAFECOMP 2009, LNCS 5775, pp. 215–228, 2009.

system that is acceptably safe (e.g., to certifying authorities). The last concern is particularly challenging to deal with: a system can fail in many ways. It may be the case that a system failure arises due to failures of individual or a small number of components. Identifying the *source and likelihood* of system failure is of substantial importance to developers and safety engineers, so that they can be sure that they have appropriately mitigated risks. Specifically, it is important that safety engineers and system developers be able to understand the consequences of individual component failures.

1.1   Current Techniques for Failure Analysis

Several approaches to failure analysis, and understanding overall system failure behaviour, have been investigated, including research on software testing (e.g., [4,5,8,9,10,13,14]) and system engineering (e.g., [2,3,6,12,15]). Largely, this body of work provides evidence that understanding system failure behaviour is more difficult than understanding specified (acceptable) behaviour. Failure analysis techniques based on software testing (especially fault-based testing and mutation analysis) include Interface Propagation Analysis (IPA) [14] and the Propagation Analysis Environment (PROPANE) [5]. Both IPA and PROPANE studied propagation behaviour at the code level. There were also studies of propagation in terms of software architecture, e.g., [10]. Most of the research from the software testing perspective focused on the study of the propagation of data error, which occurs homogeneously — "for a given input, it appears that either all data state errors injected at a given location tend to propagate to the output, or else none of them do" [9]. In practice, the failure propagation behaviour of software components may become much more complex when considering failures caused by hardware components.

There are also approaches to analysis of failure propagation behaviour from the system engineering perspective. Perhaps the most well known approach is the classical safety engineering technique *Failure Modes and Effects Analysis* (FMEA) [1], which is a manual process for identifying the failure modes of a system starting from an analysis of component failures. Generally, the process of failure analysis consists of several activities: identifying failures of individual components, modelling the failure logic of the entire system, analysing a failure's effect on other components, and determining and engineering the mitigation of potential hazards.

In safety engineering, developers and engineers general model and analyse potential failure behaviour of a system as a whole. With the emergence of component-based development approaches, investigations began exploring component oriented safety analysis techniques, mainly focusing on creating *encapsulated* failure propagation models. These failure propagation models describe how failure modes of incoming messages (input failure) together with internal component faults (internal failure) propagate to failure modes of outgoing messages (output failure). Failure Propagation Transformation Notation (FPTN) [3] was the first approach to promote the use of failure propagation models. Other relevant techniques are Hierarchically Performed Hazard Origin and Propagation

Studies (HiP-HOPS) [12] and Component Fault Trees (CFT) [6]. For specific component-based specification languages, the later two techniques allow tool-supported and automated generation of a safety evaluation model. A limitation of these safety analysis techniques is their inability to handle cycles in the control- or data-flow architecture of the system; cycles, of course, appear in most realistic systems. Fault Propagation and Transformation Calculus (FPTC) [15] was one of the first approaches that could automatically carry out failure analysis on systems with cycles by using fixed-point analysis.

This paper focuses on failure propagation behaviours at the architecture level, in which the components may be hardware or software components. Based on our experience, we found that existing failure analysis techniques have a number of limitations, in particular:

- FMEA and FPTN generally provide manual or non-compositional analysis. Such analysis is expensive, especially in a typical component-based development process, because if changes are made to components, the failure analysis has to be carried out again, and previous analysis results will be invalidated.
- FPTC does not provide facilities for quantitative analysis, particularly in terms of determining the *probability* of specific failure behaviours. Such quantitative analysis can help to provide more fine-grained information to help identify and determine suitable (cost-effective) mitigation to potential hazards.

By providing an extension of FPTC technique, we are aiming to overcome the limitations we found in existing system engineering analysis techniques.

1.2 Contribution and Structure of the Paper

In this paper, we propose a safety analysis technique, *failure propagation and transformation analysis* (FPTA), which follows the direction of FPTC [15]. The FPTA method integrates an automated failure analysis algorithm presented in [15], and it also allows the application of model checking technique as provided by the PRISM[1] model checker [7]. The approach is therefore a probabilistic safety analysis technique for component-based system development.

The structure of the paper is as follows. We begin by presenting background material. We introduce the failure analysis technique in detail and outline its underlying theory, explaining how FPTC [15] is integrated with probabilistic model checking. Finally, we demonstrate the analysis method on an illustrative safety-related application.

2 Background

The theory and techniques of FPTC were initially introduced in [15], and the implementation of a supporting standards-compliant and open-source tool was presented in [11]. We will briefly describe the modelling and analysis techniques of FPTC in the following section.

---

[1] http://www.prismmodelchecker.org/

2.1   Failure Modelling

FPTC is based on FPTN [3], and is applied to a model of system architecture. In this approach the failure behaviours of *both* components and connectors are determined and modelled. FPTC takes the view that connectors between components are communication protocols, and because a communication protocol also has its own potential failure behaviour, the protocols in the model must be treated identically to the components of the system – i.e., their failures are also modelled.

Components and connectors can (in terms of failure) behave in only a few ways [15]. They can introduce new types of failures (e.g., because of an exception or crash), or may propagate input failures (e.g., data that is erroneous when it arrives at a component remains erroneous when it leaves the component), or transforms an input failure into a different kind of failure (e.g., data that arrives late may thereafter arrive early). Finally, a component may correct or mask input failures that it receives.

Failure responses of a component to its input can be expressed in a simple language based on patterns. For example, the following expressions denote examples of failure propagation and transformation behaviours for a trivial single-input single-output component: an *omission* fault at the input may propagate through the component, but a *late* fault is transformed to a *value* fault at the output.

$$omission \longrightarrow omission \qquad (failure\ propagation)$$
$$late \longrightarrow value \qquad (failure\ transformation)$$

A typical component will have its failure behaviour modelled by a number of clauses of this form, and the effect is its overall *FPTC* behaviour.

2.2   FPTC Analysis Technique

To represent the system as a whole, every element of the system architecture – both components and connectors – is assigned FPTC behaviour. Each model element that represents a relationship is annotated with sets of *tokens* (e.g., omission, late). The architecture as a whole is treated as a token-passing network, and from this the maximal token sets on all relationships in the model can be automatically calculated, giving us the overall failure behaviour of the system. This calculation resolves to determining a fix-point [15]. For details of the algorithm, see [11]; for an argument that the fix-point calculation must ultimately terminate, see [15]. Examples describing the use of FPTC in a number of domains, including for analysis control logic and FPGAs, appear in [11].

2.3   Analysis of FPTC

FPTC overcomes the problem of handling cyclic data- and control-flow structures in a system architecture by using fix-point calculations. As well, experience from a number of case studies suggests that it can be integrated into a system design process, thus potentially reducing safety engineering overheads. FPTC nevertheless has some limitations which make it difficult to extend directly to richer forms of analysis, particularly probabilistic analysis. We summarise these limitations by example.

Example I: internal failures. Consider a simple system with a component (e.g., a hardware sensor) that may have an *internal* power failure. When a power failure occurs, there will be no output (i.e., an omission failure) from the component, no matter what its inputs are. This can be modelled implicitly in FPTC as shown in Equation 1[2].

$$input.* \longrightarrow output.omission \qquad (1)$$

This does not explicitly model the fact that there has been an internal failure in the component. This is not a problem for standard FPTC, but if we desire to extend FPTC to probabilistic analysis, we encounter difficulties: suppose an internal omission failure occurs with probability 0.01. To model this, we need to distinguish the case where an internal failure arises (described in Equation 1) from the case where an omission failure is *propagated* by the component (i.e., the omission failure occurs elsewhere in the system). This requires the addition of a new FPTC equation.

$$
\begin{aligned}
input.omission &\longrightarrow output.omission \\
input.* &\longrightarrow output.omission
\end{aligned} \qquad (2)
$$

The first line states that an omission fault on input leads to an omission fault on output. The second line indicates that any fault on input leads to an omission fault. But the first line is an instance of the second, and according to the definition of FPTC analysis in [15], is removed from calculations. But it is explicitly necessary in order to support probabilistic analysis, because we must be able to distinguish internal from external omission failure.

Unlike other techniques, such as HiP-HOPS and CFT, the FPTC technique targets software systems where component failures are only triggered by inputs. It is thus lacking in its support for modelling internal failure in the process of integrated software/hardware design and assessment. Overall, input and output failures are generally straightforward to identify, but a failure model given strictly in terms of inputs and outputs may be insufficient to adequately capture system failure behaviour, particularly when probabilities are involved.

Example II: non-determinism. Suppose we have a situation where a component may not receive the inputs it requires (i.e., an omission failure on input), and as a result, the component will, half of the time, generate no output, and the other half of the time will generate the wrong output (i.e., a value failure). In FPTC, this component can be partly modelled as in Equation 3.

$$
\begin{aligned}
input.omission &\longrightarrow output.omission \\
input.omission &\longrightarrow output.value
\end{aligned} \qquad (3)
$$

---

[2] * Indicates any input.

This FPTC model is not well-formed according to [15], because the algorithm assumes that failure behaviours on outputs are deterministic. Such behaviours cannot be automatically analysed with the existing algorithm, but being able to represent such behaviours is essential in order to support probabilistic analysis.

Summary. Overall, FPTC addresses one significant limitation of other safety analyses – handling cycles in architectures – but is still insufficient. The limitations we have identified are all related to how failures are modelled currently in FPTC; the coarse nature of failure modelling in FPTC (particularly, the inability to represent internal failures and non-deterministic failure behaviour on output) makes it difficult to extend to probabilistic analysis. In the next section, we propose an extension to FPTC models that supports probabilistic modelling, and that eliminates these problems.

3   Probabilistic Modelling Extensions to FPTC

In this section we present an extension to FPTC for supporting probabilistic modelling and that address the concerns presented above. We call this extension *failure propagation and transformation analysis* (FPTA).

3.1   Probability Property

The first limitation presented with FPTC was the inability to explicitly model internal failures in components (or connectors); this limitation is particularly important to resolve in order to describe the uncertainty of a component's transitive behaviours when considering the impact of internal failures. The overall effect of this limitation is that internal failures are masked.

To alleviate this limitation in FPTA, we extend the model of FPTC failure behaviour, by providing richer, more expressive means for modelling inputs and outputs, the *mode* that inputs and outputs are in, and the probability associated with each mode. We now explain this more precisely.

3.2   Transitive Behaviour Model

Components in FPTA (as in FPTC) are the principal processing objects of the executing system, and connectors are interaction or communication mechanisms for components. In most realistic system architectures, a component may have multiple input ports and output ports; a port is the point of interaction between component and connector. The values placed on an output port can be calculated via a function that takes all input values into account. This is called the *transition function* in FPTA. For example, a component with n input ports and m output ports will have m transition functions. An instance of a transition function can be written as:

$$\{input_1.fault, \ldots, input_n.fault\} \longrightarrow output_x.fault, \, probability \quad (4)$$

Mode is a term used in FPTA to describe the state of the contents of an input or output port. Since an output of a component may have many modes, the transition function of an output can have many instances of its possible modes. We use a tuple (*mode*, *probability*) to describe each mode of an in/output port. We call this tuple a *token*.

3.3   System Model

Connectors in an architectural model of a system are the links between components. In FPTA, we provide a different semantics to connectors than in FPTC: they are an abstraction that does not have any failure transformation behaviour. Specifically, they propagate whatever they receive from an input port to an output port. Thus, failure behaviour is modelled exclusively on components; this, as we will see, simplifies the probability calculations.

Modes are propagated by connectors at run-time one at a time. Mathematically, what is propagated by a connector is a set of all possible input or output modes. To model a connector, we define the contents propagated by a connector as a collection of tokens. Formally, this is $\{token_1, token_2, \ldots, token_n\}$ if there are n possible modes that can be propagated.

Based on this definition, the tokens of a connector should satisfy the following expression.

$$\sum_{i=1}^{n} token_i.probability = 1 \tag{5}$$

The system model is thereafter constructed by connecting the models of all its components in the same way as is done in traditional FPTC.

So far, we have explained how we model the system. Next, we will revisit the limitations of the FPTC modelling language.

3.4   Revisiting Limitations of FPTC

Given FPTA as presented in the previous subsections, we now show that it overcomes the limitations of FPTC discussed previously.

Consider the example presented in Section 2.3. Assume that a power failure occurs with probability 0.01. The failure behaviour of this component can now be expressed as:

$$
\begin{aligned}
input.omission &\longrightarrow output.omission , 0.0001 \\
input.value &\longrightarrow output.omission , 0.0001 \\
input.normal &\longrightarrow output.omission , 0.0001 \\
input.omission &\longrightarrow output.omission , 0.9999 \\
input.value &\longrightarrow output.value , 0.9999 \\
input.normal &\longrightarrow output.normal , 0.9999
\end{aligned}
\tag{6}
$$

The example in Section 2.3 described the case where a component may have different ways of reacting to the same failure on input. In particular, when there is an omission failure of input, the component will half of the time generate no output (omission) and half of the time will generate the wrong value (value failure). This failure behaviour can be described as follows.

$$
\begin{aligned}
input.omission &\longrightarrow output.omission\ ,0.5 \\
input.omission &\longrightarrow \quad output.value\quad ,0.5 \\
input.value &\longrightarrow \quad output.value\quad ,1 \\
input.normal &\longrightarrow output.normal\ ,1
\end{aligned}
\tag{7}
$$

Again, there is essential complexity that arises in modelling failure behaviour when probabilities are introduced.

3.5   Analysing the System

Once the system model is constructed by connecting models of components, we *"execute"* the model by using an algorithm similar to FPTC. Tokens in FPTA consist of two elements: a mode and its probability. The technique to deal with the computation of the modes is as same as the fix-point technique used in FPTC. The law of total probability is used to calculate the probability associated with each mode.

In FPTA, if there are n possible modes that can be transitioned to a particular failure of an output, the law of total probability says:

$$
P(output.fault) = \sum_{i=1}^{n} P(output.fault|input.mode_i)P(input.mode_i)
\tag{8}
$$

In this formula, the probability values of input modes are calculated by previous computations, and the conditional probability $P(output.fault|input.mode_i)$ is modelled in the instance of a transition function in the model of the component. At the beginning of the *"execution"*, engineers provide an initial set of probability values for modes, and then the calculation is carried out automatically until the execution stops. Because the failure set is finite, the computation will be guaranteed to reach a fix-point.

We now provide several examples. Given a component, assume that there are two possible modes in which the component can fail, namely *value* (v) and *omission* (o). As well, there is a default non-failure mode (*normal* (n)). First, we consider the case where the component has one input port and one output port. Example transitive behaviours and their probabilities (identified by a domain expert) are listed in Table 1.

Table 1. The probability of possible transitions

Input Modes	Output Modes		
	normal (n)	value (v)	omission (o)
n	0.89	0.1	0.01
r	0	0.99	0.01
nr	0	0	1

According to the data given by Table 1, the transition model of the component is:

$$
\begin{aligned}
input.n &\longrightarrow output.n &,0.89\\
input.n &\longrightarrow output.r &,0.1\\
input.n &\longrightarrow output.nr &,0.01\\
input.r &\longrightarrow output.r &,0.99\\
input.r &\longrightarrow output.nr &,0.01\\
input.nr &\longrightarrow output.nr &,1
\end{aligned}
\tag{9}
$$

We can easily determine the set of tokens for the input port on the component; this is $\{(n, 0.9), (v, 0.05), (o, 0.05)\}$. And from this, we can calculate the tokens, including the modes and their probability values, for the output port by computing the probability of every possible mode at the output port. For example,

$$
\begin{aligned}
P(output.n) &= P(input.n) \cdot P(output.n|input.n)\\
&+ P(input.v) \cdot P(output.n|input.v)\\
&+ P(input.o) \cdot P(output.n|input.o)\\
&= 0.9 \times 0.89\\
&= 0.801
\end{aligned}
\tag{10}
$$

After carrying out a similar calculation for all other possible modes, the token set at the output port is:

$$
\{(n, 0.801), (v, 0.1395), (o, 0.0595)\}
\tag{11}
$$

In a larger system, if this component is connected to another, we would take the token set, $\{(n, 0.801), (v, 0.1395), (o, 0.0595)\}$, and use them as input tokens of a component connected to this output port. This process would carry on until the calculation reaches a fix-point and stops.

3.6   Model Checking

Our component-oriented approach for analysing failure behaviour focuses on the transitions between modes of a component. Since we introduced a probability property into the failure model, we need a formal mechanism to verify the probabilistic model. Probabilistic model checking [7] is a suitable mechanism to use for verification in this situation. Probabilistic model checkers encode system models using Markov chains; in this sense, they encode the probability of making a transition between states instead of simply the existence of a transition. The probabilistic model checking process is an automatic procedure for establishing if a desired property holds in a probabilistic system model. We exploit probabilistic model checking – and, in particular, PRISM – to accomplish three purposes.

1. It can be used to formally verify the probabilistic model. Since the probability property was introduced to describe the failure behaviours of a component, the model checker can help to check criteria that the probability values must satisfy.

2. The output token set of a component can be calculated by the model checker during the analysis. When the model becomes complex (e.g., when a component has three or more input ports, or there are more than three possible modes at each port), the calculation of output token set will be very difficult without automated tool support.
3. There is also a desire that safety engineers and system developers can easily determine how critical a component is to the entire system. Ideally, it should be possible for the relationship between the failure behaviour of a component, and the entire system, can be visualised.

In order to use the PRISM probabilistic model checker, we have to precisely define the state of a component as a finite state model; note that FPTC abstracts away from internal state and represents failures as observable external behaviour. The state of a component can be formally defined by the modes of its input and output ports because they can be observed and measured directly.

Once the transitive behaviour model is expressed as a state machine, then it is very straightforward to express the model in the PRISM input language; space limitations prevent us from presenting this simple transformation. Properties can then be checked against the model by the PRISM model checker. Any counter-examples identified by the PRISM model checker can easily be mapped back to the state machine, and then manually reflected against the transitive behaviour model. Full automation of this process would be of benefit, and we are investigating the use of model transformation technology (and automated traceability management) to support this.

4   Example

We now illustrate the overall analysis process via a small, yet realistic example. The system for case study is a piece of a safety-critical control system. There are 6 components in the system —U1 to U6: Component U1 outputs the absolute value of the input; U2 outputs the product of two inputs; U3 is an amplifier (3 times); U4 generates a constant value; U5 gives the minimum value of two inputs; and U6 outputs the division of two inputs. Figure 1 shows its architecture. We applied the probabilistic failure analysis technique to a logic unit used in control systems.

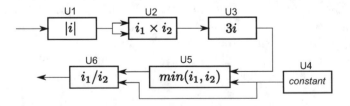

Fig. 1. Architecture of logic unit

The application is a software system (though it is normally deployed with supporting hardware, and hardware failures may lead to software failures, and vice versa). Using HAZOPs and guide-words, we identified two kinds of failure modes, *value* (v) and *omission* (o), and a default non-failure mode, *normal* (n).

Based on the knowledge of the transitive behaviours of components in the system, we modelled the components in the architecture one by one. For example, Equation 12 is the model of component U5.

$$
\begin{aligned}
\{input.n,\ input.n\} &\longrightarrow output.n\ ,0.89 \\
\{input.n,\ input.n\} &\longrightarrow output.v\ ,0.1 \\
\{input.n,\ input.n\} &\longrightarrow output.o\ ,0.01 \\
\{input.n,\ input.v\} &\longrightarrow output.v\ ,0.99 \\
\{input.n,\ input.v\} &\longrightarrow output.o\ ,0.01 \\
\{input.n,\ input.o\} &\longrightarrow output.o\ ,1 \\
\{input.v,\ input.v\} &\longrightarrow output.v\ ,0.99 \\
\{input.v,\ input.v\} &\longrightarrow output.o\ ,0.01 \\
\{input.v,\ input.o\} &\longrightarrow output.o\ ,1 \\
\{input.o,\ input.o\} &\longrightarrow output.o\ ,1
\end{aligned}
\tag{12}
$$

Based on these models of the components and the architecture of the system, we carried out several experiments. The first experiment examines the probability of the component U6 outputting *normal* values if the input of component U1 is *normal*. In this case, the input token set of component U1 is $\{(n,1),\ (v,0),\ (o,0)\}$. Applying the probabilistic FPTA technique, the automatically calculated output token set of component U6 is:

$$\{(n,0.4423),\ (v,0.4898),\ (o,0.0679)\}$$

Similarly, we calculated the case where the input tokens are: $\{(n,0),\ (v,1),\ (o,0)\}$ and $\{(n,0),\ (v,0),\ (o,1)\}$. The calculated output tokens are

$$\{(n,0),\ (v,0.9321),\ (o,0.0679)\}$$

and

$$\{(n,0),\ (v,0),\ (o,1)\}$$

Once we have obtained the input and output token sets for the individual components, we can model the entire logic unit, consisting of components U1 to U6, as follows:

$$
\begin{aligned}
input.n &\longrightarrow output.n\ ,0.4423 \\
input.n &\longrightarrow output.v\ ,0.4898 \\
input.n &\longrightarrow output.nr\ ,0.0679 \\
input.v &\longrightarrow output.v\ ,0.9321 \\
input.v &\longrightarrow output.o\ ,0.0679 \\
input.o &\longrightarrow output.o\ ,1
\end{aligned}
\tag{13}
$$

The result of our first small example shows that the FPTA technique can be applied hierarchically, which allows the decomposition of the probabilistic evaluation based on the system architecture.

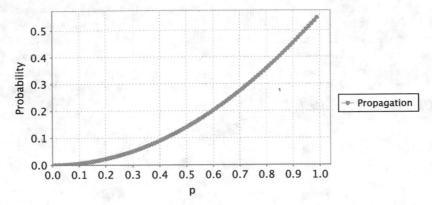

Fig. 2. Relationship of Component U4 to Overall Unit

Our second example is a variant on the first, and explores how changing a component in an architecture can affect the overall system failure behaviour. In particular, we show how we can use FPTA to explore different choices in modelling. Suppose that we are unhappy with the performance of U4 (a constant generator) in our example, and desire a design for U4 that provides a better error rate. Through experiment, we want to understand the effect of introducing a better-performing component on the entire system.

In the experiment, we model component U4 as follows:

$$input.n \longrightarrow output.n , p$$
$$input.n \longrightarrow output.v , 1 - p \qquad (14)$$

In the model (Equation 14), we introduce a variable p which is the conditional probability that the component generates a *normal* output. We transform the failure model in PRISM and set up a series of experiments in which value p is increased from 0 to 1 with step-size of 0.01. Figure 2 shows the results of experiments, where the X-axis indicates the trend for p and the Y-axis is the probability that the entire system outputs *normal* data (i.e., the output of U6 is *normal*), assuming that the input of the system (i.e., input of U1) is *normal*.

We can conclude from Figure 2 that there isn't a linear relationship between the non-failure rate of component U4 and the non-failure rate of the entire system; the better the component U4 (i.e., the smaller its error rate) is, the better the overall failure behaviour of the entire system.

In addition, suppose that we want the overall non-failure rate of the entire system to be not less than 0.5. From Figure 2 we observe that the non-failure rate of component U4 should not be less than 0.95; in fact, the overall non-failure rate of the entire system is 0.504 if the non-failure rate of U4 is 0.95 (i.e., the failure rate of U4 is 0.05).

This example shows that FPTA can be applied to analyse the criticality of a component in the system, and to help to set up criteria for component selection; this is very important in a component-based development process.

5   Conclusions

We have presented a new technique for quantitative analysis of failure behaviour for systems, based on architectural models. The proposed technique enables the assessment of failure behaviour from the analysis of components of the system, and can assess the probability of system-level failures based on failures of components. The approach has been connected to a probabilistic model checker, which allows verification of the failure models, but also helps to calculate input and output token sets and helps in exploring the model. Importantly, the approach is compositional, and can be applied to individual components and collections.

Our transformation from the failure model to input used by the PRISM tool is currently carried out manually; this can potentially lead to errors in the PRISM input. In our experience, errors are often found by PRISM, but many of these could be avoided with an automated transformation from our failure models to PRISM. We are currently building a tool which is based on our previous work [11]. The idea is that once we model the failure behaviours of all components in the system architecture, we then transform the model to PRISM model using model transformation technology. We are also exploring using customised editors to visually represent feedback from PRISM on models of system architecture.

Acknowledgements

We thank Dr. Radu Calinescu (Oxford) for his help. This research was carried out as part of the Large-Scale Complex IT Systems (LSCITS) project, funded by the EPSRC through grant EP/F001096/1.

References

1. IEC 60812. Functional safety of electrical/electronical/programmable electronic safety/related systems, analysis techniques for system reliability - procedure for failure mode and effect analysis (FMEA). Technical report, International Electrotechnical Commission IEC (1991)
2. Fenelon, P., McDermid, J.A.: New directions in software safety: Causal modelling as an aid to integration. Technical report, High Integrity Systems Engineering Group, Dept of Computer Science, University of York (1992)
3. Fenelon, P., McDermid, J.A.: An integrated toolset for software safety analysis. The Journal of Systems and Software 21(3), 279–290 (1993)
4. Hiller, M., Jhumka, A., Suri, N.: An approach for analysing the propagation of data errors in software. In: Proceedings of 2001 International Conference on Dependable Systems and Networks DSN 2001, Göteborg, Sweden, July 2001, pp. 161–172. IEEE Computer Society, Los Alamitos (2001)

5. Hiller, M., Jhumka, A., Suri, N.: Propane: an environment for examining the propagation of errors in software. In: Proceedings of the International Symposium on Software Testing and Analysis, ISSTA 2002, Roma, Italy, pp. 81–85. ACM, New York (2002)

6. Kaiser, B., Liggesmeyer, P., Mäckel, O.: A new component concept for fault trees. In: Proceedings of the 8th Australian Workshop on Safety Critical Systems and Software, SCS 2003 (2003)

7. Kwiatkowska, M.Z., Norman, G., Parker, D.: PRISM: Probabilistic symbolic model checker. In: Field, T., Harrison, P.G., Bradley, J., Harder, U. (eds.) TOOLS 2002. LNCS, vol. 2324, pp. 200–204. Springer, Heidelberg (2002)

8. Li, B., Li, M., Ghose, S., Smidts, C.: Integrating software into PRA. In: Proceedings of 14th International Symposium on Software Reliability Engineering, ISSRE 2003, Denver, CO, USA, November 2003, pp. 457–467 (2003)

9. Michael, C.C., Jones, R.C.: On the uniformity of error propagation in software. In: Proceedings of 12th Annual Conference on Computer Assurance (COMPASS 1997), pp. 68–76 (1997)

10. Nassar, D.E.M., Abdelmoez, W., Shereshevsky, M., Ammar, H.H., Mili, A., Yu, B., Bogazzi, S.: Error propagation analysis of software architecture specifications. In: Proceedings of the International Conference on Computer and Communication Engineering, ICCCE 2006, Kuala Lumpur, Malaysia (May 2006)

11. Paige, R.F., Rose, L.M., Ge, X., Kolovos, D.S., Brooke, P.J.: Automated safety analysis for domain-specific languages. In: Proceedings of Workshop on Non-Functional System Properties in Domain Specific Modeling Languages, co-located with 11th International Conference of Model Driven Engineering Languages and Systems, MoDELS 2008. LNCS, vol. 5421, Springer, Heidelberg (2008)

12. Papadopoulos, Y., McDermid, J.A., Sasse, R., Heiner, G.: Analysis and synthesis of the behaviour of complex programmable electronic systems in conditions of failure. Reliability Engineering and System Safety 71, 229–247 (2001)

13. Voas, J.M.: Pie: A dynamic failure-based technique. IEEE Transaction of Software Engineering 18(8), 717–727 (1992)

14. Voas, J.M.: Error propagation analysis for COTS systems. IEEE Computing and Control Engineering Journal 8(6), 269–272 (1997)

15. Wallace, M.: Modular architectural representation and analysis of fault propagation and transformation. Electronic Notes in Theoretical Computer Science 141(3), 53–71 (2005)

Towards Model-Based Automatic Testing of Attack Scenarios

M. Zulkernine[1], M.F. Raihan[1], and M.G. Uddin[2]

[1]School of Computing, [2]Department of Electrical and Computer Engineering
Queen's University, Kingston, Ontario, Canada K7L 3N6
{mzulker,raihan,gias}@cs.queensu.ca

Abstract. Model-based testing techniques play a vital role in producing quality software. However, compared to the testing of functional requirements, these techniques are not prevalent that much in testing software security. This paper presents a model-based approach to automatic testing of attack scenarios. An attack testing framework is proposed to model attack scenarios and test the system with respect to the modeled attack scenarios. The techniques adopted in the framework are applicable in general to the systems, where the potential attack scenarios can be modeled in a formalism based on extended abstract state machines. The attack events, i.e., attack test vectors chosen from the attacks happening in real-world are converted to the test driver specific events ready to be tested against the attack signatures. The proposed framework is implemented and evaluated using the most common attack scenarios. The framework is useful to test software with respect to potential attacks which can significantly reduce the risk of security vulnerabilities.

1   Introduction

A software vulnerable to different attacks can lead to catastrophic failure which can range from hindering normal service quality to causing dangers to human life. Therefore, software systems should be tested whether they exhibit any attack behavior when they are under potential attacks[1]. A software system under security testing is tested for security vulnerabilities with respect to specific security requirements. Model-based testing approaches provide techniques for testing system behavioral conformance to specific functional requirements [1,2]. A model-based approach to security testing involves developing models of security requirements and then testing security properties of the modeled system by automatically generating test vectors [3,4]. Testing attack behavior of a system involves modeling of attack scenarios and verifying the modeled attack scenarios against automatically generated system events. Modeling attack scenarios requires incorporating attack system attributes to the model which might not be present in a traditional modeling language. Moreover, specific testing techniques have to be developed to test the system attack behavior with respect to the modeled attack scenarios.

---

[1] For brevity, the behavior exhibited by a system under attack is called the attack behavior of the system throughout the paper.

B. Buth, G. Rabe, T. Seyfarth (Eds.): SAFECOMP 2009, LNCS 5775, pp. 229–242, 2009.

In this paper, a framework is presented for automatic model-based testing of a system with respect to potential attacks, where the attack behavior is assumed to be modeled using formalisms based on extended abstract state machines [6,8,9]. Attack scenarios are modeled to represent system attack behavior representing states, conditions, and transitions required to characterize the attacks. The attack scenarios are made executable by developing a suitable attack signature generator. An attack signature includes necessary specifications using states and transitions which are directly executable against the system events for a particular attack. The framework provides an attack test driver which generates attack signatures and tests system attack specific behavior with respect to the modeled attack scenarios. The attack test driver automatically generates attack test vectors, *i.e.*, system events. The system events are converted to attack test driver specific events before being tested against the attack scenarios. The attack test driver uses an attack testing engine which employs a generic attack testing algorithm applicable for various target systems. The framework is evaluated, and experimental results show the efficacy of the framework in testing wide range of attacks.

The overview of the attack testing framework is provided in the next section. The details of the attack testing process is presented in Section 3. Section 4 presents the implementation and experiments. The related work are discussed in Section 5. Section 6 summarizes this work and future research directions.

2   Attack Testing Framework Overview

Figure 1 presents the proposed model-based attack scenario testing framework. Attack scenarios are modeled in extended abstract machines (ASMs), where states are instrumented with specific attack attributes. ASMs incorporate attack variables in the state machines [6,8,9]. The attack variables allow more specific descriptions of system attributes corresponding to different attacks. An attack is modeled as a set of states and transitions. States represent a snapshot of different system attributes during the course of attacks. The transitions are labeled with system events that cause changes from one state to another. A state transition can take place only if certain conditions associated with the transition are satisfied. The system events need to take place in certain order to make an attack successful. Once the system reaches a state under attack, an attack report is generated (see example in Section 3.3).

The rest of the framework consists of three major modules: signature-base module, sensor module, and main module (see Section 3.1). The three modules form the architecture of the attack test driver. Signature-base module provides the executable attack test scenarios called attack signatures that are ready to be used for testing by the attack test driver. The attack signature generator is used to produce attack signatures from the modeled attack scenarios.

The sensor module generates system events for testing those against the modeled attack scenarios. The attack test vectors are generated automatically from the system events using the event generator. An attack scenario can have different representation formats based on the target system environment. Therefore, the system events have to be captured first in an appropriate format so that they can be tested against the modeled attack scenarios. The task of the attack schemas is to read system events and provide a

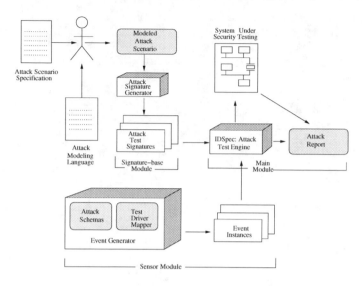

Fig. 1. Attack testing framework

way how they can used for testing. The test driver mapper converts the system events to the attack test driver specific events.

The main module contains an attack testing engine (called IDSpec) that in general requires two types of parameters: attack signatures and test driver specific system events. IDSpec tests the system based on the modeled attack scenarios and generates a report when an attack is found.

3   Testing Attack Scenarios

In this section, the testing process is described in detail following the proposed framework. The attack test driver architecture is described in Section 3.1. The attack testing engine of the architecture employs the CAAT (Context-Aware Attack Testing) algorithm (see Section 3.2). The testing process is further illustrated using the DosNuke attack in Section 3.3.

3.1   Attack Test Driver Architecture

The attack test driver consists of three principal modules (see Figure 2): signature-base, sensor, and main. The modules are discussed in the following paragraphs.

Signature-Base Module. This module contains executable attack signatures that are used by IDSpec to match the captured events with the signatures and to test potential attacks. Based on the security requirements, high-level descriptions of attack scenarios are developed. The attack scenarios are then modeled in ASMs. The attack signature generator implemented within this framework produces executable attack signature plug-ins from the modeled attack scenarios. During the course of execution, the plug-ins are loaded in the knowledge base of the attack test driver.

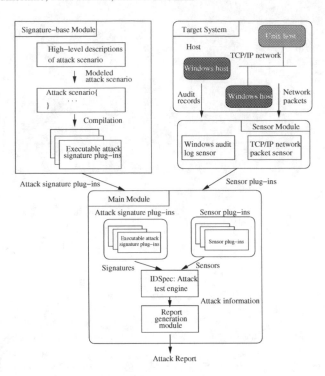

Fig. 2. Attack test driver architecture

Sensor Module. The attack test driver analyzes the events that take place in the system and identify ongoing attacks. It is assumed that attacks will leave a trace in the system activity logs. The attack signatures are written based on these events. Each log has its own format (like Windows security log and tcpdump log files). Therefore, the primary task is to read data from the event sources and convert those to the test driver specific form that can be easily analyzed by IDSpec. Figure 2 shows the target system considered in the testing process. The events from windows host are considered as audit records, while the events from TCP/IP network are regarded as network packets. However, the framework is designed in such a way so that it can incorporate other types of data sources (like Solaris BSM audit data) in its sensor module.

Main Module. The attack test driver collects events representing ongoing system activities from the sensor module. IDSpec analyzes the event streams and identifies whether there is an attack in progress. For this purpose, IDSpec matches the description of an executable attack scenario against the stream of events. Once an attack has been detected, the report generation module notifies the administrator. The notification consists of information having the time and date of an attack, the source of the attack, detailed testing information regarding the attack, and the effects it has on the system under test. IDSpec uses a generic attack testing algorithm, CAAT, presented in the following section.

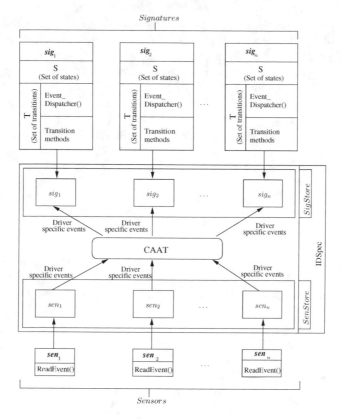

Fig. 3. Attack test driver

3.2   Context-Aware Attack Testing

The CAAT algorithm is provided in Listing 1. The algorithm takes as input a set of n attack signatures defined by *Signatures*= $\{sig_1, sig_2, \ldots, sig_n\}$. The signature plug-ins are provided by the signature-base module. Here, each sig_i represents a particular attack signature. During the course of execution of the attack test driver, each of the attack signature plug-ins are loaded in a global storage space denoted by *SigStore* located inside IDSpec. The second parameter of the algorithm is a set of m system events, $E=$ $\{e_1, e_2, \ldots, e_m\}$, which are collected by the sensor modules. Here, each e_i represents a particular system event. Let *Sensors* be the set of p sensor plug-ins, *Sensors*= $\{sen_1,$ $sen_2, \ldots, sen_p\}$, which capture events from the target system and convert them to test driver specific event format as expected by IDSpec. This set forms the third parameter of the CAAT algorithm. *SenStore* is a global storage space, where all the sensor plug-ins from the set *Sensors* are instantiated and loaded during the initialization phase of the attack test driver. IDSpec employs the algorithm, CAAT, matches the signatures from *SigStore* against the driver specific system events from *SenStore* to test any ongoing attack in the system. *SigStore*, *SenStore*, and the algorithm execution body of CAAT form IDSpec.

The following paragraphs provide the details of the algorithm by referring to the line numbers of Listing 1, while Figure 3 demonstrates the functionality of the test driver. The algorithm first initializes the signature storage *SigStore* and the test driver specific system event storage, *SenStore*. In the beginning, both sets are empty (Lines 01-02), and then *SigStore* is initialized by loading each of the attack signatures from the set *Signatures* (Lines 03-05), and *SenStore* is initialized by loading the sensor plug-ins from the set *Sensors* (Lines 06-08).

Listing 1. CAAT: Attack testing algorithm

Input: A set of *n* attack signature plug-ins (*Signatures*), a set of *m* events (*E*), and a set of *p* sensors (*Sensors*)
Output: Tests whether the events from *E* takes the system from a safe state to a state under attack by matching the events in the attack steps defined in an attack signature. (*T* is set of transitions, *F* is state transition function, *C* is set of conditions, and *X* is set of actions).

```
00. CAAT (Signatures, E, Sensors)
01.     SigStore:= ∅
02.     SenStore:= ∅
03.     FOR EACH attack signature plug-in a ∈ Signatures DO
04.         SigStore:= SigStore ∪ a
05.     END FOR
06.     FOR EACH sensor plug-in s ∈ Sensors DO
07.         SenStore:= SenStore ∪ s
08.     END FOR
09.     WHILE TRUE DO
10.         FOR EACH sensor plug-in s ∈ SenStore DO
11.             EventInstance Eₓ := s.ReadEvent()
12.             IF Eₓ = NULL THEN CONTINUE
13.             FOR EACH signature plug-ins a ∈ SigStore
14.                 a.EventDispatcher (Eₓ)
15.             END FOR
16.         END FOR
17.     END WHILE
18.     EventDispatcher (EventInstance Eₓ)
19.     FOR EACH transition t ∈ this.T
20.         IF (Satisfies (Eₓ, t))
21.             FOR EACH action statement x ∈ t.X
22.                 Execute (x)
23.             END FOR
24.         END IF
25.     END FOR
26.     Satisfies (EventInstane Eₓ, Transition t) returns Boolean
27.     Boolean bResult:= FALSE
28.     State X:= GetSourceState (t.F)
29.     FOR EACH state instance x ∈ X DO
30.         IF t.C holds for Eₓ bResult:= TRUE
31.     END FOR
32.     RETURN bResult
```

The next part of the algorithm is responsible for collecting events and performing analysis on the event stream to test any potential attack attempts. Each sensor plug-in provides an interfacing method `ReadEvent()`. This method captures data from the data sources (*e.g.*, Windows audit logs or TCP/IP networks), formats the data into test driver specific events, and returns the events to their callers. The `EventDispatcher()` method (Lines 13-14) matches each event in *SenStore* against each of the signatures of *SigStore*. The details of the `EventDispatcher()` method are provided in Lines 18-25. When the `EventDispatcher()` method receives an event, it checks

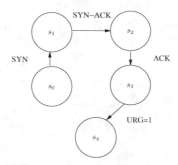

Fig. 4. State transition diagram of the DoSNuke attack

all the possible transitions of current signature instance that could be fired by the event. An event could fire a transition only if it satisfies the condition set of that transition (Lines 19-20). This is checked by the `Satisfies()` method shown in Lines 26-32. First, the method retrieves the source state of the transition by calling the method `GetSourceState()` with the state transition function F as a parameter. Then, the method checks if there exists any state variable instance in the source state that matches with event attributes specified in the condition constraint set for that transition (Lines 29-31). Depending on the positive outcome of the decision, the signature plug-in executes the set of actions associated with the transition (Lines 21-22). The set of action statements include updating state variables, making a transition to the new state, or generating an attack report in case of reaching the "state under attack". Otherwise, the current state remains unchanged.

3.3   The Testing Process Illustrated

We illustrate the testing process using the DosNuke attack. DoSNuke is a Denial of Service (DoS) attack that exploits a bug in the Windows NT operating system of a victim machine. At first, the attacker establishes a TCP connection to NETBIOS port (port number 139) and then sends a series of packets with URG bit set. The URG bit is set to represent out-of-band data (called "urgent data" in TCP) in a data stream. Figure 4 shows the state machine for the DoSNuke attack. Receiving a connection request packet (SYN packet) from the attacker changes system state from s_0 to s_1. When the receiving machine acknowledges the request with a SYN-ACK packet, the state changes from s_1 to s_2. Receiving acknowledgement from the attacker (ACK packet) establishes a TCP connection between the victim and the attacker and causes the state to transit from state s_2 to s_3. When the victim receives a TCP packet, destined to port 139, with URG bit set, it takes the system to a compromised state, (*i.e., s_4*).

While translating the modeled attack scenario to executable attack signature plug-ins, the model is instrumented with necessary data structures as shown in Figure 5. In this figure, the generic attack scenario model A has three states: S_0, S_1, and S_2 with state variables *SourceIP*, *SourcePort*, *AttackerIP*, and *AttackerPort*. Moreover, A defines three transitions T_1, T_2, and T_3, each having the form of $<F,C,X>$. Each state is implemented as a list, storing attack scenario instances, to facilitate the testing of same type of attack taking place concurrently. Different values for state variables

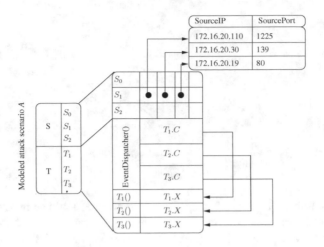

Fig. 5. Signature data structure

are stored in the list representing attack instances. For example, the three entries for S_1 ($<$172.16.20.110:1225$>$, $<$172.16.20.30:139$>$, and $<$172.16.20.19:80$>$) represent that three instances of attack type A are in progress.

Similarly, each transition presented in the modeled attack scenario is mapped to executable instructions in the signature plug-in. The condition part of each transition executes the `EventDispatcher()` method in attack signatures. As mentioned before, this method decides whether a captured system event is able to make changes in system states. Figure 5 shows that the condition parts of T_1 ($T_1.C$), T_2 ($T_2.C$), and T_3 ($T_3.C$) are merged in the `EventDispatcher()` method. The action part of each transition is mapped to a set of functions that are called by `EventDispatcher()` upon satisfying the condition set for that transition. For example, if an event satisfies $T_1.C$, then the function T_1 is called that executes the action statements corresponding to that transition (*i.e.*, $T_1.X$). Therefore, CAAT provides the flexibility to test for multiple attacks of the same kind executed at the same time by providing event matching capability to every attack signature in IDSpec. Upon the arrival of a particular system event specific to an attack scenario, the corresponding attack signature is executed by IDSpec. With the completion of an attack testing process, an attack report is generated. The attack test driver keeps track of different attack instances as it analyzes each system event with respect to the modeled attack scenarios. Figure 6 shows the DosNuke attack testing process by providing a simulation of two simultaneous DosNuke attacks against a victim machine.

Let the victim machine has IP address $P = 172.16.20.100$, and the attacker machines have IP addresses $X = 172.16.115.234$ and $Y = 172.16.115.20$. Let X and Y attempt to carry out the DosNuke attack against host P. The TCP/IP packets that are exchanged between these hosts are denoted as a tuple of the form $<$*SourceIP, SourcePort, Flag, DestIP, DestPort*$>$, where *SourceIP* and *SourcePort* denote the sender's IP address and port number respectively, while *DestIP* and *DestPort* denote the receiver's IP address and port number respectively. *Flag* represents the type of the network packet.

Attack states ⟶

Event	S_0	S_1	S_2	S_3	S_4
<X, 1216, SYN, P, 139>		<X, 1216, P, 139>			
<P, 139, SYN–ACK X, 1216>			<X, 1216, P, 139>		
<Y, 1510, SYN, P, 139>		<Y, 1510, P, 139>	<X, 1216, P, 139>		
<P, 139, SYN–ACK, Y, 1510>			<X, 1216, P, 139> <Y, 1510, P, 139>		
<X, 1216, ACK, P, 139>			<Y, 1510, P, 139>	<X, 1216, P, 139>	
<Y, 1510, ACK P, 139>				<Y, 1510, P, 139> <X, 1216, P, 139>	
<X, 1216, URG bit set, P, 139>				<Y, 1510,	<X, 1216, P, 139> DosNuke Attack
<Y, 1510, URG bit set, P, 139>					<Y, 1510, P, 139> DosNuke Attack

Time ⟶

Fig. 6. Testing for the DosNuke attack using CAAT

The DosNuke attack signature is executed when the corresponding system event is generated by the attack test driver. The first column of the table in Figure 6 represents system events related to DosNuke attack scenario. The rest of the columns simulates the different testing stages of the DosNuke attack showing successive states of the DosNuke attack signature. The different states represent different attack instances of the DosNuke attack. Moving from left to right of the table needs transitions from one state to the next state. A transition is fired upon the arrival of a corresponding system event necessary to satisfy the condition. System events in the upper rows are generated before the system events in the lower rows. For example, with the arrival of a SYN packet, transition from states s_0 to s_1 is performed by the EventDispatcher() method. A transition from states s_1 to s_2 is performed when the packet with SYN-ACK flag is generated. The system attributes are updated according to every state transition. The columns representing different states store respective system attributes related to the DosNuke attack scenario.

4   Implementation and Experiments

The three modules of the attack test driver (signature-base, sensor, and main) are implemented using C#.NET programming language. To specify attack scenarios, for the sake of widespread applications and the execution capability, a security extension of AsmL (Abstract State Machine Language) [8] called AsmLSec (Abstract State Machine Language for Security) [9] is used in this work. The attack signature generator

Table 1. Attack scenarios used in evaluating the framework

Attack Type	Attack Name	Short description
DoS	Land	Using network packets with same source and destination address
	DoSNuke	Using network packets with TCP URG bit set
	Teardrop	Using mis-fragmented UDP packets
	CrashIIS	Malformed HTTP request causes IIS server to crash
Probe	Queso	Using seven network packets with odd combination of TCP flags
R2L	Netcat	Using a trojan to create backdoor on victim machine
U2R	Sechole	Using DLL to add the user to administrator group
	Yaga	Hacking the registry adds the user to administrator group
	Anypw	Allows the attacker to logon to the system without a password
Data	NTFSDos	Allows the attacker access to NT partitions without authentication

implemented in this framework is an AsmLSec compiler. Flex [23] is used to generate the lexical analyzer unit, while Bison is used for generating the parser of the AsmLSec compiler. The output from the two phases are compiled and linked together using a C compiler. The compiler produces the AsmL representation from the modeled AsmLSec attack scenarios. The AsmL specification of the modeled attack scenarios is compiled using the AsmL compiler to generate the signature plug-ins in the form of a Dynamic Link Library (DLL).

Each event-capturing module for the sensor module is implemented as a shared library (Dynamic Link Libraries) written in *C#.NET* language. Two DLLs are implemented for the two event sensors: *WinLogPlugin.dll* for capturing Windows audit log events and *TCPIP.dll* for network packets. During the initialization phase of the attack test driver, it loads these plug-ins dynamically thus having the flexibility to add a new plug-in for another type of data source in future. Each plug-in provides a method, `ReadEvent()` that is invoked to fetch a captured event from the event generator according to the test driver specific event format. In case of *WinLogPlugin.dll*, the function returns a Windows audit log entry, *WinLogRecord*. Similarly, *TCPIP.dll* captures TCP/IP network packets and returns a record of type *FrameHeader* representing the captured ethernet frame.

The framework is evaluated for by modeling the following five most common categories of attack scenarios: *Denial of Service attacks (DoS)* are designed to disrupt a host or network service; *Remote to Local attacks (R2L)* let an attacker gain local access to a machine even though he or she does not have an account on that machine; *User to Root attacks (U2R)* allow a local user on a machine to gain administrative privileges; *Probe attacks* scan a network of hosts to discover information such as IP addresses, ports, and host operating system types; and *Data attacks* access to restricted files [7]. Table 1 presents the the attacks that are used to evaluate the framework. Experimental results show the effectiveness of the framework in testing those attacks against the target system.

5   Related Work

Blackburn *et al.* [4] propose a model-based approach to automate software security testing. The generated test vectors from the security specifications can be executed against Oracle and Interbase database servers. The security specification is written in SCR

(Software Cost Reduction) with SCRtool. SCR test specification is converted to T-VEC test specification using an SCR-to-T-VEC translator. A T-VEC tool is used to generate test vectors from T-VEC test specifications. Chandramouli and Blackburn [3,5] continue this model-based security testing approach by combining the security behavioral model and the test vectors with product interface specifications. The interface specification is provided using an object mapping file which maps between the behavioral model variables and the interface elements. The model-based testing approach in this paper tests a system attack behavior against a state-based formalism of the modeled attack scenarios. While their security testing processes use the SCR-to-T-VEC translator to translate the SCR specification into T-VEC test specification, the attack testing process of this work generates different system events and automatically converts them into attack-driver specific test vectors, *i.e.*, attack events.

Potter and McGraw [10] argue in favor of risk-based security testing which should be employed while the software is still under development. Software penetration testing technique plays a vital role in security testing, where the software is tested against all kinds of possible attacks and probing. Arkin *et al.* [11] propose that a penetration test must be structured according to perceived risk. Stytz and Banks [12] suggest an intelligent system that can test a software system while it is still in the development phase by presenting the basic concept of dynamic security testing. They argue that a software under development should be tested against all kinds of attacks. The risk-based testing, penetration-based testing, and dynamic security testing approaches have influenced the development of the attack testing framework provided in this paper. The framework can be employed early in the software development life cycle to test a system under development.

A security-critical system designed in UMLsec (Unified Modeling Language extension for security) can be tested for flaws automatically using effective tool support [13]. The UMLsec models have to be imported in an internal repository which is an XMI-specific data-binding library for the XML representation of an UML diagram. The access to this repository is provided by JMI (Java Metadata Interface) which can be used for static and dynamic checking of the model. For the dynamic analysis part, the UMLsec diagrams are translated into first-order logic formulas. Jürjens [14] provides a list of tools supporting model-based testing where the security properties are specified using UMLsec, and the model is verified automatically by a Prolog-based attack generator against the system. The modeled attack behavior in this work is tested against automatically generated system events. In this work, an automatic attack testing framework is provided where attack scenarios are modeled in state-based formalism. Executable attack signatures are generated from the modeled attack scenarios, and then they are tested against automatically generated system events.

Allen *et al.* [18] propose an architecture for testing the security of network protocol implementations. A protocol specification is converted into a finite state diagram. A valid state sequence is called a test template. Each test template accompanied with valid data is termed as a test case or message. Valid messages are separated into relevant blocks supported by protocol specifications and fuzzed to generate corrupted inputs to reveal vulnerabilities in applications. In contrast, our work uses attack signatures and matches attacks with incoming network packet sequences. Kosuga *et al.* [19] propose an SQL (Standard Query Language) injection attack (SQLIA) testing framework named Sania for the application development and debugging phase. Their approach initially constructs parse trees of intended SQL queries written by developers. Terminal leafs of parse trees typically represent vulnerable spots, which are filled with possible attack strings. The difference between the initial parse tree and the modified parse tree generated from user supplied attack string results in warnings of SQLIAs. Salas *et al.* [20] generate test cases that reveal security bugs of functional specification written in Object Constrained Language (OCL). They perform testing of SQL injection attacks based on the specification of login functionalities for web applications by injecting faults in specifications. In contrast, our work tests attacks through AsmL specification. Similarly, Wimmel *et al.* [21] generate test cases by mutating specification of cryptographic protocol. The modification includes confusion of keys or secrets, missing or wrongly implemented verification of authentication codes, etc. The implementation of the protocol is tested based on the mutated specification. Jayaram [22] proposes testing the security of cryptographic protocol specified with UML state charts. The method generates initial test data sets that are adequate for control and data flow coverage criteria. The resultant test set is measured for adequacy with respect to security mutants which must be nullified by the generated test cases.

Tal *et al.* [15] propose vulnerability testing of frame-based network protocol implementation, where the structure of a protocol data unit (PDU) is specified in a frame. Their approach captures PDUs from client machines, mutates data fields of PDUs, sends them back to the server, and observes whether the protocol daemon running in the server crashes due to segmentation violation. Ghosh *et al.* [16] mutate the internal states of program to detect vulnerabilities at runtime. They develop Fault Injection Security Tool (FIST) which injects various types of faults such as corruption of boolean, integer, and string variables, overwriting the return addresses of stacks. Du *et al.* [17] perform vulnerability testing of applications by perturbing environment variables during runtime from initialization processes, file system inputs, network packets, etc. They propose fault coverage-based test adequacy criteria. Ideally, the higher the fault coverage, the more secure the application is.

6   Conclusions and Future Work

In this work, a framework is proposed which can test software for possible attacks with respect to modeled attack scenarios. The architecture of the attack test driver is presented by describing its different modules and their interactions. A generic attack testing algorithm called CAAT (Context-aware Attack Testing) is presented. The algorithm is employed by the attack test driver to test the target system with respect to the modeled attack scenarios. The modeling and testing of attack scenarios are explained using the DosNuke attack scenario as an example. The framework is evaluated by using the five categories of attacks: DoS, R2L, U2R, probe, and data attacks. The attack testing engine compares the attack signature plug-ins against automatically generated attack test vectors, *i.e.*, system events.

This work contributes to the automatic testing of attack behavior of a system, where the attack scenarios are modeled in a formalism based on extended abstract state machines. The proposed attack testing framework can also be used to test the software under development with respect to potential attacks for discovering vulnerabilities early in the software development life cycle. The framework is applicable for various types of target systems and the most common attack scenarios. The attack testing algorithm, CAAT, provides a generalized approach to testing which greatly improves the applicability of the framework.

Attacks are of varying nature, and it is almost impossible to model and test all the attacks against a particular system using any attack modeling language and a framework. Most of the limitations and future research of this work are related to the current implementation of the attack test driver and the expressive power of the attack scenario modeling language. We will extend our work to cover more attack scenarios that the current implementation of the attack test driver fails to test. Some attacks may be carried out spanning over several login sessions or may be carried out after weeks. The attack test driver cannot keep track of such attacks and therefore fails to test system penetrations due to those attacks. Another type of attack that the driver cannot test is when the same attacker logs in with a different username and each time carries out one step of an attack. In future, AsmLSec grammar can be modified to express the varying nature of many attack scenarios. Because of the variations of the attacks in different systems and operating environments, it is not easy to measure the attack test coverage of the proposed attack testing framework. However, the framework can be extended to test more attacks.

Acknowledgment

This research work is partially funded by the Natural Sciences and Engineering Research Council (NSERC) of Canada. We would also like to thank Hossain Shahriar of Queen's University, Canada for his helpful comments to improve this paper.

References

1. Dalal, S., Jain, A., Karunanithi, N., Leaton, J., Lott, C., Patton, G., Horowitz, B.: Model-based testing in practice. In: Proc. of the Intl. Conf. on Software Engineering, USA, May 1999, pp. 285–294 (1999)
2. Rosaria, S., Robinson, H.: Applying models in your testing process. Information and Software technology 42(12), 815–824 (2000)
3. Chandramouli, R., Blackburn, M.: Automated testing of security functions using a combined model and interface-driven approach. In: Proc. of the 37th Annual Hawaii International Conference, Hawaii, USA (January 2004)
4. Blackburn, M., Busser, R., Nauman, A., Chandramouli, R.: Model-based approach to security test automation. In: Proc. of the 14th International Software and Internet Quality Week Conference, San Francisco, USA (June 2001)
5. Chandramouli, R., Blackburn, M.: Security functional testing using an interface-driven model-based test automation approach. In: Proc. of the 18th Computer Security Applications Conference, Las Vegas, USA (December 2002)

6. Barnett, M., Grieskamp, W., Nachmanson, L., Schulte, W., Tillmann, N., Veanes, M.: Towards a tool environment for model-based testing with AsmL. In: Proc. of the 3rd International Workshop on Formal Approaches to Testing of Software, pp. 252–266. Springer, Heidelberg (2003)

7. MIT Lincoln Laboratory. DARPA Intrusion Detection Evaluation (2006), http://www.ll.mit.edu/ist/ideval (accessed in April 2006)

8. Barnett, M., Schulte, W.: The ABCs of specification: AsmL, behavior, and components. Informatic (Slovania) 25(4), 517–526 (2001)

9. Raihan, M., Zulkernine, M.: AsmLSec: An extension of abstract state machine language for attack scenario specification. In: Proc. of the 2nd International Conf. on Availability, Reliability and Security, Vienna, Austria (April 2007)

10. Potter, B., McGraw, G.: Software security testing. IEEE Software Security & Privacy Magazine 2(5), 81–85 (2004)

11. Arkin, B., Stender, S., McGraw, G.: Software penetration testing. IEEE Software Security & Privacy Magazine 3(1), 84–87 (2005)

12. Stytz, M., Banks, S.: Dynamic software security testing. IEEE Software Security & Privacy Magazine 4(3), 77–79 (2006)

13. Jürjens, J.: Sound methods and effective tools for model-based security engineering with UML. In: Proc. of the 27th International Conference on Software Engineering, St. Louis, USA, May 2005, pp. 322–331 (2005)

14. Jürjens, J., Fox, J.: Tools for model-based security engineering. In: Proc. of the 28th international conference on Software engineering, Shanghai, China, May 2006, pp. 819–822 (2006)

15. Tal, O., Knight, S., Dean, T.R.: Syntax-based Vulnerabilities Testing of Frame-based Network Protocols. In: Proc. of the 2nd Annual Conference on Privacy, Security and Trust, Fredericton, Canada, October 2004, pp. 155–160 (2004)

16. Ghosh, A.K., O'Connor, T., McGraw, G.: An automated approach for identifying potential vulnerabilities in software. In: IEEE Symp. on Security and Privacy, USA, pp. 104–114 (1998)

17. Du, W., Mathur, A.: Testing for software vulnerabilities using environment perturbation. In: Intl. Conf. on Dependable Systems and Networks, New York, USA, June 2000, pp. 603–612 (2000)

18. Allen, W., Chin, D., Marin, G.: A Model-based Approach to the Security Testing of Network Protocol Implementations. In: Proc. of the 31st IEEE Conference on Local Computer Networks, November 2006, pp. 1008–1015 (2006)

19. Kosuga, Y., Kono, K., Hanaoka, M., Hishiyama, M., Takahama, Y.: Sania: Syntactic and Semantic Analysis for Automated Testing against SQL Injection. In: Proc. of the 23rd Annual Computer Security Applications Conference, Miami, December 2007, pp. 107–117 (2007)

20. Salas, P., Krishnan, P., Ross, K.J.: Model-Based Security Vulnerability Testing. In: Proc. of Australian Software Engineering Conference, Melbourne, Australia, pp. 284–296 (2007)

21. Wimmel, G., Jürjens, J.: Specification-based Test Generation for Security-Critical Systems Using Mutations. In: George, C.W., Miao, H. (eds.) ICFEM 2002. LNCS, vol. 2495, pp. 471–482. Springer, Heidelberg (2002)

22. Jayaram, K.R.: Identifying and Testing for Insecure Paths in Cryptographic Protocol Implementations. In: Proc. of the 30th Annual International Computer Software and Applications Conference, Chicago, USA, September 2006, pp. 368–369 (2006)

23. Aaby, A.: Compiler Construction using Flex and Bison, http://cs.wwc.edu/ (Accessed, April 2006)

CRIOP: A Human Factors Verification and Validation Methodology That Works in an Industrial Setting

Andreas Lumbe Aas[1,*], Stig Ole Johnsen[1,2], and Torbjørn Skramstad[1]

[1] Dept. of Computer and Information Science, Norwegian University of Science and
Technology (NTNU), Sem Saelands vei 7-9, NO-7491 Trondheim, Norway
*Phone: +47 90029602; *Fax: +47 73594466
{andreaas,stigolj,torbjorn}@idi.ntnu.no
[2] SINTEF Technology and Society, S.P. Andersens v 5, NO-7031 Trondheim, Norway
Stig.O.Johnsen@sintef.no

Abstract. We evaluated CRIOP, a Human Factors (HF) based methodology,
for the purpose of capturing the Norwegian Oil & Gas (O&G) industry's opinion of CRIOP to identify how it is used and suggest potential improvements.
CRIOP has been a preferred method in the Norwegian O&G industry and is
used for Verification and Validation (V&V) of a Control Centre's ability to
safely and effectively handle all modes of operations. CRIOP consists of one
introduction part, one checklist part and one scenario based part. We based our
study on interviews of 21 persons, an online survey with 23 respondents and
firsthand experience in workshops. The results showed that CRIOP is an effective Control Centre design V&V tool. Highlighted issues were timing, stakeholders, planning and preparation of the analysis, adapting the checklists and
the workshop facilitators' competence. We conclude that CRIOP is an effective
V&V tool, applied and appreciated by the Norwegian O&G industry.

Keywords: Human Factors, Verification, Validation, Control centre, Control
room, Offshore, Petroleum, Oil & Gas, CRIOP.

1 Introduction

Human Factors (HF) has become a significant factor in the design of any large and
complex interactive system today. HF deals with issues related to humans, human
behaviour and physical and psychological aspects of their working environment. The
UK Health and Safety Executive defines HF as *"human factors (also known as Ergonomics) is concerned with all those factors that can influence people and their behaviour"* [1]. ISO 6385 use the definition *"HF (ergonomics) is the scientific discipline
concerned with the understanding of interactions among human and other elements of
a system, and the profession that applies theory, principles, data and methods to design in order to optimize human well-being and overall system performance"* [2].
Even though there are various definitions, HF represents a system view on human
working conditions.

B. Buth, G. Rabe, T. Seyfarth (Eds.): SAFECOMP 2009, LNCS 5775, pp. 243–256, 2009.

1.1 Verification and Validation (V and V)

Verification and Validation (V&V) is an important part of any design process and thus, effective V&V tools are important to enable a good V&V process ensuring proper quality of the end product. V&V is an iterative process that must be performed in various stages in the project life cycle. This is illustrated by e.g. the V-model [3]. According to the Norwegian standard for working environment in the petroleum industry, NORSOK S-002, verification is "*confirmation by examination and provision of objective evidence that specified requirements have been fulfilled*" [4]. NORSOK S-002 refers to validation as "*confirmation by examination and provision of objective evidence that the particular requirements for a specified intended use are fulfilled*" [4]. NORSOK S-002 applies the same definitions as IEEE [5]. In CRIOP, verification is "*to satisfy stated requirements*", while validation is to "*satisfy implied needs, i.e. that the control room is usable*" [6].

There are, however, many definitions of V&V. In one of the most commonly used safety standards, IEC 61508, the objective of safety verification is "*...to demonstrate, for each phase of the overall, E/E/PE and software safety lifecycles (by review, analysis and/or tests), that the outputs meet in all respects the objectives and requirements specified for the phase*" [7]. The objective of safety validation is to "*...validate that the E/E/PE safety-related systems meet the specification for the overall safety requirements in terms of the overall safety functions requirements and overall safety integrity requirements...*" [7]. These definitions differ in level of detail, but they can be summarized as verification is to answer the question; are we building the system right? While validation is to answer the question; are we building the right system?

Most offshore petroleum installations have one or more control rooms, including a Central Control Room (CCR), in which control room operators work. The CCR and related rooms are often referred to as a Control Centre (CC). The introduction of new technology, such as Integrated Operations (IO) will give people onshore and offshore access to each other and share real time data [8] and thus change the way operators work by integrating work processes independent of physical location. IO allows for remote control of offshore installations and the formation of virtual organizations. When such major changes occur, it is vital to ensure that the available industrial tools are effective in use and up to date with current challenges. Thus, we have measured the opinion of stakeholders in the Norwegian petroleum industry regarding their use of the HF V&V methodology CRIOP.

1.2 The CRIOP Methodology

The CRIOP methodology is used to verify and validate Control Centre (CC) designs. The CRIOP methodology assumes that the design of the CC is based on the ISO 11064 development process, see Fig. 1 for an overview and ISO 11064-1 [9] for a detailed description of the entire design process.

A CRIOP analysis is typically conducted in a workshop with experts on the system to be reviewed and a facilitator who leads the workshop. CRIOP consists of three

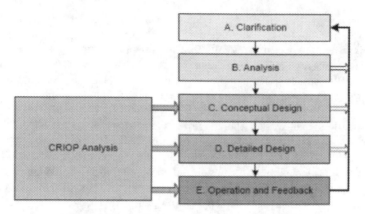

Fig. 1. Integration of CRIOP in ISO 11064 design process [6]

parts, an introduction and context of use, a general analysis checklist and a scenario analysis. A scenario is a description that contain actors, background information about them, and assumptions about their environment, their goals or objectives, and sequences of actions and events [10]. Design scenarios offer a flexible approach to help designers and design teams propose, evaluate and modify design concepts [11]. One of the most important principles of the CRIOP methodology is to verify that focus has been on important HF issues in relation to operation and handling of normal situations and abnormal situations in offshore CCs, and to validate solutions and results. Key general principles of HF design are: improve design through iteration; conduct HF analyses such as function and task analysis; form an interdisciplinary team; ensure systematic end user participation; and document the process, and these principles has been incorporated in CRIOP.

Given that the design process is iterative, CRIOP should be applied several times during the ISO 11064 design process, as indicated by the grey arrows in Fig. 1. During the last revision of CRIOP it was agreed with the industry (Statoil and Hydro) to perform three CRIOP analyses during the design process. This includes the operation phase as well as the different design phases of a control room. Note that the potential for improvements is largest during the early phases of the design process. A CRIOP analysis typically requires 2 to 5 days of effort and this is a suitably small scope to ensure proper V&V. CRIOP has been developed based on a sequential complex accident philosophy and the "safety barrier" philosophy as described by Reason [12].

A CRIOP analysis is initiated by a *preparation and organization phase*, in order to identify stakeholders, decide the scope and size of the analysis, identify relevant questions and scenarios to be elaborated and decide when the CRIOP should be performed. After the initial phase, CRIOP consists of the following two main phases:

1. *General Analysis* with checklists to verify that the CC satisfies the stated requirements based on best industry practice. This is a standard design review of the CC.

2. *Scenario Analysis* of key scenarios performed by an experienced team to validate that the CC satisfies the implied needs. Scenario analyses helps analyze actual specific accidents that may happen in the future rather than at a summary level of the traditional technical risk analysis. The analyses help to identify issues to be elaborated and resolved, such as remedial actions that will stop an accident scenario from developing.

CRIOP specifies that workers, management and the design team should meet to discuss key scenarios and the checklists in an environment supporting open and free exchange of experience. Experience from operations should be discussed with the design team and management. Issues found in co-operation should be resolved with management. The goal is to achieve double loop organisational learning as opposed to single loop organisational learning, by taking action to change the "governing variables" as CC design, procedures or work organisation.

2   Materials and Methods

This chapter describes our research design and the field data we collected during interviews, the online survey and the workshops.

2.1   Research Design

In our research design we have chosen the case study strategy, which is *"an empirical inquiry that investigates a contemporary phenomenon within its real-life context [...]"* [13]. The main objective of this study was to measure the perceived usefulness of CRIOP among its users in the Norwegian oil and gas industry. We used interviews in the exploratory phase and followed up with an online survey. Our observations from the workshops provided in-depth knowledge of the opinion of CRIOP among the stakeholders in the oil and gas industry and the application of CRIOP in industrial projects.

Data, investigator, theory and methodology are four approaches to triangulation [13]. We achieved data triangulation by comparing the interview and survey data to identify differences and similarities. We did not include the workshop data, due to the form of these. We partly achieved investigator triangulation since two authors have analyzed the survey data. Theory triangulation was not relevant for our research. We achieved method triangulation by applying three different research methods; interviews, survey and workshop facilitation, participation and observation.

2.2   Interviews

During 2006 we interviewed 21 persons regarding their use of CRIOP. A detailed description of this study can be found in Aas and Johnsen [14]. We prepared and used an interview guide and we applied the constant comparison method to analyze the interview results. In our analysis we have focused on positive and negative opinions among the interviewees, as well as their comments and suggestions. See Fig. 2 for an overview of the stakeholders.

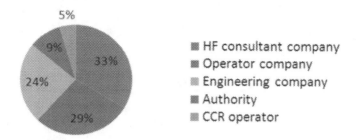

Fig. 2. Interview stakeholders (n=21)

2.3 Online Survey

During 80 days in 2008 we carried out an online survey to follow up the interview results. Out of a total of 51 respondents to the survey, 22 persons had participated in CRIOP checklist analyses and 20 persons had participated in CRIOP scenario analyses.

Before the survey was published we conducted one test survey with two HF experts, one review with five HF experts, and then one test survey with one HF expert to ensure the quality of the survey. See Fig. 3 for an overview of the stakeholders.

Fig. 3. Survey stakeholders (n=23)

We constructed the CRIOP survey questionnaire based on the research question; *Are existing supporting tools for CC design and V&V suitable for use with ISO 11064?* Our objective was to map how the opinion of this tool among the stakeholders. We used a balanced seven level Likert scale in our survey and we used visual analysis and simple statistical methods to analyze the survey results.

2.4 Workshops

We arranged and participated in several workshops involving users of the CRIOP methodology and CC users, e.g. CCR operators. The majority of the participants in these workshops had long and broad experience from the petroleum industry and several participants had good HF experience. The results of these meetings have been well documented and the reports are available at [15]. The participants had experience from the Norwegian Oil and Gas sector but there were also participants from Great Britain and USA.

3 Results

In this section we present the results obtained from the interviews, the online survey and the workshops.

3.1 Interviews

Out of the 21 interviewees, 18 had experience using CRIOP checklists and 17 had experience using CRIOP scenario analysis. We used four categories to determine the level of familiarity with CRIOP among the interviewees, and the majority had good or very good knowledge of the CRIOP methodology. See Fig. 4 for details.

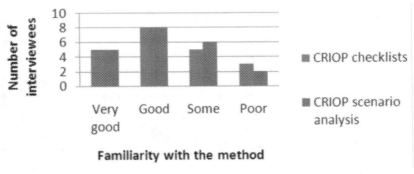

Fig. 4. Interviewees' knowledge of CRIOP

Two thirds (67%) of the interviewees specifically responded that the CRIOP checklists were *good* or *useful* (Fig 5). The majority of interviewees expressing this opinion had good or very good knowledge of the CRIOP checklists. More than half (56%), representing several types of stakeholders, responded that the checklists were suitable for self-assessment, i.e. to use them in a desktop analysis, without conducting a full scale CRIOP meeting.

The interviewees pointed out several challenges in the CRIOP checklists. One quarter (28%) of the interviewees pointed out that the checklists were too general or too superficial, while one fifth (22%) pointed out that the answers were not checked (i.e. verified), and thus one could give incorrect answers. It was also mentioned by one interviewee that people tend to focus on what is good, unwilling to reveal the potential problem areas in their system.

Another identified drawback (17%) was that there was poor traceability or too general links between some of the items in the CRIOP checklists and the corresponding requirements in standards or other public governing documents. Almost half of the interviewees (44%) also made comments on the importance of adapting the checklists to the current process stage and to the type of system in focus.

Almost one third (29%) of the interviewees answered that CRIOP scenario analysis is a good method. It was also pointed out by one quarter (24%) that scenarios were good validation or at least better than checklists. On the other hand, 18% pointed out

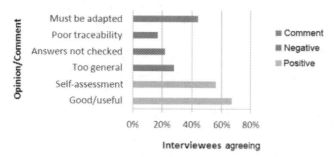

Fig. 5. Overview of CRIOP checklist interview results (n=21)

that scenario analyses were not necessarily a validation of the system, but rather a validation of the selected scenarios. The selected scenarios will normally cover only parts of the system behaviour, and thus a scenario analysis will not be a complete validation of the system.

3.2 Online Survey

Among all survey respondents (n=23), more than 80% held a Master's degree or higher and more than 70% had at least 10 years of working experience. The most significant CRIOP *checklists* results (Table 1) were that four out of five (86,4%) agreed that the CRIOP checklists are an effective tool to verify a CC design and three quarters (77,3%) agreed that they are an effective tool to validate a CC design. None of the respondents strongly agreed[1] to this.

Table 1. Overview of CRIOP checklist survey results based on the percentage agreeing to given statements (n=22)

Statement	Percent	Mean	SD	Median
Effective verification	86,4%	2,95	1,36	3,0
Effective validation	77,3%	3,27	1,64	3,0
Always used in relevant projects	50,0%	4,41	1,68	4,5
Not more appropriate for self-assessment	50,0%	3,77	1,93	3,5
Not up to date with challenges in the industry	54,5%	4,50	1,57	5,0

We also observed that half (50%) of the respondents disagreed that the checklists were more appropriate for self-assessment than to use in workshops, while almost one third (31.8%) agreed and the remaining respondents were neutral. All (100%) of the respondents who found the checklists more suitable for self-evaluation were HF-consultants.

Half (50%) of the respondents agreed that CRIOP checklists were always used in relevant projects. More than half (54.5%) meant that CRIOP checklists were up to date with the challenges in the industry while more than one third (36%) disagreed to that.

---

[1] Highest agreement level on our Likert scale.

Table 2. Overview of CRIOP scenario analysis survey results based on the percentage agreeing to given statements (n=20)

Statement	Percent	Mean	SD	Median
Effective verification	80,0%	3,05	1,19	3,0
Effective validation	75,0%	3,15	1,53	3,0
Always used in relevant projects	45,0%	3,90	1,92	4,5
Not up to date with challenges in the industry	40,0%	4,35	1,87	4,5

Twenty of the respondents had participated in CRIOP *scenario* analyses. The most significant results (Table 2) were similar to the results for the CRIOP checklists. The results showed that four out of five (80%) agreed that the CRIOP scenario analysis is an effective tool to verify a CC design and three out of four (75%) agreed that they are an effective tool to validate a CC design.

We also observed that almost half (45%) agreed that CRIOP scenarios are always used in relevant projects, while half (50%) disagreed. More than one third (40%) agreed that CRIOP scenarios are up to date with challenges in the industry, while almost half (45%) disagreed.

3.3 Workshops

Several issues were highlighted during the workshop discussions. These were timing, stakeholders' participation, planning and preparation of the CRIOP analysis and the actual results of the analysis. Timing was one of the most important of these issues. There must be a possibility to adjust the design based on the findings in the CRIOP analysis and there must be budget and time to actually implement the identified changes. Key design decisions must not be made prior to the involvement of HF experts and the CRIOP analysis. If the HF activities are performed too late, large costs could incur due to poor HF design.

Identified key issues related to the stakeholders participating in CRIOP analyses were:

- The facilitator (CRIOP leader) must have knowledge of HF and challenges regarding CCRs (or driller's cabins) offshore.
- Experienced personnel must participate in the analysis. It is important to involve technical personnel (from automation and instrument) in addition to experienced CCR operators and HF personnel.
- Communication and understanding between technical personnel and HF experts can be a challenge, thus it is important to explore opinions and create understanding between the different experts involved in the process.

One of the key issues in initiating the CRIOP analysis has been to select the relevant checklist items and scenarios during the planning and preparation phase. The identified issues should be further explored in the subsequent CRIOP analysis. The scenario analysis is an important arena for exploring challenging situations. Experienced CCR operators should be involved to identify scenarios to be explored. Given the limited time available for a CRIOP analysis, it is important not to include too many questions or too many scenarios. The CRIOP analysis must not be performed as a defence, or "cover your back"; but must be performed to increase quality and mitigate important HF issues.

During the workshops it was also mentioned that the checklist contained many questions and that the questions were somewhat academic or theoretical. Some of the questions were difficult to answer by a clear Yes or No. But even participants who initially were sceptical to CRIOP were positively surprised by the discussions and the results of the analysis.

The results of CRIOP analyses have been explored and used further in design projects. A good CRIOP analysis does result in recommendations that are implemented. The CRIOP method has been used by StatoilHydro on Oseberg C, Troll B, Njord, Visund, Troll C, Oseberg Sør, Grane and many other installations.

The participants from Great Britain (GB) and USA expressed that they found the CRIOP method useful. The references to government standards and rules and regulations had to be updated to match the legislation in GB and USA respectively, which was also done when CRIOP was used in these countries.

4 Discussion

In this section we discuss the results and we combine the results from the different methods to provide the full picture of our study.

4.1 Interviews

The CRIOP checklists appear to be appreciated and applied for V&V in the Norwegian oil and gas industry. The checklists were suitable for use both in workshops and for self-assessment, but they were perceived as general or superficial by some. One reason for this can be expectations that checklists shall require specific answers and not arguments. On the other hand, CRIOP is supposed to be used in a group setting and therefore it should be - and usually is - consensus among the participants regarding the answers given.

Another identified issue was that the answers are not checked, which could be a weakness when the facilitator does not understand the processes of the domain in question, e.g. drilling or processing of oil and gas. However, as described above, CRIOP is supposed to be used in a group setting and when consensus is achieved, the group itself ensures the quality of the answers. A check of the answers would be a verification of the verification and thus might not give a good cost/benefit ratio.

Almost half the interviewees pointed out the importance of adapting the checklists to each project, depending on scope, project size etc and to the maturity of the design, i.e. the current project phase. Such a process should be emphasized and might be an opportunity for improvement of CRIOP.

Some interviewees pointed out that there were some poor or missing specific links between the checklists and the corresponding requirements in standards or other governing documents. The checklists contain many links to standards, chapters in standards etc, but there might still be an opportunity to improve the CRIOP checklists further to make these links even clearer.

Several interviewees stated that the CRIOP scenario analysis was a better V&V tool than the CRIOP checklists. One reason for this can be that scenarios tend to be more specific about the system with a clear scope and thus are easier to relate to. But several of the interviewees also pointed out that the scenario analysis was only a validation of the scenarios, and not necessarily a validation of the entire system. Thus, the selection of scenarios is crucial for the success of such analyses.

4.2 Online Survey

4.2.1 CRIOP Checklists

Four out of five survey respondents and two thirds of the interviewees replied that CRIOP checklists are an effective tool to verify and validate CC designs. However, none of the survey respondents strongly agreed to that. This indicates that there is still room for improvement of CRIOP.

One third of the respondents agreed that the checklists were more suitable for self-assessment than for workshops and several interviewees reported the same. The majority of the stakeholders who took this position were HF consultants. One reason for this could be that the HF consultants use the checklists more than other stakeholders, e.g. engineers, who mainly participate in CRIOP workshops. Another reason could be that HF consultants sometimes use the checklists as a design tool rather than for V&V. Yet another reason could be that the checklists not were properly adapted to the workshops and thus gave unsatisfactory results.

It appears that CRIOP checklists are applied in most relevant projects, since half of the respondents stated that they are always used in relevant projects. One reason for not using CRIOP could be that other methodologies were used, e.g. that large international oil companies have in-house methodologies that are required on their projects. Our survey did however not reveal the number of projects not using CRIOP and we thus need more data to elaborate this further.

The checklists appeared not to be quite up to date with current industrial challenges, since half of the respondents took this position. One reason for this could be that the recently published ISO11064-5 "Displays and Controls" [16] is not yet incorporated in CRIOP. Another reason could be that changes in operation philosophy, e.g. following the implementation of IO, have not been well enough covered in CRIOP. CRIOP is continuously updated, but no change requirements have been filed, which could imply that there is little knowledge about how the CRIOP methodology can be changed or updated.

4.2.2 CRIOP Scenarios

Four out of five of the respondents replied that the CRIOP scenario analysis is an effective tool to verify and validate CC designs. The standard deviation values were relatively low for these questions; indicating consensus among the respondents However, only one respondent strongly agreed, and less than one third of the interviewees answered that scenario analysis was an effective tool to verify and validate CC designs. One reason for this difference could be that the interviews were open ended and thus people might focus more on weaknesses than strengths of the methodology.

Reasons why half of the respondents replied that CRIOP scenario analyses were not used in all relevant projects could be the same as the one discussed for the checklists.

Two out of five of the respondents replied that the CRIOP scenarios were not up to date with current industrial challenges. One reason for this could be that the scenario part contains a set of checklists that are known to be too complicated. Another reason could be that scenarios are considered unsuitable in general. We do however not consider this to be likely, since this was not mentioned in the interviews.

4.3 Workshops

The workshop results supports the finding that CRIOP is an effective tool to verify and validate CCs, even though CRIOP appears to focus more on verification than validation. One reason for this could be that more effort is spent on the checklists than on the scenario part. Facilitators of the methodology might spend more time and effort on the checklists than on the scenarios because the checklists are concrete, while the scenario selection requires more active participation from the system experts. Concluding on this requires further work.

The CRIOP analysis must be scheduled at a time in the design process when it is still possible to make changes and there must be budget and time to perform these changes. If the analysis is done too early there is not enough information available to perform a good analysis. If the analysis is done too late, there might not be enough time or money left to implement the changes.

It is important that the facilitator (CRIOP leader) has a background and knowledge about HF and at least some of the challenges regarding use of CCRs (or driller's cabins) offshore. The facilitator's HF knowledge is important since HF is the focus of a CRIOP analysis. The facilitator's knowledge of CRIOP, group dynamics and interpersonal relationships are important to enable good facilitation. Some domain knowledge (e.g. drilling) is important to be able to lead the discussions in the right direction and contribute in preparation of the analysis material.

When the CRIOP analysis is planned, experienced personnel must be involved in order to identify relevant issues to be explored in the subsequent CRIOP analysis. It is important to focus both on key questions to be explored and to identify key scenarios.

4.4 Suggested CRIOP Improvements

Based on the findings we have presented in this paper we have some suggestions to improve CRIOP. We suggest including a process description of how CRIOP can be prepared for specific projects and a guide to planning and timing of the analyses. We also suggest including a short scenario selection guide.

A process description should outline a step by step procedure on how to assess the relevance of each point in a checklist to match the CC design maturity and CC type, the basic assessment of when to exclude a checklist item and when to keep an item. Typically, some of the points will be easy to exclude, clearly irrelevant at a given stage in the design process, while others will be less obvious. The rationale for exclusion should be included in the CRIOP analysis documentation.

Domain specific checklists, e.g. for Central Control Rooms (CCRs) on production platforms, driller's cabins or crane cabins, can allow for a smoother adaptation of the checklists. Such an approach might however introduce the possibility of making a checklist too narrow and thus miss out points that could be relevant for a specific system.

Increased links to the requirements, e.g. standard chapters, could increase the understanding of the CRIOP checklists and their background and be an aid in the checklist project adaptation. However, all checklist points cannot necessarily be directly linked to a specific requirement. Thus including such links where applicable might be an appropriate solution.

CRIOP scenario selection was not specifically targeted in our study, but we suggest establishing a selection guide to aid the scenario selection and help ensure that the most relevant scenarios are selected and that all relevant stakeholders are identified. The checklists in the CRIOP scenario part should also be updated.

Competence requirements were identified as a weakness in the interviews and we thus suggest including a guide on how to identify the required competence for scenario analyses.

It appears to be little knowledge about how the CRIOP methodology can be updated. Change propositions can be sent to criop@sintef.no for assessment and possible incorporation in future versions.

4.5 Limitations of Our Study

One threat to the *construct validity* of our study was that we measured the participants' opinions, which may vary depending on their understanding of terms like good or great. We avoided this issue by only separating between positive and negative opinions on our analysis.

One threat to the *internal validity* of our study was that we might not have revealed all opinions of the participants. The interviews were however open-ended, and thus the interviewees could outline their personal opinions.

One threat to the *external validity* of our study was that this study only focused on the Norwegian petroleum industry, even though there were participants representing international oil and gas companies and people from GB and USA. We did not attempt to generalize our results outside of the Norwegian petroleum sector, since other countries have different legislation and thus different approaches might be in use. CRIOP has, however, been adapted and used in both GB and USA. Another threat was that we did not cover the entire Norwegian petroleum sector, only a selection. The participants did however represent a wide range of experienced stakeholders, so the most important aspects should be covered.

5 Conclusion

We conclude that CRIOP checklists and scenarios are effective V&V tools which are appreciated and used by the Norwegian petroleum industry. However, CRIOP was not used in all relevant projects. Based on the findings that CRIOP is not up to date with all challenges currently faced by the industry, we conclude that CRIOP needs to be improved. More systematic feedback appears to be required for keeping the methodology up to date with challenges faced by the industry. It also appears that CRIOP has a stronger focus on verification than it has on validation and thus it is more a verification tool than a validation tool.

We made several suggestions to improve CRIOP, including guidance for timing of CRIOP analyses and guidance to determine the appropriate competence of relevant stakeholders contributing to the analyses. The methodology must be adapted to each specific project and thus we suggested making domain specific checklists to make this process smoother.

Acknowledgements

We would like to express our gratitude to the persons who participated in the interviews, the survey respondents and the participants of the workshops.

We would also like to thank the forum Human Factors in Control (www.hfc.sintef.no) who contributed financially to allow for the travelling required to perform the interviews.

References

1. HSE: Human factors / ergonomics - health and safety in the workplace (2009), http://www.hse.gov.uk/humanfactors
2. ISO 6385: Ergonomic principles in the design work systems. International Organization for Standardization (2004)
3. Redmill, F., Rajan, J.: Human factors in safety-critical systems. Butterworth-Heinemann, Oxford (1997)
4. NORSOK S-002: Working environment. The Norwegian Oil Industry Association (OLF) and Federation of Norwegian Manufacturing Industries (TBL), Standards Norway, Lysaker, Norway (2004)
5. IEEE: IEEE standard for software verification and validation. IEEE Std 1012-1998 (1998)
6. Johnsen, S.O., Bjørkli, C., Steiro, T., Fartum, H., Haukenes, H., Ramberg, J., Skriver, J.: CRIOP®: A scenario method for Crisis Intervention and Operability analysis (accessed February 2, 2008), http://www.criop.sintef.no/The%20CRIOP%20report/CRIOPReport.pdf
7. IEC61508-1:1998: IEC 61508-1:1998 Functional safety of electrical/electronic/programmable electronic safety-related systems. International Electrotechnical Commission (1998)
8. OLF: Integrated Work Processes: Future work processes on the Norwegian Continental Shelf (2005), http://www.olf.no/getfile.php/zKonvertert/www.olf.no/Rapporter/Dokumenter/051101%20Integrerte%20arbeidsprosesser,%20rapport.pdf
9. ISO 11064-1: Ergonomic design of control centres - Part 1: Principles for the design of control centres. International Organization for Standardization (2000)
10. Go, K., Carroll, J.M.: Scenario-Based Task Analysis. In: Diaper, D., Stanton, N. (eds.) The Handbook of Task Analysis for Human-computer Interaction. Lawrence Erlbaum Associates, Mahwah (2003)

11. Stanton, N.A., Salmon, P.M., Walker, G.H., Baber, C., Jenkins, D.P.: Human factors methods: a practical guide for engineering and design. Ashgate, Aldershot (2005)
12. Reason, J.: Managing the risks of organizational accidents. Ashgate, Aldershot (1997)
13. Yin, R.K.: Case study research: design and methods. Sage, Thousand Oaks (2003)
14. Aas, A., Johnsen, S.O.: Improvement of Human Factors in Control Centre Design - Experiences Using ISO 11064 In The Norwegian Petroleum Industry And Suggestions For Improvements. In: International Petroleum Technology Conference (IPTC). Society of Petroleum Engineers (SPE), Dubai (2007)
15. Sintef: Forum for Human Factors in Control systems (HFC) (accessed February 25, 2009), http://www.hfc.sintef.no
16. ISO 11064-5: Ergonomic design of control centres - Part 5: Displays and controls. International Organization for Standardization (2008)

Reliability Analysis for the Advanced Electric Power Grid: From Cyber Control and Communication to Physical Manifestations of Failure

Ayman Z. Faza, Sahra Sedigh, and Bruce M. McMillin

Missouri University of Science and Technology, Rolla, MO, 65409-0040, USA
Phone: +1(573)341-7505; Fax: +1(573)341-4532
{azfdmb,sedighs,ff}@mst.edu

Abstract. The advanced electric power grid is a cyber-physical system comprised of physical components, such as transmission lines and generators, and a network of embedded systems deployed for their cyber control. The objective of this paper is to qualitatively and quantitatively analyze the reliability of this cyber-physical system. The original contribution of the approach lies in the scope of failures analyzed, which crosses the cyber-physical boundary by investigating physical manifestations of failures in cyber control. As an example of power electronics deployed to enhance and control the operation of the grid, we study Flexible AC Transmission System (FACTS) devices, which are used to alter the flow of power on specific transmission lines. Through prudent fault injection, we enumerate the failure modes of FACTS devices, as triggered by their embedded software, and evaluate their effect on the reliability of the device and the reliability of the power grid on which they are deployed. The IEEE118 bus system is used as our case study, where the physical infrastructure is supplemented with seven FACTS devices to prevent the occurrence of four previously documented potential cascading failures.

Keywords: reliability analysis, failure propagation, cyber-physical, power grid, FACTS devices.

1 Introduction

The advanced electric power grid is a cyber-physical system comprised of physical components, such as transmission lines and generators, and a network of embedded systems deployed for their cyber control. This cyber control is achieved by using Flexible AC Transmission System (FACTS) devices. These devices can alter the flow in the transmission lines in a fashion that can prevent failures from occurring in the system. In this paper, a transmission line failure is defined as the unanticipated outage of that line due to protective device actions. A typical cyber-physical system is shown in Figure 1 below. Figure 1(a) shows a typical physical network comprised of a number of generators, transmission lines and

B. Buth, G. Rabe, T. Seyfarth (Eds.): SAFECOMP 2009, LNCS 5775, pp. 257–269, 2009.

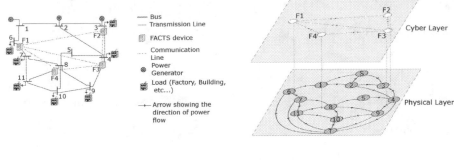

(a) Interconnected cyber and physical components

(b) Graph-theoretic view

Fig. 1. Depiction of the electric power grid as a cyber-physical system

loads. Overlaid on this physical network is the cyber network, which includes interconnected computers that control the operation of the physical network. Figure 1(b) depicts a graph-theoretic version of Figure 1(a), where these two networks are shown as parallel planes. In the lower plane, the physical layer is represented as a number of nodes connected with edges (transmission lines) in which electric power flows in one direction, while the upper plane represents the cyber components, which communicate information over bidirectional channels.

While adding cyber control to the power grid aims at improving the system's performance and increasing its overall reliability, the addition of requisite cyber components to an already complex system will further increase its complexity and will introduce new vulnerabilities. In fact, we will show in Section 4.4 that there exist cases where the deployment of a failure-prone FACTS device is detrimental to the overall reliability of the grid.

FACTS devices can fail in a number of ways, including software and hardware failures. In this paper, our main focus is on software failures of the FACTS devices, and their manifestations at the physical portion of the power grid. We use the IEEE118 bus system as our case study, and based on the results shown in [1] and [2], we simulate the deployment of FACTS devices at the locations shown in Figure 2. The goal of this deployment is to protect the power grid against potential cascading failures.

Through simulation, we examine the effect of failure of a given FACTS device on the operation of the IEEE118 bus system. The results of this simulation are then used to develop models for system reliability that correspond to various failure modes of the FACTS devices.

As presented in [3] and [4], we use the Markov chain Imbeddable Structures (MIS) technique as the basis for our reliability model. This technique requires enumeration of "safe" and "unsafe" states of the system being analyzed. System reliability is defined as the probability that the system will stay in a safe state for a given amount of time. "Safe" states are defined as the states where the system as a whole is considered functional, despite the possible failure of a number of

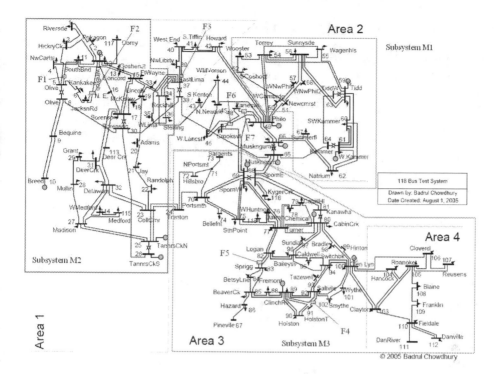

Fig. 2. The IEEE118 bus system, with FACTS devices deployed

components. "Failed" states are defined as the states where the system as a whole is considered to have failed, due to the failure of one or more components.

The main contribution in this paper is in relating the software failure modes of FACTS devices to their manifestations in the combined cyber-physical power grid, and quantification of this interdependency through the development of reliability models for the grid.

The remainder of the paper is organized as follows. Section 2 provides a summary of related literature. Section 3 describes the system used as a case study, and presents the problem in more detail, while Section 4 specifically targets the failure modes of the FACTS devices. In Section 5, we discuss fault injection as a means of refining our reliability model. Section 6 concludes the paper.

2   Related Work

Estimating the reliability of a cyber-physical system is significantly complicated by interdependencies among its cyber and physical components, as a failure in the physical network could cause a subsequent cyber failure, and vice versa. A number of studies related to this paper describe efforts to capture these interdependencies.

One such study is [5], where the authors provide a qualitative analysis of interdependencies among the electric, water, gas, oil, and telecommunication networks. The paper describes how a failure in one network, such as the power grid, can cause disruptions in other networks, such as curtailment in the production of natural gas, or disruptions in irrigation pumps in the water distribution system. Second- and third-order effects are also investigated, highlighting the importance of studying interdependencies among the systems.

In another study, Lee et al. present an algorithm that identifies vulnerabilities in the design of infrastructure systems by observing the interdependencies among them [6]. They also present an example that illustrates interdependencies between the power and telecommunication systems.

It is important to stress that in the two aforementioned studies, the analysis of interdependencies is of a qualitative nature. Our model, however, proceeds to quantitatively capture such interdependencies through semantic understanding of a specific system as an example, the physical power distribution system and the power electronics used for its cyber control.

Reliability of the physical infrastructure of the power grid has been the topic of decades of research. These studies are vital to analysis of modern power distribution systems, however, they give no consideration to cyber control, computation, or communication issues, and as such, their application to intelligent networks is limited. Notable examples of reliability analysis of physical components of the power grid include [7] and [8].

The study presented in [8] sheds light on the main challenges in modeling the reliability of the power grid. Factors cited include conceptual difficulties in defining appropriate metrics for the evaluation, challenges in choosing appropriate models, and computational limitations. Alleviating computational limitations on reliability analysis is one objective of our work.

The study in [7] presents a method for evaluating the reliability of an electric power generation system with alternative energy sources, such as solar panels and wind turbines. The model presented attempts to capture the effects of primary energy fluctuations, in addition to failure and repair characteristics of the alternative sources. The focus of this study is on the generation aspect of the power grid, and its results do not extend to the remainder of the grid, in particular the transmission lines, whose failures can cause cascading power outages.

In this paper, we go beyond the physical infrastructure to explore interdependencies among the cyber and physical components of the power grid, with regard to their semantics. Our goal is the development of a quantitative reliability model that captures such interdependencies. A number of related studies take a qualitative approach to the same problem, including [9], which analyzes interdependencies among the electric power infrastructure and the information infrastructures supporting its management, control and maintenance.

The EU Critical Utility Infrastructural Analysis initiative (CRUTIAL) also aims to understand interdependencies among the power and information infrastructures. Results published thus far include [10,11,12,13], all of which provide a qualitative analysis of security aspects in the power grid infrastructure. In [11], the authors present a detailed analysis of several potential intrusion scenarios in the power grid infrastructure in an attempt to raise the issue of security in the system and help develop methods to defend against such intrusions. The author of [11] tries to motivate the research towards increasing the security of the control systems that manage critical infrastructures. The paper presents reasons for enforcing increased security based on past attacks or potential security breaches, and provides general ideas for improving the security of those systems, in addition to identifying potential challenges. Recommendations for improvements to the reliability and robustness of intelligent power grids are made in [12].

In another study, vulnerability assessment of cyber security in a SCADA system used to control the operation of the power grid is presented in [14]. Two submodels are used for the system; a firewall model that regulates the packets flowing between the networks, and a password model, which is used to monitor penetration attempts. Petri nets are used to model the system, and simulation is used to provide an estimate of the vulnerability of the system to security attacks launched against it. This work is similar to our work, in the sense that it addresses control of the power grid; however, their focus is on security aspects of the system, rather than reliability.

A number of interesting studies have been carried out on the topic of fault injection for dependability analysis, including [15] and [16]. In [16], the authors define a methodology for dependability assessment of a hardware/software system by using fault injection tools. They explain the use of the "Messaline" fault injection tool and provide examples and experimental results. While the fault injection framework presented was mainly focused on hardware, the methodology provided will be useful in our efforts towards improving our model by implementing software fault injection schemes.

The injection of software faults into a high-speed network system and assessment of the effect of those faults on the network dependability is presented in [15]. The types of faults analyzed in this paper include message corruption, message drop, and computer hanging, which are similar to the types of software faults that can occur in the cyber network of FACTS devices. The investigation presented concerns a purely cyber system.

The work presented in this paper is part of an ongoing research project, and a continuation of the work presented in [3] and [4]. Significant advances have been made since the publication of [4], as we have investigated software failures in the cyber network of FACTS devices, and their effect on the physical portion of the power grid. The work presented here leads to the introduction of fault injection as an enabling tool for refinement of our reliability model for the power grid.

3   Effects of Cyber Control on Grid Reliability

In the absence of cyber control of the physical network, the power grid is vulnerable to cascading failures. A number of these failures can be mitigated through prudent deployment of FACTS devices, the form of cyber control investigated in this paper. In the IEEE118 bus system used as our case study, four cascading scenarios were found to be mitigated by proper FACTS placement [2]. Table 1 summarizes the cascading failures, and Table 2 shows the locations where FACTS

Table 1. Preventable Cascading Failures in the IEEE118 Bus System

Cascading Failure	Stage 1	Stage 2	Stage 3	Stage 4	Stage 5	Stage 6	Stage 7	Stage 8
1	4-5	5-11	7-12	3-5	16-17	14-15	failure	
2	37-39	37-40	40-42	40-41	failure			
3	47-69	47-49	46-48	45-49	failure			
4	89-92	82-83	91-92	100-101	94-100	95-96	94-96	failure

Table 2. Locations of FACTS Devices Required for Mitigation of Failures

Cascading Failure	Initiating Line	1st Device/Line	2nd Device/Line
1	(4-5)	F1/(5-11)	F2/(7-12)
2	(37-39)	F3/(37-40)	
3	(89-92)	F4/(91-92)	F5/(82-83)
4	(47-69)	F6/(47-49)	F7/(48-49)

devices can be deployed to prevent each cascading failure. These locations are also depicted in Figure 2.

The IEEE118 bus system includes 210 transmission lines, out of which only 143 can fail without causing the system to fail, according to our simulation. Any state where the only failed component of the physical network is one of these 143 lines is classified as a "safe" state for the grid. Any state where two or more lines have failed is considered a "failed" state. In our work, we focus on the failures of transmission lines, since the other physical components of the grid usually have sufficient backup to compensate for their failures. With those arguments in mind, application of the MIS technique yields the following model for system reliability, when no FACTS devices are included, i.e., system reliability of the purely physical grid.

$$R_{sys} = p_L^{210} + 143 p_L^{209} q_L \qquad (1)$$

where p_L is the reliability of the transmission line, and $q_L = 1 - p_L$ is the unreliability of the transmission line. For tractability, all transmission lines have been assumed to be equally reliable.

Adding FACTS devices to the system is expected to increase the reliability of the system, as the purpose of their deployment is mitigation of failure. This is reflected in the MIS model by an overall increase in the number of "safe" states, which yields higher reliability.

For example, consider the simple case where a FACTS device can never do any harm to the network, i.e., if the device fails, the system simply bypasses it and continues to operate. This is denoted as the the "fail-bypass" failure mode. In this failure mode, correct operation of the FACTS devices adds safe states to the system, and failure of these devices has no effect on system operation, as a failed device is bypassed. The additional safe states correspond to the cascading failures prevented by introducing the FACTS devices (see Table 2). The resulting reliability model is given by Equation 2.

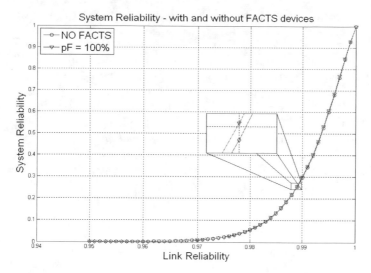

Fig. 3. System reliability, with and without FACTS devices

$$R_{sys} = p_L^{210} + 143 p_L^{209} q_L + p_L^{209} q_{L_{(4-5)}} p_{F_1} p_{F_2} + p_L^{209} q_{L_{(37-39)}} p_{F_3} \qquad (2)$$
$$+ p_L^{209} q_{L_{(89-92)}} p_{F_4} p_{F_5} + p_L^{209} q_{L_{(47-69)}} p_{F_6} p_{F_7}$$

where p_{F_i} and $q_{F_i} = 1 - p_{F_i}$ are the reliability and unreliability of FACTS device i, respectively.

If we assume that all FACTS devices are equally reliable, the model reduces to the following:

$$R_{sys} = p_L^{210} + p_L^{209} q_L (143 + 3 p_F^2 + p_F) \qquad (3)$$

An increase in system reliability is evident from comparing Equations 1 and 3. Figure 3, which depicts the system reliability with and without FACTS devices, confirms this assertion. The average increase in reliability was found to be about 0.18%. The financial savings that result from the prevention of cascading failures magnify the impact of even the smallest improvements to grid reliability.

In the following section, we investigate more sophisticated failure modes of the FACTS devices and evaluate their effect on system reliability.

4   Software-Induced Failures in Cyber Control

Faults in the software executed by the FACTS devices can lead to failures that can affect the performance of the power grid. Here, we focus on failures in software, rather than hardware, since hardware reliability is a well studied area and hardware failures can be mitigated by redundancy. This section extends the analysis of the previous section to three non-trivial failure modes of FACTS devices. A system reliability model is developed for each failure mode.

4.1   Failure Mode 1: Fail-Limit to Line Capacity

This mode occurs when a FACTS device has lost its ability to decide on an appropriate setting for the line on which it is deployed. This could be due to loss of communication with other FACTS devices in the system. In such a case, if the flow in the line carrying the FACTS device is already within the line capacity, the FACTS device leaves it as is, but if the flow begins to exceed the line capacity, the FACTS device will limit it to the line capacity. The latter will only be necessary if a line fails elsewhere in the system.

This is a localized approach that prevents failure of the line carrying the FACTS device, but could lead to overloads in other parts of the grid, and even cascading failure. Due to lack of communication capability, a FACTS device that has failed in this mode can monitor only the line on which it is deployed, and has no information about the consequences of its actions for other lines in the grid.

This situation was investigated for the IEEE118 bus system, and using simulation, we verified that cascading failure is a possible result of FACTS device failure in mode 1. The results of this simulation were used to identify the "safe" and "failed" states of the grid, leading to the reliability model of Equation 4.

$$
\begin{aligned}
R_{sys} = {} & p_L^{210} + p_L^{209} q_{L_{(4-5)}} q_{F_1} p_{F_2} p_F^5 + p_L^{209} q_{L_{(4-5)}} p_{F_1} p_{F_2} p_F^5 \\
& + p_L^{209} q_{L_{(37-39)}} q_{F_3} p_F^6 + p_L^{209} q_{L_{(37-39)}} p_{F_3} p_F^6 + p_L^{209} q_{L_{(89-92)}} q_{F_4} p_{F_5} p_F^5 \\
& + p_L^{209} q_{L_{(89-92)}} p_{F_4} p_{F_5} p_F^5 + p_L^{209} q_{L_{(47-69)}} q_{F_6} p_{F_7} p_F^5 \\
& + p_L^{209} q_{L_{(47-69)}} p_{F_6} p_{F_7} p_F^5 + 143 p_L^{209} q_L
\end{aligned}
\tag{4}
$$

Assuming all transmission lines and all FACTS devices are equally reliable, respectively, the model reduces to that of Equation 5.

$$
R_{sys} = p_L^{210} + 143 p_L^{209} q_L + 4 p_L^{209} q_L p_F^6
\tag{5}
$$

4.2   Failure Mode 2: Erroneously Set Flow to Line Capacity

In this failure mode, the FACTS device will push the flow on its corresponding transmission line to the line's capacity. This will happen even in the absence of failures elsewhere in the system, unlike mode 1, where the failure of the FACTS device only manifested when failure of a different transmission line is about to cause overload in the line bearing the device.

As in mode 1, this erroneous operation will not cause failure on the line bearing the device, but it may have consequences for other lines in the system. Simulation of this failure mode confirmed that cascading failures could occur as a result of failures in mode 2. This mode is an example of a situation where cyber control is actually detrimental to a functional physical system. This underscores the fact that only highly reliable cyber control will only improve a physical system.

Using simulation, the reliability model of Equation 6 for the grid, assuming failure mode 2 for the FACTS devices.

$$R_{sys} = p_L^{210}(p_F^7 + 4p_F^6 q_F) + 143p_L^{209}q_L(p_F^7 + 4p_F^6 q_F) + 4p_L^{209}q_L p_F^6 \qquad (6)$$

4.3 Failure Mode 3: Erroneously Set Flow to 80% of Correct Value

This case is similar to failure mode 2, in that failure of the FACTS device can cause the grid to fail, even when all physical components are functioning correctly. However, instead of pushing the flow in the transmission line bearing the FACTS device to its capacity, as in mode 2, the failure results in the flow being set to 80% of what would have been the correct value. This fault could occur due to malfunction of the maximum flow algorithm used to calculate the appropriate settings for the FACTS devices [17].

As in the failure modes 1 and 2, this incorrect operation of the FACT device will not cause an overload in the line bearing the device, but it may cause overloads elsewhere in the grid. Simulation was used to verify that FACTS device failure in mode 3 could lead to cascading failures. Results of the simulation were used to develop the reliability model of Equation 7, which assumes that the FACTS devices fail in mode 3.

$$R_{sys} = p_L^{210}p_F + p_L^{209}q_L(141p_F + 3p_F^2 + p_F^3 + 1) \qquad (7)$$

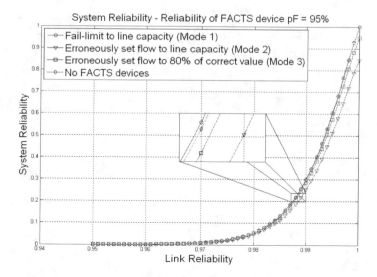

Fig. 4. System reliability in different software failure modes

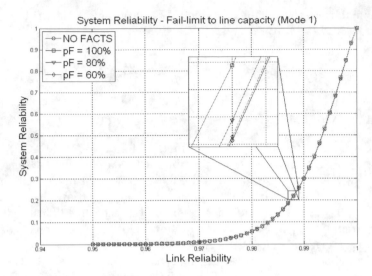

Fig. 5. System reliability - Fail-limit to line capacity (mode 1)

4.4   Comparison of Failure Modes

Figure 4 compares system reliability for the three aforementioned failure modes, using the reliability models of Equations 5 through 7. The figure shows that failure mode 2, where the flow of the line bearing the FACTS device is erroneously set to line capacity, is most detrimental to system reliability, while failure mode 1, which only limits the flow to capacity in case of an overload, is least detrimental.

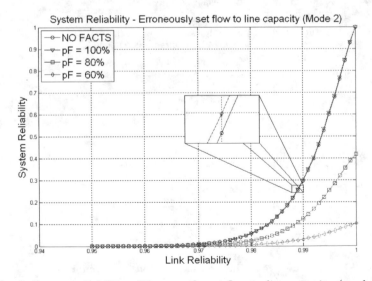

Fig. 6. System reliability - Erroneously set flow to line capacity (mode 2)

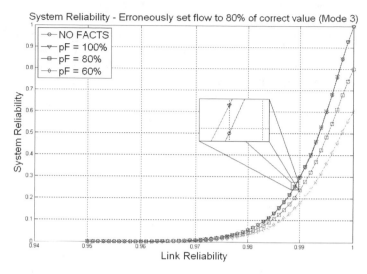

Fig. 7. System reliability - Erroneously set flow to 80% of correct value (mode 3)

The figure illustrates that needlessly changing the flow on a line, as in modes 2 and 3, generally has worse consequences than carrying out an incorrect operation when action is required, as happens in mode 1.

Figures 5 through 7 show the system reliability in failure modes 1 through 3, respectively. For failure mode 1, even an unreliable FACTS device is never detrimental to the grid reliability. At worst, a failed FACTS device will lead to the same reliability as a purely physical grid. In the other two modes, however, the FACTS devices have to be extremely reliable in order to provide an improvement to the overall system reliability. It can be seen from Figures 6 and 7 that system reliability decreases drastically as the reliability of FACTS device decreases. This underscores the potential damage that can be caused by an unreliable FACTS device, or more generally, cyber control, to even a perfectly functional physical system.

5   Software Fault Injection to the Cyber Network

The analysis presented so far describes how the impact of a faulty FACTS device on the operation of the physical part of the power grid. We have analyzed three failure modes in which failed FACTS devices could potentially cause cascading failures in the physical part of the power grid. More thorough investigation on the operation of FACTS device can help identify the causes of such failures.

In the advanced electric power grid presented in this paper, the cyber control is intended to prevent failures through control of the power flow in specific lines. The cyber network of FACTS devices runs a distributed version of the maximum flow algorithm [17] to determine appropriate settings for these transmission lines.

The main task of a FACTS device is to set the power flow in its transmission line to some predetermined value, but another very important contribution made by each FACTS device is to help determine that value. The network of interconnected FACTS devices collectively executes the maximum flow algorithm, in a distributed fashion. Three types of faults can contribute to failure in the operation of a FACTS device:

- A vertex fault
- An edge fault
- A message fault

The next stage of the research described in this paper will include injection of all three types of faults into the cyber network, as it executes the maximum flow algorithm, and investigate the effect of such faults on the operation of the FACTS devices. We anticipate that faults injected into the system will cause the FACTS device to operate in of the three failure modes discussed in Section 4. Additional failure modes are also possible. One objective of this research is comprehensive identification of the failure modes for cyber control of the grid, which will facilitate determination of the causes of failure. Our reliability model will be refined and improved as a result, and we anticipate valuable insight into increasing the efficacy of cyber control of the grid.

6   Conclusions

In this paper, we presented a reliability model for the advanced electric power grid, as a cyber-physical system, with a focus on software faults. FACTS devices, which control the flow of power in the physical infrastructure, were the tools of choice in carrying out cyber control. The effect of this form of cyber control on the overall reliability of the grid was quantitatively investigated using simulation, for different failure modes of the FACTS devices.

This research described in this paper laid the groundwork for the next stage of our analysis of cyber-physical systems: software fault injection into the cyber control. The insight gained into root causes of FACTS device failure will be used to further refine the reliability models, facilitating accurate quantitative analysis of reliability of the power grid.

References

1. Chowdhury, B.H., Baravc, S.: Creating cascading failure scenarios in interconnected power systems. In: IEEE Power Engineering Society General Meeting (June 2006)
2. Lininger, A., McMillin, B., Crow, M., Chowdhury, B.: Use of max-flow on FACTS devices. In: North American Power Symposium (2007)
3. Faza, A., Sedigh, S., McMillin, B.: Reliability Modeling for the Advanced Electric Power Grid. In: Saglietti, F., Oster, N. (eds.) SAFECOMP 2007. LNCS, vol. 4680, pp. 370–383. Springer, Heidelberg (2007)

4. Faza, A., Sedigh, S., McMillin, B.: The Advanced Electric Power Grid: Complexity Reduction Techniques for Reliability Modeling. In: Harrison, M.D., Sujan, M.-A. (eds.) SAFECOMP 2008. LNCS, vol. 5219, pp. 429–439. Springer, Heidelberg (2008)

5. Rinaldi, S., Peerenboom, J., Kelly, T.: Identifying, understanding, and analyzing critical infrastructure interdependencies. IEEE Control Systems Magazine 11(6), 11–25 (2001)

6. Lee, E.E., Mitchell, J., Wallace, W.: Assessing vulnerability of proposed designs for interdependent infrastructure systems. In: Proceedings of the 37th Annual Hawaii International Conference on System Sciences (January 2004)

7. Singh, C., Lago-Gonzalez, A.: Reliability Modeling of Generation Systems Including Unconventional Energy Sources. IEEE Transactiosn on Power Apparatus and Systems PAS-104(5), 1049–1056 (1985)

8. Endrenyi, J., Bhavaraju, M., Clements, K., Dhir, K., McCoy, M., Medicherla, K., Reppen, N., Salvaderi, L., Shahidehpour, S., Singh, C., Stratton, J.: Bulk Power System Reliability Concepts and Applications. IEEE Transactions on Power Systems 3(1), 109–117 (1988)

9. Laprie, J.C., Kanoun, K., Kaaniche, M.: Modelling interdependencies between the electricity and information infrastructures. In: Saglietti, F., Oster, N. (eds.) SAFECOMP 2007. LNCS, vol. 4680, pp. 54–67. Springer, Heidelberg (2007)

10. Dondossola, G., Garrone, F., Szanto, J., Fiorenza, G.: Emerging Information Technology Scenarios for the Control and Management of the Distribution Grid. In: Proc. of the 19th Int'l Conf. on Electricity Distribution (2007)

11. Geer, D.: Security of Critical Control Systems Sparks Concern. Computer 39(1), 20–23 (2006)

12. Rigole, T., Vanthournout, K., Deconinck, G.: Interdependencies Between an Electric Power Infrastructure with Distributed Control, and the Underlying ICT Infrastructure. In: Proc. of Int' Workshop on Complex Network and Infrastructure Protection (CNIP 2006), Rome, Italy, March 2006, pp. 428–440 (2006)

13. Deconinck, G., Belmans, R., Driesem, J., Nauwelaers, B., Lil, E.V.: Reaching for 100% Reliable Electricity Services: Multi-system Interactions and Fundamental Solutions. In: Proc. of the DIGESEC-CRIS Workshop 2006 Influence of Distributed Generation and Renewable Generation on Power Systemm Security, Magdeburg, Germany (December 2006)

14. Ten, C.W., Liu, C.C., Govindarasu, M.: Vulnerability Assessment of Cybersecurity for SCADA Systems. IEEE Transactions on Power Systems (to appear, 2009)

15. Stott, D.T., Ries, G., Hsueh, M.C., Iyer, R.K.: Dependability Analysis of a High-Speed Network Using Software-Implemented Fault Injection and Simulated Fault Injection. IEEE Transactions on Computers 47(1), 108–119 (1998)

16. Arlat, J., Aguera, M., Amat, L., Crouzet, Y., Martins, E., Powell, D.: Fault Injection for Dependability Validation: A Methodology and Some Applications. IEEE Transactions on Software Engineering 16(2), 166–182 (1990)

17. Armbruster, A., Gosnell, M., McMillin, B., Crow, M.L.: Power transmission control using distributed max flow. In: Proc. of the 29th Annual Int'l Computer Software and Applications Conf (COMPSAC 2005), Washington, DC, USA, pp. 256–263. IEEE Computer Society, Los Alamitos (2005)

Increasing the Reliability of High Redundancy Actuators by Using Elements in Series and Parallel

Thomas Steffen[1], Frank Schiller[2], Michael Blum[2], and Roger Dixon[1]

[1] Control Systems Group, Department of Eletronic and Electrical
Engineering, Loughborough University, Loughborough LE11 3TU, UK
{t.steffen,r.dixon}@lboro.ac.uk
www.lboro.ac.uk.departments.el

[2] Institute of Information Technology in Mechanical Engineering,
Technische Universität München, Boltzmannstr. 15,
D-85748 Garching near Munich, Germany
{Blum,Schiller}@itm.tum.de
www.itm.tum.de

Abstract. A high redundancy actuator (HRA) is composed of a high number of actuation elements, increasing both the travel and the force above the capability of an individual element. This provides inherent fault tolerance: if one of the elements fails, the capabilities of the actuator may be reduced, but it does not become dysfunctional. This paper analyses the likelihood of reductions in capabilities. The actuator is considered as a multi-state system, and the approach for k-out-of-n:G systems can be extended to cover the case of the HRA. The result is a probability distribution that quantifies the capability of the HRA. By comparing the distribution for different configurations, it is possible to identify the optimal configuration of an HRA for a given situation.

Keywords: high redundancy actuator (HRA), fault-tolerance, fault mode and effect analysis (FMEA), multi-state system, k-out-of-n:G system, failure probability, dependable systems.

1   Introduction

1.1   Fault Tolerance

Fault tolerance is about dealing with faults in technical systems [Blanke et al., 2006]. Its goal is to prevent a component fault from becoming a system failure [Blanke et al., 2001].

So far, most theoretical considerations have focused on sensor and controller faults. These redundant structures are very efficient. Obviously, the probability of a fault in several identical components is much lower than the probability of a fault in a single one. In order to avoid common causes of failures in redundant components, redundant diversity approaches are applicable. This could mean

B. Buth, G. Rabe, T. Seyfarth (Eds.): SAFECOMP 2009, LNCS 5775, pp. 270–282, 2009.

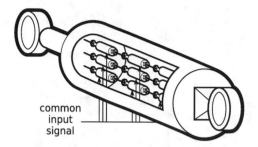

common
input
signal

Fig. 1. High Redundancy Actuator

e.g. to measure the same physical quantity by different principles, or to measure different physical quantities with a known correlation. Whilst significant achievements have been made for sensors and controllers, many of these results are not directly applicable to faults in actuators.

The reason for the difference is the effect of redundancy for actuators. Whereas redundancy for sensors and controllers is always realized by parallel configurations, the adequate configuration of actuators depends on the failure mode. For instance, a blocked valve in the closed position can be tolerated by means of a redundant valve in parallel, but a blocked valve in the open position by means of a redundant valve in series. Therefore, networks of redundant actuators with respect to their specific faults and failure modes have to investigated.

Most existing approaches for the treatment of actuator failures are derived from the information view used to handle sensor faults. For example, the observer based approach has been extended to cover actuator faults in the form of the virtual actuator [Steffen, 2005]. Likewise, the idea of analytical redundancies in sensors [Frank, 1990] has its equivalent for actuators in the form of dynamic gain scheduling and control allocation [Oppenheimer and Doman, 2006].

Consequently, the classical fault tolerant approach for actuation is replication, the same strategy usually used for sensors. Typically, 2, 3 or 4 actuators are used in parallel, very much like redundant sensors. Each actuator is strong enough to meet the performance requirements by itself. This leads to a significant amount of over-engineering and consequently a less efficient system (e.g. because of a higher weight). Also these parallel arrangements fail if one element locks up, and additional counter-measures are necessary to reduce the impact of such lock-up faults.

1.2   High Redundancy Actuator

The most general way to improve reliability in an efficient way is to use a greater number of smaller actuation elements. For example, a system with ten elements may still work with only eight of them operational. The reliability improves because two faults can be accommodated. At the same time, the overall capacity is only over-dimensioned by 25 %, making the system more efficient. This is the central idea of the high redundancy actuator (HRA).

This idea is inspired by the human musculature. A muscle is composed of many individual fibres, each of which provides only a minute contribution to the force and the travel of the muscle. This allows the muscle as a whole to be highly resilient to damage of individual fibres.

In an HRA, actuation elements are used both in parallel and in series (see Fig. 1). This increases the available travel and force over the capability of an individual element, and it makes the actuator resilient to faults where an element becomes loose or locked up. These faults will reduce the overall capability, but they do not render the assembly functionless.

So far, the research has focused on the modelling and control of simple configurations with four elements [Du et al., 2006, 2007]. Previous studies on the reliability of complicated electromechanical assemblies are rare: the reliability of electro-mechanical steering is discussed by Blanke and Thomsen [2006], and electrical machines and power electronics are analysed by Ribeiro et al. [2004].

This paper presents a method to analyse the reliability of an HRA of any size, as long as it can be interpreted as a hierarchy of parallel and series configurations. It is based on the concepts developed using graph theory in Steffen et al. [2007]. The main new contribution of this paper is a systematic treatment of configurations with multiple layers and the comparison of configurations for the 4 × 4 grid case.

A similar duality can also be found in transport networks, such as pipelines, roads or communication channels. They use channels in parallel to increase the capacity, and channels in series to increase the reach. Since the same basic equations apply, the results from this paper are directly applicable.

1.3   List of Symbols

This paper follows the notation used in the first part of Pham [2003], supplemented by the application specific interpretation of the capability c. This leads to the following symbols.

$P(\cdot)$ probability of an event,
q failure probability (unreliability) of an element, typically close to 0,
p reliability of an element, typically close to 1,
c_t, c_f travel and force capability,
$r_x(c)$ probability of capability c of system x:
$$r_x(c) = P(c_x = c),$$
$R_x(c)$ reliability of system x wrt the requirement c,
$$R(c) = P(c_x \geq c).$$
$R_{fx}(c_f)$ reliability of x wrt. the force requirement c_f.
$R_{tx}(c_t)$ reliability of x wrt. the travel requirement c_t.

1.4   Structure of the Paper

Section 2 deals with the basic terms and concepts used for the reliability assessment, and it defines the behaviour of individual actuation elements. In Section 3, the effect of series or parallel arrangement of elements on reliability is investigated. In Section 4, the special cases of series-in-parallel and parallel-in-series configuration is analysed for a simple 2 × 2 system. In Section 5, this concept is extended to configuration with multiple layers, and an exhaustive study of 4 × 4 systems is presented. The paper finishes with some conclusions in Section 6.

2   Specification of Actuation Elements

The individual actuation elements of the HRA are specified using a number of different measures. From an abstract perspective, they can be divided into two types: physical measures and reliability measures. The first kind contains physical parameters related to the mechanical movement, such as force, speed, acceleration, or distance. The second kind of parameters describes the probability of a fault.

2.1   Specification of the Nominal Performance

An actuation element can perform a one-dimensional mechanical movement (expansion or contraction) in response to a control input as shown in Fig. 2a. To simplify the analysis, only the static case is considered in the following. So the central performance measurements of an element are the force f it can produce and the amount of travel t it can provide.

While it is entirely possible to use the measurements in physical units (Newton for the force and meter for the travel), this paper will use normalised values instead. The force capability c_f and travel capability c_t of a nominal element are defined to be one (without unit). The use of integer values simplifies the probability analysis significantly, because discrete distributions can be used.

2.2   Specification of Faults

The two capability measures lead to two main fault modes of an element: loss of force (loose fault, see Fig. 2b) and loss of travel (lock-up fault, see Fig. 2c).

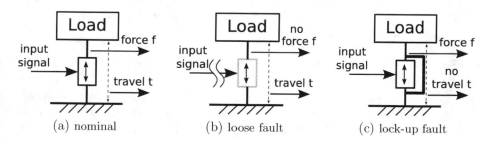

(a) nominal   (b) loose fault   (c) lock-up fault

Fig. 2. A Single Actuation Element

Table 1. Influence of Faults on Capabilities

Fault	Force Capability	Travel Capability
None	nominal (1)	nominal (1)
Loose	affected (0)	nominal (1)
Lock-Up	nominal (1)	affected (0)
Both	affected (0)	affected (0)

Both faults are assumed to be complete: a fault reduces the relevant capability to zero (see Table 1).

Because both faults are considered to be independent, they can also appear together. It may seem impossible to have an element that is both loose and locked-up at the same time. However, this analysis is concerned with the guaranteed performance of an element, and it is perfectly possible that it cannot reliably provide neither force nor travel.

It is also assumed that a locked-up element is fixed in its neutral position (this would be the medium length if the nominal travel is symmetric to both sides). This requirement is for convenience only and can be relaxed later.

2.3   Specification of Reliability

In practical applications, different ways can be used to describe the reliability of an element, such as mean time to failure (MTTF), availability, failure probability over a given time, or failure probability during a specified mission. The relevant specification depends very much on the application. However, all measures are based on probabilities or probability densities over time. These functions over time can then be interpreted using any of the above measures. Therefore, this paper will use fault probabilities as a generic way to measure reliability:

$$P(\text{loose}) = P(c_f = 0) = q_f$$
$$P(\text{lock-up}) = P(c_t = 0) = q_t.$$

2.4   Capability Distributions

Together with the corresponding OK-probability $P(c_f = 1) = p_f = 1 - q_f$ and $P(c_t = 1) = p_t = 1 - q_t$, these values span the two capability distributions

$$r_f(i) = P(c_f = i)$$
$$r_t(j) = P(c_t = j).$$

Because there are two capabilities, the state space is two-dimensional. However, to avoid the complexity of two-dimensional distributions, this paper deals with one capability at a time in the following. This separation is possible because both fault modes are assumed to be statistically independent.

In some cases, the cumulative capability distributions

$$R_f(i) = P(c_f \geq i) = \sum_{k=i}^{c_{f,\max}} P(c_f = k) = \sum_{k=i}^{c_{f,\max}} r_f(k)$$

$$R_t(j) = P(c_t \geq j) = \sum_{k=j}^{c_{t,\max}} P(c_t = k) = \sum_{k=j}^{c_{t,\max}} r_t(k)$$

are used for determining the reliability of more complex configurations.

3   Aggregation on a Single Level

The main reason for using several elements is that they serves to increase the capabilities (see Fig. 3, Table 1). Two elements in parallel can produce twice the force, and two elements in series can achieve twice the travel. In the following, it is assumed that n equal elements are combined, and that the capability distribution for one individual element is known.

This effect is not only observed in mechanical systems, but in most networks. Transport networks for example have the two properties (distance and capacity) that follow the same law. So the results found here should be generally applicable to most uses of networks.

3.1   Limiting Capabilities

Some capabilities do not increase when subsystems are combined. Instead, the capability of the resulting system is determined by the weakest part. This happens e.g. with the force capability c_f for actuation elements used in series (see Fig. 3b)

$$c_{fS}(\mathbf{c}_f) = \min\{c_{f1}, c_{f2}\}   ,\tag{1}$$

where $\mathbf{c}_f$ denotes the vector $(c_{f1}\ c_{f2})^T$. The same equation also applies to the travel capability of elements in parallel

$$c_{tP}(\mathbf{c}_t) = \min\{c_{t1}, c_{t2}\}\tag{2}$$

(see Fig. 3a). These equations follow directly from the specification and physical laws, so they will be assumed as given for the reliability analysis.

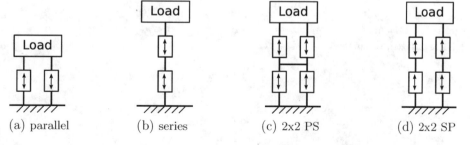

Fig. 3. Basic Configurations

(a) parallel   (b) series   (c) 2x2 PS   (d) 2x2 SP

Table 2. Configurations and Capabilities

Configuration	Force Capability	Travel Capability
Parallel	increased (sum)	unchanged (min)
Series	unchanged (min)	increased (sum)
Grid	increased (times columns)	increased (times rows)

In both cases, the capability of such a combined system is the minimum capability over all the subsystems or elements:

$$c_{\lim}(\mathbf{c}) = \min\{c_1, \ldots, c_n\}. \tag{3}$$

This represents a classic series arrangement of multi-state subsystems (MSS), and the reliability has been well studied in the literature. Here, a new operator is introduced to calculate the new cumulative reliability distribution for the overall system.

Theorem 1: If n elements with the cumulative reliability distributions $R_i(c)$ are connected so that the overall capability is limited by the weakest element according to Eqn. (3), the cumulative reliability distribution $R_{\lim}(c_{\lim})$ of the new system can be calculated as

$$R_{\lim}(c) = R_1 \oplus R_2 \oplus \ldots \oplus R_n(c) \tag{4}$$

with the operator

$$(R_1 \oplus R_2)(c) = R_1(c)R_2(c). \tag{5}$$

Proof: According to the definition, the reliability $R_{\lim}(c)$ is the probability that the overall capability is at least c:

$$c_{\lim} \geq c.$$

Because of Eqn. (3), this inequality holds if and only if all elements have at least this reliability:

$$\forall_i : c_i \geq c.$$

Since the capability of the elements c_i are considered to be independent, the probability of this condition can be calculated as the product of the probabilities of the individual terms:

$$P(\forall i : c_i \geq c) = \prod_i P(c_i \geq c) = \prod_i R_i(c).$$

This is exactly the result defined by the operator $\oplus$.

Since the original Eqn. (3) is applicable in two cases, the same is true for the resulting operator $\oplus$. It can be used to describe the force of elements in series

$$R_{fS} = R_{f1} \oplus R_{f2} \tag{6}$$

or the travel for elements in parallel

$$R_{tP} = R_{t1} \oplus R_{t2}. \tag{7}$$

3.2   Additive Capabilities

If several actuation elements are used together, the capability of the combined system may increase above the capability of any element. In fact, this increase is the motivation for using several element in the first place.

In contrast to the maximum operator in Eqn. (1), the sum applies to the force capability of two elements in parallel (see Fig. 3a),

$$c_{fP}(\mathbf{c}_f) = c_{f1} + c_{f2} \tag{8}$$

and to the travel capability of two elements in series (see Fig. 3b)

$$c_{tS}(\mathbf{c}_t) = c_{t1} + c_{t2}. \tag{9}$$

In both cases, the relevant capabilities of the elements add up to the capability of the overall system:

$$c_{\mathrm{add}}(\mathbf{c}) = c_1 + c_2 + \ldots + c_n. \tag{10}$$

This is unlike typical multi-state systems [Jenab and Dhillon, 2006], because the state space of the system c_{add} can be larger than the state space of any element c_i. Again, a new operator $\otimes$ is introduced to calculate the cumulative reliability distribution of the combined system of two elements.

Theorem 2: If n elements with cumulative reliability distributions $R_i(c_i)$ are arranged so that the capabilities add up according to Eqn. (10), the cumulative reliability distribution $R_{\mathrm{add}}(c_{\mathrm{add}})$ of the resulting system is defined by

$$R_{\mathrm{add}}(c) = R_1 \otimes R_2 \otimes \ldots \otimes R_n(c) \tag{11}$$

with the operator

$$(R_1 \otimes R_2)(c) = \sum_{i=0}^{c} (R_1(i) - R_1(i+1)) R_2(c - i). \tag{12}$$

Proof: It is easier to work with the same statement in terms of reliability distributions r. Because only integer capabilities are used, it follows from the definition of R and r that $r(i) = R(i) - R(i+1)$. Therefore, the following equation is equivalent to (12):

$$r_{\mathrm{add}}(c) = \sum_{i=0}^{c} r_1(i) r_2(c - i) \quad . \tag{13}$$

Central to this proof is the set of all capability combinations c_1 and c_2 that lead to the same overall capability $c_{\mathrm{add}} = c$. According to Eqn. (10), this set is

$$\mathcal{C}(c) = \{(c_1, c_2) \in \mathbb{N}_0^2 : c_1 + c_2 = c\}.$$

The probability of the two elements to have the capabilities (c_1, c_2) is

$$P(c_1, c_2) = P(c_1)P(c_2) = r_1(c_1)r_2(c_2)$$

because both are considered to be independent. Now the probability of a given overall capability of c can be calculated as:

$$P(c_{\text{add}} = c) = \sum_{(c_1, c_2) \in \mathcal{C}(c)} P(c_1)P(c_2)$$

which is equivalent to Eqn. (13).

This operator $\otimes$ is applicable in two situations: the force of elements in parallel

$$R_{fP} = R_{f1} \otimes R_{f2} \tag{14}$$

and the travel for elements in series

$$R_{tS} = R_{t1} \otimes R_{t2}. \tag{15}$$

4   Hierarchical Aggregation

An HRA contains elements in series and in parallel. Thus it is important to analyse the reliability resulting from multiple levels of aggregations. Assuming that the configuration is given, this section explains how to find the reliability distribution of the overall system by combining the operators defined above.

Any structure can be analysed using an iterative bottom-up approach. From the capability distribution of the individual elements, it is possible to calculate the distributions for the basic subsystems, which are either parallel or series arrangements of elements. Basic subsystems can be aggregated to more complex subsystems, and this can be repeated until the reliability of the overall system is found. For a successful application of this iterative approach, it is required that the actuator configuration is described as a series-parallel network.

4.1   Notation and Formalism

For the examples used here, it is assumed that two equal subsystems are used in series or in parallel. A series configuration is denoted with the letter S, and the parallel configuration with the letter P (cf. Section 3). A sequence of letters denotes a hierarchical configuration, from the bottom level of aggregating individual elements up to the complete system.

So two series elements, duplicated in parallel, are called SP. The dual configuration (two parallel elements, and two of these blocks arranged in series) is denoted as PS. Using two SP systems in series leads to an SPS configuration and so on. It is also possible to have identical levels following each other, for example a PP configuration consists of 4 elements in parallel.

Several examples are shown in Fig. 4. All systems defined by this notation are highly regular and symmetrical, which simplifies the analysis considerably. Following the notation from Section 3, the cumulative force capability of a configuration x is denoted with $R_{fx}(c_f)$, and the cumulative travel capability with $R_{tx}(c_t)$. This allows an easy comparison between different configurations. In the following, all elements are assumed to be identical as specified using the properties defined in Section 2.

4.2   Iterative Reliability Calculation

In each iterative step, two equal subsystems with a known reliability distribution are combined to a new system. The configuration of a subsystem is assumed to be x, and the cumulative force and travel reliability distributions are $R_{fx}(c_f)$ and $R_{tx}(c_t)$.

For a parallel configuration (xP) of two identical subsystems x, the force increases ($c_{f1}+c_{f2}$), and the travel is limited by the weaker subsystem ($\min\{c_{t1},c_{t2}\}$). As discussed in Section 3, the following two operators can be used to calculate the cumulative reliability distributions.

Theorem 3: The cumulative reliability distributions for a system of two identical parallel subsystems are

$$R_{fxP} = R_{fx} \otimes R_{fx} \tag{16}$$
$$R_{txP} = R_{tx} \oplus R_{tx} \quad . \tag{17}$$

Similarly, in a series configuration (xS), the force is limited by the weakest element ($\min\{c_{f1}, c_{f2}\}$), and the travel increases ($c_{t1} + c_{t2}$). So the cumulative reliability distributions are determined by the other operator, respectively.

Theorem 4: The cumulative reliability distributions for a system of two identical subsystems in series are

$$R_{fxS} = R_{fx} \oplus R_{fx} \tag{18}$$
$$R_{txS} = R_{tx} \otimes R_{tx} \quad . \tag{19}$$

The proofs for these two theorems are analogue to the proofs of Theorems 1 and 2 in Section 3. Instead of the two individual elements assumed there, two identical subsystems specified by R_{fx} and R_{tx} are used. These subsystems satisfies all the assumptions made about the elements, including the independence.

5   Examples

Some representation examples of 4×4 configurations will be discussed in this section.

Therefore each configuration contains 2 parallel and 2 serial levels, but they appear in different order, as shown in Fig. 4. In the nominal state, all configurations are identical: both force and travel capability are four times the value of a single element.

However, the response to faults (especially multiple faults) differs significantly. The two Eqns. (16) and (18) are used to determine the cumulative reliability distribution for series and parallel connections.

The results are produced using the symbolic toolbox in MATLAB, and they are shortened by omitting coefficients of little interest. The reliabilities for a capability of 2 out of 4 is:

$$R_{fSSPP}(2) = 1 - 16q_f^3 + 12q_f^4 + 96q_f^6 \ldots + 81q_f^{16}$$
$$R_{fSPSP}(2) = 1 - 32q_f^3 + 56q_f^4 - 16q_f^5 \ldots + q_f^{16}$$

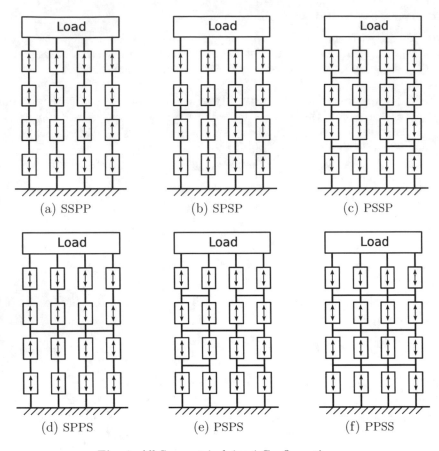

Fig. 4. All Symmetrical 4×4 Configurations

$$R_{f\text{PSSP}}(2) = 1 - 64q_f^3 + 192q_f^4 - 240q_f^5 \ldots + 9q_f^{16}$$
$$R_{f\text{SPPS}}(2) = 1 - 64q_f^3 + 240q_f^4 - 352q_f^5 \ldots - q_f^{16}$$
$$R_{f\text{PSPS}}(2) = 1 - 128q_f^3 + 640q_f^4 - 1248q_f^5 \ldots - q_f^{16}$$
$$R_{f\text{PPSS}}(2) = 1 - 256q_f^3 + 1920q_f^4 - 7104q_f^5 \ldots + 3q_f^{16} \ .$$

A number of observations are interesting for high integrity systems:

1. All reliabilities have the same polynomial structure: they start at 1, the first non-constant factor is q_f^3, and order is q_f^{16}.
2. The reliabilities maintain a partial order

$$R_{f\text{SSPP}}(2) > R_{f\text{SPSP}}(2) > R_{f\text{PSSP}}(2),$$
$$R_{f\text{SPPS}}(2) > R_{f\text{PSPS}}(2) > R_{f\text{PPSS}}(2)$$

for all admissible q_f in $[0 \ldots 1]$.
3. The reliability of travel ($R_t(2)$) follows the opposite order. So the conflict between reliable force and reliable travel is confirmed.

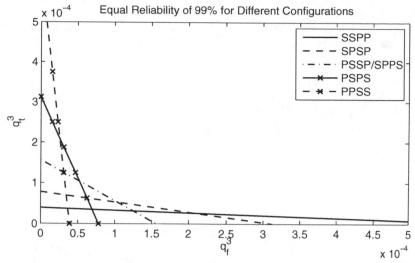

Fig. 5. Comparison of Overall Reliability 0.99

Based on these results, it is possible to calculate the failure probability due to insufficient force and the probability of insufficient travel. These cases are not 100% exclusive, but it is safe (conservative) to assume so. So the sum determines the overall failure probability, which can be compared directly to determine the best configuration for a given combination of q_t and q_f.

The pareto-optimality of the different configurations is graphically shown in Fig. 5. The coloured lines denote combinations of q_f^3 and q_t^3 that lead to the same overall reliability of 99 %. The further right and up the line goes, the better the reliability of the configuration, as the system is less sensitive to the element faults. The Pareto optimal front is a combinate of all five lines, which means that each configuration is the best choice for a certain ratio $q_f : q_t$ between the two fault modes. It is worth noting that the range of ratios where this is happening is rather small, so in practical cases it is highly likely that one of the two extreme configurations (SSPP or PPSS) is ideal.

6   Conclusions

This document has shown how to calculate the reliability of an HRA. Due to the high number of actuation elements, a new generic approach had to be developed. Using probability distributions, the problem can be solved with a low computational effort and using well understood operations.

Different configurations consist of several levels series and parallel connections are considered and modelled using multi-state systems. The results show that even with the same number of elements in the same two dimensional arrangement, the selection of the best suitable configuration (as determined by the lateral connections) has a significant influence on the reliability of the HRA.

The influence is especially important when high element fault rates are considered, as planned for the HRA. A more comprehensive analysis is planned in a forthcoming journal paper.

Acknowledgements. The HRA project is a cooperation of the Control Systems group at Loughborough University, the Systems Engineering and Innovation Centre (SEIC), and the actuator supplier SMAC Europe limited. The project is funded by the Engineering and Physical Sciences Research Council (EPSRC) of the UK under reference EP/D078350/1.

References

Blanke, M., Thomsen, J.S.: Electrical steering of vehicles - fault-tolerant analysis and design. Microelectronics reliability 46, 1421–1432 (2006)

Blanke, M., Staroswiecki, M., Wu, N.E.: Concepts and methods in fault- tolerant control. In: Proceedings of the American Control Conference 2001, vol. 4 (2001)

Blanke, M., Kinnaert, M., Lunze, J., Staroswiecki, M.: Diagnosis and faulttolerant control. Springer, New York (2006)

Du, X., Dixon, R., Goodall, R.M., Zolotas, A.C.: Assessment of strategies for control of high redundancy actuators. In: Proceedings of the ACTUATOR 2006 (2006)

Du, X., Dixon, R., Goodall, R.M., Zolotas, A.C.: Lqg control for a high redundancy actuator. In: Proceedings of the 2007 IEEE/ASME International Conference on Advanced Intelligent Mechatronics (2007)

Frank, P.M.: Fault diagnosis in dynamic systems using analytical and knowledge- based redundancy- a survey and some new results. Automatica 26(3), 459–474 (1990)

Jenab, K., Dhillon, B.S.: Assessment of reversible multi-state k-out-of- n:g/f/load-sharing systems with ow-graph models. Reliability Engineering & System Safety 91(7), 765–771 (2006)

Oppenheimer, M.W., Doman, D.B.: Control allocation for overactuated systems. In: Proceedings of the 14th Mediteranean Conference on Control Automation (June 2006)

Pham, H.: Handbook Of Reliability Engineering. Springer, Heidelberg (2003)

Ribeiro, R.L.A., Jacobina, C.B., da Silva, E.R.C., Lima, A.M.N.: Faulttolerant voltage-fed pwm inverter ac motor drive systems. IEEE Transactions on Industrial Electronics 51(2), 439–446 (2004)

Steffen, T.: Control reconfiguration of dynamical systems: linear approaches and structural tests. LNCIS. Springer, New York (2005)

Steffen, T., Davies, J., Dixon, R., Goodall, R.M., Zolotas, A.C.: Using a series of moving coils as a high redundancy actuator. In: Proceedings of the 2007 IEEE/ASME International Conference on Advanced Intelligent Mechatronics (2007)

AN-Encoding Compiler:
Building Safety-Critical Systems with
Commodity Hardware

Christof Fetzer, Ute Schiffel, and Martin Süßkraut

Technische Universtät Dresden
Department of Computer Science
Dresden, Germany
firstname.lastname@se.inf.tu-dresden.de
http://wwwse.inf.tu-dresden.de

Abstract. In the future, we expect commodity hardware to be used in safety-critical applications. However, in the future commodity hardware is expected to become less reliable and more susceptible to soft errors because of decreasing feature size and reduced power supply. Thus, software-implemented approaches to deal with unreliable hardware will be needed. To simplify the handling of value failures, we provide failure virtualization in the sense that we transform arbitrary value failures caused by erroneous execution into fail-stop failures. The latter ones are easier to handle. Therefore, we use the arithmetic AN-code because it provides very good error detection capabilities. Arithmetic codes are suitable for the protection of commodity hardware because guarantees can be provided independent of the executing hardware. This paper presents the encoding compiler EC-AN which applies AN-encoding to arbitrary programs. According to our knowledge, this is the first in software implemented complete AN-encoding. Former encoding compilers either encode only small parts of applications or trade-off safety to enable complete AN-encoding.

1 Introduction

Historically, hardware reliability has been increasing with every new generation. However, one expects that in the future, decreasing feature size of hardware will not lead to more reliable but to less reliable hardware. Borkar in [8] impressively describes the effects of reduced feature sizes. Even today's CPUs already have a variation in operating frequency of about 30% which is dealt with by using die binning. But this variability will increase further with decreasing feature sizes. Indeed, [16] shows that even today's large computing systems—e. g., the Los Alamos Neutron Science Center—experience failures because of soft errors. The conclusion is that the uncontrollable variety of the production process will make processor designs more and more unpredictable. Furthermore, smaller transistors age faster and thus become faster unreliable and smaller features are more susceptible to soft errors since supply voltages decrease with decreasing feature

B. Buth, G. Rabe, T. Seyfarth (Eds.): SAFECOMP 2009, LNCS 5775, pp. 283–296, 2009.

size. It is expected that the amount of failures caused by soft errors will increase exponentially with every new technology generation.

Nowadays, safety related systems are typically built using special purpose hardware. However, these solutions are expensive because the effort put into design and production is much higher and the number of units is much smaller than for commodity systems [3]. Also, such hardware is usually an order of magnitude slower than commodity hardware because it lags behind new developments. We expect that in the future there will be economic pressure to use commodity hardware for dependable computing. Furthermore, systems will become *mixed mode*, i. e., both critical and non-critical applications will be executed on the same computer system built from unreliable hardware because it is faster and cheaper. Such mixed mode systems will require new dependability mechanisms which make it possible to cope with the restrictive failure detection capabilities of commodity hardware. One crucial step in providing such mechanisms is *failure virtualization*, i. e., the transformation of a (more difficult to handle) failure model into another (easier to handle) failure model. We aim at turning difficult to handle erroneous output into easier to handle crash failures.

Encoding software using *arithmetic codes* facilitates software-implemented hardware error detection. In contrast to replication, arithmetic codes enable also the detection of permanent errors. Furthermore, the error detection capabilities of arithmetically encoded applications can be determined independent of the used hardware (see Sect. 3).

In this paper we present an encoding compiler (EC-AN) which transforms arbitrary integer applications into their AN-encoded versions (see Sect. 3). In contrast to similar previous approaches such as [20,10,34], we encode the whole application with the same powerful code. This includes memory, logical operations, and handling of external functions whose source code is not available for encoding. We do not yet support encoding applications using floating point instructions. Those applications have to be modified to use a integer-based software implementation of floating point instructions. Section 4 evaluates both the runtime overhead generated by our AN-encoding compiler and the error detection capabilities.

2   Related Work

Usually soft-error tolerant hardware uses replication of large hardware parts and voting for error detection and correction [38,27,4]. Currently research efforts include more sophisticated approaches than simple replication. [18] reuses testing circuitry for error detection and correction and [17] extends hardware with built-in soft error resilience which is able to detect and correct soft errors and even to predict a soon hardware failure. The hardware design presented in [26] on-the-fly replicates executed instructions. [23] checks consistency of data independent parts of instruction fetch and decoding for repeated traces within an application. For this to be useful, it is required that an application consists to large parts of traces which are repeated often. All those approaches only aim at protecting the execution logic. Memories have to be protected by separate means such as error correcting codes. Of course this list of hardware approaches is far from complete. There are several more but all of them have in common that custom hardware is typically very expensive—too expensive for application in mixed-mode systems which execute both safety-critical and non-safety criti- cal applications. Furthermore, most of these approaches are in contrast to our approach not able to detect permanent hardware errors. The intention is that by providing a software-implemented error detection mechanism up-to-date hard- ware can be also used in safety-critical systems which require certification. The precondition is that the error detection probability of the mechanism is indepen- dent of the actually used hardware. This can be provided by using arithmetic codes such as the AN-code.

Control flow checking, which can be implemented in hardware [15,9,6] or soft- ware [2,30,7,29], provides means to recognize invalid control flow for the executed program, that is, execution of sequences of instructions which are not permitted for the executed binary. In contrast to AN-encoding control flow checking cannot detect errors which do only influence processed data.

Algorithm based fault tolerance [13,28] and self-checking software [36,5] use invariants contained in the executed program to check the validity of the gen- erated results. This requires that appropriate invariants exist. These invariants have to be designed to provide a good failure detection capability and are not easy—if not impossible—to find for most applications.

Other software approaches work with replicated execution and comparison of the obtained results. The protected software is modified during or before compilation—rarely, dynamic binary instrumentation is used [24]. Replication can be implemented at different levels of abstraction. Some approaches dupli- cate single instructions and execute them in one thread [22,19,10,25,24,6]. Other approaches execute duplicates of the whole program within several threads and provide synchronization means for them [31,12,32]. For all those approaches which are based on redundant execution of the same program instructions, it is not possible to provide guarantees with respect to permanent hardware errors or soft errors which disturb the voting mechanism.

Instead of duplication, or additionally, arithmetic codes can be used to detect errors. In that case, the program and the processed data are modified. ED4I [20], for example, duplicates instructions but the duplicated instructions do not pro- cess the original data but a k-multiple of it, which is a so-called AN-code. All results of duplicate instructions have to be k-multiples of the original results. In this way, most hardware errors are recognizable. However, whenever a pro- gram contains logical operations, the authors choose a factor k which is a power of two to make those operations encodable. Thereby they reduce the detection capabilities immensely. The resulting code cannot detect bit flips in the higher order bits of data values. But those bits contain the original functional value. Furthermore, the authors do not discuss overflow problems with AN-codes which we pointed out in [33]. Over- and underflows in arithmetic operations are not conserved when AN-encoded values are used e. g. in an addition. If for example the result of an addition overflows, ED4I will detect an error. This is a false positive because the C standard expects over- and underflows to work correctly for unsigned integers, i. e. to form a ring. For signed integers overflows are also required to be correct since the addition of a negative number in the end results in an overflow in its unsigned representation. [10] did also use an AN-code but only for operations which easily can handle encoded values such as additions and subtractions. They did also ignore the over-/underflow issue. Furthermore, the encoding is only applied to registers and not to memory. In the end that leaves supposedly only small parts of applications which are AN-encoded. As should be expected their fault injection experiments show a non-negligible amount of undetected failures for most of the tested applications.

Forin's Vital Coded Processor (VCP) [11] and our previous work Software Encoded Processing (SEP) [34] use an even more powerful arithmetic code which is an AN-code extended with per-variable specific signatures and timestamps. This code does not only facilitate detection of faulty execution of operations or modification of data. It also detects the usage of wrong operands which might be caused by address line errors and the usage of wrong operators. VCP adds the encoding on source code level. But VCP can only be applied to applications which do not use dynamic memory and make no use of instructions other than arithmetic operations `add`, `sub`, and `mult` without over- or underflows. SEP on the other hand, encodes applications on runtime and can be applied to arbitrary applications. SEP generates very high runtime overhead. Furthermore, support for encoded logical operations, shift operations, casts, unaligned memory access and arbitrary external functions is not included in SEP.

This paper presents the encoding compiler EC-AN which in contrast to [11,20,10,34] encodes arbitrary applications completely with an AN-code. In the future, we will extend this compiler to support AN-code with signatures and timestamps.

3   AN-Encoding of an Application

A long known technique to detect hardware errors during runtime are *arithmetic codes*. Arithmetic codes add redundancy to processed data which results in a larger domain of possible words. The domain of possible words contains the smaller subset of valid code words. Arithmetic codes are conserved by correct arithmetic operations, i. e., a correctly executed operation taking valid code words as input produces a result which is also a valid code word. On the other hand, faulty arithmetic operations destroy the code with a very high probability, i. e., result in a non-valid code word [1].

The *AN-code* is one of the most widely known arithmetic codes. Encoding is done by multiplying the information part x_f of variable x with a constant A. Thereby, the encoded version x_c is obtained. Only multiples of A are valid code words and every operation processing AN-encoded data has to conserve this property. Code checking is done by computing the modulus with A. which is zero for a valid code word. A variable is checked before it is used as a parameter of an external function, or before it influences data or control flow.

If A requires k bits and we encode values with a maximum size of n bits, we need $n + k$ bits to store encoded values. Assuming a failure model with equally distributed bit flips and that the Hamming distance between all code words is constant the resulting probability p of not detecting an error is: $p = \frac{\text{number of valid code words-1}}{\text{number of possible words}} \approx \frac{2^n}{2^{n+k}} = 2^{-k}$ Thus, the error detection capability is independent of the actually used hardware—it just depends on the choice of A. A should be as large as possible and should not be a power of two because then multiplication by A only shifts the bits to the left and no bitflips in the higher bits can be detected. Furthermore, A should have as few factors as possible to reduce the probability of undetected operation errors. Hence, most large prime numbers are a good choice for A.

For encoding a program with an AN-code, every instruction and every variable has to be replaced with its appropriate AN-encoded version. We use a 64-bit data type for encoded values and support encoding up to 32-bit integers. That leaves 32-bit for A. The encoded value is always a 64-bit type regardless of the bitwidth of the unencoded value. We do the instrumentation statically on compilation time because: (1) The protection starts with the encoding. The earlier the encoding is done, the larger is the sphere of protection. Any errors introduced by the steps following encoding, e. g., lowering the code to an executable binary, are detectable. (2) We do not introduce further slowdowns because of dynamic instrumentation. See [35] for a detailed discussion of advantages and disadvantages of encoding on compile vs on runtime. We implement compile time encoding using the LLVM compiler framework [14]. We encode LLVM's bitcode which is a static single assignment assembler-like language. It clearly distinguishes static data flow which occurs within LLVM-registers and dynamic data flow which is implemented using load and store instructions accessing memory. The advantage of LLVM's bitcode, in comparison to any native assembler, is its manageable amount of instructions for which we have to provide encoded versions and the LLVM framework for analyzing and modifying LLVM bitcode.

For example, the following simple C-code snippet:

```
if(d + e == b) return 1; else return 0;
```

is equivalent to the following LLVM bitcode

```
bb:   %tmp = add i32 %d, %e
      %c = icmp eq, i32 %tmp, %b
      br i1 %c, label %eq, label %ue
eq:   ret i32 1  ue:   ret i32 0
```

whose encoded version with enlarged data types, replaced operations, and encoded constants looks like that:

```
bb:   %tmp_c = call i64 @add_an(i64 %d_c, i64 %e_c)
      %c_c = call i64 @eq_an(i64 %tmp_c, i64 %b_c)
      %c = call i1 decode(i64 %c_c); includes if c_c is a valid code word
      br i1 %c, label %eq, label %ue
eq:   ret i32 65521  ; comment: A is 65521 ue:  ret i32 0
```

Note, that with AN-encoding the control flow itself, i. e. the actual jump, is not encoded. Only the condition is checked if it is a valid code word. In the future, we will extend the encoding compiler EC-AN with signatures as used by

[11,34]. Thereby, we will provide control flow checking within basic blocks and between basic blocks. In this case, a variable is not only multiplied with A but additionally a variable-specific signature is added.

For AN-encoding LLVM bitcode, we solved the following problems:

(1) We need encoded versions of all operations supported by LLVM. For arithmetic, logical boolean and shift operations we did reuse our already existing but improved implementations for the AN-code with signatures which were presented in [33]. But for type casting, arithmetic right shift and bitwise logical operations new solutions had to be developed since they were not supported by previous solutions.

(2) For the encoding of memory content, a specific word size had to be chosen: All memory accesses have to be aligned to that word size because only whole encoded words can be read.

(3) We have to provide encoded versions of all constants and intialization values.

(4) We have to handle calls to external libraries. Those are not encoded because we have no access to their sources.

Arithmetic Operations. For arithmetic operations we use by hand encoded operations These operations take encoded operands and produce valid encoded results without decoding the operands for the computation. [33] describes the implementation of these encoded arithmetic operations for an AN code with signatures. The described problems and solutions can be applied to AN codes likewise. Since the operations have to implement the expected overflow behavior of normal integer operations, i. e., modulo arithmetic, their implementation is non-trivial and will generate noticeable slowdowns. Furthermore, the multiplication of two encoded values of 64 bit size results in a 128-bit value. The division requires to multiply the dividend with A before executing the actual division which then has to be 128-bit division. The usage of 128-bit integer operations results in especially large slowdowns for multiplication and division. Our new overhead measurements are presented in Sect. 4.

Replacement Operations. Since encoding by hand is a tedious and error-prone task we automated as much of the remaining encoding tasks as possible. Thus, we provide a library of so-called *replacement operations*. Those contain implementations of the following operations: shifts, casts, bitwise logical operations, (unaligned) memory accesses and the LLVM instruction `getElementPtr` which implements address calculation. The replacement operations are written in such a way that they can be automatically encoded by the actual encoding pass of our encoding compiler EC-AN. Before executing the encoding pass, the EC-AN replaces all otherwise non-encodable operations with their appropriate encodable replacement operations which are described in the following.

Shift Operations. Encoded versions of arithmetic and logic shift operations can be implemented using division and multiplication with powers of two since $a \ll k$ is equivalent to $a * 2^k$ and $a \gg k$ is equivalent to $\frac{a}{2^k}$. For obtaining 2^k we use a tabulated *power-of-two* function with precomputed values. An arithmetic right-shift additionally requires a sign-extension to be made if the shifted value is negative. The following pseudo-code represents the encodable variant of the 8-bit arithmetic right shift operations. It shifts `val` k bits to the right:

```
int8_t ashr8 (int8_t val, int8_t k){
    const static uint8_t signExt[]={0,0x80,0xC0,0xE0,0xF0,
                                     0xF8,0xFC,0xFE,0xFF};
    if (val < 0){
        uint8_t shifted = (uint8_t)val / (uint8_t)powerOfTwo((uint8_t)k);
        return shifted + signExt[(uint8_t)sh];
    }else{
        return val / powerOfTwo((uint8_t)k);
    }
}
```

Cast Operations. Cast operations also have to be emulated using encoded operations. For downcasts, i. e., casts from a larger to smaller-sized type, this can be done by doing a modulo computation which can be implemented in an encodable way using division, multiplication, and subtraction. If, for example, the 32-bit integer a is downcasted to 8 bit, we compute its new value using the encoded version of $a \mod 2^8$. Unsigned upcasts from smaller to larger unsigned types require no further actions. Signed upcasts need to check if the casted number is negative and if so, a sign extension has to be made by adding the appropriate sign bits. Assume the 8-bit integer a is negative, i. e., its sign bit is set, and it is casted to a 16-bit signed integer, we would have to execute the encoded version of $a = ff00_{hex} + a$.

Logical Operations. Encoding boolean logical operations can be emulated using arithmetic operations. This implementation of boolean logical operations requires that the processed functional values are either 1 (for *true*) or 0 (for *false*):

original	emulation	original	emulation
x || y	$x + y - x * y$	! x	$1 - x$
x && y	$x * y$	x ^ y	$(x + y) \mod 2$

Realizing encoded bitwise logical operations is more difficult. The naive approach using shift and addition operations to compute every bit individually would generate a huge overhead. We decided to use tabulated results of logical operations. Since tabulating all possible results for 8-, 16-, and 32-bit integers would require way too much memory, we only tabulate smaller chunks: 16-bit for the **not** operation and 8-bit for the other operations. To combine those chunks, we use arithmetic operations. The following pseudocode demonstrates this approach for the 32-bit **not** operation. The other bitwise logical operations use a two dimensional array and smaller chunks but are otherwise implemented similarly:

```
0xFFFD, ...};

uint32_t not (uint32_t a){
    a1 = a / 0x10000; a2 = a % 0x10000;
    r1 = notTab[a1]; r2 = notTab[a2];
    return r1 * 0x10000 + r2;
}
```

Memory Encoding. We chose to encode the memory at 32-bit granularity because we assume that most programs mainly operate on 32-bit values. This means every 32-bit word in memory is stored as an encoded 64-bit word. Thus,

Fig. 1. Execution of an unaligned load at address 66. The upper part represents the memory layout of the original program, the lower part that of the encoded program but with unmapped addresses.

we need to adapt every load and store operation because they have to map the original address to the appropriate address of the encoded value. Furthermore, all memory accesses in the program to encode have to be aligned to 32-bit boundaries. Thus, we replace before encoding the program all unaligned loads and stores with implementations which implement those operations using aligned loads and stores. As Fig. 1 demonstrates, this requires for an unaligned 32-bit load to read both affected 32-bit words (at addresses 64 and 68) and to use logical operations to put together the result 32-bit word (at address 66).

Unaligned stores require to read at least one affected 32-bit word, e. g., when executing an 8-bit store, and in worst case two if it is a 32-bit unaligned store. The read words are than modified accordingly and written back. To prevent accessing unallocated memory when executing an unaligned store, we adapt the size of all allocated memory regions to be a multiple of 32 bits. Note that we zero-initialize all allocated memory regions.

Since pointers are treated like other data items and we restrained the encodable data size to at most 32 bit, we have to ensure that when compiling and executing on 64-bit architectures the encountered addresses do not exceed the 32-bit address range. Therefore, we brought all memory allocations under our control.

getElementPtr. The getElementPtr LLVM instruction implements address calculations. It does not access memory. Its operands are a pointer to a (possibly nested) structure or an array and several indices which describe the indexed element of the structure or array. Before encoding an application, we replace all getElementPtr instructions with explicit address computations. Therefore, we take the architecture dependent type sizes into account and replace getElementPtr using addition and multiplication. This step makes the resulting LLVM binary architecture dependent.

Constant Encoding. LLVM enables us to find and modify all initialization values of variables and constants. We replace them with appropriate multiples of A. In LLVM-bitcode non-integer constants are accessed using load and store, i. e. as memory. Thus, those constants are encoded according to our rules for memory, that is they are divided into 32-bit chunks. Therefore, we ensure that their size is a multiple of 32 bit.

External Calls. In contrast to dynamic binary instrumentation, static instrumentation does not allow for protection of external libraries whose source code is not available on compilation time. For calls to those libraries, we currently provide hand-coded decoding wrappers which decode parameters and after executing the unencoded original, encode the obtained results. For implementing those wrappers, we rely on the specifications of the external functions. Using the specifications of external libraries, those wrappers can be generated automatically.

Last, we want to point out that AN-encoding leads to unexpected performance modifications. Some operations whose unencoded versions are very fast, such as, casts, shifts, bitwise logical operations, multiplications and divisions suddenly induce very large overheads. Therefore, programmers should avoid these operations if developing explicitly for a system protected by AN-codes.

4   Evaluation

We evaluated our approach using five small examples:

(1) `md5` calculates the md5 hash of a 20,000 characters long string,

(2) `quicksort` sorts an array of 10000 integers,

(3) `bubblesort` sorts an array of 1000 integers,

(4) `primes` calculates all prime numbers up to 10,000 and

(5) `pid` runs 500,000 steps of a Proportional-Integral-Derivative controller [37].

Performance. Figure 2 compares the runtimes of an on compile time AN-encoded application to an on runtime encoded application using SEP by depicting the achieved speedup. In general it can be seen that the compiled version is much faster than the interpreted version. That has several reasons: (1) We are comparing an AN-code with an AN-code with signatures and timestamps. The latter one induces larger overheads for all encoded operations. After extending the encoding compiler EC-AN to an AN-code with signatures and timestamps, the resulting speedups surely will be smaller. (2) With EC-AN all encoding is done at compile time as an LLVM compiler extension. Thus, the overhead at runtime compared to SEP is smaller because the binary is natively executed.

We observe that the obtained speedups largely depend on the executed program. The reason for this is the incompleteness of SEP which does not support encoded versions of logical operations, shift operations, casts, and unaligned memory access. Those operations are just executed unencoded in SEP while they are encoded with the help of the described *replacement operations* by EC-AN.

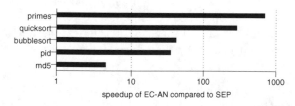

Fig. 2. Speedup of EC-AN (AN-code) compared to SEP (AN-code with signatures and timestamps)

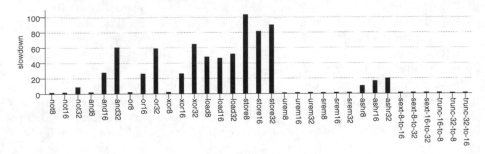

Fig. 3. Slowdowns of encodable versions of replacement operations compared to their native versions

Those operations generate already in their encodable but yet unencoded version large slowdowns compared to their native versions. See Fig. 3. Thus, applications using many of those operations such as md5 result in a smaller speedup.

Furthermore, we see that the encodable versions of unaligned loads (load$x$) and stores (store$x$) are also very expensive. Arithmetic right shifts (ashr$x$) are not as expensive but still between 10 and 20 times slower than their native counterparts. Whereas the encodable versions of the signed and unsigned modulo operations (srem$x$ and urem$x$), and upcast and downcast operations (sext-x-to-y and trunc-x-to-y) are very cheap.

Figure 4 evaluates the slowdowns of our AN-encoded arithmetic operations compared to their native counterparts. We compare two versions: One implements the required 128-bit operations in software while the other one uses the SSE-extensions of the processor. Both are as far as possible compiled using LLVM with optimizations.

Since 128-bit operations are only used for multiplications and divisions, we see only for them a difference – but that is immense. Nevertheless, the slowdowns are very large. For the future, we plan to extend EC-AN so that it supports adaptive encoding. As stated in [21] not all calculations are equally important. We want to enable the programmer to identify safety-critical parts of an application. The encoding will then only be applied to those parts thereby reducing the performance impact. The rest of the program (e.g. book-keeping, user interface) could run unencoded with native speed.

Furthermore, those safety-critical parts should be written for encodability: All memory accesses should be aligned which would remove the overhead introduced by implementing encoded aligned memory accesses. Developers should try to avoid bitwise logical operations and shifts. By sticking to the same data type, they can avoid explicit and implicit casts. Depending on the application, programmers would like to check by themselves for overflows. In this case, they could use faster encoded operations without overflow correction.

Error Detection. Figure 5 shows the results of our error injection experiments. The used error injection tool was also implemented using LLVM. It inserts the following types of errors according to Forin's error model [11]:

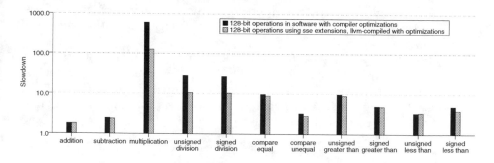

Fig. 4. Slowdowns of encoded arithmetic operations compared to their native versions for two versions: (1) 128-bit arithmetic implemented as software library and (2) implemented using the processors SSE extensions

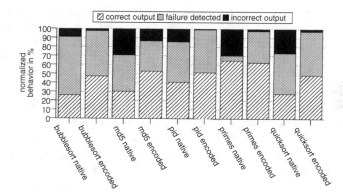

Fig. 5. Error injection results for injection of: operation, operand and lost update errors

(1) **operation errors**: the result of an operation is wrong.

(2) **operand errors**: an operand is modified, e. g. by an bitflip.

(3) **lost updates**: a store operation is unsuccessful.

In each injection run exactly one error is inserted. We performed 3000 injection runs for the native, i. e. unprotected versions, and the AN-encoded versions of our programs.

We see that for all runs a large part of the injections does not result in a failure (*correct output*), that is the program neither crashed nor produced erroneous results. *Failure detected* means that the application crashed. That is our intended error model. We want to turn difficult to handle value failures (*incorrect output*) into easier to detect and thus to handle crash failures. For all AN-encoded versions of the programs the amount of runs which produced *incorrect output* is smaller than for the unprotected versions. But it is not zero for several reasons:

(1) An AN-code does not provide protection from exchanged operand errors, e. g., a store which reads the wrong address, neither from lost updates or modified control flow.

(2) In contrast to SEP external functions such as `printf` are unprotected.

We also see that the relation of the amount of undetected errors between native and AN-encoded version varies largely with the executed program. For md5 the improvement compared to native is rather small compared to the other programs. We believe, the reason for this is that the AN-code does not detect loads and stores to/from the wrong address.

5   Conclusion

We presented the AN-encoding compiler EC-AN which applies the arithmetic AN-code to arbitrary programs. In contrast to earlier approaches the encoding is applied to the whole program. In contrast to existing solutions we do also encode bitwise logical operations completely using a powerful AN-code. Existing solutions did either not encode bitwise logical operations at all [11,10,34] or did if a program contained them switch to a much less safe code variant for the whole program [20]. The measurements show that the approach is successful in detecting errors but there are still undetected incorrect outputs in the presence of errors. This further motivates our ongoing work to extend EC-AN to support AN-encoding with signatures and timestamps. Compared to the in principle safer SEP [34] the runtime overhead produced by with EC-AN encoded programs is far lower. This is promising for EC-AN's extension to support signatures and timestamps which will make its error detection capabilities equal to those of SEP and in the end even better since EC-AN does a more complete encoding. Nevertheless, the observed slowdowns require actions to be taken to mitigate them. We will research the concept of adaptive safety, that is to apply the encoding only to the most safety-critical parts of an application.

References

1. Avizienis, A.: Arithmetic error codes: Cost and effectiveness studies for application in digital system design. Transactions on Computers (1971)
2. Bagchi, S., Kalbarczyk, Z., Iyer, R., Levendel, Y.: Design and evaluation of preemptive control signature(PECOS) checking. IEEE Transactions on Computers (2003)
3. Barnaby, H.J.: Will radiation-hardening-by-design (RHBD) work? Nuclear and Plasma Sciences, Society News (2005)
4. Bernick, D., Bruckert, B., Vigna, P.D., Garcia, D., Jardine, R., Klecka, J., Smullen, J.: Nonstop advanced architecture. In: Proceedings of the International Conference on Dependable Systems and Networks, DSN (2005)
5. Blum, M., Luby, M., Rubinfeld, R.: Self-testing/correcting with applications to numerical problems. In: STOC 1990: Proceedings of the twenty-second annual ACM symposium on Theory of computing. ACM Press, New York (1990)

6. Bolchini, C., Miele, A., Rebaudengo, M., Salice, F., Sciuto, D., Sterpone, L., Violante, M.: Software and hardware techniques for SEU detection in IP processors. J. Electron. Test. 24(1-3), 35–44 (2008)
7. Borin, E., Wang, C., Wu, Y., Araujo, G.: Software-based transparent and comprehensive control-flow error detection. In: Proceedings of the International Symposium on Code Generation and Optimization (CGO), pp. 333–345. IEEE Computer Society, Washington (2006)
8. Borkar, S.: Designing reliable systems from unreliable components: The challenges of transistor variability and degradation. IEEE Micro (2005)
9. Budiu, M., Erlingsson, Ú., Abadi, M.: Architectural support for software-based protection. In: ASID 2006: Proceedings of the 1st workshop on Architectural and system support for improving software dependability, pp. 42–51. ACM, New York (2006)
10. Chang, J., Reis, G.A., August, D.I.: Automatic instruction-level software-only recovery. In: Proceedings of the International Conference on Dependable Systems and Networks (DSN), Washington, USA (2006)
11. Forin, P.: Vital coded microprocessor principles and application for various transit systems. In: IFA-GCCT, September 1989, pp. 79–84 (1989)
12. Gomaa, M., Scarbrough, C., Vijaykumar, T.N., Pomeranz, I.: Transient-fault recovery for chip multiprocessors. In: International Symposium on Computer Architecture (2003)
13. Huang, K.-H., Abraham, J.A.: Algorithm-based fault tolerance for matrix operations. IEEE Trans. Computers 33(6), 518–528 (1984)
14. Lattner, C., Adve, V.: LLVM: A compilation framework for lifelong program analysis & transformation. In: Proceedings of the international symposium on Code generation and optimization (CGO), Washington, DC, USA, vol. 75. IEEE Computer Society, Los Alamitos (2004)
15. Li, X., Gaudiot, J.-L.: A compiler-assisted on-chip assigned-signature control flow checking. In: Asia-Pacific Computer Systems Architecture Conference (2004)
16. Michalak, S.E., Harris, K.W., Hengartner, N.W., Takala, B.E., Wender, S.A.: Predicting the number of fatal soft errors in Los Alamos National Laboratory's ASC Q supercomputer. In: IEEE Transactions on Device and Materials Reliability (2005)
17. Mitra, S.: Globally optimized robust systems to overcome scaled CMOS reliability challenges. In: Design, Automation and Test in Europe, DATE 2008 (2008)
18. Mitra, S., Seifert, N., Zhang, M., Shi, Q., Kim, K.S.: Robust system design with built-in soft-error resilience. Computer 38(2), 43–52 (2005)
19. Nicolescu, B., Velazco, R.: Detecting soft errors by a purely software approach: Method, tools and experimental results. In: Design, Automation and Test in Europe, DATE 2003 (2003)
20. Oh, N., Mitra, S., McCluskey, E.J.: ED4I: Error detection by diverse data and duplicated instructions. IEEE Trans. Comput. 51 (2002)
21. Pattabiraman, K., Grover, V., Zorn, B.G.: Samurai: protecting critical data in unsafe languages. In: Eurosys 2008: Proceedings of the 3rd ACM SIGOPS/EuroSys European Conference on Computer Systems 2008, pp. 219–232. ACM, New York (2008)
22. Rebaudengo, M., Reorda, M.S., Violante, M., Torchiano, M.: A source-to-source compiler for generating dependable software. In: Proceedings of the First IEEE International Workshop on Source Code Analysis and Manipulation, SCAM (2001)
23. Reddy, V., Rotenberg, E.: Inherent time redundancy (itr): Using program repetition for low-overhead fault tolerance. In: DSN 2007: Proceedings of the 37th Annual IEEE/IFIP International Conference on Dependable Systems and Networks, Washington, DC, USA. IEEE Computer Society, Los Alamitos (2007)

24. Reis, G.A., Chang, J., August, D.I., Cohn, R., Mukherjee, S.S.: Configurable transient fault detection via dynamic binary translation. In: Proceedings of the 2nd Workshop on Architectural Reliability, WAR (2006)
25. Reis, G.A., Chang, J., Vachharajani, N., Rangan, R., August, D.I., Mukherjee, S.S.: Design and evaluation of hybrid fault-detection systems. In: ISCA 2005: Proceedings of the 32nd annual international symposium on Computer Architecture, Washington, USA. IEEE Computer Society, Los Alamitos (2005)
26. Rhod, E.L., Lisbôa, C.A., Carro, L., Reorda, M.S., Violante, M.: Hardware and software transparency in the protection of programs against SEUs and SETs. J. Electron. Test. 24(1-3), 45–56 (2008)
27. Slegel, T.J., Averill, R.M., Check, M.A., Giamei, B.C., Krumm, B.W., Krygowski, C.A., Li, W.H., Liptay, J.S., MacDougall, J.D., McPherson, T.J., Navarro, J.A., Schwarz, E.M., Shum, K., Webb, C.F.: IBM's S/390 G5 microprocessor design. IEEE Micro 19, 12–23 (1999)
28. Stefanidis, V.K., Margaritis, K.G.: Algorithm based fault tolerance: Review and experimental study. In: International Conference of Numerical Analysis and Applied Mathematics (2004)
29. Vemu, R., Abraham, J.A.: CEDA: Control-flow error detection through assertions. In: IOLTS 2006: Proceedings of the 12th IEEE International Symposium on On-Line Testing, Washington, DC, USA. IEEE Computer Society, Los Alamitos (2006)
30. Venkatasubramanian, R., Hayes, J.P., Murray, B.T.: Low-cost on-line fault detection using control flow assertions. In: Proceedings of the 9th IEEE On-Line Testing Symposium (IOLTS), p. 137 (2003)
31. Vijaykumar, T.N., Pomeranz, I., Cheng, K.: Transient-fault recovery using simultaneous multithreading. SIGARCH Comput. Archit. News 30(2), 87–98 (2002)
32. Wang, C., Kim, H.s., Wu, Y., Ying, V.: Compiler-managed software-based redundant multi-threading for transient fault detection. In: International Symposium on Code Generation and Optimization, CGO (2007)
33. Wappler, U., Fetzer, C.: Hardware failure virtualization via software encoded processing. In: 5th IEEE International Conference on Industrial Informatics, INDIN 2007 (2007)
34. Wappler, U., Fetzer, C.: Software encoded processing: Building dependable systems with commodity hardware. In: Saglietti, F., Oster, N. (eds.) SAFECOMP 2007. LNCS, vol. 4680, pp. 356–369. Springer, Heidelberg (2007)
35. Wappler, U., Müller, M.: Software protection mechanisms for dependable systems. Design, Automation and Test in Europe, DATE 2008 (2008)
36. Wasserman, H., Blum, M.: Software reliability via run-time result-checking. J. ACM (1997)
37. Wescott, T.: PID without a PhD. Embedded Systems Programming 13(11) (2000)
38. Yeh, Y.: Triple-triple redundant 777 primary flight computer. In: Proceedings of the 1996 IEEE Aerospace Applications Conference, vol. 1, pp. 293–307 (1996)

Component-Based Abstraction in Fault Tree Analysis

Dominik Domis and Mario Trapp

Fraunhofer Institute for Experimental Software Engineering, Fraunhofer-Platz 1,
67663 Kaiserslautern, Germany
{dominik.domis,mario.trapp}@iese.fraunhofer.de

Abstract. To handle the complexity of safety-critical embedded systems, it is
not appropriate to develop functionality and consider safety in separate tasks, or
to consider software only as a black box in safety analyses. Rather, safety aspects have to be integrated as tightly as possible into the system and software
development process and its models. But existing safety analyses and models
do not fit well with software development tasks such as architectural design and
do not take advantage of their strengths. To solve this problem, this paper extends fault tree analysis by hierarchical component-based abstraction, enabling
fault tree analysis to be integrated into a component-oriented model-based design approach and to handle the complexity of software architectural design.

1 Introduction

In many different domains, the relevance of software has increased rapidly over the
last decades. For example, health professionals are supported by visualization devices
that help diagnose illness or injuries, and by irradiation units for cancer therapy. In the
automotive domain, many functions have been developed that assist the driver and
ensure active and passive safety, such as airbags or driving stability control systems.
Because of the growing size of such functions, their complexity has increased at the
same time. For such systems, guaranteeing high quality and safety is a difficult task.
To handle the increasing complexity, rigorous development processes must be followed and relevant dependability aspects have to be considered from the earliest development phases on as an integrated part of the overall development process. This
has to include the software, in particular, because of its high impact on the dependability of the entire system.

For this reason, more and more standards and guidelines for the development of
safety-relevant systems demand safety analyses for the system and the software as
part of a rigorous development process. Examples of this are IEC 61508 [1], IEC/TR
80002 [2], MISRA safety analysis guidelines [3], and ISO 26262 [4]. ISO 26262 is a
committee draft for the development of road vehicles. It defines requirements on the
development of electrical and electronic systems and particularly requirements on the
development of software, which include qualitative safety analysis for software architecture as well as for software unit design. However performing a qualitative safety
analysis technique such as failure mode and effect analysis (FMEA) or fault tree
analysis (FTA) on software architectural design is a complex task. One reason for this
is that safety analyses do not fit well with software architectural design and do not

B. Buth, G. Rabe, T. Seyfarth (Eds.): SAFECOMP 2009, LNCS 5775, pp. 297–310, 2009.

take advantage of basic software engineering principles that help to handle complexity such as hierarchical abstraction. Component-based Software Engineering (CBSE) [5] uses hierarchical abstraction in software architectural design to focus at one point in time only on one component at one hierarchy level and to systematically abstract from details of the levels below. In this way, unnecessary information is hidden from the engineer and each component of every hierarchy level is kept simple. In top-down development, this helps to iteratively refine and analyze the design in order to find weak points as early as possible and to avoid late changes. Bottom-up, it helps to abstract from unnecessary details as well as from complexity, and gives users a compact and precise specification of how to use or reuse a component. Additionally, in distributed development, hierarchical abstraction guarantees information hiding and protection of intellectual property (IP). Existing qualitative safety analysis techniques of software architectures are not able to appropriately reflect hierarchical abstraction. Instead, they either reflect hierarchy or the data flow through the system, but they cannot show the relevant information on each level of hierarchy. Because of this, they are not able to appropriately handle the complexity of software architectures.

In order to transfer the principles of CBSE such as hierarchical abstraction to safety analyses of software architectural design, we previously integrated safety analysis into a component-oriented model-based design approach, called Safe Component Model (SCM) [6], which will be presented in chapter 2. In this paper, we define hierarchical component-based abstraction of FTA and explain how existing fault tree evaluation algorithms can be reused to automate hierarchical fault tree abstraction. The problem of missing hierarchical abstraction in fault tree analysis is analyzed in more detail in chapter 3. In chapter 4, the requirements on hierarchical fault tree abstraction are derived. Chapter 5 explains how existing algorithms can be used to implement abstraction. In chapter 6, the related work is discussed and chapter 7 gives a short summary and conclusion.

2   Safe Component Model

Following the principles of CBSE, hierarchical abstraction is implemented in SCM by **rigorously separating specification and realization**, i.e., the model of a component is divided into component specification and component realization.

The component realization shows how a component is realized. The realization of simple components, which can be implemented directly, consists of models that specify the implementation in detail and on a very low level of abstraction, such as state machines or code, if this is appropriate. These are called modules. Complex components cannot be implemented directly, but have to be divided into smaller subcomponents (**divide and conquer**). The realization of such components shows the subcomponents that are used by the component and how they collaborate with each other. For example, Figure 1a shows the functional realization of the component *SpeedControl (S)*, which is a component of the traction control system of an electrical model car. From this data flow model it can be seen that *SpeedControl* consists of two subcomponents: *LogicalSensor(A)* and *Controller (B)*. *LogicalSensor* requires the wheel revolutions per minute of the car at the functional input *A.I1* and the acceleration value of the car measured by an acceleration sensor at *A.I2*. With these values,

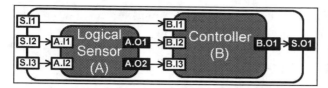
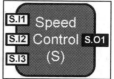

Fig. 1. a) Functional realization and b) functional specification of *SpeedControl*

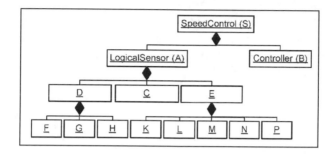

Fig. 2. Containment tree of the component *SpeedControl*

LogicalSensor calculates the reference speed of the car at the functional output *A.O1* and the reference acceleration at *A.O2*. *A.I1* receives its value from functional input *S.I2* and *A.I2* from *S.I3*. *Controller* requires the reference speed of the car at *B.I2* from *A.O1*, the reference acceleration at *B.I3* from *A.O2*, and the set value of the speed of the car at *B.I1* from *S.I1*. From these the *Controller* provides the new set value of the motor power at *B.O1*, which is directly connected with *S.O1* of *SpeedControl*. In this way, the functional realization shows how *SpeedControl* is realized by using the sub-components *LogicalSensor* and *Controller*.

In contrast to the realization, the specification of a component has to abstract from and hide all inner details of the realization. It has to show only the externally visible properties of the component and how a component has to be used, i.e., it specifies its functionality, its external interfaces, and, e.g., its pre- and post-conditions. For example, the functional specification of *SpeedControl* (Figure 1b) specifies only that it requires the wheel revolutions per minute at S.I2, the acceleration value at S.I3, and the speed set value at S.I1 to provide the set value of the motor power at S.O1. However, it abstracts from its subcomponents. Two other examples, of functional specifications are the information about *LogicalSensor* and *Controller* that is used in the functional realization of *SpeedControl*. From this can be seen that the component realization only knows the specifications of its direct subcomponents, but not how these subcomponents are realized. For example, the containment tree in Figure 2 of *SpeedContol* shows that *Controller* is a module and that *LogicalSensor* consists of many subcomponents. These subcomponents are completely hidden in the realization of *SpeedControl*, in order to hide complexity and keep the component simple and manageable. This makes it easier for engineers to focus in large systems on the relevant properties of a single component on a single hierarchy level. Additionally, it supports distributed development, because different components can be developed by different groups of people. Moreover, if components are developed by different companies, hierarchical abstraction guarantees the protection of intellectual property. The main advantage of abstraction, however, is the handling of complexity.

Functional specification and functional realization are the functional views of a component. These views are models that describe the desired data flow through a component on different levels of abstraction. Other functional and non-functional properties of a component, such as resource consumption, quality of services, or dependability, are modeled and separated by additional views (models). For example, the propagation of failures through a component is modeled by a failure specification and a failure realization view. The view concept helps to focus on a single property of a component and thus helps to handle complexity. In this paper, we focus only on the functional views and on the failure views already explained above, which are the results of fault tree analysis of the component. This analysis, the resulting failure specification and failure realization, as well as the relationship between both views will be discussed in the remainder of this paper.

3   Challenge: Fault Tree Analyses of Architectural Design

Three different possibilities exist for performing fault tree analysis of, e.g., the component realization of *SpeedControl*. The first one is to use the FTA to decompose failure modes of the component into failure causes of its subcomponents, which is the original idea of FTA for hardware. Following this process, the fault tree is built up vertically along the component hierarchy. For example, Figure 3a shows an excerpt of the vertical Component Fault Tree (**CFT**) [7] of *SpeedControl* based on the containment tree in Figure 2. The top event (filled triangle) is the **output failure mode** *S.O1-FM1*, i.e., a wrong set value of the motor power (*S.O1*). The *FMs* represent the failure types [6] of the failure modes. For example, *FM1* represents the failure type *value*, *FM2 high*, *FM3 low* and *FM4 late*. The output failure mode can be caused, e.g., by the **input failure mode** (triangle, open at the bottom) *S.I3-FM1* of the functional input *S.I3*. Determining this cause-and-effect chain requires detailed information about the failure propagation paths through the subcomponents of *SpeedControl*, which is not reflected in the vertical CFT. This information is important, e.g., for selecting appropriate subcomponents and for initiating failure detection or mitigation measures. Because of this, the vertical fault tree shows the hierarchic structure of the components, but neglects the failure propagation paths. It is difficult to build up manually and prone to errors.

For software and other systems that contain a flow of data, mass, or energy, it is more appropriate to build the fault tree up horizontally along this flow through the system [8]. This method is also used for automating safety analyses [9][10] and is called Failure Logic Modeling (**FLM**) [11].

In FLM, the failure propagation through every component is modeled, e.g., by a fault tree, and then composed into the fault tree of the entire system. Figure 3b shows the horizontally defined CFT of *S.O1-FM1*. From this can be seen how *S.I3-FM1* is

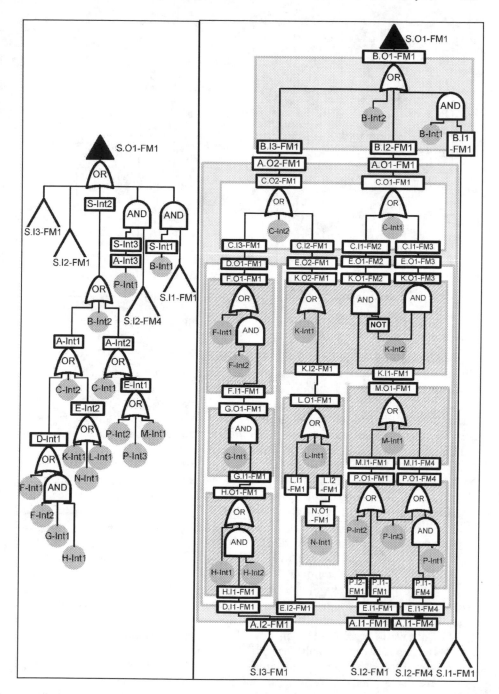

Fig. 3. a) Vertical fault tree b) Horizontal (FLM) fault tree

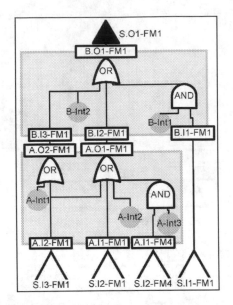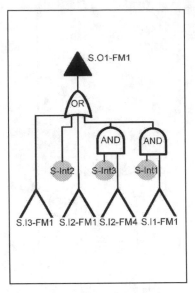

Fig. 4. a) Failure realization and b) Failure specification of *SpeedControl*

propagated through *SpeedControl* before it can cause *S.O1-FM1*. However, it does not only show the two direct subcomponents of *SpeedControl*, *LogicalSensor* and *Controller*, but shows all subcomponents and modules of *LogicalSensor* in addition. Imagine a distributed development in which *LogicalSensor* is a Component off the Shelf (COTS): Why do we have to see every single failure mode of module *H* in FTA if we are only responsible for the realization of the component *SpeedControl* and do not know that *H* exists and that *H* is a subcomponent of *D* and *D* a subcomponent of *LogicalSensor (A)*? In order to hide such details as well as intellectual property, and to provide, at the same time, exactly the information that is needed to analyze the safety of the component *SpeedControl*, hierarchical abstraction of this fault tree is necessary. The abstract CFT of the realization of *SpeedControl* has to show only the failure modes of exactly the two direct subcomponents *LogicalSensor* and *Controller* as well as the failure modes of *SpeedControl* itself. Accordingly, the CFT of the specification has to show only the failure modes of *SpeedControl* itself. These requirements are fulfilled by the failure realization in Figure 4a and the failure specification in 4b.

Of course, like Figure 3b, Figures 4a and 4b can also be built by FLM: To get Figure 3b, all modules of Figure 2 have to be analyzed manually; to get Figure 4b, *SpeedControl* has to be analyzed manually; and to get Figure 4a, *LogicalSensor* and *Controller* have to be analyzed manually. However, this approach does not ensure a formal relation between the fault trees of Figures 3b, 4a and 4b, and thus, they may be inconsistent with each other, i.e., the higher-level fault trees might not be abstractions of the levels below and the levels below not refinements of the levels above.

FLM is able to reflect the failure propagation of software, but not the hierarchical abstraction of the software architectural design. In contrast to this, vertical fault trees (e.g., Figure 3a) support hierarchical abstraction and refinement, but cannot appropriately handle the complex failure propagation of software. Because of this, a new kind of hierarchical abstraction for fault trees is necessary that is able to reflect failure propagation like FLM and hierarchical abstraction like vertical fault trees, and that is consistent with the principles of software architectural design and CBSE.

4 Abstraction Requirements

Abstraction is "a view of an object that focuses on the information relevant to a particular purpose and ignores the remainder of the information" [12]. So, to define hierarchical abstraction from the failure realization to the specification, the difference between their purposes has to be determined, which is only the hierarchy level. This means that the specification has to abstract from the same information as the realization, plus from the inner details of the component that are shown in the realization. For the hierarchical abstraction of the functional specification from the functional realization this means that the subcomponents and their collaboration are hidden, as well as that the functionality of the component is specified only in terms of the component itself. The failure realization must have the same level of hierarchical abstraction as the functional realization and the failure specification the same level as the functional specification. This requirement is true for *SpeedControl*. The hierarchy level of the failure realization in Figure 4a is consistent with its functional realization in Figure 1a, because it only shows failure modes of the functional in- and outputs as well as failure modes of the subcomponents that are shown in the functional realization. The hierarchy level of the corresponding failure specification in Figure 4b is consistent with the functional specification in Figure 1b, because it hides all details of the subcomponents and only shows the failure modes of *SpeedControl (S)*.

In the following, the *SpeedControl* example is used to determine, first, the information that is contained in the failure realization, and, afterwards, the information that should remain in the failure specification and the information that must be abstracted. The failure realization, as shown for example in Figure 4a, contains the following information:

- The failure modes that can occur at the outputs of the component. (*S.O1-FM1*)
- The failure modes that can occur at the inputs of the component. (*S.I3-FM1*, *S.I2-FM1*, *S.I2-FM4*, and *S.I1-FM1*)
- The internal failure modes that are failure modes of the component or its subcomponents (*B-Int2*, *A-Int1*, and *A-Int2*). Internal failure modes may also include (failed) failure detection or mitigation measures (*A-Int3* and *B-Int1*).
- The (Boolean) conditions for mitigating, propagating, or transforming [8] internal and input failure modes to output failure modes of the component, which are specified by the fault tree gates (e.g., AND- and OR-gates).
- The failure propagation paths of every internal and input failure mode through the component realization, including its direct subcomponents and their interfaces (e.g., *A.O2-FM1* and *B.I3-FM1*).
- A detailed specification of every failure mode including name, corresponding component or functional interface, failure type, failure attributes, description, and probability distribution, if applicable.

The failure specification of *SpeedControl* (Figure 4b) still has the same output failure mode (*S.O1-FM1*) as the failure realization, and the input failure modes *S.I3-FM1* as well as *S.I2-FM1* remain single points of failures. *S.I2-FM4* and *S.I1-FM1* are still covered by independent measures, but the specification of the measures has changed: *A-Int3* is renamed to *S-Int3* and *B-Int1* to S-*Int1*. The internal failure modes of the realizations *A-Int1*, *A-Int2*, and *B-Int2*, which have the same effects on *S.O1-FM1* under the same Boolean conditions of input failure modes, are disjunctively merged into the abstract internal failure mode *S-Int2*. Additionally, the tree structure is changed, by removing all in- and output failure modes of the subcomponents. The CFT of the failure specification is the disjunction of its Minimal Cut Sets (MCS) and, if the described mappings are considered, equivalent to the failure realization in Figure 4a. According to this, the following four requirements are defined that have to be fulfilled by hierarchical fault tree abstraction to derive the failure specification:

1. The input and output failure modes as well as the (Boolean) conditions under which the input failure modes are mitigated, propagated, or transformed into output failure modes of the component must remain *equivalent*.
2. The specification must only show internal failure modes that can be seen and distinguished externally, i.e., the number of internal failure modes is minimized by abstracting from the realization to the specification. This is done by removing internal realization failure modes if they cannot cause an output failure mode and by merging internal realization failure modes if they have the same effects on the output failure modes under the same Boolean conditions of the input failure modes.
3. The failure propagation paths must be changed in such a way that no information about the inner structure and subcomponents is disclosed, i.e., the structure of the failure specification CFT must be independent of the structure of the failure realization CFT apart from the Boolean conditions of requirement 1.
4. Apart from the input and output failure modes, any information about the inner details of the component must be removed from the specification of any remaining internal failure mode, gate, or intermediate event. For this purpose, names, descriptions, and references to objects of the component realization have to be changed to the component specification.

In some cases, it may be not applicable or necessary for both failure views to be equivalent to each other. For example, if we consider only coherent fault trees, it may be acceptable that the failure realization only *implies* the specification, i.e., every time an output failure mode in the realization is true, it is also true in the specification. In such a case, the specification is a pessimistic or conservative approximation of the realization. In a quantitative FTA, the probabilities of the output failure modes, which depend on the probabilities of the input failure modes, can be used to define other relations. For example, it can be requested that the output probabilities of the realization are either equal or below the probabilities of the specification, or between two thresholds. However, if any relation other than equality is used, the type of relation between the specification and the realization must be specified as part of the failure specification in order to use the component correctly. Additionally, the changes and mappings between the failure specification and the failure realization have to be known and stored as part of the component realization, in order to be able to check and guarantee equivalence or any other relation between the failure specification and the realization.

Through this kind of hierarchical fault tree abstraction, the failure specification of a component can be derived from the failure realization and will be consistent with the failure realization and the hierarchy level of the component specification. In this way, unnecessary details and complexity of the levels below are hidden and only the information that is required to evaluate and assess the failure behavior of the current component is provided. Additionally, it can be checked and guaranteed that fault trees of different hierarchy levels are consistent with each other.

5 Abstraction Algorithms

Like the evaluation of fault trees, hierarchical fault tree abstraction cannot be done manually for larger systems, because of the complexity, error-proneness, and effort needed. Thus, for the application of hierarchical fault tree abstraction, it is mandatory to have an appropriate degree of automation and tool support. For this purpose, algorithms are needed that take a failure realization as input, automatically generate an abstract failure specification from it, and check that both are consistent to each other.

In order to realize the requirements of hierarchical fault tree abstraction, different fault tree evaluation algorithms have been reviewed. The results of this survey and the requirements led to three major steps that can be used to abstract from a given failure realization. These three steps are: merging internal failure modes, building a structure-independent form, and changing the information of internal events.

Changing the information of internal events is the straightforward implementation of requirement 4. All information about the component realization is removed from internal failure modes and gates of the fault tree. For this purpose, the names of and the references to the component realization are substituted by the name of or references to the component specification, as done in the abstraction of the *SpeedControl* failure realization. After this step, gates and internal failure modes represent only information about the component specification and not about the realization.

5.1 Structure-Independent Form

To hide detailed failure propagation paths (req.3), the CFT is transformed into a form that is independent of the original structure of the tree. For this purpose, different forms could be used, but the best known form of coherent fault trees are minimal cut sets (**MCS**). The MCS of a fault tree are the sets of basic events (internal and input failure modes), where every event must be true for the top event to become true. MCS are used for qualitative analyses of fault trees: They show only the minimal failure combinations and abstract from the structure and the failure paths of the tree. Because MCS are only applicable for coherent fault trees, prime implicants (**PI**) have to be used for non-coherent ones, since these also include negated literals (variables). MCS/PI show the fault tree in its minimal disjunctive normal form (DNF), which is independent of the original structure of the tree, but mathematically equivalent. Other normal forms could also be used for abstracting from the structure, but MCS and PI are the most appropriate and proven ones for fault trees. Additionally, MCS and PI contain only failure modes that can cause an output failure mode. Failure modes that are contained in the tree, but cannot cause the output failure mode and, thus, cannot be observed from the outside, are also hidden by calculating MCS or PI. The sequence of the variables of MCS and PI depends on the algorithms that are used to calculate them. Thus, the sequence can also depend on the original structure of the tree. This structural dependency can be easily avoided by changing the sequence of the variables.

One problem of PI, in particular, is that fault trees can have a huge number of them ($O(3^n)$, n number of FT variables) and that their calculation is very time consuming. Different algorithms exist that can be used to calculate a reduced or minimal cover of PI that is equivalent to the original set of PI, but they require additional computation time [13][14]. The advantage of a **minimal cover** of PI would be that less PI have to be stored and considered in subsequent analysis steps. But if computation time becomes too long, fault tree evaluation as well as abstraction are hard to apply. If the failure specification does not have to be equivalent to the failure realization, Minimal P-Cuts or Truncation [15] can be used instead of PI. **Minimal P-Cuts** are MCS for non-coherent fault trees, i.e., they calculate PI, but leave out negated variables. In this way, Minimal P-Cuts are a pessimistic approximation, because the failure realization would imply the failure specification as described before. Truncation uses the algorithms to calculate PI, but sorts out PI that consist of more variables than a given threshold (**truncation of order**) or that have a probability lower than a given threshold (**truncation of probability**). In this way, PI with a low probability or high order are simply left out, decreasing the probabilities of the output failure modes. Because of this, truncation is an optimistic approximation and the failure specification would imply the failure realization, but not the other way around. This is only applicable for abstraction if the calculation error is bounded. However, truncation of probability is not possible for software, because probabilities are unknown, and for the truncation of order it can only be assumed that PI with a very high order are sufficiently improbable, but this cannot be guaranteed. Because of this, MCS are the best structure-independent form for coherent fault trees and PI for non-coherent fault trees to be used in hierarchical fault tree abstraction. For example, MCS are used for abstracting from the failure realization of *SpeedControl* (Figures 4a and 4b).

5.2 Merging Internal Failure Modes

By building a structure-independent form and changing the information of internal events, the abstraction requirements 1, 3, and 4 are fulfilled, but every failure mode in the realization would still have exactly one corresponding failure mode in the specification. However, many internal failure modes can exist that, under exactly the same conditions of the input failure modes, have the same effects on the output failure modes such as *A-Int1*, *A-Int2*, and *B-Int2* in Figure 4a. Because of this, they cannot be distinguished from the outside of the component and are disjunctively merged into *S-Int2* in the failure specification of *SpeedControl* (Figure 4b). Such a combination of internal failure modes that cannot be distinguished from the outside of the component constitutes an **internal module**.

A fault tree module is a subtree that is completely independent of the rest of the tree and, thus, can be analyzed separately and considered as a single event by the rest of the tree. In fault tree evaluation, modules are used to reduce the complexity of calculations [16] or to combine different calculation techniques [17]. Modules can be identified by the linear time algorithm presented in [18], but in many trees, additional modules can be laid open by simple Boolean transformations, which eliminate, for example, repeated events. These transformations are called reduction [16] and combination, and were used in [17] to identify independent modules that contain dependent failure modes. After reduction and combination, the fault tree is still equivalent to the original one, has its most concise form [16], and contains all modules that will be identified by the modularization algorithm. For hierarchical fault tree abstraction, these algorithms have been adapted to identify only modules of internal events (internal modules) in the CFT of the failure realization. Each internal module of the failure realization becomes an abstract internal failure mode of the failure specification, which hides the internal module, because its internal failure modes cannot be distinguished from the outside. Reduction also changes the structure and the failure propagation paths of the tree, and can be used to remove internal failure modes that cannot cause the output failure modes, but this produces a structure-independent form only in some cases.

If it is sufficient that the failure realization only implies the failure specification, but does not need to be equivalent, internal failure modes can also be merged if they do not constitute an internal module. For example, if the user of a component only needs to know that it has a detection mechanism for some input failure modes, all internal failure modes of the realization that represent the relevant detection mechanisms can be merged into an abstract internal detection failure mode of the failure specification [6]. In this way, all internal failure modes or any combination, such as all internal failure modes of the same failure type, can be merged into a new abstract internal failure mode, e.g., through the disjunction of the old ones. If probabilities are used, probabilities for the new internal failure modes of the specification can be calculated based on the probabilities of the failure realization.

Independent of how the internal failure modes are merged and what other abstraction algorithms are applied, the mapping between the realization and the specification must be specified as part of the realization. Additionally, the kind of relation must be specified as part of the specification. Only in this way is it possible to guarantee traceability and to check if the assumed relation between failure realization and specification is true. For example, if modularization is used, the internal modules of the failure realization and the corresponding internal failure modes of the specification must be known in order to check equivalence. This is also true if the internal failure modes are only "renamed" from the realization to the specification. To efficiently check the equivalence or other qualitative relations between failure specification and realization, Binary Decision Diagrams (BDDs) are used.

5.3 Example

The basic abstraction algorithms and consistency checks are already implemented as part of SCM in the ComposeR tool [6] and were used in the development of the traction control system. So, the failure specification of *SpeedControl* in Figure 4b was generated by abstracting from its failure realization in Figure 4a by reducing the OR-Gates as well as the input and output failure modes of *LogicalSensor (A)* and

Controller (B), merging the internal module (*A-Int1* ∨ *A-Int2* ∨ *B-Int2*), and renaming *A-Int3* and *B-Int1*. Calculation of MCS has no effect here, because reduction and modularization have already transformed the tree into its MCS structure.

Reduction, modularization, MCS, and changing information of internal events were also applied to abstract over two hierarchy levels from the CFT in Figure 3b and generate the failure specification of *LogicalSensor (A)* in Figure 4a. In the first step of reduction, all subsequent OR-gates were contracted [16] into a single one. After contraction, *S.I3-FM1* is a direct input of the OR-gate *C.O2-FM1* and the law of absorption [16] is used to remove its edge to the AND-gate of *H*, as well as to remove the AND-gate of *H* and the internal failure mode *H-Int2*. Then, the internal module of *LogicalSensor* (*C.Int2* ∨ *K.Int1* ∨ *L.Int1* ∨ *N.Int1* ∨ *F.Int1* ∨ (*F.Int2* ∧ *G.Int1*∧ *H.Int1*)) under the OR-gate *C.O2-FM1* is combined into the internal failure mode *A-Int1*. At the OR-gate *C.O1-FM1*, the distributive law is used to remove the internal failure mode *K-Int2*, the NOT-gate, and the two corresponding AND-gates of *K* from the tree, and make *M.O1-FM1* a direct input to the OR-gate *C.O1-FM1*. After this, the new subsequent OR-gates are contracted and, then, the internal module (*C.Int1* ∨ *M.Int1* ∨ *P.Int2* ∨ *P.Int3*) is combined to *A-Int2*. During reduction, the input and output failure modes of the subcomponents of *LogicalSensor (A)* were also removed. In the last step of the abstraction, *P-Int1* is renamed to *A-Int3*. Calculation of MCS is already done by reduction and modularization, in this case. Considering the abstraction mappings, the resulting failure specification of *SpeedControl* in Figure 4a is equivalent to the original CFT in Figure 3b, but shows only failure modes of *Logical-Sensor (A)* and *Controller (B)*, while hiding all inner details as well as the complexity of *LogicalSensor*. This is consistent with the functional realization (Figure 1a) and fulfills the requirements of hierarchical abstraction.

Now, it can be seen easily and without tool support that all four fault trees of *SpeedControl* in this paper are consistent to each other. Compare the failure specification in Figure 4b and the vertical fault tree in Figure 3a. Both have the same top-level OR-gate with actually the same five inputs. The only difference is that in Figure 3a, each internal failure mode of the failure specification in Figure 4b is recursively substituted by the definition of its internal failure modes or modules from the next-lower hierarchy level. So, by the new definition of hierarchical fault tree abstraction, the advantages of the vertical (Figure 3a) and the horizontal FTA (Figure 3b) have been combined with the separation of specification and realization of CBSE. In this way, on each component level, exactly the relevant failure information is provided to the user and unnecessary complexity is hidden, according to the hierarchical abstraction of software architectural design.

6   Related Work

Hierarchical component-based abstraction is a new topic for FTA and a challenge for safety analyses of software architectures. Because of this, hierarchical abstraction has also been proposed by other approaches, but not for qualitative safety analysis such as FTA. In the Rich Component Model (RCM) [19], formal state machines are used to model the failure behavior of components. To abstract in the (black-box) specification from the realization (gray-box specification), all or only some combinations (e.g., "single failure", "no failure", and "multi failure") of the realization failure configurations are represented as a state in the specification. Additionally, a fault tree that is generated by Fault Injection [11] from the state machine of the realization also becomes a part of the specification. So, hierarchical abstraction in RCM only works on state machines, and the FT is a side product derived automatically from these.

State machines are also used in the AADL error model annex [20] to describe the failure behavior of components, but in contrast to RCM, these are compiled into generalized stochastic petri nets (GSPNs) for evaluation. Hierarchical abstraction of the failure behavior is applied by summarizing states of the subordinated hierarchy level and building the state machine of the current component in this way. But there is no further guidance or automation regarding abstraction. To the best of our knowledge, we can say that there is no other approach that systemizes hierarchical abstraction of fault tree analysis similar to SCM.

7 Summary and Conclusion

To handle the complexity of safety analysis of software architectural design, this paper has provided a new definition of hierarchical component-based abstraction for FTA. It combines vertical structural decomposition and horizontal data flow-oriented failure propagation with the hierarchical abstraction of CBSE. For this purpose, the fault trees of the entire system are built up or lie in background, while the user only chooses and navigates through the component-oriented failure views that are appropriate for his/her purpose. In this way, the user focuses on the relevant information about the functionality and the failure behavior of the components, and unnecessary information as well as complexity are hidden. Consistency between the fault trees of all components on all hierarchy levels can be guaranteed at all times. This facilitates the application of FTA on software architectural design and enables the integration of safety analysis into software architectural design. Furthermore, hierarchical component-based abstraction of fault trees also guarantees protection of intellectual property and supports distributed development as well as the reuse of components that have already been analyzed.

References

1. IEC 61508: Functional safety of electrical/electronic/programmable electronic safety-related systems, International Electrotechnical Commission (1999)
2. IEC/TR 80002-1 Ed.1: Medical device software - Guidance on the application of ISO 14971 to medical device software, International Electrotechnical Commission (2009)
3. MISRA: Guidelines for safety analysis of vehicle based programmable systems. MIRA Limited, Warwickshire (2007)
4. ISO/CD 26262, Road vehicles, Functional Safety Part 6: Product development software. Committee draft (2008)
5. Atkinson, C., Bayer, J., Bunse, C., Kamsties, E., Laitenberger, O., Laqua, R., Muthig, D., Peach, B., Wüst, J., Zettel, J.: Component-based Product Line Engineering with UML. Addison-Wesley, London (2001)

6. Domis, D., Trapp, M.: Integrating Safety Analyses and Comopnent-based Design. In: Harrison, M.D., Sujan, M.-A. (eds.) SAFECOMP 2008. LNCS, vol. 5219, pp. 58–71. Springer, Heidelberg (2008)
7. Kaiser, B., Liggesmeyer, P., Mäckel, O.: A New Component Concept for Fault Trees. In: Lindsay, P., Cant, T. (eds.) Conferences in Research and Practice in Information Technology Series, vol. 33, pp. 37–46. Australian Computer Society (2003)
8. Fenelon, P., McDermid, J.A., Pumfrey, D.J., Nicholson, M.: Towards Integrated Safety Analysis and Design. ACM Computing Reviews 2(1), 21–32 (1994)
9. Papadopoulos, Y., McDermid, J.A.: Hierarchically Performed Hazard Origin and Propagation Studies. In: Felici, M., Kanoun, K., Pasquini, A. (eds.) 18th International Conference on Computer Safety, Reliability and Security. LNCS, vol. 1608, pp. 139–152. Springer, Heidelberg (1999)
10. Grunske, L.: Towards an Integration of Standard Component-Based Safety Evaluation Techniques with SaveCCM. In: Hofmeister, C., Crnković, I., Reussner, R. (eds.) QoSA 2006. LNCS, vol. 4214, pp. 199–213. Springer, Heidelberg (2006)
11. Lisagor, O., McDermid, J.A., Pumfrey, D.J.: Towards a Practicable Process for Automated Safety Analysis. In: 24th International System Safety Conference, pp. 596–607 (2006)
12. IEEE Standard Glossary of Software Engineering Terminology, IEEE Std. 610.12-1990
13. Coudert, O., Madre, J., Henri, F.: A new viewpoint on Two-Level Logic Minimization. In: 30th ACM/IEEE Design Automation Conference, Dallas, TX, USA, pp. 625–630 (1993)
14. Coudert, O., Madre, J., Henri, F.: New Qualitative Analysis Strategies in Metaprime. In: Annual Reliability and Maintainability Symposium, Anaheim, CA, USA, pp. 298–303 (1994)
15. Dutuit, Y., Rauzy, A.: Exact and Truncated Computations of Prime Implicants of Coherent and non-Coherent Fault Trees within Aralia. In: Reliability Engineering & System Safety, vol. 58, pp. 127–144 (1997)
16. Remenyte-Prescott, R., Andrews, J.: Prime Implicants for modularized non-coherent fault tress using binary decision diagrams. Int. J. Reliability and Safety 1(4), 446–464 (2007)
17. Sun, H., Andrews, J.: Identification of independent modules in fault trees which contain dependent basic events. Reliability Engineering & System Safety 86, 285–296 (2004)
18. Dutuit, Y., Rauzy, A.: A Linear Time Algorithm to Find Modules of Fault Trees. IEEE Transactions on Reliability 45, 422–425 (1996)
19. Damm, W., Votintseva, A., Metzner, A., Josko, B., Peikenkamp, T., Böde, E.: Boosting Re-use of Embedded Automotive Applications Through Rich Components. In: Proceedings of the Foundation of Interface Technology Workshop. Elsevier Science B.V, Amsterdam (2005)
20. Feiler, P., Rugina, A.: Dependability Modeling with the Architecture Analysis & Design Language. Technical Report CMU/SEI-2007-TN-043, Carnegie Mellon University (2007)

A Foundation for Requirements Analysis of Dependable Software

Denis Hatebur[1,2] and Maritta Heisel[1]

[1] Universität Duisburg-Essen, Germany, Fakultät für Ingenieurwissenschaften
maritta.heisel@uni-due.de
[2] Institut für technische Systeme GmbH, Germany
d.hatebur@itesys.de

Abstract. We present patterns for expressing dependability requirements, such as confidentiality, integrity, availability, and reliability. The paper considers random faults as well as certain attacks and therefore supports a combined safety and security engineering. The patterns - attached to functional requirements - are part of a pattern system that can be used to identify missing requirements. The approach is illustrated on a cooperative adaptive cruise control system.

1 Introduction

Dependable systems play an increasingly important role in daily life. More and more tasks are supported or performed by computer systems. These systems are required to be safe, secure, available, reliable, and maintainable.

Safety is the *in*ability of the system to have an undesirable effect on its environment, and **security** is the *in*ability of environment to have an undesirable effect on the system [16]. To achieve safety, systematic and random faults must be handled. For security, in contrast, certain attackers must be considered. Security can be described by confidentiality, integrity and availability requirements. **Confidentiality** is the absence of unauthorized disclosure of information. **Integrity** is the absence of improper system, data, or a service alterations [15]. **Availability** is the readiness for service (up-time vs. down-time) [14][1]. Also for safety, integrity and availability must be considered. For safety, integrity and availability mechanisms have to protect against random (and some systematic) faults. **Reliability** is a measure of continuous service accomplishment [14]. A safety-critical system has to perform its safety-functions with a defined reliability (or integrity) [2]. In this case, reliability describes the probability of correct functionality under stipulated environmental conditions [4]. This paper shows that reliability requirements can be defined not only from a safety point of view, but also from a security point of view. **Maintainability** is the ability to undergo modifications and repairs [2]. Maintainability can be achieved by additional interfaces for updates (of the whole software or components), by a maintainable structure of the software itself (e.g., documentation, appropriate architectures, comments in the source code), and by maintenance plans (e.g., restart the software once a week to reduce memory fragmentation). Maintainability is not considered in this paper.

---

[1] Availability, in contrast to reliability, does not require correct service.
[2] If the system can for example be safely deactivated, it is sufficient to define the integrity requirement and the actions to be performed in case of an integrity error.

B. Buth, G. Rabe, T. Seyfarth (Eds.): SAFECOMP 2009, LNCS 5775, pp. 311–325, 2009.
© Springer-Verlag Berlin Heidelberg 2009

Dependability requirements must be described and analyzed. Problem frames [12] are a means to describe and analyze functional requirements, but they can be extended to describe also dependability features, as shown in earlier papers [7,8]. In Section 2, we present problem frames and the parts of the problem frames meta-model [10] used for the formalization of dependability features. In Section 3, we define a set of patterns that can be used to describe and analyze dependability requirements. Section 4 describes how to integrate the use of the dependability patterns into a system development process. The case study in Section 5 applies that process to a cooperative adaptive cruise control system. Section 6 discusses related work, and the paper closes with a summary and perspectives in Section 7.

2   Problem Frames

Problem frames are a means to describe software development problems. They were invented by Jackson [12], who describes them as follows: *"A problem frame is a kind of pattern. It defines an intuitively identifiable problem class in terms of its context and the characteristics of its domains, interfaces and requirement."* Problem frames are described by *frame diagrams*, which consist of rectangles, a dashed oval, and links between these (see Fig. 1). All elements of a problem frame diagram act as placeholders, which must be instantiated to represent concrete problems. Doing so, one obtains a problem description that belongs to a specific problem class.

Plain rectangles denote *problem domains* (that already exist in the application environment), a rectangle with a double vertical stripe denotes the *machine* (i.e., the software) that shall be developed, and *requirements* are denoted with a dashed oval. The connecting lines between domains represent interfaces that consist of *shared phenomena*.

Shared phenomena may be events, operation calls, messages, and the like. They are observable by at least two domains, but controlled by only one domain, as indicated by an exclamation mark. For example, in Fig. 1 the notation *O!E4* means that the phenomena in the set *E4* are controlled by the domain **Operator**.

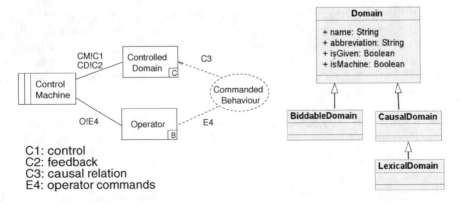

C1: control
C2: feedback
C3: causal relation
E4: operator commands

Fig. 1. *Commanded Behaviour* problem frame

Fig. 2. Inheritance structure of different domain types

A dashed line represents a requirements reference. It means that the domain is referred to in the requirements description. An arrow at the end of such a dashed line indicates that the requirements constrain the problem domain. Such a constrained domain is the core of any problem description, because it has to be controlled according to the requirements. Hence, a constrained domain triggers the need for developing a new software (the machine), which provides the desired control. In Fig. 1, the **Controlled-Domain** domain is constrained, because the **ControlMachine** has the role to change it on behalf of user commands for achieving the required **Commanded Behaviour**.

Jackson distinguishes the domain types **CausalDomain**s that comply with some physical laws, **LexicalDomain**s that are data representations, and **BiddableDomain**s that are usually people. In Fig. 1, the C indicates that the corresponding domain is a **CausalDomain**, and B indicates that it is a **BiddableDomain**. In our formal meta-model of problem frames [10] (see Fig. 2), **Domains** have **names** and **abbreviations**, which are used to define interfaces. According to Jackson, domains are either **designed**, **given**, or **machine** domains. These facts are modeled by the boolean attributes **isGiven** and **isMachine** in Fig. 2. The domain types are modeled by the subclasses **BiddableDomain**, **CausalDomain**, and **LexicalDomain** of the class **Domain**. A lexical domain is a special case of a causal domain. This kind of modeling allows to add further domain types, such as **DisplayDomain**s as introduced in [3].

Problem frames support developers in analyzing problems to be solved. They show what domains have to be considered, and what knowledge must be described and reasoned about when analyzing the problem in depth. Other problem frames besides the commanded behavior frame are *required behaviour*, *simple workpieces*, *information display*, and *transformation*.

Software development with problem frames proceeds as follows: first, the environment in which the machine will operate is represented by a *context diagram*. Like a frame diagram, a context diagram consists of domains and interfaces. However, a context diagram contains no requirements, and it is not shown which domain is in control of the shared phenomena (see Fig. 3 for an example). Then, the problem is decomposed into subproblems. If ever possible, the decomposition is done in such a way that the subproblems fit to given problem frames. To fit a subproblem to a problem frame, one must instantiate its frame diagram, i.e., provide instances for its domains, phenomena, and interfaces. The instantiated frame diagram is called a *problem diagram*.

Successfully fitting a problem to a given problem frame means that the concrete problem indeed exhibits the properties that are characteristic for the problem class defined by the problem frame. A problem can only be fitted to a problem frame if the involved problem domains belong to the domain types specified in the frame diagram. For example, the Operator domain of Fig. 1 can only be instantiated by persons, but not for example by some physical equipment like an elevator.

To describe the problem context, a **ConnectionDomain** between two other domains may be necessary. Connection domains establish a connection between other domains by means of technical devices. Typical connection domains are **CausalDomain**s, e.g., video cameras, sensors, or networks.

Since the requirements refer to the *environment* in which the machine must operate, the next step consists in deriving a *specification* for the machine (see [13] for details). The specification describes the machine and is the starting point for its construction.

3 Patterns for Dependability Requirements

We developed a set of patterns for expressing and analyzing dependability requirements. An important advantage of these patterns is that they allow dependability requirements to be expressed without anticipating solutions. For example, we may require data to be kept confidential during transmission without being obliged to mention encryption, which is a means to achieve confidentiality. The benefit of considering dependability requirements without reference to potential solutions is the clear separation of problems from their solutions, which leads to a better understanding of the problems and enhances the re-usability of the problem descriptions, since they are completely independent of solution technologies.

Our dependability requirements patterns are expressed as logical predicates. They are separated from functional requirements. On the one hand, this limits the number of patterns; on the other hand, it allows one to apply these patterns to a wide range of problems. For example, the functional requirements for data transmission or automated control can be expressed using a problem diagram. Dependability requirements for confidentiality, integrity, availability and reliability can be added to that description of the functional requirement.

For each dependability requirement, a textual description pattern and a corresponding predicate pattern are given. The textual description helps to state dependability requirements more precisely. The patterns help to structure and classify dependability requirements. For example, requirements considering integrity can be easily distinguished from the availability requirements. It is also possible to trace all dependability requirements that refer to a given domain.

The logical predicate patterns have several parameters. The first parameter of a predicate is the domain that is constrained by the requirement, whereas the other parameters are only referred to. The predicate patterns are expressed using the domain types of the meta-model described in Figure 2, i.e., **Domain**, **BiddableDomain**, **CausalDomain**, and **LexicalDomain**. From these classes in the meta-model, subclasses with special properties are derived:

- An **Attacker** is a **BiddableDomain** that describes all subjects (with their equipment) who want to attack the machine.
- A **User** is a **BiddableDomain** that describes subjects who have an interface to the machine.
- A **Stakeholder** is a **BiddableDomain** (and in some special cases also a **CausalDomain**) with some relation to stored or transmitted data. It is not necessary that a stakeholder has an interface to the machine.
- A **ConstrainedDomain** is a **CausalDomain** that is constrained by a functional or dependability requirement.
- An **InfluencedDomain** is a **CausalDomain** that is influenced by the machine to fulfill the dependability requirement (it can be the same domain as the **ConstrainedDomain**, but also another domain).
- A **Display** is a **CausalDomain** used to inform the user of the machine.
- **StoredData** is a **CausalDomain** or **LexicalDomain** used to store some data as defined by the functional requirement. Also the machine domain may include some (transient) stored data that must be considered.
- **TransmittedData** is a **CausalDomain** or **LexicalDomain** used to transmit data (e.g., a network).

– A *Secret* is a *StoredData* or *TransmittedData* that is used to implement a set of security requirements.

To use the predicate patterns for describing the dependability requirements of a concrete problem, the domains of the problem diagram (and in the context diagram) must be derived from the domains given in the dependability patterns. They must be described in such a way that it is possible to demonstrate that the dependability predicate holds for all objects of this class. The parts of the pattern's textual description printed in **bold and italics** should be refined according to the concrete problem.

The instantiated predicates are helpful to analyze conflicting requirements and the interaction of different dependability requirements, as well as for finding missing dependability requirements.

The patterns for integrity, reliability, and availability considering random faults are expressed using probabilities, while for the security requirements no probabilities are defined. We are aware of the fact that no security mechanism provides a 100 % protection and that an attacker can break the mechanism to gain data with a certain probability [17]. But in contrast to the random faults considered for the other requirements, no probability distribution can be assumed, because, e.g., new technologies may dramatically increase the probability that an attacker is successful. For this reason we suggest to describe a possible attacker and ensure that this attacker is not able to be successful in a reasonable amount of time.

3.1 Confidentiality

A typical confidentiality requirement is to

Preserve confidentiality of *StoredData / TransmittedData* for *Stakeholder*s and prevent disclosure by *Attacker*s.

The security requirement pattern can be expressed by the confidentiality predicate $conf_{att} : CausalDomain \times BiddableDomain \times BiddableDomain \rightarrow Bool$. The suffix "att" indicates that this predicate describes a requirement considering a certain *att*acker.

To apply the confidentiality requirement pattern, subclasses of *StoredData* or *TransmittedData*, *Stakeholder*, and *Attacker* must be derived and described in detail. For example, a special *TransmittedData* may be the *PIN of a bank account*, a special *Stakeholder* may be the *bank account owner*, and a special *Attacker* may be the class of all *persons with no permission, who want to withdraw money and have access to all external interfaces of the machine*. The instances of *Stakeholder* and *Attacker* must be disjoint. The *Stakeholder* is referred to, because we want to allow the access only to *Stakeholder*s with legitimate interest [5]. The reference to an *Attacker* is necessary, because we can only ensure confidentiality with respect to an *Attacker* with given properties.

Even if data is usually modeled using lexical domains, we derive *StoredData* or *TransmittedData* from *CausalDomain*, because in some cases the storage device and not the data is modeled. A *LexicalDomain* is a special *CausalDomain*. The following patterns can be used to define confidentiality requirements:

$\forall sd : StoredData; \ s : Stakeholder; \ a : Attacker \bullet conf_{att}(sd, s, a)$

$\forall td : TransmittedData; \ s : Stakeholder; \ a : Attacker \bullet conf_{att}(td, s, a)$

They express the informal requirement given above as a logical formula. The confidentiality predicate is often used together with functional requirements for data transmission and data storage.

3.2   Integrity - Random Faults

Typical integrity requirements considering random faults are that

> With a probability of P_i, one of the following things should happen: service (described in the functional requirement) **with influence on / of** the **Constrained-Domain** must be correct, or **a specific action** must be performed.

The specific action could be, e.g.:
- write a log entry into **InfluencedDomain**
- switch off the actuator **InfluencedDomain**
- do **not** influence **ConstrainedDomain**
- perform the same action as defined in the functional requirement on **Constrained-Domain**.
- inform **User**

For this requirement it is important to distinguish **ConstrainedDomain** and **Influenced-Domain**. The **ConstrainedDomain** is the domain that should work correctly or should be influenced correctly as described in the functional requirement. The **InfluencedDo-main** is the domain that should react as described in the dependability requirement. The **InfluencedDomain** could be, e.g., an actuator or a log file. The last specific action directly refers to the **User**. The **User** must be informed by some technical means, e.g. a display. The assumption that the **User** sees the **Display** (being necessary to derive a specification from the requirements) must be checked later for validity.

The requirement can be expressed by the integrity predicate int_{rnd} : $CausalDomain \times Domain \times Probability \rightarrow Bool$. The suffix "rnd" indicates that this predicate describes a requirement considering random faults.

The probability is a constant, determined by risk analysis. The standard ISO/IEC 61508 [11] provides a range of failure rates for each defined safety integrity level (SIL). The probability P_i could be, e.g., for SIL 3 systems operating on demand $1 - 10^{-3}$ to $1 - 10^{-4}$.

The following patterns can be used to define the integrity requirements for a given probability P_i:

$\forall cd : ConstrainedDomain;\ u : User \bullet int_{rnd}(cd, u, P_i)$
$\forall cd : ConstrainedDomain;\ id : InfluencedDomain \bullet int_{rnd}(cd, id, P_i)$
$\forall cd : ConstrainedDomain \bullet int_{rnd}(cd, cd, P_i)$

The predicate $int_{rnd}(cd, cd, P_i)$ expresses that the specific action is either that the **Con-strainedDomain** is **not** influenced any longer, or that it is influenced as described in the functional requirement (same action).

3.3   Integrity - Security

A typical security integrity requirement is that

> The **influence (as described in the functional requirement) on / data in** Con-strainedDomain must be either correct, or in case of any modifications by some **Attacker a specific action must be performed**.

The specific action may be the same as described for random faults in Section 3.2. In contrast to the dependability requirement considering random faults, this requirement can refer to the data of a domain (instead of the functionality), because security engineering usually focuses on data. For security the **ConstrainedDomain** in the functional requirement is usually a display or some plain data. The security requirement pattern can be expressed by the integrity predicate int_{att} : $CausalDomain \times Domain \times BiddableDomain \to Bool$.

Similarly to Section 3.2 the following patterns can be used to define integrity requirements:

$\forall cd : ConstrainedDomain; \ u : User; \ a : Attacker \bullet int_{att}(cd, u, a)$
$\forall cd : ConstrainedDomain; \ id : InfluencedDomain; \ a : Attacker \bullet int_{att}(cd, id, a)$
$\forall cd : ConstrainedDomain; \ a : Attacker \bullet int_{att}(cd, cd, a)$

3.4   Availability - Random Faults

A typical availability requirement considering random faults is that

> The service (described in the functional requirement) **with influence on / of** the **ConstrainedDomain** must be available for **User** with a probability of P_a.[3]

The requirement can be expressed by the availability predicate $avail_{rnd\_user}$: $CausalDomain \times BiddableDomain \times Probability \to Bool$.

P_a is the probability that the service (i.e., the influence on the **ConstrainedDomain**) is accessible for defined users.   A probability P_a of $1 - 10^{-5}$ means that the service (influence on the **ConstrainedDomain**) may be unavailable on average for 315 seconds in one year. The following pattern can be used to define the availability requirements for a given probability P_a:

$\forall cd : ConstrainedDomain; \ u : User \bullet avail_{rnd\_d\_user}(cd, u, P_a)$

3.5   Availability - Security

When we talk about availability in the context of security it is not possible to provide the service to everyone due to limited resources and possible denial-of-service attacks. Availability can be expressed with the predicate $avail_{att\_user}(cd, u, a)$ similar to the availability requirement considering random faults.

3.6   Reliability, Authentication, Management, and Secret Distribution

Reliability is defined in the same way as availability with the predicates rel_{rnd_user}, rel_{rnd}, and rel_{att_user}. The same failure rates as for integrity (see Section 3.2) can be used. Other important security requirements are authentication ($auth_{att}(cd, sh, a)$) to permit access for **Stakeholder** (sh) and deny access for **Attacker** (a) on **ConstrainedDomain** (cd), security management ($man_{att}(sd, sh, a)$) to manage security-relevant **StoredData** (sd) (e.g., configure an access rule), and **Secret** (s) distribution ($dist_{att}(s, sh, a)$) that additionally keeps the managed secret s confidential.

4   Working with Dependability Requirement Patterns

This section describes how to work with the modular construction system built up on the predicates defined in Section 3. It can be used to find possible interactions with other

---

[3] In [6], a variant that does not refer to users is presented ($avail_{rnd}$).

Table 1. Selected dependability dependencies

Requirement	Generic mechanism	Possible interaction	Introduced / considered domains	Necessary conditions	Conditions to be established before	Related
$int_{rmd}(c_1, u, P_i)$	checksums	$avail_*(c_1, *)^4$	$di : Display$	$int_{rmd}(m, u, P_i) \wedge$ $int_{rmd}(di, u, P_i) \wedge$ user sees display message	-	int_{att}
$int_{rmd}(c_1, c_2, P_i)$	checksums	$avail_*(c_1, *)^4$	-	$int_{rmd}(m, c_2, P_i) \wedge rel_{rmd}(c_2, P_i)$	-	int_{att}
$int_{att}(d, u, a)$	MAC	$avail_*(d, u, *)^4$	$s_{Snd}, s_{Rcv} : Secret$ $di : Display$	$conf_{att}(m, u, a) \wedge int_{att}(m, u, a) \wedge$ $int_{att}(di, u, a) \wedge$ $conf_{att}(s_{Snd}, u, a) \wedge$ $int_{att}(s_{Snd}, u, a) \wedge$ $conf_{att}(s_{Rcv}, u, a) \wedge int_{att}(s_{Rcv}, u, a)$	$dist_{att}(s_{Snd}, u, a) \wedge$ $dist_{att}(s_{Rcv}, u, a)$	$conf_{att}$
	cryptographic signature	$avail_*(d, u, *)^4$	$s_{Snd} : SenderSecret$ $s_{Rcv} : ReceiverSecret$ $di : Display$	$conf_{att}(m, u, a) \wedge int_{att}(m, u, a) \wedge$ $int_{att}(di, u, a) \wedge int_{att}(s_{Snd}, u, a) \wedge$ $conf_{att}(s_{Rcv}, u, a) \wedge int_{att}(s_{Rcv}, u, a)$	$dist_{att}(s_{Snd}, u, a) \wedge$ $dist_{att}(s_{Rcv}, u, a)$	$conf_{att}$
$avail_{rmd\_user}(c_1, u, P_a)$	reliable hardware and software		-	$rel_{rmd\_user}(m, u, P_r)$	-	rel_{att}
$rel_{rmd}(c_1, P_r)$	reliable hardware and software		-	$rel_{rmd}(m, P_r)$	-	rel_{att}
$auth_{att}(d, u, a)$	dynamic authentication using random numbers (symmetric)	$avail_*(d, *)$	$s_{Mchn}, s_{Ext} : Secret$	$conf_{att}(m, u, a) \wedge int_{att}(m, u, a) \wedge$ $conf_{att}(s_{Mchn}, u, a) \wedge$ $int_{att}(s_{Mchn}, u, a) \wedge$ $conf_{att}(s_{Ext}, u, a) \wedge int_{att}(s_{Ext}, u, a)$	$dist_{att}(s_{Mchn}, u, a) \wedge$ $dist_{att}(s_{Ext}, u, a)$	
$dist_{att}(d, u, a)$	see dynamic authentication	...	...	...	...	...

---

4 Availability may be descreased if modified data is just deleted.

dependability requirements and helps to complete the dependability requirements by a set of defined necessary conditions for each mechanism that can be used to solve dependability problem. To apply the dependability patterns, we assume that **hazards and threats are identified and a risk analysis** is performed. The next step is to **describe the environment**, because dependability requirements can only be guaranteed for some specific intended environment. For example, a device may be dependable for personal use, but not for military use with more powerful attackers or a non-reliable power supply. The **functional requirements are described** using patterns for this intended environment (see Section 2). The requirements describe how the environment should behave when the machine is in action. To describe the requirements, domains and phenomena of the environment description should be used. From hazards and threats an **initial set of dependability requirements can be identified**. These requirements are usually linked to a previously described functional requirement.

For each dependability requirement, a pattern from our pattern catalog should be selected, using the informal description of the dependability requirements given in Section 3. After an appropriate pattern is determined, is must be "instantiated" with the concrete domains from the environment description. To instantiate the domains that represent potential attackers, a certain level of skill, equipment, and determination of the potential attacker must be specified. Via these assumptions, *threat models* are integrated into the development process using dependability patterns. The values for probabilities can be usually extracted from the risk analysis. For each dependability requirement stated as a predicate, we **select a generic mechanism** that solves the problem; for example, to achieve integrity (int_{att_bidd}) message authentication codes (MACs) can be used. Table 1 lists for each dependability requirement pattern a set of possible mechanisms. The dependability requirement predicates in the table refer to all instances d of **TransmittedData** or **StoredData**, the **ConstrainedDomain**s c_1 and c_2, the **user**s u, the **Attacker**s a, and the **Machine** with all relevant connection domains m.

Table 1 supports the analysis of conflicts between the dependability patterns. For some of the mechanisms, **possible interactions** with other dependability requirements are given in the third column. These possible conflicts must be analyzed, and it must be determined if they are relevant for the application domain. In case they are relevant, conflicts can be resolved by modifying or prioritizing the requirements. For example, if the MAC protection mechanism is applied and the specific action is to delete modified data, we may have a contradiction with the availability of that data.

For many mechanisms, additional **domains must be introduced or considered**. MAC protection, e.g., requires a **Secret** s_{Snd} used to calculate the MAC and another **Secret** s_{Rcv} used to verify the MAC. For asymmetric mechanisms, **SenderSecret** and **ReceiverSecret** need to be introduced. They are special **StoredData**. For dynamic authentication, the **Secret** s_{Mchn} (stored in the machine) and the **Secret** s_{Ext} (known by the subject) are necessary. Such introduced domains must be **added to the description of the environment**.

The next step is to **inspect the necessary conditions and the conditions to be established beforehand**. The generic mechanisms usually have a set of *necessary conditions* to be fulfilled. These necessary conditions describe conditions necessary to establish the dependability requirement when a certain mechanism is selected. For example, the introduced secrets for the MAC protection must be kept confidential, and their integrity must be preserved. Before the mechanism is applied, some other activities are necessary, e.g., a secret must be distributed before it can be used for MAC calculation (*conditions to be established beforehand*). Two alternatives are possible to guarantee that the necessary conditions hold: either, they can be *assumed* to hold, or they have to be *established* by instantiating a further dependability requirement pattern, that matches the necessary condition. What assumptions are reasonable depends on the hazards to be avoided and the threats the system should be protected against. Assumptions cannot be avoided completely, because otherwise it may be impossible to achieve a dependability requirement. For example, we must assume that the user sees a warning messages on a display or keeps a password confidential. Only in the case that necessary conditions *cannot* be assumed to hold, one must instantiate further appropriate dependability patterns, and the procedure is repeated until all necessary conditions of all applied mechanisms can be proved or assumed to hold. The dependencies expressed as necessary condition are used to develop a consolidated set of dependability requirements and solution approaches that additionally cover all dependent requirements and corresponding solution approaches, some of which may not have been known initially.

The next step is to check the **Related** column. There, dependability requirements that are commonly used in combination with the described dependability pattern are mentioned. This information helps to find missing dependability requirements right at the beginning of the requirements engineering process. The dependencies for security requirements are based on previous work [9].

Table 1 only shows some important dependencies used in Section 5. A comprehensive version can be found in our technical report [6]. The next step in the software development life-cycle is to **derive a specification**, which describes the machine and is the starting point for its development.

5   Case Study

The approach is illustrated by the development of a cooperative adaptive cruise control (CACC) maintaining string stability. Such a system controls the speed of a car according to the desired speed given by the driver and the measured distance to the car ahead. It also considers information about speed and acceleration of the car ahead which is sent using a wireless network[5] The **hazard** to be avoided is an unintended acceleration or deceleration (that may lead to a rear-end collision). The considered **threat** is an attacker who sends wrong messages to the car in order to influence its speed.[6] Examples for domain knowledge of the CACC in the **described environment** are physical properties about acceleration, breaking, and measurement of the distance (relevant for safety). Other examples are the assumed intention, knowledge and equipment of an attacker. We assume here that the attacker can only access the *WAVE/WLAN interface*. The context diagram for the CACC is shown in Fig. 3. The **functional requirement** for the CACC is to maintain string stability.

R1 The CACC should control the speed of a *Car* using the *MotorActuator_Break* according to the desired speed given by the *Driver* and the measured *Distance* to the car ahead (commanded behaviour, see Section 2).

---

[5] cf. United States Patent 20070083318.

[6] The **risk analysis** is left out here.

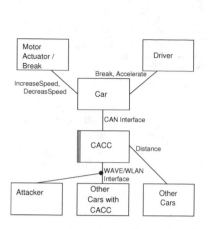

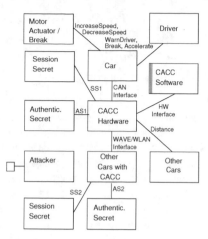

Fig. 3. CACC context diagram

Fig. 4. CACC context diagram after mechanisms have been selected

R2 The CACC should also consider information about speed and acceleration of ***Other Cars with CACC*** ahead which is sent using a wireless network (*WAVE/WLAN interface*) (required behaviour).

The next step is to **identify an initial set of dependability requirements**. For the functional requirement **R2**, the following security requirement can be stated using the textual pattern from Section 3.3:

> The ***influence (as described in the functional requirement) on*** the ***MotorActuator_Break*** must be either correct, or in case of any modifications by some ***Attacker the ConstrainedDomain should <u>not</u> be influenced <u>and</u> the Driver must be informed***.

These requirements can be expressed using the integrity predicates

$$\forall\, mab : MotorActuator\_Break;\ dr : Driver;\ a : Attacker \bullet$$

$$int_{att}(mab, mab, a) \wedge int_{att}(mab, dr, a) \tag{1}$$

The first occurrence of the variable *mab* in Equation 1 refers to the influenced domain as described in the functional requirement, and the second occurrence of *mab* expresses that this domain is not influenced in case of an attack.

A safety requirement is to keep a safe distance to the car ahead while being activated (see **R1**). For each safety requirement the integrity or the reliability must be defined. For the CACC only integrity is required, because it is safe to switch off the functionality and inform the driver in case of a failure. The risk analysis performed in the first step showed that a probability of at most 10^{-6} untreated random errors per hour (that may lead to an accident) can be accepted. Hence, for **R1** it can be stated that

> With a probability of $1 - 10^{-6}$ ***per hour***, one of the following things should happen: service (described in the functional requirement) ***with influence on*** the ***MotorActuator_Break*** must be correct, or ***the ConstrainedDomain should <u>not</u> be influenced <u>and</u> the Driver must be informed***.

The corresponding predicates are:

$$\forall\, mab : MotorActuator\_Break;\ dr : Driver \bullet$$

$$int_{rnd}(mab, mab, 1 - 10^{-6}) \wedge int_{att}(mab, dr, 1 - 10^{-6}) \tag{2}$$

Additionally, to satisfy the drivers buying the CACC:

> The service (described in the functional requirement) **with influence on** the
> **MotorActuator_Break** must be available with a probability of $1 - 10^{-4}$.

This requirement can be expressed with the predicate

$$\forall mab : MotorActuator\_Break \bullet avail_{rnd}(mab, 1 - 10^{-4}) \tag{3}$$

For availability, we only consider random faults, because for the corresponding security requirement we have to limit the group of users (the service is provided for) as described in Section 3.5, and this is not possible in the described environment.

The next step is to **Select appropriate generic mechanisms** for each dependability requirement expressed as a predicate. Depending on the generic mechanism, additional **domains must be introduced or considered**.

To establish Equation 1 messages authentication codes (MACs) can be used to check integrity and authenticity of the messages (position, acceleration and speed data) from other cars with trusted CACCs. According to Table 1, **Secret**s for sender and receiver are necessary to calculate and verify the MAC. We decide to use **SessionSecret**s for Sender (ss_2) and Receiver (ss_1). A **SessionSecret** has the advantage that it has a short life-time: even if the attacker is able to obtain this secret, it can only be used for a short time period. The "**necessary conditions**" column of Table 1 shows for the MAC mechanism that the secrets (ss_1 and ss_2) and the machine processing the secrets ($cacc$) must be protected from modification and disclosure. In case of any modification by the **attacker**, the **driver** is informed, and there will be no influence on **MotorActuator_Break** (Equation 4). The "**conditions to be established beforehand**" column of Table 1 shows that the secrets must be distributed beforehand (Equation 7), as stated with the following predicates:

$$\forall cacc : CACC;\ ss_1, ss_2 : SessionSecret;$$
$$mab : MotorActuator\_Break;\ dr : Driver, a : Attacker \bullet$$
$$conf_{att}(cacc, dr, a) \wedge int_{att}(cacc, dr, a) \wedge int_{att}(cacc, mab, a) \wedge \tag{4}$$
$$conf_{att}(ss_1, dr, a) \wedge int_{att}(ss_1, dr, a) \wedge int_{att}(ss_1, mab, a) \wedge \tag{5}$$
$$conf_{att}(ss_2, dr, a) \wedge int_{att}(ss_2, dr, a) \wedge int_{att}(ss_2, mab, a) \wedge \tag{6}$$
$$dist_{att}(ss_1, cacc, a) \wedge dist_{att}(ss_2, cacc, a) \tag{7}$$

The integrity and confidentiality of the **CACC** with its data, in particular the **SessionSecret** ss_1 (required by Equations 4 and 5), can be established by some physical protection. The **SessionSecret** ss_2 is stored in the **OtherCarsWithCACC**. Its confidentiality and integrity (Equation 6) are also established by physical protection. To establish Equation 7, a dynamic authentication mechanism with random numbers can be used. With this authentication mechanism additionally a session key can be generated. Since replay attacks cannot be avoided in the described context, random numbers are used for authentication (cf. *CSPF Dynamic Authentication* in [7]). The necessary conditions for this mechanism are similar to those for MAC protection. Integrity and confidentiality of the machines and secrets are established in the same way as for the MAC protection. Secure distribution of the **AuthenticationSecret**s is assumed to be done in the production environment of the **CACC**.

To establish Equation 2, we regard the machine **CACC** as consisting of two parts: the **CACCSoftware** $cacc_{SW}$ and the **CACCHardware** $cacc_{HW}$. For the hardware we use, a reliability of only $1 - 10^{-4}$ is guaranteed. For our software we assume (and try to achieve using several quality assurance activities, see ISO/IEC 61508 [11, Part 3]) a reliability of $1 - 10^{-6}$. Therefore, our software must check the hardware and initiate the required actions. Several checks on the hardware have to be performed as given, e.g., in the standard ISO/IEC 61508, Part 2, Tables A.1 to A.15 [11]. The first row of Table 1 shows for the checksum mechanism (as one example from [11]) that the integrity of the **Machine** and of the **Display** have to be ensured; i.e., if these domains are not able to forward the warning to the user, the user must be informed by other means. The **Machine** is here the **CACC Hardware**, and the **Display** is here (to simplify the example) the **Car** used in the following predicates (Equation 8). The warning is given acoustically and visually to increase the probability that the **Driver** recognizes the warning. Additionally, it is necessary that in this case there is no automatic control of the speed of the car, i.e., no influence on the **MotorActuator_Break** (Equation 9).

$$\forall \, cacc_{HW} : CACCHardware; \; car : Car; \; dr : Driver; \; mab : MotorActuator\_Break \; \bullet$$

$$int_{rnd}(cacc_{HW}, dr, 1 - 10^{-6}) \wedge int_{rnd}(car, dr, 1 - 10^{-6}) \wedge \qquad (8)$$

$$int_{rnd}(cacc_{HW}, mab, 1 - 10^{-6}) \wedge int_{rnd}(car, mab, 1 - 10^{-6}) \wedge \qquad (9)$$

The first part of Equations 8 and 9 cannot be assumed, because of the reliability of the hardware is only $1 - 10^{-4}$. Therefore, our solution for this contradiction consists of two parts. The first one is the dependability requirements for the software:

> With a probability of $1 - 10^{-6}$, one of the following things should happen: service (described in the functional requirement) *of* the **Hardware** must be correct, or *the CACC must be switched off using* **SwitchOffPartsOfCAC-CHardware** $cacc_{HW\_OFF}$ (omitted in Fig. 4).

$$\forall \, cacc_{HW} : CACCHardware; \; cacc_{HW\_OFF} : SwitchOffPartsOfCACCHardware \; \bullet$$

$$int_{rnd}(cacc_{HW}, cacc_{HW\_OFF}, 1 - 10^{-6}) \qquad (10)$$

To establish Equation 10, the pre-requisites according to Table 1 can be fulfilled by a reliability of $1 - 10^{-6}$ for the **CACCSoftware** and the **SwitchOffPartsOfCACCHardware**, which is also assumed.

The second part of the solution is that the **Car** has to detect a switched-off **CACC**. In this case the **Car** should warn the driver, and the **Car** should not use the output of the **CACC** to control the **MotorActuator_Break**. For this requirement (R_{car}), the following reliability (stated as a predicate) is necessary and must be assumed for the CACC development[7]:

$$\forall \, car : Car \; \bullet \; rel_{rnd}(car, 1 - 10^{-6}) \qquad (11)$$

To establish Equation 3, reliable hardware and software can be used, because $rel_{rnd}(c, P) \Rightarrow avail_{rnd}(c, P)$. The required reliabilities of the machine and all relevant connection domains are assumed as shown in [6]. The new context diagram for the CACC resulting from applying dependability requirements patterns is shown in Fig. 4. New domains were **added to the description of the environment**, and the connection of the attacker to the *WAVE/WLAN Interface* is replaced by the more generic "window to the world", because the new domains **SessionSecret AuthenticationSecret**, and the **CACC** itself are of great interest for the **Attacker**. Additionally, the machine **CACC** is split into **CACCHardware** and **CACCSoftware**. Since some dependability requirements state that the **Driver** must be informed, the additional phenomenon *WarnDriver* is introduced.

By using the dependencies given in Section 4, we systematically developed more than 27 dependability requirements to be inspected from the 3 initial dependability requirements.

---

[7] Equation 11 expresses together with the functional requirement R_{car} the same requirements as Equations 8 and 9.

6 Related Work

We are not aware of any similar approach for modeling a wide range of dependability requirements. However, the Common Criteria [1], Part 2 define a large set of so-called *Security Functional Requirements (SFRs)* with explicitly given dependencies between these SFRs. But some of these SFRs directly anticipate a solution, e.g. the SFR *cryptographic operation* in the class *functional requirements for cryptographic support* (FCS_COP) specifies the cryptographic algorithm, key sizes, and the assigned standard to be used. The SFRs in the Common Criteria are limited to security issues. The dependencies given in the Common Criteria are re-used for our pattern system. Our dependability requirements can be regarded on the level of Security Objectives that have to be stated according to Common Criteria, Part 3, before suitable SFRs are selected. For example, for int_{att_d} the SFRs *Cryptographic operation (FCS_COP)*, *Cryptographic key management (FCS_CKM)*, and Stored data integrity (FDP_SDI) can be instantiated.

7 Conclusions and Future Work

In this paper, we have presented a set of patterns for expressing and analyzing dependability requirements. These patterns are separated from the functional requirements and expressed without anticipating solutions. They can be used to create re-usable dependability requirement descriptions for a wide range of problems.

This paper also describes a pattern system that can be used to identify missing requirements in a systematic way. The pattern system is based on the predicates used to express the requirements. The parameters of the predicates refer to domains of the environment descriptions and are used to describe the dependencies precisely. The pattern system may also show possible conflicts between dependability requirements in an early requirements engineering phase.

In summary, our pattern system has the following advantages:
- The dependability patterns are re-usable for different projects.
- A manageable number of patterns can be applied on a wide range of problems, because they are separated from the functional requirements.
- Requirements expressed by instantiated patterns only refer to the environment description and are independent from solutions. Hence, they can be easily re-used for new product versions.
- The patterns closely relate predicates and their textual descriptions. The textual description helps to state the dependability requirements more precisely.
- The patterns help to structure and classify the dependability requirements. For example, requirements considering integrity can be easily distinguished from availability requirements. It is also possible to trace all dependability requirements that refer to one domain.
- The predicates are the basis of a modular construction system used to identify dependencies and possible interactions with other dependability requirements.

In the future, we plan to elaborate more on the later phases of software development. For example, we want to apply our patterns to software components to show that a certain architecture is dependable enough for its intended usage. Additionally, we plan to systematically search for missing dependability requirements and dependencies using existing specifications (e.g., public Security Targets).

References

1. Common Criteria for Information Technology Security Evaluation, Version 3.1 (September 2006), http://www.commoncriteriaportal.org/public/expert/
2. Avizienis, A., Laprie, J.-C., Randall, B., Landwehr, C.: Basic concepts and taxonomy of dependable and secure computing. IEEE Transactions on Dependable and Secure Computing 1(1), 11–33 (2004),
   http://se2c.uni.lu/tiki/se2c-bib_download.php?id=2433
3. Côté, I., Hatebur, D., Heisel, M., Schmidt, H., Wentzlaff, I.: A systematic account of problem frames. In: Proceedings of the European Conference on Pattern Languages of Programs (EuroPLoP 2007). Universitätsverlag Konstanz (2008)
4. Courtois, P.-J.: Safety, reliability and software based systems requirements. In: Contribution to the UK ACSNI Report of the Study Group on the safety of Operational Computer Systems (June 1997)
5. Gürses, S., Jahnke, J.H., Obry, C., Onabajo, A., Santen, T., Price, M.: Eliciting confidentiality requirements in practice. In: CASCON 2005: Proceedings of the 2005 conference of the Centre for Advanced Studies on Collaborative research, pp. 101–116. IBM Press (2005)
6. Hatebur, D., Heisel, M.: A foundation for requirements analysis of dependable software (technical report). Technical report, Universität Duisburg-Essen (2009),
   http://swe.uni-due.de/techrep/founddep.pdf
7. Hatebur, D., Heisel, M., Schmidt, H.: Security engineering using problem frames. In: Müller, G. (ed.) ETRICS 2006. LNCS, vol. 3995, pp. 238–253. Springer, Heidelberg (2006)
8. Hatebur, D., Heisel, M., Schmidt, H.: A pattern system for security requirements engineering. In: Werner, B. (ed.) Proceedings of the International Conference on Availability, Reliability and Security (AReS), IEEE Transactions, pp. 356–365. IEEE, Los Alamitos (2007)
9. Hatebur, D., Heisel, M., Schmidt, H.: Analysis and component-based realization of security requirements. In: Proceedings of the International Conference on Availability, Reliability and Security (AReS), IEEE Transactions, pp. 195–203. IEEE, Los Alamitos (2008)
10. Hatebur, D., Heisel, M., Schmidt, H.: A formal metamodel for problem frames. In: Czarnecki, K., Ober, I., Bruel, J.-M., Uhl, A., Völter, M. (eds.) MODELS 2008. LNCS, vol. 5301, pp. 68–82. Springer, Heidelberg (2008)
11. International Electrotechnical Commission IEC. Functional safety of electrical/electronic/programmable electronic safty-relevant systems (2000)
12. Jackson, M.: Problem Frames. Analyzing and structuring software development problems. Addison-Wesley, Reading (2001)
13. Jackson, M., Zave, P.: Deriving specifications from requirements: an example. In: Proceedings 17th Int. Conf. on Software Engineering, Seattle, USA, pp. 15–24. ACM Press, New York (1995)
14. Laprie, J.-C.: Dependability computing and fault tolerance: Concepts and terminology. Fault-Tolerant Computing – Highlights from Twenty-Five Years, 2–13 (June 1995),
   http://lion.ee.ntu.edu.tw/Class/FTDS_2008/Laprie-Definitions.pdf
15. Pfitzmann, A., Hansen, M.: Anonymity, unlinkability, unobservability, pseudonymity, and identity management - a consolidated proposal for terminology. Technical report, TU Dresden and ULD Kiel, 5 (2006),
   http://dud.inf.tu-dresden.de/Anon_Terminology.shtml
16. Røstad, L., Tøndel, I.A., Line, M.B., Nordland, O.: Safety vs. security. In: Stamatelatos, M.G., Blackman, H.S. (eds.) Safety Assessment and Management - PSAM 8, Eighth International Conference on Probabilistic. ASME Press, New York (2006)
17. Santen, T.: Stepwise development of secure systems. In: Górski, J. (ed.) SAFECOMP 2006. LNCS, vol. 4166, pp. 142–155. Springer, Heidelberg (2006)

Establishing a Framework for Dynamic Risk Management in 'Intelligent' Aero-Engine Control

Zeshan Kurd[1], Tim Kelly[1], John McDermid[1],
Radu Calinescu[2], and Marta Kwiatkowska[2]

[1] High Integrity Systems Engineering Group
Department of Computer Science
University of York, York, YO10 5DD, UK
{zeshan.kurd,tim.kelly,john.mcdermid}@cs.york.ac.uk
[2] Computing Laboratory, University of Oxford,
Wolfson Building, Parks Road, Oxford, OX1 3QD, UK
{radu.calinescu,marta.kwiatkowska}@comlab.ox.ac.uk

Abstract. The behaviour of control functions in safety critical software systems is typically bounded to prevent the occurrence of known system level hazards. These bounds are typically derived through safety analyses and can be implemented through the use of necessary design features. However, the unpredictability of real world problems can result in changes in the operating context that may invalidate the behavioural bounds themselves, for example, unexpected hazardous operating contexts as a result of failures or degradation. For highly complex problems it may be infeasible to determine the precise desired behavioural bounds of a function that addresses or minimises risk for hazardous operation cases prior to deployment. This paper presents an overview of the safety challenges associated with such a problem and how such problems might be addressed. A self-management framework is proposed that performs on-line risk management. The features of the framework are shown in context of employing intelligent adaptive controllers operating within complex and highly dynamic problem domains such as Gas-Turbine Aero Engine control. Safety assurance arguments enabled by the framework necessary for certification are also outlined.

1 Introduction

The use of Artificial Intelligence (AI) in highly critical roles has long been a subject of scepticism and controversy within the safety community. Although such technology is being increasingly acclaimed for its qualities and performance capabilities their inherent unpredictability has gained limited recognition within current safety development standards and guidelines [1]. At the macro level, AI paradigms such as Multi-Agent Systems may be employed in the complex simulation management and control of Systems of Systems [2]. At the micro-level, intelligent machine learning paradigms can be employed for control systems such as Artificial Neural Networks (ANNs) and Fuzzy Logic Systems (FLSs).

B. Buth, G. Rabe, T. Seyfarth (Eds.): SAFECOMP 2009, LNCS 5775, pp. 326–341, 2009.
© Springer-Verlag Berlin Heidelberg 2009

There are many motivations for using AI paradigms - some of which include addressing incomplete specifications, uncertainty, unexpected conditions, complexity and changing environments. Many of these AI paradigms fall into the category of self-* or autonomous systems. These are Self-Managed systems that are capable of self-configuration, self-adaptation, self-healing, self-monitoring and self-tuning [3].

The emergence of self-governing or autonomous solutions to address complex, highly dynamical and unpredictable real world problems has led to major challenges in achieving compelling and acceptable safety assurance necessary for certification. Previous work on the safety of Intelligent Adaptive Systems [4-6] has addressed these issues by employing design features and a set of behavioural (functional) safety bounds within which such paradigms are able to learn and adapt their behaviour once deployed. This can be achieved using self-* algorithms such as self-tuning and self-generation [5]. Although this may be sufficient for problems where the functional safety requirements are well defined in some other problems it may be necessary to change the defined safety bounds themselves post certification in the event of unexpected failures or system degradation.

In section 2, the problem of managing unexpected operating conditions is highlighted in context of the Gas Turbine Aero-Engine. Section 3 of the paper presents an argument about how such operating conditions can be addressed through adaptive systems. Section 4 presents a framework detailing key activities, how they contribute to safety assurance and major safety challenges in context of Gas Turbine Aero-Engine control.

2 Problem Definition: Managing Changing Requirements

Gas Turbine Engines (GTE) are a real world example of a complex and a highly dynamical system that is comprised of many interconnected components. GTEs are

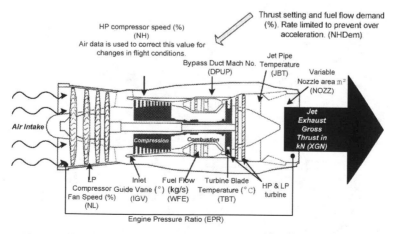

Fig. 1. Typical Mechanical Layout of a Twin-Spool Gas Turbine Aero-Engine

internal combustion heat engines which convert heat energy into mechanical energy. There are three main elements within the GTE namely; compressor, combustion chamber and a turbine placed on a common shaft. The GTE illustrated in Figure 1 shows the typical mechanism for producing thrust and highlights the engine acronyms. The initial stage involves atmospheric air entering the engine body. Air that is drawn in then enters the compressor which is divided into the LP and HP (Low and High Pressure) compressor units (twin-spool). Air pressure is first raised by the LP Compressor unit and then further increased by the HP Compressor unit. The Inlet Guide Vane (*IGV*) is used to match the air from the fan to the HP compressor characteristics. Pressurised air then reaches the combustion chamber where engine fuel is mixed with the compressed air and ignited at constant pressure. This results in a rise in temperature and expansion of the gases. A percentage of the airflow is then mixed with the combusted gas from the turbine exit. This is then ejected through the jet pipe and variable nozzle area to produce a propulsive thrust.

At the system-level, a major engine hazard is engine 'surge' which can lead to loss of thrust (XGN – ref. Figure 1) or engine destruction. Engine surge is caused by excessive aerodynamic pulsations transmitted across the engine and is of particular concern during high thrust demand. For typical GTEs, there is a 'surge line' which is used as a measure of aerodynamic stability. As shown in Figure 2 the 'surge line' defines various surge points across the engine speed range. To provide safety assurance that the risk of engine surge is controlled a 'working line' is defined that specifies an extreme of allowable engine behaviour at the system level.

At the local level of the engine there are various controllers designed to fulfil engine design objectives and performance efficiency. An example of such objectives is shown in the "expected operating conditions" column in Table 1.

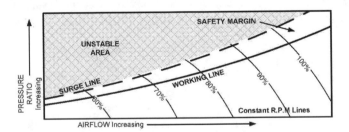

Fig. 2. Typical engine surge margins and working lines

Table 1. Operating Context Dependant Engine Safety Objectives

Objectives for Expected Operating Conditions	Objectives for Collision Avoidance
LPSM ≥ 6.6%, HPSM ≥ 6.6% JPT ≤ 833°C, TBT ≤ 813°C dTBT/dt ≤ 1320°/s $NH ≤ 101\%, NL ≤ 101\%$	LPSM ≥ 1%, HPSM ≥ 1% TBT ≤ 1730°C ...

LPSM and HPSM are Low and High Pressure Surge Margins that indicate how close the engine is to instability and the surge condition. To avoid control system design flaws in such complex systems, rigorous analytical techniques are needed to cope with various types of *changes*. Such changes include changing goals, user requirements and operational and system conditions. Engine control is typically designed to accommodate for predicted changes such as *expected* engine degradation and wear between service intervals. Suitable AI controllers can be employed to address operating context changes given specified safety objectives. For example, previous work [7] has demonstrated the use of fuzzy logic systems for control of Inlet Guide Vanes, fuel flow (WFE), and engine nozzle (NOZZ) using Mamdani and Takagi-Sugeno [8] fuzzy rules. Such work has been shown to offer improved performance (such as thrust maximisation) over linear or non-linear polynomial schedulers [7].

In real world scenarios the engine may be expected to perform in the event of 'unexpected' changes such as *unexpected* and abrupt excessive turbine blade wear or excessive turbine blade over-heating (i.e. prolonged TBT > 2000°C resulting in high risk of imminent blade failure). Such emergency scenarios may arise when the engine is on-line, in operation and where immediate maintenance is unavailable. For such cases, the assumed safety objectives may no longer be valid. For example, column "objectives of collision avoidance" in Table 1 defines appropriate safety objectives that enable maximum thrust to avoid imminent collision. These safety objectives are far more flexible than that defined for 'normal' expected operating contexts but are not suitable for 'normal' operating conditions. The implication of such changes in the objectives is that the intelligent controllers can adapt themselves to offer a suitable solution from a context-specific solution space. Forcing intelligent controllers to adapt according to a single fixed set of objectives could result in the inability of the adaptive system to find an appropriate solution to address the current operating conditions given engine capabilities and constraints. Such 'intelligent' solutions could contribute to exacerbating the risk of an accident when they are forcibly (an unavoidably) used out of context. Addressing unexpected engine changes through the use of intelligent self-* systems can greatly increase the probability of achieving system or mission goals when operating in stochastic environments.

As an example, our previous work employed the Safety Critical Artificial Neural Network [5] (SCANN) within the GTE. SCANN is a 'hybrid' nonlinear function approximator that exploits both fuzzy and neural network paradigms for mutual benefit and overcomes many problems traditionally associated with ANNs [9]. Through manual hazard analysis (prior to deployment) functional safety barriers (that only allow actions to be executed once defined preconditions are satisfied [10]) for the SCANN function are derived and guarante behaviour to lie within derived behavioural bounds and prevent the occurrence of identified failure modes [4]. However, during on-line learning and adaptation the behavioural bounds are always fixed thereby leading to possible adaptations within a single pre-defined operating context. This means that under unexpected conditions the behavioural bounds may instantly become invalid and safety assurance can no longer be provided that the risk of hazard occurrence or accident can be minimised. Furthermore, it is shown that such low-level behavioural bounds are impractical for safety engineers to determine for multiple-input controllers [4]. Further difficulties arise since each adaptive controller cannot be considered independently of other adaptive controllers. To address the problem of control under *unexpected* engine operating conditions safety assurance needs to be provided for determining valid controller solutions "on-the-fly".

3   Dynamic, Real-Time, On-Line Risk Management

The term 'risk' is defined in Defence Standard 00-56 [11] as *the combination of the probability, or frequency, and the consequence of an accident.* Thus an argument that a system is 'safe' is primarily based upon demonstrating that an acceptable level of risk has been achieved. Risk management as defined in [11] comprises of six main activities which are hazard identification, risk analysis, estimation, evaluation, reduction and acceptance. There are many risk management techniques employed when the system (engine) is off-line and during service intervals. For example, Grid computing [12] and multi-agent engine scheduling [13] are some approaches that employ artificially intelligent paradigms for diagnosis and prognosis. To address cases when the engine control system is required to operate outside the defined operating conditions an on-line risk management scheme is needed. This scheme is termed hereafter as *Dynamic Risk Management.* Already there are several domains that deal with the problem of Dynamic Risk Management in the field of robotics [14], financial critical decisions [15], security [16] and many others. However, such approaches need to address the key issue of providing compelling safety assurance required for certification and operation within 'safety-critical environments'. So far, most forms of evidence are based upon empirical performance analysis results [15]. Sole reliance on such forms of evidence is inappropriate for certification.

Figure 3 presents the top level of a dynamic risk management safety assurance argument for using intelligent adaptive systems to manage risk in unexpected operating conditions. The argument is expressed using Goal Structuring Notation (GSN) [17] and is commonly used for composing safety case argument patterns. The focus of the argument is to capture product evidence-based safety arguments (that is in the spirit of current UK Defence Standard 00-56 [11]).

The top goal of the argument G1 abstractly refers to an "adaptive system". This might be a single or *n* interconnected system of systems that have the ability to achieve evolving objectives through self-* algorithms. The instantiated definition of an adaptive system is defined by context C1 e.g. SCANN. The constraints associated with employing an adaptive system are that the behaviour must be controllable to address failures common across all operating conditions. For example, assurance must be provided that the behaviour of a neural network non-linear function approximator does not exhibit discontinuity of output. As captured by context C3, goal G1 requires a known and intentionally complete list of hazards that may be generated through well known conventional safety processes (i.e. Preliminary Hazard Identification). The 'sufficiency' of the risk reduction as stated in context C2 is dependent on the nature of the overarching argument G1 is used within. The management of risk is performed on-line, post certification and whilst the system is in operation as stated by C5.

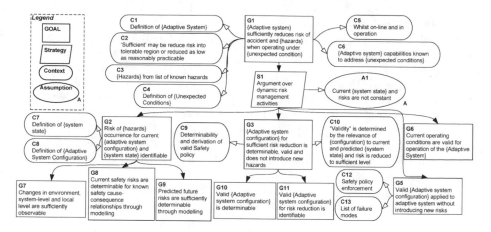

Fig. 3. GSN safety argument for Dynamic On-Line Risk Management

Context C4 is concerned with the operating conditions for which the argument is applicable. 'Unexpected' conditions are not the same as 'unknown' conditions - overly-high TBT is 'unexpected' because of regular engine maintenance but such a condition is not 'unknown' in that it can be preconceived during safety analyses. Another example of *unexpected* but *known* condition is excessive environmental temperature changes - where a change of only one degree centigrade in external can increase internal temperatures by several tens of degrees [18]. Context C4 is specific to the type of problems addressed and the requirements of the solution – such as component failures (blade material random failures) or degradation. As required for certification, context C4 delineates the scope of applicability of the adaptive system.

Strategy S1 decomposes the argument over major activities associated with managing risk "on-the-fly" and autonomously. As acknowledged by assumption A1, the dynamic risk management activities have to be conducted with the view that the system states are not constant during these activities. Strategy S1 breaks the argument into five sub-goals. The first sub-goal G2 is concerned with determining the level of risk associated with the identified hazards. This presents a "situational awareness" of the current state in terms of the risk associated with known hazard occurrence. The achievement of G2 will rely upon *sufficient* and *appropriate* monitoring of the environment as stated by G7. This may include inputs from all levels of the system, environment, components (such as current system state – health of components), safety objectives, mission objectives, current adaptive system configuration, their capabilities, status etc. If there are faulty sensors resulting in incorrect or delayed readings then such issues may lead to unrepresentative risk determination and result in unnecessary or incorrect action (in terms of risk management). Work presented on smart sensors [19] attempt to address such problems. Goals G8 and G9 aim to assess risk for current and predicted future states. The prediction of risk is extremely important because of the on-line, real-time nature of the risk management. Without such prediction, risk reduction plans may become immediately outdated and the process of risk management may never reach the execution of a suitable risk reduction plan (thereby becoming stuck in 'observation' and 'orientation' modes). The length of prediction of future risks in the temporal sense can be used later to 'life' proposed solutions and provide valid stopping conditions. For example, when attempting to address the issue of excessive NH shaft speed, in the time taken to find a solution the system enters a condition where TBT is over the prescribed limits. As a result, non-functional temporal issues will play an important role and must be addressed through prediction and 'validity' of plans based on non-functional temporal properties. Prediction will rely upon the provision of a suitable model that captures the cause-consequence relationship of relevant variables. Failures with the modelling and it's output would result in 'invalid' risk reduction plans and could introduce new risks. The argument of high fidelity modelling and how associated failure modes are addressed will therefore involve decomposition of goal G9.

The next step for risk management is assuring that an adaptive system 'configuration' or 'solution' can indeed by determined and that such a solution does not result in introducing new and unnecessary safety risks (G3). For example, safety risks can be prioritised based on the system level effects – maximising thrust to avoid an accident is acceptable given that risks associated with over-TBT and shaft overspeed are of lower priority. Risks are therefore managed depending on the highest level of risk and the solution (which may be non-dominant). This gives rise to the notion of *determinability* of managing such risks through an adaptive system configuration as stated in G10. Approaches to identify valid solutions can be used to further decompose goal G11.

The behaviour of the adaptive components must comply with the derived adaptive system configuration solution (G5). One safety concern is that the enforcement itself may introduce new risks and failures especially since it is performed in real-time and whilst the system is in operation. For example, defining new functional safety barriers for the SCANN may result in problems with the current operating control point – this may result in a control output spike (or high derivative changes) resulting in local-level failure modes.

Finally, G6 provides assurance that the applicability of the adaptive system for the context in which it has been defined is valid.

Due to space constraints a fully decomposed safety argument is not shown here. The following section shows how activities within a self-management framework can contribute to generating suitable forms of safety argument and assurance for Figure 3.

4 A 'Safe' Self-management Framework

A conceptual framework is illustrated in Figure 4 and aims to address the safety argument goals in Figure 3. The framework is based on the three layer architecture conceptual model for self-management of autonomous agent and intelligent systems [20].

The *Component Control Layer* consists of a set of adaptive interconnected and interdependent controllers that will adhere to a derived risk reduction solution. For example, this may contain SCANN non-linear function controllers for IGV, WFE and NOZZ whose function can be adapted using self-* intelligent algorithms. This layer can report current status of its *components* to higher layers such as the current configuration (i.e. fuzzy rules that define their current function or behaviour) in addition to component health, degradation and faults. Such data contributes to the internal situation awareness model of the current state that is used for analysis and prediction.

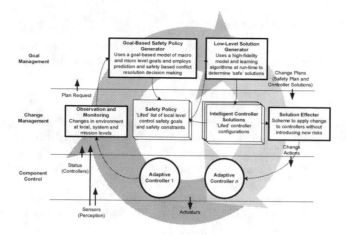

Fig. 4. Conceptual framework for unexpected operating conditions on-line

The *Change Management Layer* observes relevant environmental changes, maintains plans and effects changes *to the Component Control Layer*. The *Change Management Layer* responds to new states reported by the *Component Layer* and responds to new objectives required of the system introduced from the operating conditions and environment. This layer contains the "what" must be done, "why" it should be done and "how" in the form of a *Safety Policy* [21]. This layer also contains *solutions* generated from self-* intelligent algorithms and manages changes upon the adaptive controller behaviour in on-line fashion without introducing new risks. Because of the on-line application of the framework and the dynamic nature of the problem this layer also manages the 'life' or the 'validity' of the plans and solutions generated and *requests* re-planning if the assumptions of the plans and solutions no longer hold for the current operating conditions.

The *Goal Management Layer* deals with dynamic risk reduction through generating suitable planning and solutions using high-fidelity models for *situation awareness* and *prediction*. This layer takes as input the current states, safety goals, performance goals and constraints. A hierarchical relationship is formed from the operational\mission (macro) level down to local (micro) levels. This layer produces a *Safety Policy* that expresses what current prioritised safety (risk related) objectives need to be achieved, why they need to be achieved and by whom (adaptive controllers that will fulfil the Policy). In addition, the layer also generates solutions based on the input of the Safety Policy. Multi-Objective intelligent algorithms are employed with a high-fidelity model of the system and prediction techniques. 'Prediction' of risk and future states has a major role in defining the 'validity' of the plans and solutions.

The entire framework operates on-line and continuously thereby becoming the main approach for adaption of the controllers. The framework operation has also been defined in the spirit of the Observe-Orient-Decide-Act (OODA) loop commonly employed for highly dynamic environments for safety-based risk management. To understand how the framework contributes to the safety assurance argument the following section proposes possible solutions in context of the GTE.

4.1 Goal Based Safety Policy Generator

Control in GTEs often requires the satisfaction of competing performance and safety objectives that are related to engine degradation, stability, structural integrity, steady-state, transient accuracy, thrust performance, stall margins and many others (Table 1). Multi-objective optimisation is the process by which optimal solutions are sought for two or more competing objectives under specified constraints. For highly complex problem domains it may become apparent that there is no single ideal optimal solution. An improvement in one of the objectives will lead to degradation in one or more of the remaining objectives. For example, in an effort to minimise fuel flow and reduce turbine blade temperature (safety objective) the maximum thrust force is reduced (degrading the performance objective). Such solutions are known as 'non-dominated' solutions. An additional problem is that whilst the engine is in operation, each of these objectives can be related to a *safety* or *performance* classification depending on the current operating conditions and risk levels. For example, for an aircraft to avoid an impending collision, "maximise fuel flow" may be seen as a safety objective during an abrupt manoeuvre. Such a solution would be non-dominant since it would negatively impact the engine temperatures and reduce the surge margins (*LPSM* and *HPSM*). Alternatively, for a non-threat scenario "maximise fuel flow" can be classed as a 'performance' objective (whereby risk of platform destruction is no longer in the intolerable region).

The *Goal-Based Safety Policy Generator* is used to address the problem of 'what' should be done and 'why' based on sound safety reasoning. The inputs into this block are many and include goals and their status from the operational\mission\macro level (e.g. "*avoid collision risk*", "*no threat*"). At the platform system level we may have goals (e.g. *max(Thrust) immediately*, *min(Fuel Consumption) over 1 hour*) and status e.g. "*High NHDem*", "*Low Fuel*". At the boundary of the engine level there may be goals i.e. min(TBT) immediately, $TBT \leq 813^{o}C$ and conditions e.g. "*Excessive Turbine Blade Degradation*", "*TBT = 813°C*". At the local component level there are controllers, with health conditions that must be chosen to fulfil the hierarchy of identified safety objectives i.e. *NOZZ & WFE control* or *WFE control* only. There is a clear need to model the decomposition of goals, criteria\objectives, conditions, risk and temporal properties in real-time, such that guidance is provided on 'how' the self-* algorithms must adapt the controllers in order to address the prominent and prioritised set of risks.

The problem can be managed through the derivation and maintenance of a Safety Policy whilst the engine is in operation. A Safety Policy describes how the physical integrity of the system can be protected, what must be done to protect the system and reasoning using dynamic system relationships. Figure 5 shows an example of an aero-engine safety policy for high thrust demand during "Collision Avoidance".

There are several challenges associated with generating such a safety policy. The first is 'perception' – there must be sensors that reliably determine the current system and world state. Sensor flaws would result in invalid policy derivation (out of context) whereby risk of accident occurrence may not be reduced or even identified. With appropriate 'perception' there needs to be an appropriate model of the current goals and how such goals can be suitably decomposed. The model needs to capture objectives from mission level to component level. This can be achieved through safety

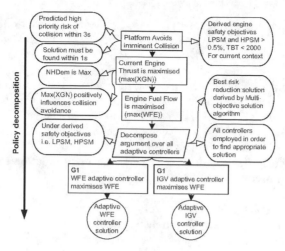

Fig. 5. Example of engine safety policy decomposition for collision avoidance

analyses performed prior to certification and deployment and would include identification of engine level objectives outlined in section 2. Missing or superfluous goals would mean solutions are not generated or do not address current operating conditions. The cause-effect relationship between local objectives and system level effects (e.g. engine surge, turbine blade failure etc.) also needs to be understood and modelled (e.g. *increase* in WFE *increases* XGN, *increase* in NH *increases* TBT). These relationships form a knowledge base and enable automated policy decomposition. Failures in the relationships would also result in a flawed policy that could in turn, lead to increased risk of hazard occurrence.

Another aspect that must be addressed is defining the current safety objectives e.g. *LPSM*. These must be derived based on predictive techniques that understand short term and long term goal satisfaction. In the example presented in Figure 5, the collision avoidance is the current highest risk to the platform therefore surge margins can be drastically reduced. Although this may increase the risk of failure in the long term the new objective (*LPSM* > 0.5%) enables appropriate solutions to address the most highly prioritised safety risks. This also means that the risks associated with goals need to be determined dynamically, whilst on-line and prioritised. Current state information input into the Safety Policy generator would include the current risk levels associated with the current state e.g. turbine blades have degraded (medium risk), imminent collision (High Risk) etc. Such risk levels can determine the goal decomposition of the Safety Policy. Contradictions and conflicts when deriving a suitable safety policy can occur where there are several high risks that need to be addressed simultaneously. For example, this may include conflict of resources, duties and objectives as detailed in [21]. The occurrence of unexpected conditions at run-time is when such policy conflicts may arise. Such problems can be addressed through the use of high-fidelity models and decision making for on-line conflict prevention and resolution [21]. On-line detection of safety policies that are unable to be fulfilled due to temporal resource constraints need to be resolved by other 'governing' components or agents within the system e.g. Full-Authority-Digital-Electric-Control (FADEC).

Non-functional temporal issues and prediction play an important role in generating the Safety Policy. Validity of the policy will be dependent on the current operating context. To reduce the probability of a generated safety policy requiring re-planning and drastic change, prediction techniques can be employed through the use of a suitable high-fidelity model. The prediction would determine expected future states of the system e.g. TBT is near limits, engine is being used heavily therefore the predicted time before blade failure is t. Time t can then be used to provide a 'life' of validity of the Safety Policy and where risk management techniques need to accomplish their activities within the allocated predicted temporal resources. To complete the Safety Policy, low level controller solutions need to be generated that define how current safety risks are addressed.

The approach of using 'intelligent' solutions to solve multi-objective problems involving risk is not a new problem especially in the domain of finance [15] and security [16]. For Safety Policy decomposition we have identified the challenge of addressing numerous risk-related objectives well above the level of adaptive controller solutions. Techniques in Operations Research such as Non-linear Programming (NLP) [22] can be used to address such problems through minimising weighted sum of deviations from goals. Other techniques such as lexicographic goal programming described in [22] categorises goals into levels such that a goal of a particular-level may be of greater priority than one assigned at a different level. For safety, this approach is appealing because it enables the distinction between performance and safety related objectives and is particularly effective when there is a clear priority ordering amongst the goals to be achieved. This can be achieved by inputting risk associated with known hazards and relating the current and predicted states to determine prioritisation. The safety challenge is to generate Pareto-efficient solutions thereby resulting in the most effective risk reduction plan possible given the capabilities of the system. A sub-optimal plan could result in exacerbating existing risks. 'Governor' agents and multi-agent architectures [23] are seen as approaches to address such problems. In any case, safety assurance needs to be provided that the safety policy has been appropriately decomposed, and that the safety policy is 'valid' for the current and predicted future operating contexts.

4.2 Component (Controller) Solution Generator

The *Component Solution Generator* adopts a bottom-up approach to determine 'how' adaptive controllers will meet the defined safety policy which is provided as input. Existing approaches to address unexpected operating conditions using adaptive controllers include the Situational Controller Methodology (SCM) [18] which has been applied to GTE control. SCM uses neural network pattern recognition algorithms and predefined controller solutions to determine the ideal controller for the current operating context. Such a solution is 'rigid' in that the actual scenario may not fall into any particular pre-defined situation and there is no opportunity for re-planning using existing scenario-based solutions (interpolation problems). As highlighted in [18] this greatly limits the potential for acceptable risk reduction strategies by focussing on a limited and potentially inadequate solution space. Other work on the use of Evolutionary algorithms for devising optimal Engine schedulers include the Multi-Objective Genetic Algorithm (MOGA) [7]. As described in [7] MOGA has been

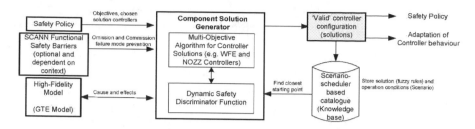

Fig. 6. Approach for 'safe' dynamic control of solution space

shown to be a competent algorithm for finding optimal fuzzy schedulers for GTE control. MOGA is composed of three levels and uses genetic algorithms to search for an optimal controller solution of fuzzy control rules. The first two levels generate and analyse the performance (using objectives in Table 1) of potential solutions at different engine operation points (such as 54, 65, 75, 85, 95% NH). The last level selects the best fuzzy solution (by making trade-offs between objectives). However, such a scheme is limited to off-line aero-engine design and there is little or no safety assurance that the behaviour of the scheduler will not lead to system-level hazards (such as discontinuity of function output). An alternative solution introduced here uses a combination of the above mentioned approaches (including the SCANN) for mutual benefit (in terms of safety assurance) and is illustrated in Figure 6.

As depicted in Figure 6, the *Component Solution Generator* works on the principle of using high-fidelity cause-effect models of the system to generate valid risk reduction controller solutions. The first step is to input the safety policy which is generated in the previous phase of the framework and specifies safety objectives e.g. *LPSM >* 0.5%, safety goals e.g. max(XGN) and the proposed actions *contracted* out to IGV and WFE adaptive controllers. The adaptive controllers (whether they are fuzzy, neural, reactive or deliberative agents) must address failure modes associated with their behaviour that are common to all possible configurations that may be applied (e.g. functional safety barriers). For example, failure modes such as 'omission' and 'commission' of output given an input are applicable to *all* potential desired controller functions. The safety argument must therefore assure that the adaptive controller addresses such failures through appropriate design features or otherwise as described previously with the SCANN [4]. Such a safety argument can contribute to the decomposition of goal G5 in Figure 3 whereby the adaptive controller will be able to adhere to proposed solutions without causing failures modes that are common to all potential system states.

In Figure 6, the main role of the scenario-scheduler knowledge base is to reduce the time taken for Multi-Objective intelligent algorithms to find a valid solution and contribute to goal G12. The knowledge base would consist of a catalogue of known (foreseeable but unexpected) and unknown (self-generated) operating conditions, respective safety policies and controller based solutions (e.g. Takagi-Sugeno fuzzy rules that define controller behaviour). Part of the catalogue can be preconceived through safety analyses and updated through during post-deployment use when valid solutions are found. Through the philosophy of 'expect the unexpected' the time taken to generate a valid solution and re-planning can contribute to achieving non-functional temporal goals (e.g. avoid imminent collision). It is likely that the actual operating conditions may not match precisely with any particular item in the knowledge base. Instead, the mappings in the knowledge base can be used as a 'starting' point for multi-objective solution searches. The unexpected conditions detailed in 'C4' of the safety argument can provide input into this knowledge-base and provide assurance that a solution is determinable in the time provided if it is sufficiently close to the actual operating conditions.

The next step is for the safety-based multi-objective learning and adaptation algorithms to find potential solutions (and contribute to G10). This step must consider solutions and effects of the proposed solutions for all controllers defined in the safety policy. Employing MOGA is ideal in this case however given the inter-relationship of controlled variables, treating each controller independently would lead to flawed and conflicting solutions. As a result, this would lead to problems in providing assurance that a valid solution can be provided within the allocated temporal resources (G4). To further address the temporal resource and 'validity' issues, the knowledge base can be used as 'seeds' of the MOGA solution finding. Therefore MOGA is tasked with the role of finding a valid solution given the safety policy for all controllers simultaneously. This approach addresses the 'rigidity' of the SCM and solution space limitations of the SCANN. The engine operating conditions are likely to be continuously changing and as a result, the *Component Solution Generator* is likely to continuously iterate. For each solution finding iteration, the current control scheme can be used as a starting point if the operating context is on a predicted path. If the operating context changes abruptly then the knowledge base can be used for a new 'seed'. If none is available (or even close enough) then the multi-objective search algorithm can devise a solution using a default schedule.

To address the safety concern that the generated solutions might be invalid for the current operating context the high-fidelity model is used to assess the risk reduction of the derived solution based on the safety policy. To delineate valid and invalid solutions a dynamic *safety discriminator function* can be employed and also used as a stopping condition. This function takes in as input the proposed solutions, a high-fidelity engine model and the safety policy. Predictive techniques are then used to determine whether the solution is an acceptable risk reduction plan. Unlike existing approaches, the *safety discriminator function* is required to identify the current states and predict future states (in accordance with G2 and G3). As the accuracy of any model can be affected significantly by even minute changes in the behaviour or state of the modelled system, special mechanisms need to be employed to maintain the high-fidelity of the model through these changes. Examples of such mechanisms include system state monitors and on-line machine learning modules that continuously adjust the model in line with the actual behaviour of the system. Similarly strict requirements must be fulfilled by the on-line model analysis that determines valid controller solutions (e.g. function parameters) from the high-fidelity model. In particular, accurate predictions and a fast response time are essential for the dynamic risk management to be effective. Failures in the model and it's fidelity would mean that the proposed solution may introduce or exacerbate risks. To address failures of the *safety discriminator function* it must be argued through product-based analytical and empirical means that the model of the system is indeed of high-fidelity (for G3 and G4). Potential safety argument goals for high-fidelity simulation and modelling

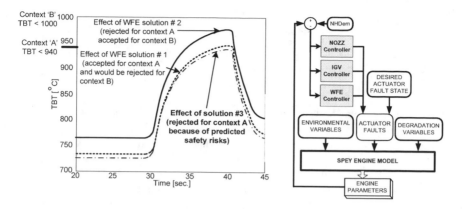

Fig. 7. (a) Delineation of solutions through prediction (b) block diagram of the Rolls Royce Aero-Engine Model

defined in [24] can be used to decompose such a safety argument goal. Safety requirements defined for the Situation Awareness Model defined in [14] also apply to the high-fidelity system model and contribute to decomposing goals G2, G3 and G4.

Determining potential controller solution failures such as function derivatives and function output extremes will rely upon the effects exhibited by the high-fidelity model. The limitation of such an approach is that every proposed solution needs to be checked against the model. This can be time consuming and places heavy reliance on the system model. An example of the safety discriminator function is presented in Figure 7 (a) and shows how controller solutions are rejected or accepted based on various current and predicted risk factors. This is produced using a Matlab and Simulink model of a Rolls Royce GTE as shown in Figure 7 (b). The model accommodates degradation variables of various parts of the engine as well as actuator faults and is an ideal example for analysing the benefits of 'dynamically' changing functional safety requirements.

To address goal G3 in Figure 3, assurance needs be provided that the devised solutions can be 'safely' enforced and applied to the current on-line control of actuators. The actual solution will inevitably depend on the precise nature of the adaptive systems employed. In this case, if we consider the SCANN operating within the GTE, the 'old' controller behaviour must be switched with the 'new' controller behaviour. An approach to address this problem is to employ additional 'smoothing' functions that enable the transition between the solutions. Such 'smoothing' functions would address derivative changes that would introduce new risks in terms of hardware failure e.g. if the rate of opening the engine nozzle is too fast. Such limiters can be defined on the boundaries of the adaptive controller function and must be designed to enable transition within the 'life' and temporal validity of the safety policy. The provision of modifications within the *component layer* of the framework i.e. component creation, deletion and interconnection provides the necessary capabilities to address the failure modes associated with enforcing a safety policy.

5 Conclusions

This paper has shown the challenges of exposing 'intelligent' adaptive systems to unexpected operating conditions in the context of a highly dynamical and complex problem domain. The presented self-management framework identifies key activities and shows how they contribute to the dynamic risk management safety argument. The framework has shown how behaviour-based approaches for generating safety arguments are highly reliant on the provision of high-fidelity models. Through the framework, low level component solutions are shown to be highly dependent on the management of a hierarchy of goals and constraints. Also outlined is how features of the framework enable controller solutions to be generated on-line and how prediction and historical knowledge base can contribute to addressing identified safety challenges such as validity and non-functional resources. Much work remains for a complete solution and the focus of remaining work includes the provision of safety assurance for automated safety policy generation, high-fidelity modelling and employing a multi-agent architecture for problem solving that would enable a highly scalable and modular solution.

Acknowledgements

The work described in this paper was funded by the EPSRC under the LSCITS (Large Scale Complex Information Technology Systems) programme. We are also grateful to Parta Dutta from SRC Rolls-Royce for providing useful domain knowledge.

References

1. IEC, 61508: Fundamental Safety of Electrical / Electronic / Programmable Electronic Safety Related Systems, International Electrotechnical Commission (1999)
2. Heo, J.S., Lee, K.Y.: A multi-agent system-based intelligent control system for a power plant. In: IEEE Power Engineering Society General Meeting, vol. 2, pp. 1050–1055 (2005)
3. Calinescu, R., Kwiatkowska, M.: Using quantitative analysis to implement autonomic IT systems. In: Proceedings of the 31st International Conference on Software Engineering (ICSE 2009), Vancouver, British Columbia, Canada (2009)
4. Kurd, Z.: Artificial Neural Networks in Safety Critical Applications, PhD Thesis, Department of Computer Science, University of York, York (2005)
5. Kurd, Z., Kelly, T.P.: Using Safety Critical Artificial Neural Networks in Gas Turbine Aero-Engine Control. In: Winther, R., Gran, B.A., Dahll, G. (eds.) SAFECOMP 2005. LNCS, vol. 3688, pp. 136–150. Springer, Heidelberg (2005)
6. Kurd, Z., Kelly, T.: Using Fuzzy Self-Organising Maps for Safety Critical Applications. Reliability Engineering & System Safety 92(11), 1563–1583 (2007)
7. Chipperfield, A.J., Bica, B., Fleming, P.J.: Fuzzy Scheduling Control of a Gas Turbine Aero-Engine: A Multiobjective Approach. IEEE Trans. on Indus. Elec. 49(3) (2002)
8. Sugeno, M., Takagi, H.: Derivation of Fuzzy Control Rules from Human Operator's Control Actions. In: Proc. of the IFAC Symp. on Fuzzy Information, Knowledge Representation and Decision Analysis (1983)

9. Kurd, Z., Kelly, T.P.: Safety Lifecycle for Developing Safety-critical Artificial Neural Networks. In: Anderson, S., Felici, M., Littlewood, B. (eds.) SAFECOMP 2003. LNCS, vol. 2788, pp. 77–91. Springer, Heidelberg (2003)

10. Hollnagel, E.: Accidents and Barriers. In: Proceedings of Lex Valenciennes, Presses Universitaires de Valenciennes, pp. 175–182 (1999)

11. MoD, Defence Standard 00-56 Issue 3: Safety Management Requirements for Defence Systems, Issue 3, Part 2, UK Ministry of Defence (2004)

12. Austin, J.: A Grid Based Diagnostics and Prognosis System for Rolls Royce Aero Engines: The DAME Project. In: 2nd International Workshop on Challenges of Large Applications in Distributed Environments (CLADE 2004), Honolulu, Hawaii, USA. IEEE Computer Society, Los Alamitos (2004)

13. Stranjak, A., et al.: A multi-agent simulation system for prediction and scheduling of aero engine overhaul. In: Proceedings of the 7th international joint conference on Autonomous agents and multiagent systems, International Foundation for Autonomous Agents and Multiagent Systems: Estoril, Portugal, pp. 81–88 (2008)

14. Wardzinski, A.: Safety Assurance Strategies for Autonomous Vehicle. In: Harrison, M.D., Sujan, M.-A. (eds.) SAFECOMP 2008. LNCS, vol. 5219, pp. 277–290. Springer, Heidelberg (2008)

15. Subramanian, H., et al.: Designing safe, profitable automated stock trading agents using evolutionary algorithms. In: Proceedings of the 8th annual conference on Genetic and evolutionary computation, pp. 1777–1784. ACM, Seattle (2006)

16. Torrellas, G.A.S.: A Framework for Multi-Agent System Engineering using Ontology Domain Modelling for Security Architecture Risk Assessment in E-Commerce Security Services. In: Proceedings of 3rd IEEE International Symposium on Network Computing and Applications (NCA 2004), pp. 409–412. IEEE Computer Society, Cambridge (2004)

17. Kelly, T.P.: Arguing Safety – A Systematic Approach to Managing Safety Cases, Ph.D. Thesis, Department of Computer Science, University of York, York, UK (1998)

18. Andoga, R., Madarasz, L., Fozo, L.: Digital Electronic Control of a Small Turbojet Engine - MPM 20. In: Proceedings of International Conference on Intelligent Engineering Systems (INES 2008). IEEE, Miami (2008)

19. Bishop, P., et al.: Justification of smart sensors for nuclear applications. In: Winther, R., Gran, B.A., Dahll, G. (eds.) SAFECOMP 2005. LNCS, vol. 3688, pp. 194–207. Springer, Heidelberg (2005)

20. Magee, J., Kramer, J.: Self-Managed Systems: an Architectural Challenge. In: International Conference on Software Engineering 2007 Future of Software Engineering, Washington, DC, USA, pp. 259–268. IEEE Computer Society, Los Alamitos (2007)

21. Hall-May, M., Kelly, T.P.: Towards Conflict Detection and Resolution of Safety Policies. In: Proceedings of 24th International System Safety Conference, System Safety Society, Albuquerque, USA (2006)

22. Deb, K.: Non-linear Goal Programming Using Multi-Objective Genetic Algorithms, in Computational Intelligence, Universität Dortmund (2004)

23. Hall-May, M., Kelly, T.P.: Using Agent-based Modelling Approaches to Support the Development of Safety Policy for Systems of Systems. In: Górski, J. (ed.) SAFECOMP 2006. LNCS, vol. 4166, pp. 330–343. Springer, Heidelberg (2006)

24. Alexander, R.: Using Simulation for Systems of Systems Hazard Analysis, PhD Thesis, Department of Computer Science, University of York, York (2007)

Author Index